GLOBAL WARRING

AND THE

LAND OF ZINJ

GLENN H. DOWNING

Global Warring
and the
Land of Zinj

Contents

Appendices

Preface

"Kings of the earth stand ready, and princes conspire together against the Lord and his anointed king. 'Let us break their fetters,' they cry, 'let us throw off their chains".   *Psalms 2:2-3 (Revised English Bible)*

Conspiracy, cabal, and junta are words that refer to a group who have joined forces for some secret purpose which is looked upon as evil and often has to do with the displacement or discrediting of an established authority or government.[1]

Revisionist or conspiracy history literature has developed no less than eight theories to explain the purposes and activities of the single conspiracy each describes. I call these <u>The Octopus Theories</u>.[2]

Included are Jesuits, Illuminati, Freemasonry, Jews, Communists, World Bankers, multinational corporations, and most recently the Oligarchy, ("Pretenders" to the old European thrones).[3]

From second grade on, I have been an avid reader. Initially it was an escape from some irksome task such as cleaning my room. Later, it opened a world of adventure and excitement. My responsibilities in the United States Marine Corps included ground training of Marine enlisted men. This was during the "Cold War" when Communism was the enemy. My reading carried me into studying various conspiracy concepts and Biblical prophecy. Much of this reading was pretty scary and caused fear in those who listened to my lectures. I stopped lecturing but continued reading.

As time went on, the dire predictions of the revisionists failed to materialize. I began to agree with Mark Twain's observations: "I am an old man and have known a great many troubles, but most of them never happened."[4] The verses following Psalm 2:3 provided the reason:

---

[1]S.I. Haykawa, *Use the Right Word,* (United States of America, Reader's Digest Books, Inc., 1968), 122.

2 John Daniels, *Scarlet and the Beast,* (Longview, TX, Day Publishing, 2007), 6.

[3] Ibid., 6.

[4] Lloyd Cory, *Quote Unquote,* (Wheaton, IL, Victor Books, 1977), 343.

He who sits in the heavens laughs, The Lord scoffs at them. Then He will speak to them in his anger and terrify them in His fury, saying, 'But as for Me, I have installed My King upon Zion, My Holy Mountain.[5]

The event in history that reset the calendar for the Western world was the resurrection of Jesus Christ. We are more than 2,000 years into the Christian era, and wars appear to be proliferating. World War I alone destroyed 8.5 million combatants, and the following influenza epidemic took another twenty million lives worldwide.

Peace on earth is rare. Less than 8% of the time, since the beginning of recorded history, has the world been entirely at peace. In a total of 3,530 years, 286 have been warless. Eight thousand treaties have been broken in this time.[6]

World War I was the first world conflict in the 20th century. According to Norman Podhoretz, it was followed by World War II, the Cold War which was World War III, and now we are engaged in World War IV or Islamofascism.[7] Worldwide conflicts dominated the 20th century and have extended into the 21st. I was born in Kenya in 1935, the year Italy invaded Ethiopia just north of Kenya. My parents, Herbert and Mildred Downing, with my sister Gayle and me, traveled to the United States in November 1937 on their first mission furlough. War broke out in Europe in 1939 and Dad became involved in WW II war training in the US. A second term on the mission field in Kenya, beginning in 1947, brought our family of six (with Brother Ed and Sister Ruth) to the United States in 1952.

After three years of college I enlisted in the Naval Aviation Cadet Flight Training program. I received my wings in 1957 and spent a total of 13 years on active duty in the United States Navy and Marine Corps. While flying commercially for the airlines, I completed eight years in the Marine Corps Reserve. My life has been governed by Global Wars.

The Persian name for the 2,000 mile shore line of tropical East Africa was Zinj, the land of the Black People. My paternal grandfather, Lee Downing, entered Kenya, in 1901 as a pioneer missionary. Both my father and I were born there. So the title of the book suitably describes a native of Zinj navigating through global wars. My personal peace has been the deliberate adjustment of my life to my perception of the will of God. It has been a daring but exciting adventure.

---

[5] The New American Standard Bible Updated Edition, Psalms 2:4-6.
[6] Lloyd Cory, *Quote Unquote*, Ibid., 232.
[7] Norman Podhoretz, *World War IV*, (New York, NY, Doubleday, 2007), 14-15.

The plan is to take you with me on many of my travels, describe significant events, and try to show how they have influenced my peculiar weltanschauung (worldview).

I have written this book at the request of my son, Lt. Col. Jonathan Downing, USAF. He was concerned that my children and grandchildren could not experience the unusual adventures I have enjoyed.

Glenn H. Downing

Introduction

When this project began, the title, general outline, plan, and travel itinerary were settled. However, the evolution of chapter contents was occasionally surprising to me.

Almost two years were spent investigating the reason for the world wide magnitude of the British Empire. Growing up under the Union Jack in Kenya favorably disposed me towards *Pax Brittanica*. The correlation of British animosity towards Israel's birth as a nation, and the rapidity of the empire's subsequent demise was a major clue.

The antagonists in World War IV naturally lead us back in history to Father Abraham. The course of events becomes clearer with the Biblical background of the adversaries in today's conflict. Coupled with Biblical prophecy, current events appear to be moving rapidly towards a global climax.

Come with me then, in my safaris around the world and see things from a Zinjian point of view.

This account would not have been possible without the help of my wife. "Tweet's" sense of propriety, her computer skills, and her ability to decipher my hurried hand writing were priceless. I am deeply indebted to my editor, Lee Troup, who patiently taught me to minimize adjectives and adverbs. His support was invaluable. The enthusiasm of my surrogate father, Charles White, was especially encouraging. And my number three grandson, Matthew Chamberlain, proof read every chapter as each was written. He was the one who discovered the powerful poem used in the last paragraph.

Above all is my conviction that this was in response to the Voice of God. I believe He quite clearly said: "Don't spill your guts! I'll tell you what to write." Sometimes this came in an easy flow of words. Other times it was thoughts that were implanted in the middle of the night. Whatever the medium, I trust He will use this witness to strengthen His sheep and advance His Kingdom.

AFRICA
Trip from Nairobi to New York – 1952

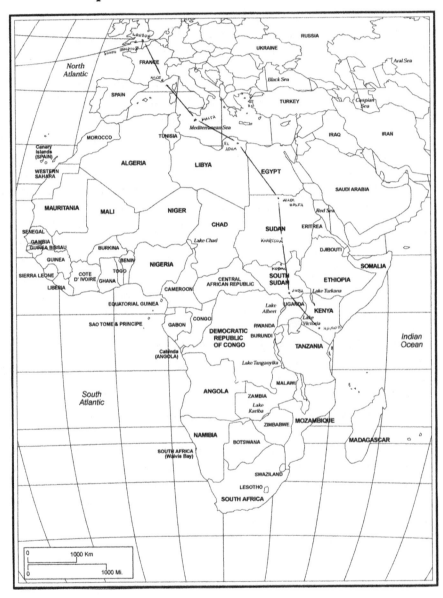

Down the Nile by Air

"If I take the wings of the morning and dwell in the uttermost part of the sea, even there shall thy hand lead me and thy right hand shall hold me." Psalm 139: 9 & 10

Saturday, 24 May, 1952, Eastleigh Airport, Nairobi, Kenya Colony, East Africa. British Empire Day and Queen Victoria's Birthday.

It was about six weeks since I had received my high school diploma from Kenya's Rift Valley Academy. The days were filled with packing, storing keepsakes, and getting travel immunizations. This climaxed 5-1/2 of the best years of my life.

My older sister, Gayle and I, were returning to the United States to attend college. Our family of six, which included two parents, a younger brother, and sister, was scheduled to fly to Great Britain on an aircraft operated by Airwork Ltd. This was a scheduled furlough for my parents.

As we filed out of the terminal building, we approached an aircraft that crudely resembled an old *Douglas DC-3*. The *DC-3* first flew in 1935, the same year I was born.

Just before we mounted the steps behind the left wing, my father, Herbert Downing, noted that the wing and tail units were fabric covered. This seemed unusual for an aircraft that first flew less than seven years before. The Ministry of Aircraft Production had ordered a passenger aircraft from Vickers-Armstrong Limited in 1944. The *Viking* was the result. To speed development, the aircraft used the wing and undercarriage design from the Vickers Wellington medium bombers of WW II. The fuselage was new and carried 21 passengers. The proto-type had flown on 22 June, 1945, just 15 days after Germany's unconditional surrender.[8]

The interior of the aircraft had a single aisle, with two seats on the right and one on the left. Mine was the left seat in the last row. With a window all to myself, I could see the ground clearly behind the left wing.

---

[8] An interesting note: In 1948 another *Viking*, temporarily fitted with two Rolls Royce turbojet engines, became the first entirely jet powered airliner. It flew from London to Paris in thirty-four minutes!

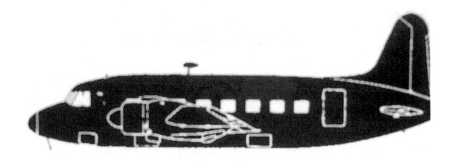

The Viking

The crew of four included a pilot, co-pilot, radio operator/navigator, and one tall, good looking stewardess. The cockpit crew was hidden away behind the cockpit door most of the time. The flight attendant caught my attention, welcoming all aboard in high heels. After the door was closed, she changed to low heels and did her best to spoil us with coffee, tea, and tasty snacks.

We became airborne about 8:00 A.M. As things were getting smaller, and my perspective of the earth was expanding, I began to realize the advantages of three dimensional freedom of flight. This was not my first experience in an aircraft, having previously accompanied my father when he flew a single engine *Piper Cub*. However, it was my first opportunity to travel a long distance through the air in a commercial aircraft. Little did I realize how many hours I would later spend in airplanes during my lifetime, both as a passenger and pilot.

Our route took us from Eastleigh Airport, more than a mile above sea level, past the Nairobi National Park. We had spent many happy outings there, enjoying sights of big game animals. This reserve is a protected area of about 40 square miles, less than half an hour from Nairobi. Nearly all wild animal species left in Africa passed through this park.

About 30 miles northwest of Nairobi, we passed over Kijabe, my birth place, and home for the past 5 1/2 years. I had thoroughly enjoyed growing up in such a pleasant environment, more than 7,000 feet above sea level. The temperature was always mild, even though we were less than a degree south of the Equator.

The Great Rift Valley has been described as one of the most startling landscapes on earth. This 4,000 mile valley is part of the most extensive fault on the earth's surface. Two extinct volcanoes rise from the floor of the valley below Kijabe. Every house on our mission station faced this magnificent view. I'll always remember seeing the morning sun illuminate the tip of the closest volcano, and then move slowly down the mountain until the valley floor was flooded with golden sunshine. Kijabe was my home.

Fifteen miles further along our route, we passed Lake Naivasha. I had been duck hunting there with Dr. Propst, one of my mentors, and one of his guests. On the right were the Aberdare Mountains, on the plateau above Kijabe. The tallest peak is more then 13,000 feet high. This is the home area of the Aberdare elephant, supposedly one of the largest elephants in Africa, though it never seems to carry the heaviest ivory. Once, my father was taking a picture of an old bull when he found himself the object of an aggressive charge. In his haste to escape, he fled down into a rather deep valley. At the bottom he looked up on the other side and noticed the Africans who had been with him, calmly looking back at him. They apparently lost their nerve before he did.

As we leveled off, our cruising speed was approximately 260 miles per hour. I had never traveled so fast. We were covering in hours what had previously taken days driving over dusty roads. As I sat in my comfortable seat, enjoying the attention of our efficient flight stewardess, in air-conditioned comfort, I turned to my mother and said: "This is the life." She never failed to chuckle when she frequently reminded me of this comment.

We crossed the Kenya/Uganda border as we flew over Mt. Elgon, the seventh highest mountain in Africa, at over 14,000 feet above sea level.

To our left was the railroad and highway I had traveled to the Belgian Congo. We had visited missionary friends there on two occasions. Travel from the rail head was by automobile. The highway wound down to Pakwach on the Albert Nile, which was crossed on a native propelled ferry. It was fruitless to be in a hurry on such occasions.

The Victoria Nile enters the Albert Nile at the northern end of Lake Albert. The Albert Nile flows into the White Nile at Nimule, 100 miles north of Pakwach. Some 100 miles further down the White Nile was Juba, our first fuel stop.

On our descent for landing at Juba, things on the ground became gradually larger.

We were approaching from the southeast and flew parallel to the landing runway. I noticed that we made a left turn to land, so from my seat the whole approach was visible. I was fascinated, wondering how the pilot could judge his altitude when he was so high over the field. Dad mentioned the use of an altimeter, but I was still intrigued.

After landing and taxiing to the terminal, the high heels were put back on and the door was opened by the flight stewardess. After refueling, we took off again. The next two legs would take us down the Nile River.

Early explorers expended much effort, arduously seeking the source of the Nile River, the longest river in the world. It originates in the tributaries of Lake Victoria and empties into the Mediterranean Sea, 4,132 miles down stream. Lake Victoria is the second largest fresh water lake in the world, although rather shallow. The Nile begins at Jinja, flowing northward over the Ripon Falls. (Subsequently, submerged since the construction of the Owen Falls Dam in 1954.)

Juba is located 65 miles north of Uganda in Southern Sudan. Sudan, the largest country in Africa, stretches 1,270 miles from south to north and 980 miles from east to west at its widest. It covers an area of nearly a million square miles. In comparison, it is almost 1 1/2 times the size of Alaska, and 3 1/2 times the size of Texas. Consequently our next two legs of 723 miles and 439 miles, respectively, kept us within its borders.

Some 300 miles north of Juba is Kodok, a small village on the west bank of the Nile. In 1898 this was known as Fashoda, and the scene of an extremely significant, international confrontation. Great Britain and France were actively involved in linking their separated colonial possessions in Africa. Great Britain was pushing south toward Uganda hoping to create a cape to Cairo railroad. France was pushing eastward from the west coast, aiming to extend its dominion across central Africa and the Sudan.

In January of 1897, French major Jean Baptiste Marchand was sent from Brazzaville, in the French Congo across Central Africa to Fashoda on the White Nile, a straight line distance of more than 1,500 miles. His party fought with warring Africans, struggled with fever, climbed mountains and penetrated dense jungles. Five days and five nights they were submerged up to their necks in swamp water. They finally accomplished their mission on the 10th of July, 1898, after 18 months enroute. Of the 150 men who began this journey, only 80% survived.[9]

The British Army under General Kitchner was sent to meet Major Marchand, further up the White Nile from Egypt. Due to cataracts and low

---

[9] Winston S. Churchill, *The River War*, (United States of America, Seven Treasures Publications, 2007), 179-184.

water levels during the dry season, a railroad was required to move up the river. On the first of January, 1897, the first spade full of sand was turned for General Kitchener's Desert Railway. From Wadi Halfa, on the southern Egyptian border, the railroad extended to Atbara, about 150 miles northeast of Khartoum. It was finally completed on the third of July, 1898. With this means of rapid supply, General Kitchener was able to command an army of two divisions with their artillery and a flotilla of gunboats, in all a force of 26,000 men. On the second of September, 1898, Kitchener defeated some 40,000 of the Mahdists forces that opposed him. The result was the extinction of Islamic Mahdism in the Sudan, and the establishment of British dominance.

General Kitchener did not reach Fashoda until 18 September, 1898, more than two months after Major Marchand's arrival. The two commanders decided to fly the French, Egyptian, and British flags over the fort until their respective governments resolved the impasse! Finally, on 4 November, 1898, France withdrew its force and Pax Britannica imposed stability on the Anglo Egyptian Sudan until 1956.[10]

Khartoum, our next refueling stop, is the capital of Sudan, located just south of the confluence of the White Nile and the Blue Nile. The Blue Nile originates high in the mountains of Ethiopia, and is the source of 70% of the Nile's flood water at Khartoum. Begun in 1821 as an Egyptian army camp, it grew into a military town.

In 1877 General Charles Gordon was appointed governor general of Sudan by the khedive, the Turkish Viceroy of Egypt. General Gordon had previously served 2 1/2 years as governor of the Equatorial province. B Forrest Clayton stated that "Gordon was a faithful Evangelical Christian who gave all the credit to Jesus Christ, the Son of the Living God." He also said that he had "practically single handedly, without an army at his disposal, put an end to the slave trade in the Sudan."[11]

Estimates of the slaves taken from Africa range from 30 million to 100 million. Restricting such a lucrative industry created strong animosities among its practitioners. All they needed was a strong leader. Mohammed Ahmed, a charismatic Muslim priest, provided that leadership. "The Mahdi" led a dervish (a Muslim religious sect) revolt against the Egyptian government. British General Hicks, on 1 November, 1881, led a 10,000 man

---

[10] Encyclopedia Britannica, 15th.ed., s.v. "Fashoda Incident."
[11] B. Forest Clayton, *Suppressed History III*, (Cincinnati, OH, Armistead Publishing, 2007), 31.

Egyptian force to quell this revolt. His army was completely wiped out by the Mahdi's primitive troops.

General Gordon was sent by the British government to evacuate the Egyptians from Khartoum. He arrived 22 February, 1884, and evacuated those he could down the Nile River. That same month a 3,500 man evacuating Egyptian force, under a British officer, was wiped out. Consequently, Gordon chose to defend Khartoum. He did a magnificent job building a defensive perimeter around the city. The siege began in March and continued for 10 months.

Eventually, the low water level of the Nile opened a breach in his defenses. The enemy came through, destroying the city, its inhabitants, and General Gordon, two days before a relief force arrived.

Winston Churchill wrote, "That one man, a European among Africans, a Christian among Mohammedans, should by his genius... have offered a vigorous resistance to the increasing attacks of an enemy though cruel, would yet accept surrender (with submission to Islam) during a period of 317 days, is an event perhaps without parallel in history."[12]

That, in a nutshell was the history of our second refueling stop. It was characteristic of the chaos in Africa, when my grandfather, Lee Downing, helped found the Africa Inland Mission.

Our third flight of the day was between Khartoum and Wadi Halfa, a distance of 439 miles. This was a direct flight over mostly desert, because of two big loops in the Nile River.

The Sahara is the largest desert in the world, covering most of North Africa. There is a line that runs east and west, just south of Khartoum. Everything north of this line receives less than 10 inches of rain per year. Rainfall increases south of this line producing tropical rainforests near the equator. Only about 20% of the Sahara is covered with sand dunes, which are rich in Stone Age relics, containing fishhooks on old lake bottoms, artifacts, pottery, and tombs. In fact, earth satellites have led to several notable discoveries, such as, drainage patterns in Sahara, relics of a period when this region was not arid.

About 240 miles from Khartoum we crossed the Nile River, finally landing at Wadi Halfa about sunset. Leaving the air-conditioned comfort of the airplane; we stepped into what felt like a gigantic oven. The red sky in the west indicated that the "heating element" was still glowing red hot.

---

[12] Winston S. Churchill, *The River War*, Ibid., 72.

We were transported by bus to a pleasant hotel accommodation, with ceiling fans, to counter the stifling desert heat. We enjoyed the dining room that evening. I was interested in tasting a fresh date, but it was not that much different from the dried ones. This complex was probably submerged by Lake Nasser when the Aswan High Dam was completed in 1970.

Saturday night, 24 May, 1952. We had flown almost 1,500 miles, farther than any day's travel in my life. Sleep was difficult because of high temperatures and humidity from the river. The next morning, I noticed that the flight crew had pulled their beds onto the deck outside their rooms. They obviously had been there on previous occasions.

World War II in North Africa

Sunday, 25 May, 1952. Wadi Halfa Airport, Anglo Egyptian Sudan. North Africa. Islamic Ramadan began.

At 0720 A.M. we were airborne in the Airwork *Viking*, on the fourth and longest leg of our journey to London. Our next refueling stop was the RAF airbase at El Adam, in Libya, approximately 850 miles from Wadi Halfa.

We crossed the Nile River for the last time about 20 miles northwest of Wadi Halfa. Our track took us across the Libyan Desert. This desert's rocky plateaus and stony or sandy plains are described by the Encyclopedia Britannica as harsh, arid, and inhospitable. The very few inhabitants are concentrated in isolated oases, where a perennial supply of water is available, mainly from underground sources.[13] Approximately 265 miles northwest of Wadi Halfa, we passed abeam the Dakhla oasis. The water for this settlement is supplied from sandstone aquifers whose intake is possibly 500 miles away. All Arab oases dwellers depend upon the date palm as the main source of food. In its shade are grown citrus fruits, figs, peaches, apricots, vegetables, and cereals such as wheat, barley, and millet. As a result, two-thirds of the population of the Sahara is sedentary.

As we crossed the Libyan border, 280 miles further along, we were abeam the Quattara Depression, located roughly 150 miles northeast of our track. This area of about 7,000 square miles contains salt lakes and marshes. It descends to 435 feet below sea level. This is less than one-third as low as the Dead Sea but about one and one-half times as low as Death Valley in California. During WW II, because it was impassible to military traffic, this depression formed a natural anchor for the southern end of the British defense lines.

In July 1942, Gen. Montgomery stopped the final advance of Field Marshall Rommel's German army at Al Alamein, nearly 10 years before our journey to London.

At El Adam, we climbed out over the fortress of Tobruk. I could clearly see defensive earthworks and piles of war materials left from WW

---

[13]Encyclopedia Britannica, 15 ed., s.v. "Libyan Desert."

II. Tobruk had been the scene of heavy fighting from January 1941 until October 1942.

When WW II began, Libya had been ruled by the Italians since 1912. On 10 June, 1940, when it became obvious that Hitler was over-running France, the Italians came into the war. Intending to unseat England from her position in the Mediterranean and Africa, the time appeared to be ripe for Italy to add to its overseas possessions.

When Italy declared war against Great Britain, Marshall Graziani had nearly 300,000 men in Cyrenaica, eastern Libya. The British commander in chief in the Middle East was Gen. Sir Archibald Wavell. His responsibilities included protecting the North African approaches to the Suez Canal. His command encompassed not only Egypt but also East African fronts against the Italians entrenched there. He had only 36,000 men against Italy's 300,000 in Libya.[14]

The conflict opened when Marshall Graziani invaded western Egypt and established a chain of widely separated camps. On 7 December, 1940 Gen. Wavell sent Maj. General O'Conner against this incursion with 30,000 men and 275 tanks. On 24 January, 1941, Tobruk was captured and held by the British until 21 June, 1942. By 7 February, 1941 the British had captured approximately 135,000 Italian prisoners.[15]

On 6 February, 1941, Hitler appointed a young general to command two mechanized divisions of the Afrika Korps that were to be sent to help the Italians. His name was Erwin Rommel.

Gen. Rommel was born in southern Germany in 1891. Both his father and grandfather had been teachers. At age 19, Erwin became an officer cadet in an infantry regiment. As a lieutenant in WW I, he was known for his deep understanding of his men, unusual courage, and a natural gift of leadership. He preferred being in the infantry as a front line officer to doing general staff work.

Possessing a pronounced talent for teaching, he was appointed to posts at military academies. His experiences in WW I, combined with his ideas on training young soldiers in military thinking, were incorporated in a military text book entitled *Infantry Attacks*, published in 1937.[16]

Rommel's chance to prove himself as a combat commander came in February 1940. He assumed command of the 7th Panzer Division in France. He had never commanded armoured units, but quickly grasped the

---

[14] Encyclopedia Britannica, 15th. ed., s.v. "Egypt and Cyrenaica, 1940-summer 1941."
[15] Ibid.
[16] Encyclopedia Britannica, 15th. ed. s.v. "Rommel, Erwin (Johannes Eugen)."

tremendous possibilities of mechanized and armored troops on the offensive. His raid on the French channel coast provided the first proof of his boldness and initiative.[17]

His arrival in North Africa immediately affected the tide of war to the detriment of depleted British Forces. His audacity, boldness, and tactics drove the allied forces back into Egypt on one of the longest British retreats in history. He attempted to take the fortress at Tobruk, but was repulsed by the 9th Australian Division under Gen. Leslie Morshead.

Twice Gen. Wavell attempted to relieve the beleaguered fortress at Tobruk, and both attempts failed. Finally Churchill, determined to win the war in North Africa, deployed needed men and equipment. Wavell was replaced by General Sir Claude Auchinleck, in the summer of 1941. Gen. Wavell had enjoyed one definitive triumph before Churchill removed him from his command in the Middle East. That triumph was the destruction of Italian East Africa, eliminating any threat to the Suez Canal from the south or to Kenya from the north. The irony was that Gen. Rommel had carried a book with him throughout this time period titled, *Generals and Generalship;* the author of that book, Gen. Archibald Wavell.[18]

One of the victorious British generals in the Italian East African campaign was Gen. Sir Alan Cunningham. In August 1941, he led the 8th army in General Auchinleck's Libyan Desert offensive, called 'Operation Crusader'. The early failures in this campaign led him to advocate its termination, whereupon he was relieved of command and returned to England.[19]

Gen. Cunningham was replaced by Gen. Neil Ritchie, who forced the Afrika Korps south to the El Agheila bottleneck. The British were finally able to reach and reinforce Tobruk at this time. Rommel, however, was meagerly re-enforced and after repulsing a British attack, on 26 December, 1941, began a counter offensive. By June 14, the British were forced to retreat back towards Egypt leaving a garrison of 33,000 men and an immense amount of material at Tobruk. Retaining this fortress was dictated by Churchill himself.[20]

On 21 June, 1942, Rommel successfully conquered Tobruk, took 33,000 British prisoners, and captured needed supplies to continue his

---

[17] Ibid.

[18] Encyclopeida Britannica, 15th. Ed. s.v. "Internation Relations – East Africa."

[19] Encyclopedia Britannica, 15th. Ed. s.v. "Cunningham, Sir Alan Gordon."

[20] Charles Herridge, *Pictorial History of World War II*, (Norwich, England, The Hamlyn Publishing Group Limited, 1975), 116.

offensive. This disaster for the British ranked second only to the surrender of Singapore. Soon they were in full retreat back into Egypt with Rommel in hot pursuit. Rommel's forces finally "ran out of steam" about 60 miles from Alexandria at El Alamein.

Inasmuch as history is written by the winners, it is difficult to sort through the varying historical accounts to determine what really happened. The clearest picture was written by a respected eyewitness from the ranks, Derek Prince. A few brief portions of his little book, *Shaping History Through Prayer and Fasting* will clarify the issues.

From 1941 to 1943, I served as a hospital attendant with the British forces in North Africa. I was part of a small medical unit that worked with two British armored divisions-the First Armored Division and the Seventh Armored Division.

At the time the morale of British forces in the desert was very low. The basic problem was that the men did not have confidence in their officers. I myself am the son of an army officer, and many of the friends with whom I grew up were from the same background. I thus had some valid standards of judgment. As a group, the officers in the desert at that time were selfish, irresponsible, and undisciplined. Their main concern was not the well-being of the men, or even the effective prosecution of the war, but their own physical comfort.

The result of all this was the longest retreat in the history of the British army-about 700 miles in all-from a place in Tripoli called El Agheila to El Alamein, about fifty miles west of Cairo. Here the British forces dug in for one final stand. If El Alamein should fall, the way would be open for the Axis powers to gain control of Egypt, to cut the Suez Canal, and to move over into Palestine. The Jewish community there would then be subjected to the same treatment that was already being meted out to the Jews in every area of Europe that had come under Nazi control.

About 18 months previously, in a military barrack room in Britain; I had received a very dramatic and powerful revelation of Christ. I thus knew in my own experience the reality of God's power. In the desert, I had no church or minister to offer me fellowship or counsel. I was obliged to depend upon the two great basic provisions of God for every Christian; the Bible and the Holy Spirit. I early came to see that, by New Testament standards, fasting was a normal part of Christian discipline. During the whole period that I was in the desert, I regularly set aside Wednesday of each week as a special day for fasting and prayer.

During the long and demoralizing retreat to the gates of Cairo, God laid on my heart, a burden of prayer, both for the British forces in the desert and for the whole situation in the Middle East. Yet I could not see how God could bless leadership that was so unworthy and inefficient. I searched in my heart for some form of prayer that I could pray with genuine faith and that would cover the needs of the situation. After a while, it seemed that the Holy Spirit gave me this prayer: "Lord, give us leaders such that it will be for Your glory to give us victory through them."

I continued praying this prayer every day. In due course, the British government decided to relieve the commander of their forces in the desert and to replace him with another man. The man whom they chose was a general named W. H. E. "Strafer" Gott. He was flown to Cairo to take over command, but he was killed when his plane was shot down. At this critical juncture the British forces in this major theater of the war were left without a commander. Winston Churchill, then Prime Minister of Britain, proceeded to act largely on his own initiative. He appointed a more-or-less unknown officer, named B.L. Montgomery, who was hastily flown out from Britain.

Montgomery was the son of an evangelical Anglican bishop. He was a man who very definitely fulfilled God's two requirements in a leader of men. He was just and God-fearing. He was also a man of tremendous discipline. Within two months, he had instilled a totally new sense of discipline into his officers and had thus restored the confidence of the men in their leaders.

Then the main battle of El Alamein was fought. It was the first major allied victory in the entire war up to that time. The threat to Egypt, the Suez Canal and Palestine was finally thrown back, and the course of the war changed in favor of the Allies. Without a doubt, the battle of El Alamein was the turning point of the war in North Africa.

Two or three days after the battle, I found myself in the desert a few miles behind the advancing Allied forces. A small portable radio beside me on the tailboard of a military truck was playing a news commentator's description of the scene at Montgomery's headquarters as he had witnessed it on the eve of the battle. He recalled how Montgomery publicly called his officers and men to prayer, saying, "Let us ask the Lord, mighty in battle, to give us the victory." As these words came through that portable radio, God spoke very clearly to my spirit, "That is the answer to your prayer."

How well this incident confirms the truth about promotion that is stated in Psalm 75:6-7. The British government chose Gott for their commander, but God set him aside and raised up Montgomery, the man of His own choosing. God did this to bring glory to His own name, and to answer a prayer which, by the Holy Spirit, He Himself had first inspired me to pray. By this intervention, God also preserved the Jews in Palestine from coming under the control of the Axis powers.

I believe that the prayer which God gave me at that time could well be applied to other situations, both military and political: "Lord, give us leaders such that it will be for Your glory to give us victory through them."[21]

We crossed the North African coast line at 1:40 P.M. on our way to Malta, leaving the Fortress at Tobruk, a grim memorial to global warring.

The next few hours were flown over the Mediterranean Sea. As far as sightseeing is concerned, nothing is more boring than staring down at open water. Time was passed by reading. We finally descended and landed on the island of Malta.

Admiral Mahan, the great theoretician of naval power, emphasized the importance of naval bases. Inasmuch as Great Britain was a maritime power, their need for naval bases had been recognized for centuries. Well-equipped bases were indispensable for the re-supply and maintenance of sea-going forces.

Malta was ruled by Britain from 1814 until its independence in 1964. Due to its central position, Malta played a decisive role in the war in the Mediterranean. From autumn 1940 the British submarines, cruisers, and aircraft based there were able to disrupt Italian communications with Libya.[22]

When the Germans intervened in North Africa, the Luftwaffe tried to interrupt British naval shipping in the Mediterranean, and to neutralize Malta. The Germans laid siege to it from the air for two and a half years, losing as many airmen as there were casualties on the ground. Malta was the first air siege in history. The 'aircraft carrier island' continued its resistance, despite intensive bombardment. It made an important contribution cutting off supplies to German troops in North Africa, thus playing a decisive role in the defeat of Rommel.[23]

After landing on Malta, the Airwork passengers were bussed to the Phoenicia Hotel. We dined that evening in a beautiful, high ceiled dining room. The waiters were all handsome Maltese young men, well supervised by an older maitre'd.

---

[21] Derek Prince, *Shaping History Through Prayer and Fasting*, (Charlotte, NC, Derek Prince Ministries-International, 1973), 77-82.

[22] *The World Almanac, 2008*, "Malta,"

[23] Larousse, *The Second World War in Color*, (Stanford, CT, Longmeadow Press, 1991), 201.

I'll never forget a matronly lady at a nearby table. After dinner she lit a cigarette. There was something strange about her smoking technique, as she was obviously blowing instead of inhaling.

After supper we walked down the street. The air was balmy, and people were enjoying the evening with laughter and the light hearted music from stringed combos. What a nice memory!

War Scars in London

Monday, 26 May, 1952. Hotel Phoenicia, Malta

That morning, it was still dark when we boarded the bus. The road to the airport was long and lumpy. One of the younger British men made it quite clear that he was not used to such early morning exercises. Finally, we re-boarded our *Viking* Aircraft and were airborne about 0630.

Our flight took us over the western tip of Sicily. A little over nine years before, 10 July, 1943, the beaches below were assaulted by 467,000 allied troops. Because Hitler refused to approve a Dunkirk type evacuation of German troops from North Africa the previous May, Sicily was defended by only 60,000 Germans. By August, German troops had escaped across the Straits to Italy.[24] The fall of Sicily forced Mussolini from power and resulted in the signing of an Italian armistice on 3 September, 1943.

Our flight continued northwest over the island of Corsica. Seventy-five miles to the east was the island of Elba, the site of Napoleon's first exile, 1814-1815. Within a couple of years, it was to become the scene of the most thorough and important aircraft accident investigation ever.

The British Overseas Aircraft Corporation (BOAC) had acquired ten De Havilland *Comet* jet aircraft. On 2 May, 1952, two weeks before we left Nairobi, the first jet passenger service from London to Johannesburg, South Africa was inaugurated.[25]

The *Comet* carried 36 passengers at 40,000 feet in near silence, twice as fast as piston powered aircraft. 30,000 passengers were carried in the first year, and 50 aircraft were ordered by BOAC and other airlines.

The first hit on the *Comet's* safety record occurred on 26 October, 1952. The BOAC *Comet I* with a tail number of G-ALYZ crashed on take off at Rome's Ciampino Airport. There were 35 passengers on board and fortunately, no fatalities. The cause of the accident was attributed to pilot over rotation on take-off.[26]

---

[24] Don McCombs & Fred L. Worth, *World War II, 4,139 Strange and Fascinating Facts,* (Avenel, NJ,Wings Books, 1994), 543.

[25] *Jane's Encyclopedia of Aviation,*ed. Michael J. H. Taylor, (New York, NY, Portland House, 1989, s.v. "de Havilland D. H. 106 Comet."

[26] Robert Jackson, *The History of AVIATION,* (New York, NY, Barnes & Noble, 2007), 269.

During WW II, the Germans lost several pilots when they first flew the *Messerschmitt ME 262*. A jet engine produces thrust and not horsepower as does a propeller. Take-off technique in a jet requires a much slower rotation rate and a lower angle of attack. It took time for pilots to learn the new technique.[27]

The first fatal accident happened on 3 March, 1953. *Comet UN* over-rotated at Karachi. The wing struck a bridge, the aircraft crashed, burned, and eleven people on board died.

Two months later *Comet YV* disintegrated in a thunderstorm shortly after take-off from Calcutta. All 37 passengers and six crew were killed. Thunderstorms have proven to be dangerous ever since men have been on earth. They are especially hard on aircraft.

On 10 January, 1954, 20 minutes after take-off from Ciampino Airport, *Comet YP* broke up in flight with the loss of all 35 people on board. With no apparent reason for this accident, the entire fleet was grounded. Any time an aircraft breaks up in flight, the wreckage is spread over a wide area. Inasmuch, as this occurred near the island of Elba, much of the wreckage landed in the Mediterranean Sea. The investigators located the first wreckage two days later. The Royal Navy conducted recovery operation using underwater television cameras for the first time. By August, 70% of the main structure, 80% of the power section, and 50% of the equipment had been recovered. Investigators concluded that the primary cause was most likely fire, and a number of changes were recommended. *Comet* flights resumed on 23 March, 1954.

Two weeks later, *Comet YY* crashed off Stromboli Island, just north of eastern Sicily. There were no survivors, and there was no apparent cause. The entire fleet was again grounded for investigation under the direction of the Royal Aircraft Establishment. Prime Minister Winston Churchill tasked the Royal Navy with helping to locate and retrieve the wreckage. One of the largest and most thorough inquiries ensued.[28]

In February 1955, the remnants of the two Italian crashes were brought to the surface and shipped to the United Kingdom for exhaustive testing. The identical airframe of YU was subjected to repeated re-pressurization and over pressurization until it failed after 3,057 flight cycles. (1,221 actual and 1,836 simulated)[29]

---

[27] University of Southern California, Professor J. Nielsen, "Naval Aviation Safety Officers School."

[28] De Havilland Comet – Wikipedia, the free encyclopedia, "Comet disasters of 1954," http://www.enwikipedia.org/wiki/De-Havilland-Comet, (accessed November 12, 2009).

[29] Robert Jackson, *The History of AVIATION*, Ibid., 271.

The square windows were redesigned to oval, skin sheeting was slightly thickened, larger engines were installed, and a much improved *Comet IV* was introduced. This was the first jet airliner to enter transatlantic service. The *Comet* did not resume commercial airline service until four years later in 1958.

According to John Cunningham, chief test pilot for DeHavilland aircraft, representatives from American manufacturers such as Boeing and Douglas, "admitted that if it hadn't been for our problems, it would have happened to one of them."[30]

Today's traveling public owes the success of modern air travel to the persistence and integrity of the *Comet* accident investigators. We enjoy the safest and quickest long distance travel the world has ever known.

From Corsica we proceeded across the Ligurian Sea to Nice, France. Nice is a seaport and resort on the French Riviera, between Cannes and the independent principality of Monaco, about half way between Malta and London.

After landing, the passengers proceeded to the terminal, where we were served breakfast. My brother, Eddie, and I will never forget that meal. The waitress brought a large plate of fresh cherries, and we devoured more than our fair share. Needless to say, we became accomplished "water closet" (toilet) spotters in London the next few days.

With our fuel tanks serviced, we proceeded across France, crossed the English Channel, and landed at Blackbush Aerodrome at 2:55 that afternoon. A large comfortable coach whisked us to the London Victoria Bus terminal, where we engaged one of those quaint London taxis. As with most vehicles in England, this was a right hand drive. To the left of the driver was a platform, large enough to conveniently hold all of our luggage. Our family of six piled into the passenger compartment in the rear, and we were off to the House of Rest on 10 Finchley Road.

As we left downtown London, we traveled through suburban areas that were still devastated from the bombing, seven years before. London had still not recovered from WW II. We began to appreciate the horror of terror bombing.

The first case of terror bombing occurred on 26 April, 1937. German aircraft, from the Condor Legion sent to help General Franco, during the Spanish Civil War, were testing ground support tactics in preparation for

---

[30] Comet disasters of 1954, "BOAC Flight 781 and South African Airways Flight 201," http://www.enwikipedia.org/wiki/De-Havilland-Comet. (accessed November 12, 2009).

WW II. The Spanish town of Guernica was attacked at noon on a Monday market day. A large portion of the population was then outdoors. High explosive bombs, followed by incendiaries and strafing, killed 1,654 people and wounded 869 more, out of a population of 7,000. A well known painting by Picasso depicts this event.[31]

Britain declared war on Germany, 3 September, 1939. German and Allied forces faced each other across borders without either attacking until 9 April, 1940. This period was known as the phony war or SITZKRIEG. It was terminated when Germany invaded Denmark and Norway.[32]

After Germany invaded France, 338,000 British and France troops were rescued at Dunkirk, from 27 May to 4 June, 1940.[33] Hitler was hoping to open peace negotiation with Britain, but Churchill did not respond. Germany's invasion plan, Operation Sea Lion, was set for September 1940. On 5 August, Hitler ordered Herman Goering, the commander of the German Luftwaffe, to launch an aerial assault on Britain.

Initially, both Germany and Great Britain limited their air strikes to military targets, and carefully avoided bombing civilian population centers. But on the night of 24 August, 10 German aircraft became lost and accidentally bombed London, killing civilians.

The next night, the British retaliated and sent 80 planes to bomb Berlin. This raid provoked the Germans to begin regular bombing raids on London. From 6 September, 1940 to 3 November, 1940, for 57 consecutive nights, German bombs rained down on civilians in London.

It is impossible to calculate the destruction and devastation precipitated by this disoriented German flight leader. The escalation caused not only the bombing of civilians in London, but the destruction of Hamburg, Dresden, and Berlin. By the end of the war, an estimated 250,000 German and 52,000 English civilians were killed in bombing raids.[34] When the last bomb fell on Berlin, on 21 April, 1945, 6,340 acres in the heart of the city had been destroyed. Before the war, the terrain around Berlin was flat. After VE Day, all the rubble was bulldozed into seven hills that transformed the appearance of the city.[35]

---

[31] Don McCombs & Fred L. Worth, *World War II*, Ibid., 223.

[32] Ibid., 404.

[33] Ibid., 158.

[34] Thomas Ayers, *A Military Miscellany*, (New York, NY, Bantam Dell, 2006), 96-97.

[35] Don McCombs & Fred L. Worth, *World War II*, Ibid., 53.

Other air raids on London continued throughout the winter with the exception of February 1941. A final flare up in March and April concluded this phase of the air war.

More than three years later, 12 June, 1944, the first *V-1 (Vengeance)* rocket fell on London. Within two weeks the rockets had killed 2,752 Londoners. The *V-1* was a relatively cheap weapon that delivered a ton of explosives. It flew at a speed of 370 miles per hour, a distance of 150 miles, between 2,000 to 3,000 feet. It was powered by a pulse jet engine which had a distinctive sound signature. When it arrived over its programmed target, the engine shut down, and the rocket plunged towards its target. Because of its speed and small size, it was difficult to spot, and British aircraft were hard pressed to overtake it. Before the launching sites were overrun by British forces, 8,564 *V-1's* were launched against London. The total number of hits recorded was 2,419.

On 8 September, 1944, about the time pilots were learning to shoot the *V-1's* down, a more sophisticated *V-2* rocket struck the city. The *V-2* flew a distance of 230 miles to a height of 120 miles. There was no warning sound as it made its final plunge with a 2,000 pound war head. At over 2,000 miles per hour, it was more accurate than the *V-1* and made a 30 foot crater on impact. A total of 1,145 were aimed at London.[36]

When the conflict ended, 2 September, 1945, British civilian casualties numbered 52,000. Of the armed forces of the United Kingdom, 300,000 lost their lives and Britain lost one-fourth of its national wealth. As far as London was concerned, air attacks killed more than 30,000, injured more than 50,000, damaged most public buildings, and in certain sections, obliterated whole sections of the street system.

The end of hostilities brought a gradual return of many evacuees back to London, resulting in a housing shortage made worse by the ravages of dry rot. Reconstruction began at once, hampered by the shortage of most materials.[37] It was no wonder that the scars of war were still evident seven years after the conflict ended.

The House of Rest, a large dwelling for traveling Christians, provided pleasant accommodations from 26 May to 3 June, 1952.

Breakfast was memorable. It was the only time I have ever eaten boiled bacon. We were informed that such things as butter were still rationed, and were told how we could obtain our ration cards. That was

---

[36] Ibid., 612-613.
[37] Encyclopedia Britannica, 15th. Ed., s.v. "Reconstruction after World War II."

our first order of business. Afterwards, we visited Madame Tussaud's Swiss Waxworks Exhibition.

We traveled on the public transportation system, which included the tube and double decker buses, lunched at the Berkeley Restaurant, had tea at the Selfridges Store, and returned to House of Rest that evening.

On 28 May, 1952, we visited the Tower of London and saw the Crown Jewels. The Yeoman of the guards in their "Beefeaters" uniforms were traditionally distinctive.

We passed through Trafalgar Square, and saw Admiral Horatio Nelson's Monument. Admiral Nelson destroyed Napoleon's French and Spanish fleet off Cape Trafalgar 21 October, 1805.[38]

Then we visited St. Paul's Cathedral, the only building in the heart of London to survive the German incendiary attack of 29 December, 1940. It became the symbol for British resolve during the Battle of Britain.[39]

On 29 May, Dad visited the Africa Inland Mission office and wrote the Brooklyn office, giving our sailing date.

On 30 May, we saw the parade of the horse guard, bands, and foot guards in front of Buckingham Palace. King George VI had died in February while Princess Elizabeth and her husband were in Kenya. She was proclaimed Queen Elizabeth 6 February, 1952, and crowned 2 June, 1953. She had only been Queen for a few months when we visited London. Later we took a boat trip up the Thames River to Kew Gardens.

On 31 May, we visited Windsor Castle. This was the primary weekend residence of King George VI during the Battle of Britain. Lord Beaverbrook, Winston Churchill's minister of supply, used the grounds as temporary storage for fighter aircraft until they could be delivered to RAF squadrons.[40]

We boarded the train in London, traveled to South Hampton, and embarked on the SS *Liberte*, bound for New York.

---

[38] Walter Russell Mead, *God and Gold,* (New York, NY, Alfred A. Knopf, 2007), 107.
[39] Don McCombs & Fred L. Worth, *World War II,* Ibid., 519.
[40] Ibid., 642.

The Atlantic Barrier

"Therefore its name was called Babel, because there the Lord confused the language of the whole earth and from there the Lord scattered them abroad over the face of the whole earth." Genesis 11:9 (NASB)

The Atlantic Ocean was a natural barrier between Europe and the Western Hemisphere for centuries. It wasn't until the Viking sailors of Scandinavia, looking for a better place to live, ventured west to Iceland and Greenland. In AD 987, Bjarni Herjolfsson was blown off course and sighted North America. His sightings interested another Viking sailor, Leif Erikson, who in 1002 landed in Newfoundland and spent the winter. Others followed, but became discouraged after three winters, and they all left.[41]

Almost 500 years later Christopher Columbus persuaded the Queen of Spain to finance his venture across this barrier.

There is a fascinating quote from Christopher Columbus in Peter Marshall and David Manuel's book, *The Light and the Glory.*

It was the Lord who put into my mind (I could feel His hand upon me) the fact that it would be possible to sail from here (Europe) west to the Indies. All who heard of my project rejected it with laughter, ridiculing me. There is no question that the inspiration was from the Holy Spirit, because He comforted me with rays of marvelous inspiration from the Holy Scripture[42]

The year 1492 was favorable to Columbus because in January, Spain had finally driven the Moors out of the Iberian Peninsula. This was the end of what the Muslims call the "First Great Jihad."[43]

In 1805, the battle of Trafalgar pitted 33 French and Spanish ships against 27 British ships under Lord Nelson. It was Napoleon's final attempt to conquer British maritime strength. The British lost Lord Nelson, but

---

[41] Fiona MacDonald, *Vikings,* (London, England, Quarto Publishing, 1993), 19.

[42] Peter Marshall & David Manuel, *The Light and the Glory,* (Old Tappan, NJ, Fleming H. Revell Company, 1977), 17.

[43] Larry Abraham, "The Clash of Civilizations and the Great Caliphate," http://f414.mail.yahoo.com/ym/ShowLetter?Msgld=5755-88236-22-1974-28594-0-6. (accessed May 25, 2004).

sank 22 enemy ships while losing none of their own.[44]   This was the beginning of British worldwide maritime ascendancy.   By 1830, the way was opened for a mass migration of missionaries from Europe and Britain to evangelize the world.[45]

Millions of immigrants moved from Europe to North America until the 1920's.   Two significant events affected this traffic.   The 18th amendment went into effect in 1920, prohibiting the manufacture, sale, or transportation of alcoholic beverages.   This prohibition initiated travel from the United States to Europe and back by wealthy Americans for "party" purposes.   In 1921, Congress sharply curbed immigration by setting a national quota system.   These events enabled ship builders to make large, fast luxurious ships.

Germany built two ocean liners for transatlantic passenger service. Both the SS Bremen and SS Europa were launched in 1928.   The SS Europa was launched one day before the SS Bremen, but because of a fire, at the equipment dock, she did not make her maiden voyage until March 1930, eight months after SS Bremen's.   The SS Bremen took the Blue Riband for the fastest Atlantic crossing both ways on her first two voyages.[46]   The SS Europa took the westbound Blue Riband on her maiden voyage from SS Bremen.   SSBremen lost the eastbound Blue Riband to SS Normandie in 1935.   Both of these German ships were originally equipped with aircraft catapults between the funnels.   These were to speed mail service, but were later removed because they were too expensive and complex.

In 1935, the SS Normandie was the world's largest and fastest passenger ship.   To this day, she remains the most powerful steam turbo-electric propelled passenger ship ever built, though not a commercial success, needing French government subsidy.   She made 139 westbound transatlantic crossings, and one less return.   During WW II, the United States seized her.   While being fitted as a troop transport, she caught fire and capsized at the pier.[47]

After the war the SS Europa was turned over to the French as a war reparation.   After refitting her for passenger service, the Compagine

---

[44] Walter Russell Mead, *God and Gold*, Ibid., 107.

[45] Ibid., 113.

[46] The Blue Riband was won by the passenger ship with the fastest transatlantic time.

[47] Normandie,
    http://www.en,wikipedia.org/wiki/ss-Normandie. (accessed December 22, 2009).

Generale Transatlantique renamed her *SS Liberte.* She sailed for New York on her maiden voyage in 1950.[48]

SS Liberte

Wednesday, 4 June, 1952, the Herbert Downing family of six departed Southampton on one of the largest transatlantic liners in the French line fleet, the *SS Liberte.* Our cabins were in the third class section at the rear of the ship. Upon entering open water, the four huge propellers throbbed beneath us. As our speed increased the throb became a pronounced vibration.

One of the first orders of business on passenger ships was a lifeboat drill. This was designed to acquaint every passenger with the location and donning of life vests, and the path to assigned lifeboats. Next, was locating the dining room. One of the major differences between English and French Cuisine was the superior palatability of the French. Bottles of wine on every table fascinated us, and we were shocked to see even little French children drinking the stuff. Our parents objected to our tasting this readily available beverage, so it was years before I learned that most of it tastes dry to connoisseurs, acrid to me.

We soon settled into a comfortable routine, wandering about our third class section. The seas were relatively calm, and the big ship cruised along

---

[48]SS Europa (1928) – Wikipedia, the free encyclopedia,
http://en.wikipedia.org/wiki/SS-Europa-(1928). (accessed December 20, 2009).

at 27 knots or so. The ship's passenger capacity was almost 2,200 with a crew of 965. Its length was over 935 feet. I believe the SS *Liberte,* like her sister ship SS *Bremen,* had a Taylor bulbous bow. This provided buoyancy below the water line near the bow, which improved hull speed and reduced pitching. The SS *Europa's* original squat funnels were too short, coating lower class passengers with soot. The funnels were twice lengthened, once by the Germans and then by the French. Our voyage lasted about six days.

A notorious example of the perils of transatlantic travel occurred 50 years before. The SS *Titanic,* the largest movable object ever built, departed South Hampton on its maiden voyage. This was the most luxurious ship afloat. It had been constructed with a double bottomed hull with 16 water-tight compartments. Supposedly four of these compartments could be flooded and the ship still remains afloat. She was believed to be unsinkable, so she had only 1,178 lifeboat spaces for 2,224 passengers. On 14 April, 1912, the SS *Titanic* cruising at 22 knots collided with an iceberg and soon sank with the loss of 1,513 lives!

In 1985, the wreckage of the *Titanic* was discovered about 400 miles south of Newfoundland at a depth of 14,000 feet. Investigations by submersible vehicles surprised everyone; there was no gash in the ship's hull from the iceberg. A survivor's account of the collision indicated that there was little impact felt aboard the ship upon contact with the ice.[49]

The best analysis of the accident, in my opinion, is in Robert M. Williams' book, *The Sinking of the Titanic.* Inasmuch as 85% of an iceberg is submerged, he believes that the SS *Titanic* missed the visible part and ripped the bottom out on a submerged shelf. This would explain why the ship sank so quickly.[50]

The result of this disaster was an International Convention for *Safety of Life at Sea* in London in 1913. It required that every ship have lifeboat space for each person aboard, that lifeboat drills be held during each voyage, that ships maintain a 24 hour radio watch, and that The International Ice Patrol be established to warn of icebergs in North Atlantic shipping lanes.

At least three movies have been made about this disaster: SS *Titanic* (1953 in Hollywood,) centering on the shipboard story; *A Night to Remember* (1958 British) documentary-style account, far superior to

---

[49] Encyclopedia Britannica, 15th. ed. s.v. "Titanic."
[50] Robert M. Williams, "True Causes of the Titanic Disaster," http://www.rmexplorations.com/theories.htm. (accessed January 24, 2011).

Hollywood's presentation; and finally Hollywood's 1997 *SS Titanic*, which has grossed almost two trillion dollars.

We approached New York Harbor on Tuesday morning, 10 June, 1952. In preparation for disembarkation, all class barriers were dropped, and we were allowed almost anywhere on the ship. I was amazed by the opulence of the first class section: crystal chandeliers, expensive wood paneling, wall hangings, paintings, and wide winding wooden staircases. Looking back, it's not difficult to understand why so many of these ships had a history of internal fires which gutted the ship, *SS Liberte* included.

As we entered the harbor, I was at the base of the forward funnel with a young English gentleman. We felt pretty smart, looking down on the Captain's bridge, until the ship's horn blew only a few feet above us. It felt like a wooden box around my head had been slammed with a sledge hammer. We quickly vacated that position.

I was surprised to learn that educationally, English students were rated by an exam taken after junior high. This determined their qualification for college. He was surprised that Americans had no such screening system.

As we passed the Statue of Liberty, my emotions were stirred. The Empire State building, the tallest in the world, came into view, and the Englishman thought it was sort of cheating to have that tall tower on top of the building to achieve preeminence. I later learned that it had been designed as a dirigible mooring mast, so that passengers could be deposited in the heart of New Your City.

The closer we got to the pier, the more interesting the activities became. Tugboats approached and waited patiently for their cues. The dock was lined with people waiting for passengers. Longshoremen were standing by to handle the heavy hawsers for mooring the ship.

Our family had repacked our luggage and moved it to an assembly point. We then joined the passengers at the railing looking for those that were meeting us. Finally at 1:00 PM the gangways were in place, and we left the ship.

The piers for the large liners were on the west side of Manhattan. Each pier could moor two ships. The *SS Liberte* was on the north side with the south side empty. The pier became tumultuous, as 2,000 plus passengers and crew members descended into the mass of greeters, officials, and dock workers.

We gathered with our baggage, while Dad looked for the mission representative. Customs officials and immigration officers had to be con-

SS Liberte Docking

tacted. Luggage stowed in the hold had to be located and porters employed.

Meantime, one of the dock workers told me that the SS *United States* would be moored on the south side of that pier. This took place 11 days after our arrival on 21 June, 1952. The SS *United States* departed on her maiden voyage at 12:07 PM, on 3 July, 1952. She won the Blue Riband on her first two crossings and never lost them.[51]

---

[51] The Blue Ribbon or Blue Riband Atlantic Passenger Boat Record, "Competition," http://www.bluebird-electric.net/net-the-blue-ribband.htm. (accessed December 24, 2009).

The *SS United States* was the fastest transatlantic liner ever built. She was built in a U.S. Navy yard to Navy standards of safety. She had a steel hull with an aluminum superstructure. Her designer would not allow any flammable material in the vessel, with one exception. The piano manufacturer had to prove that its wood finish would not support a flame.[52]

The first airplane to conquer the Atlantic Ocean was the large Boeing 314 flying boat. Pan American Airways inaugurated a mail service between New York and Marseille, France on 28 July, 1939. Twelve of these aircraft were ordered and continued to operate throughout WW II. [53]

Douglas built a four engine transport that could cross the Atlantic in 1942. One thousand were built by war's end, and almost 8,000 crossings were made with the loss of only three aircraft. This airplane was continually improved until 1958.[54]

1952 was in the middle of the development stage of transatlantic air travel. Air transportation costs were much higher than ocean liners; at that time most missionaries traveled as we did.

1957 was the first year that airplanes carried more passengers across the north Atlantic than passenger ships. In October 1958, one month after the *SS United States* logged its one-millionth mile inbound to the Statue of Liberty, the first transatlantic jet, a *Comet 4*, crossed the Atlantic. This became the death knell to these beautiful ships.

After a couple hours of chaos, we found ourselves moving slowly through the confusion of New York traffic towards the Africa Inland Mission offices in Brooklyn. The mission had living accommodations, which we occupied until Saturday, 14 June, 1952. Mother's brother, Ed Houk, and his wife Sally, borrowed an Oldsmobile station wagon from one of his church members, and drove us to his home in Philipsburg, Pennsylvania.

---

[52] SS United States-Wikipedia, the free encyclopedia,
http://en.wikipedia.org/wiki/SS United States.
[53] Robert Jackson, *The History of Aviation*, (New York, NY, Amber Books Ltd., 2007), 128-129.
[54] Ibid., 263-267.

Guidance

"And do not be conformed to this world, but be transformed by the renewing of your mind so that you may prove what the will of God is, that which is good and acceptable and perfect." Romans 12: 1 & 2 (NASB)

For 5 1/2 years my parents had been busy with the responsibilities of the Rift Valley Academy (RVA). Dad was the principal, and mother was a full time high school teacher. It is virtually impossible for people, confined in one culture, to comprehend the complications of life in a second culture without being there.

RVA, a school for missionary children in the highlands of Kenya, East Africa, was started shortly after the Africa Inland Mission (AIM) began ministry there at the beginning of the 20th century. Lee H. Downing, my paternal grandfather, was in the third party of AIM missionaries, entering Africa in 1901. My father, born at Kijabe in 1905, was one of the first students at RVA.

Dad completed his education at Muskingum College in New Concord, Ohio, met and married my mother there, and returned to Kijabe in 1933. He was well qualified for his responsibilities. He was accepted by the Africans who worked at the school, speaking the Kikuyu language fluently. He had school administrative experience in Forest Hills, Pennsylvania, and had undergone the challenge of being a "Third Culture Kid" (TCK) himself.

Students at RVA are generally the product of parents who have left a native culture to work in a second culture. The children are part of neither the original nor the second culture. They form a third culture. The anomalies of their experiences make cultural assimilation in first or second cultures challenging.

Mother was a very bright student and an excellent teacher. She was the daughter of the Presbyterian minister in New Concord. Going to Africa was not easy for her. But working on a large mission station in an established school was not pioneer mission work. She was a professional teacher, influencing the lives of many students over her years at RVA.

Working in a faith mission was difficult for mother. A qualified educator, she was much more comfortable working for a contracted salary. It pained her to have to beg (make her needs known) and accept support, (live on charity so to speak.) But of all the missionaries I knew, she was the most faithful in corresponding with those who supported our family. Very seldom did she resort to a form letter. She spent hours writing personal letters on fold up air forms.

Kijabe was a large station of 2,000 acres, and had many different activities. There were no motels for guests, so visitors were accommodated in missionary homes. Mother was very adroit at handling unexpected visitors. I never knew whether I would be sleeping in my bed or on a camp cot under the eaves.

Five and a half years of problem solving with (1) immature TCK's in boarding school, (2) second culture Africans, and (3) teachers and staff in foreign circumstances, had taken their toll on Dad's health. He needed a break.

It should be emphasized that furloughs for "faith missionaries" are not vacations. Our family's arrival in the States simply changed priorities. An administrative routine became nonroutine fund raising. My father's diary for this period in 1952 was sketchy, but indicated a wide variety of activities. For transportation, a 1948 Chevy Fleet line, two door fast back sedan was acquired. I loved driving that car with its vacumatic gear shift. It eventually towed a 21 foot house trailer to the West Coast and back.

One of my father's interests was photography. He had filmed the visit of mission officials from the United States, and was involved with the home office in their editing.

Living accommodations were provided in Coshocton, Ohio by my mother's brother-in-law, Judge C.M. Ross. A large comfortable home, that needed some maintenance, became our temporary residence. I learned to scrape and paint the outside of the house. Dad repaired the front porch, and put a new counter-top in the kitchen. It was commodious and comfortable.

Mother was a good housekeeper and cook. Before college, I recall picking cherries and helping her pit and can them. We always ate our meals together, enjoying good food. Mom and Dad felt it was better to buy healthy food than spend money on medicines. They took good care of our medical and dental health.

Once settled into our house, mission deputation began in earnest. Dad and Mom both spoke to different groups from Iowa to the eastern seaboard. Like his father, Dad did not preach but spoke in a conversational

Downing Itinerants in Coshocton

manner. He was not a "pulpit pounder" but could hold an audience with his quiet delivery.

As the summer wore on, my sister and I prepared to leave for college. The head of the AIM, Dr. Howard Ferrin, was also president of Providence Bible Institute. His previous visit to Africa had played a part in our choice of schools. My plan at the time was to get the necessary Bible training for mission work. Ultimately, I hoped to get an engineering degree and return to Africa as a technical missionary.

In 1925, Grandfather Downing was in Washington D.C. for a missionary convention. On January 16th he wrote in his diary, "Have enjoyed the Lord's presence." The next day he recorded a physical exam listing his height, 5'8", and weight, 130 pounds. Three days later, on the 19th, he wrote: "I spoke at the Bible Institute of Washington D.C. at 8 PM on How Can I Best Execute God's Plan (Galatians 2:20)." On the 23rd: "Wrote an article on God's Plan…" On February 3rd, he gave Alice Updegraff the revised manuscript to type. Thus came into being his pamphlet *How May I Know God's Plan for my Life?* This was used by AIM for decades to help people learn to hear God's voice. I became acquainted with it when I was quite young, and have used his practical guidance for every major decision in my adult life, including my college choice. It is included as appendix A because of its significance.

Grandfather Downing

The copy of *God's Plan,* as published by the AIM, did not include the post script that was originally in Appendix A. This illustrated the practical outworking of his exhortation, and revealed the guidance that characterized his ministry in Africa from 1901 until his death there in 1942.[55]

Coshocton, Ohio is on the Muskingum River, at the confluence of the Tuscarawas River and the Walhonding River, 80 miles ENE of Columbus. The city, laid out in 1802, was originally named Tuscarawas, but nine years later became the Coshocton County seat, and was renamed Coshocton.[56]

Until 1781, Coshocton had been a Delaware Indian village. Delaware Indians had originally occupied the eastern seaboard, but were displaced by the advancing Europeans. During the Revolutionary War the tribe had been divided in its allegiance. The side that sought neutrality settled at Coshocton until American Andrew Brodhead destroyed the village. The surviving Indians fled from eastern Ohio.

The completion of the Ohio and Erie Canal in 1827 connected Lake Erie with the Ohio River. This canal followed four river valleys, including the Muskingum Valley that connected Coshocton with the Ohio River at Portsmouth, Ohio. Our family picture collection records the canoe trip my father, his brother, and a college friend made down this river. Tourists can still see remnants of this canal with boats and towing paths at the restored canal town of Roscoe Village.[57]

Canal transportation was slow and seasonal, with droughts and winter freezing. They also required excessive maintenance. Canal boats could move very heavy loads at about four miles per hour. This opened the

---

[55] Dr. F.B. Meyer, mentioned in *God's Plan* is the author of *The Consecrated Life.* Just before my father returned to Africa in 1954, he gave me a copy. It has been a helpful guideline ever since, and is included as Appendix B.

[56] Encyclopdia Britannica, 15th. ed., s.v. "Coshocton."

[57] Coshocton, Ohio-Ohio History Central – A product of the Ohio Historical Society, http://www.lhiohistorycentral.rg/entry.php?rec=693. (accessed January 31, 2010).

movement of grain from the farmlands of eastern Ohio, making Coshocton a major commercial center. The canal's heyday was from 1830-1860 when railroads began to speed up the movement of heavy freight. Canals were gradually superseded until the flood of 1931 wiped them out.[58]

Railroads were initially dangerous and unreliable, but the steel wheel on a steel rail was the most efficient means of land transportation ever developed. It helped make the United States one of the wealthiest countries in the world.

One evening, the first week of September 1952, my sister and I boarded the train in Coshocton for Providence, Rhode Island. The Pennsylvania Railroad crossed the Allegheny Mountains near Altoona, Pennsylvania. My father had talked of the famous Horseshoe Curve, so I stayed awake to see it.

Horseshoe Curve has been considered the eighth wonder of the modern world. The Allegheny Mountains presented a formidable barrier to railroads. The maximum grade was 1.8% (a rise of 1.8 feet in 100 feet of distance). In the late 1840's, J. Edgar Thompson solved the problem with a horseshoe curve that doubled back on itself. Work began in 1851. Four hundred immigrants, mostly Irish, using pickaxes, shovels, gun-powder, horses and drags, completed the project in three years on 15 February, 1854. It has been in continuous use since then.

It was so vital that Union soldiers guarded it during the Civil War. During WW II the Germans recognized its significance and planned to destroy it with operation PASTORIUS. It was one of the top 10 targets for the Germans. Seeing it personally was worth the loss of sleep.[59]

We arrived at the Pennsylvania Station in New York City the following morning. The next leg of our journey was on the New York, New Haven, and Hartford Railroad which left from Grand Central Station. Ralph Davis, from the AIM, escorted us through New York traffic to meet our next train.

The railroad tracks paralleled the sea coast most of the way. My most indelible memory was the guy with a cooler box, trying to sell ORY-JUICE. I never determined whether he had a cold or a speech impediment.

---

[58] *Encyclop0edia of Cleveland History:* "Ohio and Erie Canal," http://ech.cwrsu.edu/ech-cgi/aarticle.pl?id=OAEC. (accessed November 5, 2011).
[59] Visit the World Famous Horseshoe Curve, Pennsylvania mountains of attractions, "A Pennsylvania Historical Wonder – The World Famous Horseshoe Curve," http://www.pennsylvania-mountains-of-attractions.com/hoursehoe-curve.html. (accessed November 10, 2011).

The Providence train terminal is just below the Rhode Island State House. This beautiful building was built in 1895 of Georgia white marble.[60] It has the fourth largest unsupported marble dome in the world, (after St. Peters Basilica in Rome, the Minnesota State Capital, and the Taj Mahal in Agra, India). This dome is 50 feet in diameter at its base and is topped by an 11 foot statue of "Independent Man" covered with gold leaf. This edifice was the only thing of beauty in the whole city, from my point of view.

We engaged a taxi to take us to Providence Bible Institute just behind the State House. The cramped campus consisted of two and three story frame buildings grouped on two small city blocks. The one fairly new brick building, called Winn Hall, served as an auditorium for school convocations, with a dining room below.

My dormitory room was on the third floor of building 59. Having missed sleep on the train, I was happy to have a bed. Feeling a bit homesick, I delayed buying text books just in case the money was needed for a ticket back to Ohio.

It was depressing to realize that the carefree life I had enjoyed in Africa was gone forever. This attitude surfaced at an evening meeting designed to welcome new students. We were being introduced by home states. Since Ohio was my home of record, I was called to speak briefly about my coming. I decided to clarify my status with a saying from a huge Norwegian settler in Kenya. It went like this:

Kenya born
Kenya bred,
Strong in the body
Weak in the head.

This broke the ice and got back to my folks, at a mission meeting in New York, thanks to Dr. Carlton Booth. My heart was still in Africa, the land of my roots!

---

[60] Encyclopedia Britannica, 12th. ed., s.v. "Providence."

Roots

"Content is the man who delights in the Law of the Lord. (A law of faith in contrast to the Law of works, Romans 3:27) He is like a tree planted by streams of living water which produces seasonal fruit. And everything he does shall prosper." Psalm 1:1-3 (my paraphrase)

The seed of my roots in Africa was sown in Glasgow, Scotland in 1873. Two notable raw unordained Americans evangelists, Dwight L. Moody and Ira D. Sankey, preached to a crowd of 3,000 in the city hall. In the crowd was a six year old boy named Peter Scott. Peter's teacher described how his dislike of the accent and informality evaporated as soon as he heard Sankey sing *I am So Glad That Jesus Loves Me*. Moody's preaching brought tears to his eyes. It was a new concept for these Scottish people that God loved sinners. They believed that God loved only saints. Peter Cameron Scott became a "tree" planted by the living waters of Jesus Christ which prospered in Kenya, East Africa.[61]

The Scott family emigrated to Philadelphia, PA after one of their six children died in Scotland. One of Peter's gifts was a good voice. Trained under an Italian maestro, he was headed towards a professional operatic career. But hearing the voice of God, he gave up this endeavor to become a missionary, in obedience to the Holy Spirit.

Peter trained at the New York Missionary Training College, and was accepted by the International Missionary Alliance for service in West Africa. After being ordained to the Gospel ministry by A.B. Simpson, he sailed for the Port of Banana at the mouth of the Congo River.[62] He was under 24 years old when he arrived in January 1891. Two years later, he became so ill with fever that he was carried unconscious back to Banana, and returned to England. Mr. and Mrs. Brodie in London recalled his arrival as they were entertaining a few enthusiastic new missionaries one foggy November evening. A cab arrived, and a pathetic figure was helped out. Seated in the group with the obvious effects of his illness, Peter looked

---

[61] Dick Anderson, *We felt like Grasshoppers*, (Nottingham, Great Britain, Crossway Books, 1994), 17-18.

[62] Kenneth Richardson, *Garden of Miracles*, (London, Great Britain, Africa Inland Mission, 1968), 24-25.

around and said, "Well, friends, you are going forth—I have come back. It is no child's play; it is a battle!"[63]

Physical recovery was slow. During a visit to Westminster Abbey, Peter Scott was drawn to David Livingston's tombstone. The words under the name caused him to kneel and pray for Africa. *"Other sheep I have which are not of this fold: them also I must bring."* Later he said that he envisioned a line of mission stations passing through East Africa and on and on into the mysteries of the Sahara Desert. "Your young men will see visions." Joel 2:28

Scott read all he could about Africa. He became aware of Arab traders up the Nile into Africa's heartlands, in search of slaves and converts. A new line of Christian outposts might halt that advance. The mountains along the line of his vision attracted his attention. Disease took a heavy toll on missionaries' lives in the low lying areas. By living in the hills, they might escape the fatal fevers. He hoped that Africans, more resistant to malaria, could be trained to evangelize the people on the plains.

Finally recovered, (as "recovered" as a malaria patient can be,) he returned to Philadelphia. His enthusiasm infected not only his family, but also an interested mission support group. Arthur Pierson and Charles Hurlburt not only shared his dream but enlarged on it, establishing three organizations in 1895: Africa Inland Mission, Pennsylvania Bible Institute, and Central American Industrial Mission. PBI became the home base for the supporting missionary council and a school for training missionaries.[64]

Scott set off with six others in August 1895. By October, they had arrived in Zanzibar, East Africa's most important port and the main center of British influence. In mid November, four men set out to find a base for their work. The safari included about 300 porters and 42 camels. By December, they reached the area of Mount Nzawi. A site was selected at 4,000 feet elevation, some 250 miles from the coast, and building began.

In the first year, missionaries were positioned in four locations: Nzawi, Sakai, Kilungu, and Kangundo. Peter overcame the Wakamba tribal resistance with humor, exhibitions of juggling, tumbling, and balancing acts. In his annual report, he noted he had walked 2,600 miles. All of the missionaries had intermittent bouts with malaria. Scott was finally forced into bed on the 3 December, 1896 and died the next day at the age of 29![65]

---

[63] Kenneth Richardson, *Garden of Miracles*, Ibid., 25.
[64] Dick Anderson, *We felt like Grasshoppers*, Ibid., 19-20.
[65] Kenneth Richardson, *Garden of Miracles*, Ibid., 29-35.

When news of Scott's death reached the missionary council, Charles Hurlbert, its president, felt called to take his place. The council considered whether God was closing down AIM and calling another mission to take over. Dr. A.R. Pierson, a council member, said, "Gentlemen, the hallmark of God on any work is death. God has given us that hallmark. Now is the time to go forward."[66]

Charles Hurlburt was appointed AIM's general director in 1897. In 1900 he made a two month tour of Kenya, when man-eating lions on the railroad at Tsavo were at their worst. He returned to America with a great burden for Africa's people.

Mr. Hurlburt left for Africa in October 1901 with his wife and five children and my paternal grandparents, Lee and Blanche Downing. This was an exceptional act of faith and courage in those days.[67]

Lee Downing was born on a farm in Belmont County, Ohio. His father, Alexander Downing, was a generation older than his second wife, Margaret Harper. She bore two sons, John Alexander on 16 April, 1865 and Lee Harper 28 June, 1866.

Lee's father, Alexander, died when Lee was six years old, and his mother died before he was 10. The two Downing orphans lived with their legal guardians, John and Famie Caldwell. Famie took them in, loved, and raised them to manhood.

Lee Downing's father was 6'4" tall and his brother John was over 6'. Because of allergies and asthma, Lee was only 5'8" tall and never weighed more than 130 pounds. People considered him frail because of his size, but he was wiry and had big strong hands. Interestingly, he never suffered from allergies in Africa. He was an artist with an ax and rode thousands of miles in central Africa on a bicycle, but never drove a car. He outlived his brother by 13 years, dying in Nairobi in 1942, age 76.[68]

Lee attended Franklin College in New Athens, Ohio for two years. Franklin was later absorbed by Muskingum College. At 26, he graduated from Washington and Jefferson College in 1892, the valedictorian of his class.

In 1896, when Lee was 30, Charles Hurlburt appointed him lecturer in New Testament Greek at Pennsylvania Bible Institute. From the start, Hurlburt trusted him and invited him to be a college trustee and treasurer of the Philadelphia Missionary Council. One of Lee's students, Blanche

---

[66] Dick Anderson, *We felt like Grasshoppers,* Ibid., 31.
[67] Kenneth Richardson, Ibid., 41.
[68] Lucile Downing, *My Childhood in Africa,* (unpublished), 4-7.

39

Hunter, became his wife in October 1899. Two years later they arrived at Kangundo with the Hurlbut family.[69]

My father's older sister, Lucile, was born at Kangundo in November 1902, the first white child born in that area. She was a real curiosity to the local Africans! Soon, Mr. Hurlbut moved the main center to Kijabe where my father, Herbert, and his younger brother, Kenneth, were born. It continues to be an active mission enterprise.

Evidently the original choice of real estate had been Lake Naivasha. The deal had almost been finalized when one of the government officials got wind of it and disapproved. The higher elevation of Kijabe proved to be much healthier, as the extra thousand feet put it out of the malaria area. Interesting!

All three Downing children were educated at Rift Valley Academy and graduated from Muskingum College in New Concord, Ohio.[70] After mother and dad's engagement in March, 1929, she became aware of his commitment to helping the Kikuyu people in Kenya. Before their wedding in June 1931, they both applied and were accepted by the AIM.

From 1931 to 1933, they lived in Forest Hills, Pennsylvania, where dad was the Junior High School principal. At midnight 10 March, 1933, Grandfather and Grandmother Downing, mother and dad with my older sister, Gayle, and Uncle Kenneth, departed New York on the *SS Hamburg*, arriving in Mombasa aboard the *SS Nyassa* five weeks later.

This marked the earliest arrival of second generation AIM missionaries returning to Kenya. Herbert and Kenneth Downing were back home!

Mother wrote: "Our second child, and first son Glenn Herbert, arrived at Kijabe Hospital on January 22, 1935. I walked up to the hospital in the middle of the night with Herbert and Blanche Wakala helping me. Two nurses (no doctor!) awaited us. Next morning on the station telephone system, Father Downing gave the general ring and proudly announced Glenn Herbert's arrival to the local and visiting missionaries (the annual conference was in session). Miss Bessie Stevenson was the nurse in charge. Miss Ida Rhodes and Salome, the African nurse, also helped."[71]

An explanation of mother's note is enlightening. She miscarried not long before I was conceived. She and dad were doing double duty at RVA because of limited staff. Kijabe is perched on the side of the Great Rift Valley which is about 25 miles wide. The valley floor is savanna and

---

[69] Dick Anderson, *We Felt Like Grasshoppers*, Ibid., 78.
[70] Lucile Downing, *My Childhood in Africa*, Ibid., 48.
[71] Mildred Downing, from an undated autobiographical letter in my possession.

absorbs heat from the tropical sun during the day time. At night the rising heat from the valley sucks cold air down the side of the mountains and at 7,000 – 8,000 foot elevations it is quite chilly. We had a fire in the fireplace every evening.

Dad's only transportation was a one cylinder Harley-Davidson motorcycle, hardly suitable for the occasion. Urgency required a hike of about a quarter mile up the hill. Diminished oxygen at 7,000 feet is quite noticeable. Perhaps this will give you an idea of the conditions encountered when mother brought me into the world.

The Blaikie House

Mother describes the new home as: "the Blaikie House, a dark, rat infested house." She wrote: "I met my first lizard staring at me from a cupboard top. Our first adjustments were learning to cook on a wood stove in a kitchen separate from the main house, trying to communicate with African help, getting oil lamps and other needed supplies at the Indian dukas at Kijabe railway station and in Nairobi, washing clothes with a washboard, and learning to iron with flat irons."[72]

---

[72] Ibid.

The Blaikie House was basically a rectangular structure made out of light weight lava ash blocks. Lava ash, quite accessible in that area, could be cut with hatchets and chisels. The blocks were laid up in clay and the faces pointed with cement. The ceilings were roughly 10 feet high and covered with plywood recovered from bicycle crates. It had a wooden floor above a crawl space. A single chimney served fireplaces in the living room and dad's office. Originally, there were four rooms. There were long verandas on the front and back of the house. A small bedroom and bathroom were added on the back veranda. The kitchen was behind a floored open space. The main structure was roofed with cedar shingles and the kitchen with corrugated iron. The kitchen roof collected drinking water in a large metal tank.

My father restructured the "dark house" by putting windows in the doors, connecting the living room and dining room with an arch, building a stairway to the attic, and putting a tall window above the landing. He was a meticulous cabinet maker, and the stairs and arch were built of natural finished cedar. It was beautiful!

Mother in her Living Room

The attic was made into two bedrooms, lined with reed mats and used as temporary guest rooms. The toilet was an outhouse up the hill behind the kitchen. South of the privy path was a large garden with rabbit runs, fruit trees, and vegetables. This was home!

Little Grey House in the Weeds

Blanche Wakala was our cook and became my ayah (or nursemaid) while mother was teaching. I was known as a "gifted breakfast eater." In the kitchen, I would eat hot cereal up to a certain point, and stop until I saw eggs cooking. I made sure the next course was on its way before I ran out of food!

Among my early recollections was my second birthday cake with two white birds on it, the sour porridge that the African girls let me taste, and being in the big classroom at RVA when one of the students put a lion head outside the window. I was below the main school building when dad was on the roof and pretended to go down a chimney. Most of my memories were prompted by pouring over the three gray picture albums dad made up for relatives in the States. There were slides shown in deputation talks. One picture of me standing with my double felt hat and a big grin, when I had washed my face with garden dirt, always got a chuckle. Dad's presentations always ended with a brightly colored picture of a sunset behind the mountains across the valley.

One significant experience that has impacted my life was learning to sing Kikuyu songs with African Peter Gitau. We would sing together on the back porch in the evening. This gift has opened doors to many exciting adventures.

This was my only permanent home until I was married, had two children, and bought my first house. Wars have impacted my life from birth. In 1935 Mussolini invaded Ethiopia to the north of Kenya. WW II was incubating in Europe. Kenya was characterized by tribal wars and power struggles. Conflict was everywhere! Reduced to simplest terms, there are only two types of people on planet earth: "sheep" and "goats".[73] There is a God given enmity between the 'seed of the woman' (sheep) and the 'seed of the serpent' (goats).[74] There will never be peace on earth until the Prince of Peace is on His throne in Jerusalem. God's plan for my life has been a series of world-wide journeys prompted by these wars.

Zinj was the ancient Persian name for East Africa, the source of wealth and slaves for the Indian Ocean Empires. Conflict and slavery continue today. Hence the title: *Global Warring and the Land of Zinj*. The first of four world wars is the subject of the next chapter.

---

[73] Matthew 25:31-33. 31 "But when the Son of Man comes in His glory, and all the angels with Him, then He will sit on His glorious throne. 32 All the nations will be gathered before Him; and He will separate them from one another, as the shepherd separates the sheep from the goats; 33and He will put the sheep on His right, and the goats on the left." (New American Standard Bible Updated Edition.)

[74] Genesis 3:14-15. 14 The Lord God said to the serpent, "Because you have done this, cursed are you more than all cattle, and more than every beast of the field; On your belly you will go, and dust you will eat all the days of your life; 15 And I will put enmity between you and the woman, and between your seed and her seed; He shall bruise you on the head, and you shall bruise him on the heel." (NASB – Updated Edition.)

Dirty Face Glennie

World War I

"...And when you hear of wars and insurrections, do not panic. These things are bound to happen first, but the end does not follow at once... Nation will go to war against nation, kingdom against kingdom; there will be severe earthquakes, famines, and plagues in many places, and in the sky terrors and great signs from heaven." Luke 21:9-11. (Revised English Bible).

Norman Podhoretz, a neo-conservative Jew, has helped drive the central political and intellectual debates in the United States. He powerfully argues that the world has been subjected to four world conflicts within the last 100 years. Everyone has recognized World War I and World War II, but he maintains the "Cold War" was World War III and that we are presently engaged in World War IV, a struggle against Islamofascism.[75]

Two thousand years ago, Jesus taught that wars would be harbingers of the end of the age. He concluded by saying that the Good News of His kingdom would be proclaimed throughout the earth as a testimony to all nations, and then the end will come.[76] W.R. Mead in *God and Gold* states that after the Battle at Waterloo in 1815: "Throughout the world, British missionaries began to preach the Gospel in the unlikeliest places: that Christianity is a global religion today is in considerable part due to the efforts begun then."[77]

Few are aware of the cause of these wars. Fewer still are aware of who planned them, their ultimate goals, and the coincident results. The assassination of Archduke Francis Ferdinand in Bosnia was only the trigger of a carefully devised plot in WW I. The objectives of the intrigue included the destruction of the Ottoman Empire, the overthrow of monarchies, the degradation of the Catholic Church, and the foundation of a world republic. Details of these machinations are carefully spelled out in John Daniel's book *Scarlet and the Beast.*[78]

---

[75] Norman Podhoretz, *World War IV*, (New York, NY, Doubeday, 2007), 5.
[76] Matthew 24:14.
[77] Walter Russell Mead, *God and Gold*, (New York, NY, Alfred A. Knopf, 2007), 113.
[78] John Daniel, *Scarlet and the Beast*, (Longview, TX, Day Publishing, 2007), 523.

Since it was a conflict between the Central Powers and the Allies, Europe was where the carnage proliferated. It was, however, a war which affected the rest of the world. East Africa was no exception.

Fred and Alta Hoyt arrived in Mombassa in October 1911. Fred was 32 years old, and Alta 30. They had gone to Africa with their two sons, Howard and Paul, to work at the Lumbwa Industrial Mission under a Mr. Hotchkiss. Later, they joined the Friends Africa Industrial Mission, and spent more than 30 years at Kaimosi. My parents frequently spoke fondly of a vacation they spent with the Hoyts. They never forgot the pineapples that hung upside down after picking, so the sugar would permeate the whole fruit.

Fred built roads, ran a sawmill, taught the Africans carpentry, and showed them how to form and burn bricks. It was my father's opinion that churches built with this kind of leadership produced stronger more mature Christian communities. Not only were they wealthier, but they were prepared more quickly to accept the responsibilities of leadership and evangelism.

In 1949, Mr. Hoyt spent time in our home at Kijabe when he returned from the States, after retirement, to collect specimens for the Friends University Museum. I will never forget this big man, with his dry sense of humor.

Alta Hoyt wrote a book entitled *We Were Pioneers*. This is a fascinating read. I was particularly interested in her diary entries during 1914:

August 12, 1914- War has been declared between Germany and England and all Europe is mixed up in it. Our protectorate here is now under martial law and Mr. Andersen has had to take his and Rassmussen's mules, saddles and bridles to Kapsabit for government use. All the British settlers have volunteered...

Yes, the government commandeered our mules also and took them away after paying us cash for them. But in a few days they brought back Conover's and Dr. Blackburn's mules saying they were too mean to handle. But ours they kept.

One must recall that the next colony south of Kenya was German East Africa. Word came that the Germans had taken Kisi, 40 miles from us, and officials had ordered all white women and children to come into Kisumu at once. But our men folks asked the officials to let us all stay at our mission since we're neutral Americans, and felt safer at the mission than in Kisumu.

Fortunately the next day word came that the English had retaken Kisi so we were allowed to stay, thank God.[79]

Volume II of *Permanent Way*, written by M.F. Hill, gives a detailed account of the battle between British and the Germans in East Africa. What follows is a synopsis.

Few are aware of this conflict, for history is written by the winners. The first major confrontation ended in one of the "most ignominious reverses ever inflicted on British arms...Not for several months were the British people allowed to read news of the reverses at Tanga and Longido, and steps were taken to prevent the news spreading in India." A Prussian Lt. Col. succeeded in tying up thousands of allied troops for the duration that could have made a difference in Europe.

Mr. Hill states: *Before August 1914, little thought was given, either in Great Britain or in Germany, to what might happen in East Africa if war broke out in Europe. The Act of Berlin of 1885 contained clauses relating to neutrality within the Congo Conventional Zone, and it was widely believed that they would check the spread of war from Europe to Africa. Only the Belgian Congo had been declared permanently neutral: elsewhere within the zone, the powers concerned had the option of declaring their territory neutral in the event of war; if any did so, the other signatory powers were bound to respect the declarations of neutrality. At the outbreak of the First World War neither Great Britain nor Germany gave notice of neutrality in East Africa.*[80]

Both Germany and Britain had trained and equipped military forces to deal with internal unrest and maintain law and order. The British had 20 companies of Kings African Rifles (KAR), of 75 to 125 men each, and a camel company.

In January 1941, Lt. Col. Paul von Lettow-Vorbeck was appointed commander of the German Defense Force. This consisted of fourteen Feldkompagnies (abbreviated F.K.) which totaled 260 Germans and 2,472 Africans. Lt. Col. von Lettow-Vorbeck was a Prussian officer, of considerable experience, with outstanding ability and personal qualities.

---

[79] Alta Howard Hoyt, *We were Pioneers*, (unpublished, 1971), 42.

[80] M. F. Hill, *Permanent Way, Volume II,* (Nairobi, Kenya, Hazzell Watson and Viney LTD, 1957), 109.

He proved to be an exceptional trainer of troops, a brilliant and determined commander in the field, and a master of strategic retreat.

He immediately engaged in extensive tours throughout German East Africa. The FKs were reorganized, re-equipped and subjected to intensive training. His request for upgraded arms and ammunition was filled, just before the outbreak of war.[81]

Inasmuch as the KAR was widely scattered at the beginning of the war, and not under one command, the advantage lay with the Germans. The British East Africa protectorate and the Uganda Protectorate were entirely unprepared for war.

Dr. Heinrich Schnee, the governor of German East Africa, detested the idea of war. He bitterly resented the inevitable disruption of his work on the economic development of the German Protectorate. He regarded internal security as his first essential and clung to the hope of neutrality. He forbade any attempt to defend the ports against attack from the sea, and reluctantly agreed to collective concentrated troop training, but insisted it must not be near the frontier.

Von Lettow-Vorbeck believed his small forces might divert enemy troops that would otherwise be used in Europe, and that British East Africa should be attacked or at least threatened at a sensitive point. The Uganda Railway was the obvious objective. In *My Rememberences of East Africa*: von Lettow-Vorbeck wanted his forces to be concentrated, "to grip the enemy by the throat and compel him to use his forces in self defense."

On August 7th Captain von Prince at Moshi received a telegram from von Lettow-Vorbeck stating: "The Congo Treaty is not in force. Destruction of Uganda Railway and telegraph line to take place in several places... quick action promises good results."

During the first weeks of the war, British East Africa was fortunate that the Germans were unable, or failed, to take greater advantage of their weakness.

Steps were quickly taken to reinforce the defense of British East Africa. Dispersed KAR units were concentrated. Nearly 1,800 volunteers were enrolled in Nairobi. The largest volunteer unit was the East African Mounted Rifles (EAMR) with 335 men mounted on ponies and mules. The country was infested with tsetse flies which destroyed pack animals, requiring large numbers of human porters. It was assumed that additional troops would come from India.

---

[81] M. F. Hill, *Permanent Way, Volume II*, Ibid., 110-111.

The colonial office, not the war office, was responsible for all defense matters in the protectorate. Three Indian Infantry Battalions were sent to reinforce the KAR at its request.

In the planning stages of these moves, an expedition from India to capture a German sea port was proposed. India had already provided troops for the war in Europe and Kenya, but was tasked with this additional responsibility. B.G. Aitken was charged with planning the operation with the aid of Mr. Norman King, a previous British consul in Dar so Salaam.

From the summary of the operation in the *Official History of the Great War*-_'Military Operations, East Africa,'_ compiled by Lt. Col. Charles Hordern, chapters IV and V:

There can be no doubt that the expedition to Tanga contained from the beginning all the elements of a disaster. Founded upon a plan devised in London, on scanty and far from reliable information, by a committee of officials of the India Office, Colonial Office and Admiralty, its conception was accepted by the Offensive Sub-committee unquestioningly and without reference to the military experts of the General Staff. In that acceptance lay the root cause of one of the most notable failures in British military history. Other causes...contributed to make failure doubly certain.

From a military point of view the defects of the project are only too apparent. A scratch force some 8,000 strong, with no knowledge of African warfare, a considerable percentage of whose troops were quite unsuited to the purpose, was in the first place to land on a hostile coast as to which little was known, immediately after a fortnights sea-voyage under debilitating conditions...With a curious blend of optimism and misapprehension of German mentality, it was suggested that the enemy might yield to the moral effect of this advance; that a large area of his territory might be occupied...

The impracticability of these hopeful designs was destined to be finally and cruelly demonstrated at the first attempt to put them into execution...[82]

The failure prompted the British to reconsider the offer of volunteers they had previously rejected. The Legion of Frontiersmen, better known as "the old and bold," came into existence. Col. Daniel "Jerry" Driscoll raised the 25th battalion of Royal Fuseliers composed of the "zaniest group ever to put on uniforms." This unit attracted comedians, border gunmen, Moroccan bandits, Chinese generals, ex-Members of Parliament,

---

[82] 125-126.

cowboys, prize fighters, ex-regular officers, a one-time submarine commander, painters, singers, acrobats, professional composers, and professional hunters!

The Fuseliers arrived in Africa with 1,100 men in 1915. Six months later they had been reduced to 700. Six months later only 450 were left. The biggest cause of fatalities on the British side, which was mostly white, was disease. Malaria and dysentery killed three times as many men as were killed in combat.

Lt. Gen. J.C. Smuts landed in Mombasa in February 1916. He became the commander of 13,000 British, 3,250 Indian, and 2,150 African troops. His South African strategy of envelopment, persistently maintained, despite one disappointment after another, would continue to be opposed by von Lattow-Vorbeck with a technique of the most skillful retreat. The German took no risk that imperiled the ability of his forces to continue the struggle. Moreover, he never forgot that his essential task was to keep in the field, the greatest possible number of troops, and thereby reduce the effective effort of his countries enemies in far more important theatres of war.

In January 1917, Lt.Gen. Smuts was called to London and replaced by Lt. Gen. A.R. Hoskins. 15,000 South Africans returned home and were replaced by a Nigerian brigade and by new battalions of the KAR. Before operations with the replacement units began, Lt. Gen. Hoskins was replaced by Lt. Gen. Van Devanter.

Throughout 1917, the Germans in ever dwindling numbers evaded decisive action. Von Lettow-Vorbeck's skill in the art of strategic retreat, and his gift for leadership, grew as the odds were weighted against him. Three times he was wounded, but he never left his troops; he insisted on being carried about in a litter "to prevent the half-resistance that leads to surrender."[83] In 1918, the British fought almost entirely with their KAR. It was a steady pursuit of the remnants of the evasive von Lettow-Vorbeck's troops, first in Portuguese East Africa, and then into Northern Rhodesia.

The Germans agreed to surrender, after the armistice in Europe was signed. "In view of the gallant and prolonged resistance maintained by the German force in East Africa, Lt.Gen. Van Deventer allowed von Lettow-Vorbeck and his officers to retain their swords. So ended a campaign

---

[83] M.F. Hill, *Permanent Way, Volume II*, Ibid., 166.

which, as a test of human endurance, had no equal in the history of warfare." [84]

The Wheaton College archives at the Billy Graham Center has a transcript of an interview of my father, Herbert Downing, by Robert D. Shuster. Almost as an aside, Dad said:

We were on the mission field during World War I and experienced some difficulty in getting food, at least the right kind of food, because of a long drought followed by a long heavy raining season. So there were several years (with)… very little food produced right in Kenya. I remember one of the things I thought I could never look at again, was rice and tomatoes. (chuckles) (We) raised tomatoes by irrigation and there was an Indian storekeeper at the railway station who provided us with rice. I have since learned to enjoy both rice and tomatoes. [85]

Alta Hoyt wrote of "a very bad earthquake" on 11 May, 1916 while eating breakfast. It rattled dishes in the cupboard and pictures on the wall swung back and forth. [86]

In 1918, influenza killed an estimated 20 million people worldwide, 548,000 in the United States. [87] "Then He (Jesus) continued by saying to them, 'Nation will rise against nation and kingdom against kingdom, and there will be great earthquakes, and in various places plagues and famines…' " [88]

---

[84] Ibid., 132-166.
[85] Billy Graham Center Archives, Collection 251, Herbert C. Downing T1 Transcript, 2.
[86] Alta Hoyt, *We were Pioneers,* Ibid., 48.
[87] *The World Almanac 2008,* (New York, NY, World Almanac Books, 2008), 481.
[88] Luke 21:10-11a, New American Standard Bible.

Isaac

One day in the late 19th Century, Queen Victoria of England reportedly asked her Prime Minister, Benjamin Disraeli: "Mr. Prime Minister, what evidence can you give me of the existence of God?"

Disraeli thought for a moment and replied, "The Jew, Your Majesty."[89]

Walter Russell Mead in *God and Gold* discusses 'The Father of History in the following excerpts:

> *...somebody in the ancient Middle East first believed that the life of his or her people was shaped by the call of God ...the sacred story isn't "proven" by the antiquity of the manuscripts in which it is written, but rather by the way the fulfillment of God's promise to Abraham has dominated the history of the subsequent millennia. Something happened in the Middle East that has reshaped the way people think, act, hope, believe in every corner of the earth... the civilizations of half the world owe their primary ideological foundations to the revolutionary idea of a single all-powerful God determined to intervene in human history, to judge every human soul, and to establish His perfect kingdom among us...*
>
> *...Whether we owe the monotheistic tradition to Abraham or to another Middle Eastern prophet of the same name, roughly half the world's population today believes that God's promise to him is the great lever of history and the proportion of believers is growing. More than two billion of Christians and more than one billion Muslims trace the origin of their faith to the desert patriarch... it is clear that more lives have been touched by the Abraham tradition than any other... Those developments would be astonishing if there really was a historical Abraham; they are nothing short of miraculous if there wasn't.[90]*

The oldest and most widely read record of antiquity is the Bible. Though proscribed by the "goat" culture (the seed of the serpent) this is the only record that claims to be a communication to human beings from an all powerful, loving God. More than any other document, it has stood the test of time, survived the most vehement opposition and outlived its most

---

[89] David Brog, *Standing with Israel*, (Lake Mary, FL, FrontLine, 2006), 212.
[90] Walter Russell Mead, *God and Gold*, (New York, NY, Random House, Inc., 2007), 275-276.

dedicated enemies. Any honest person in search of truth must examine its evidence.

God's call to Abraham, according to the New American Standard Bible, is as follows:

Now the Lord said to Abram, "Go forth from your country, and from your relatives and from your father's house, to the land which I will show you; And I will make you a great nation, and I will bless you, and make your name great; And so you shall be a blessing; And I will bless those who bless you, and the one who curses you I will curse. And in you all the families of the earth will be blessed."[91]

Briefly the Biblical story is this: In obedience to God's directive, Abram at 75 left his father, accompanied by his wife, Sarai, a half sister who was 65. They traveled by stages toward the Negeb. When a famine struck, they went to Egypt. Abram feared for his life because of his wife's beauty and convinced her to say she was his sister. This ploy worked twice, once with Pharaoh and later with King Abimelech of Gerar. God intervened in both cases. Pharaoh was afflicted with plagues and Abimelech was threatened in a dream.

Abram had no heir because Sarai was barren. She convinced Abram to produce an heir through Hagar, her Egyptian slave, since infertility frequently caused torment and humiliation. Upon her conception, Hagar's attitude toward her mistress changed to contempt and resulted in reactive ill-treatment. Sarai was so harsh that Hagar became a pregnant runaway slave.

The angel of the Lord spoke to her near a spring of water, commanding her to return to Sarai and submit to her authority. He further told Hagar that she would bear a son called Ishmael (God hears,) who would be a wild donkey of a man. His hand would be against everyone, and everyone's hand would be against him.

When Abram was 100, God informed him that Sarai would bear a son to him. Both Abram and Sarai's names were changed. Abram became Abraham (Father of Many,) and Sarai became Sarah (Mother of Nations.) Thus Isaac was born, a miraculous fulfillment of God's promise. From him has come a race of people who have indeed been blessed, and have

---

[91] New American Standard Bible Updated Edition, Genesis 12:1-3.

been a channel of God's blessing to all the families of the earth. God's ultimate blessing was the gift of His Son, Jesus, the Savior of the world.

An illustrious example of God's blessing upon these people is the reign of King Solomon. His kingdom extended from Gaza northeast to the Euphrates River. The Bible describes his wealth in I Kings 10:14:

The weight of gold which Solomon received in any one year was 666 talents, in addition to the tolls levied by the customs officers, the profits on foreign trade, and the tribute of the kings of Arabia and the regional governors." [92]

An estimated 666 talents are between 20 and 25 tons of gold, roughly a billion dollars per year at 2011 prices.

The finest sailors in that time were Phoenicians from Tyre. They sailed through the straits of Gibraltar, down the west coast of Africa, south of the equator. Solomon built a fleet of ships at Ezion Geber on the Red Sea, and crewed them with Tyrian sailors. They made three year voyages, bringing back gold, silver, ivory, apes, and monkeys.

"Thus King Solomon outdid all the kings of the earth in wealth and wisdom." [93]

David Brog, in his 2006 book *Standing with Israel,* quotes Pat Robertson:

"Think of it. According to Disraeli the primary evidence that God exists is the existence of the Jewish people. A people who in 586 B.C. were deported to Babylon, yet returned after 70 years to rebuild a nation. Who were again brutally massacred and dispersed by the Romans in A.D.70, yet after countless centuries of Diaspora, expulsions, pogroms, ghettos, and attempts at genocidal extermination, have clung to their faith, their customs..." [94] *In fact, the Jews have never lost their identity as a people.*

Jonathan Cahn, in his October 1, 2010 <u>Sapphires</u> wrote:

---

[92] Revised English Bible, I Kings 10-14.
[2] Ibid., I Kings 10:23.
[94] David Brog. Ibid., *Standing With Israel,* 212, quote from Pat Robertson, "Why Evangelical Christians Support Israel", speech before The Herzliya Conference, Herzliya, Israel, December 17, 2003.

Recently two genetic studies were completed, the first to use genome-wide scanning devices to study Jewish people throughout the world. The studies included Jewish communities widely scattered and several communities long separated from other Jewish communities.

The findings? It turns out that all the Jewish communities studied contained the same genetic make up as in all the other Jewish communities, even those Jewish communities separated from other Jewish communities for over 2,000 years. This could never be, unless the Jewish people today are the same as the Jewish people in the Bible. Further, it was discovered that the common genes shared among Jewish people throughout the world go back to the Middle East. In other words, despite their living in other lands for most of the past 2,000 years, the Jewish people today are primarily Middle Eastern people.

So modern 21ˢᵗ-century advanced genetic technology has finally caught up with the Bible. In Jeremiah 31 is an amazing prophecy: "This is what the Lord says, who appoints the sun to shine by day, and decrees the moon and stars to shine by night...

Only if these decrees vanish from my sight... will the children of Israel cease from being a nation before Me."[95]

Consider the mystery of the British Empire's success. According to Winston Churchill; Britain was *"the greatest empire the globe has ever known, comprising one-fourth of the earth's surface and a quarter of the world's population, thrice the size of the Roman Empire at full flush."*[96]

What was the underlying secret of Britain's financial world supremacy? Was it because England was one of the first to have the Bible in the common language of the people? Was it because of the religious revivals in Wales and Scotland? Was it the result of the industrial revolution? Was it the quality of leadership developed in their public schools? Was it because they were able to keep the balance of power between the nations in Europe? Was it the size of their navy? Was it because the water around the British Isles allowed them to have smaller land armies than European countries?

---

[95] Jonathan Cahn, "The DNA Surprise and the Jewish People." _Sapphires_, October 1, 2010, http://failedmessiah.typepad.com/failed-messiah.com/2010/06/second-wider-genetic-study. (accessed January 19, 2011).
[96] Winston Churchill, *My Early Life,* (New York, NY, Touchstone, 1930), X1.

All of these may have been factors, but the primary reason appears to be a result of the Glorious Revolution of 1688. The end of Jewish life in England had taken place in 1290 with the expulsion of some 16,000 Jews[97] Jews were not allowed to return to England until 1656. The fundamental motive came from Oliver Cromwell, then Lord Protector of the Commonwealth. He was a realist and England was in an intense trade competition with Holland, Spain, and Portugal, all leading maritime powers. By readmitting the Jews into the country, Cromwell thought he would strengthen England's commercial position… The claims of Jews for civil equality in England had at last found many defenders in liberal Christian circles, beginning with John Locke.[98]

Liberation of Jews in England drew a member of the Rothschild family to its shores. Nathan Rothschild was the second and most gifted of Mayer Amschel Bauer's five sons. Bauer had changed his name to Rothschild and became the first truly international banker.[99]

With banks in Berlin, Vienna, Paris, Naples, and London, the Rothschilds developed the most efficient communication system in the world. This allowed Nathan to know, several hours in advance, the outcome of the Battle of Waterloo in 1815. He used this time to dump his consuls and collapse the stock market. His timing was perfect and he bought up every consul in sight for just "a song."[100] (A British consul was a 19th century bond issued by the British government which paid a set nominal fee of interest forever, a perpetual bond without a maturity date.)[101]

"A short time later the 'official' news arrived in the British capital. England was now the master of the European scene."[102] Napoleon had 'met his Waterloo.' Nathan had bought control of the British economy. Overnight the Rothschild's already vast fortune was multiplied 20 times over.

Not only were Jewish bankers instrumental in Britain's ascendancy, but Benjamin Disraeli, a baptized Jew, became Chancellor of the Exchequer, then Prime Minister twice.

---

[97] Nathan Ausubel, *Pictorial History of the Jewish People,* (New York, NY, Crown Publishers, Inc., 1961), 117.

[98] Ibid., 118.

[99] Des Griffin, *Descent into Slavery,* (South Pasadena, CA, Emissary Publications, 1984), 18.

[100] Ibid., 28.

[101] "What is a Perpetual Bond?"

http://www.wisegeek.com/what-is-a-perpetual-bond.htm. (accessed November 5, 2011).

[102] Des Griffin, Ibid., 28.

Unlike his predecessor, Disraeli had good relations with Queen Victoria. She approved of his imperialist views and his desire to make Britain the most powerful nation in the world. The reform bill, which introduced universal male suffrage, was piloted through the House of Commons in 1867 by Disraeli. This paved the way for the phenomenal growth of the British Empire across all of Africa and the Middle East.[103] In 1876, Queen Victoria agreed to his proposal that she should accept the title of Empress of India. In 1878 Disraeli gained great acclaim for his success in limiting Russia's power in the Balkans at the Congress of Berlin.

So it appears that the success of the British Empire could be attributed to God's blessing upon the seed of Isaac and Jacob. "And in you all families of the earth will be blessed." (Genesis 12:3)

The Diaspora[104] spread Isaac's progeny all over the world, and with few exceptions they met with "expulsions, pogroms, ghettos, and attempts at genocidal exterminations."[105] The obvious question is why? The Russian Tsar attempted to force the Jews in his country to amalgamate with the rest of Russia. They refused and became objects of Anti- Semitism. This resulted in miserable living conditions with no hope of escape. So the dream of a homeland of their own became fantasy. Thus was Zionism born.

It could be concluded then, that Anti-Semitism is the product of Jewish differences they are unwilling to give up. What are these differences?

Denis Prager and Joseph Telushkin wrote a book entitled *Why the Jews? The Reason for Anti-Semitism*. Their views are summed up by a quote from the National Conference of Catholic Bishops: *"It was Judaism that brought the concept of a God-given universal moral law into the world. ...The Jew carries that burden of God in history (and) for this has never been forgiven."*[106]

[103] Martin Sieff, *The Politically Incorrect Guide to the Middle East*, (Washington, DC, Regnery, 2008), 199.
[104] Diaspora - The dispersion of the Jews after the Babylonian exile.
[105] David Brog, quote from Pat Robertson, "Why Evangelical Christians Support Israel", speech before The Herzliya Conference, Herzliya, Israel, December 17, 2003, 212.
[106] Dennis Prager and Joseph Telushkin, *Why the Jews? The Reason for Anti-Semitism*, (NY, Touchstone, Division of Simon & Schuster, 2003), 7-8.

George Gilder takes exception to this position in his book *The Israel Test*.

> *All the sage observations by Prager and Telushkin miss the heart of the matter, which is Jewish intellectual and entrepreneurial superiority. As eminent Russian pro-Semite writer Maxim Gorky put it, "Whatever nonsense the anti-Semites may talk, they dislike the Jew only because he is obviously better, more adroit, and more capable of work than they are..." The source of anti-Semitism is Jewish superiority and excellence.*
>
> *The entire debate over Israel currently rides on a tacit subtext of crucial matters that cannot be discussed, such as the central contributions of Jews to global science, technology, art, and prosperity; properties that cannot be transgressed, such as pointing to the comparative brutality and barrenness of its adversaries; and immense realities that cannot be broached, such as the manifest supremacy of Jews over all other ethnic groups in nearly every intellectual, commercial, and cultural endeavor.*
>
> *...The Bell Curve by Charles Murray and Richard Herrnstein pointed to the massive superiority in IQs of Ashkenazi (Eastern European) Jews over all other genetically identifiable groups. The upside tail of the curve is massively Jewish.*
>
> *What matters in human accomplishment is not the average performance but the treatment of exceptional performance and the cultivation of genius... Murray explains, "The key indicator for predicting exceptional accomplishment (like winning a Nobel Prize) is the incidence of exceptional intelligence... The proportion of Jews with IQs of 140 or higher is somewhere around six times the proportion of everyone else..."* [107]

Not only are the Jews demonstrably more intelligent than other groups, they are

> *...also heavily overrepresented among entrepreneurs of the technological businesses that lead and leaven the global economy. Edward B. Roberts of Massachusetts Institute of Technology's Sloan School of Management said: 'The largest factor in predicting an entrepreneurial career in technology was an entrepreneurial father' ...he discovered that Jews were five times more likely to start technological enterprises than other MIT graduates.* [108]

---

[107] George Gilder, *The Israel Test*, (USA, Richard Vigilante Books, 2009), 31-33.
[108] Ibid., 35-36.

In countries where the descendants of Isaac are free to invent and create, as in the United States, they pile up conspicuous wealth. In an information age, achievements of mind have shown that Jews have forged much of the science and wealth of the era. It is obvious that the United States, which has more Jews than any other country except Israel, has been financially blessed by Jewish accomplishments. The standard of living here has attracted more immigrants than any other. Even our poor enjoy amenities unheard of in other nations.

"And in you (Abraham) all the families of the earth will be blessed."[109]

---

[109] The New American Standard Bible, Genesis 12:3b.

Ishmael

The Arabian Peninsula looks like an Eskimo muk-luk, with its toe pointing north east towards Afghanistan. The back of the boot has mountains running from top to bottom. The heel also has mountains along the coast towards the boot's shank. Another line of mountains is at the toe. At the instep is the Rub'al Khali (or Empty Quarter). This is the largest area of continuous sand in the world, covering 250,000 square miles. Just above the ankle is a plateau that extends from the desert running up the front of the boot to the mountains at the rear.

Boston University scientist Farouk El-baz, had long wondered about the pebbles of granite and basalt found in abundance in Kuwait at the boot's laces. The nearest source of these rocks was the Hejaz Mountains 650 miles to the west. Upon examining satellite photos, he detected a dry river bed known today as Wadi al Batin. The channel disappeared when it reached the sand dunes; however, an extended line followed patterns in the sand, which could only be explained by an underground river along a fault line.

This river fulfills all the descriptive elements of one of the four rivers associated with the Garden of Eden. Genesis 2:11-12 states:

"The name of the first is Pishon; it flows around the whole land of Havilah, where there is gold. The gold of that land is good; the bdellium and the onyx stones are there."

The forefather of the people who inhabited the southern area of the Arabian boot was Joktan. Havilah was one of his 13 sons who settled the land drained by this river.

There is only one place in Arabia that has a noteworthy deposit of gold. This is the famous site known as the "Cradle of Gold," located about 125 miles south of Medina, halfway up the back of the boot. It was rediscovered in 1932 by American mining engineer Karl Twitchell. As of 1996, it was producing more than five tons of gold a year.[110]

Another of Joktan's sons was Sheba who settled at the heal of the boot, around 1000 B.C. Southern Arabia's coast line along the Arabian Sea gets

---

[110] John D. Keyser, "The First River of Eden,"
(http:// www.hope-of –israel.org/riveden.htm. (accessed November 30, 2010).

regular rain and has a surprising variety of plant life. This area is well known for its tropical plants and beautiful cities. Frankincense and myrrh were valuable exports. The residents were non- nomadic, living in cities and relying upon agriculture for their food. Two rainy seasons, one in spring and one in autumn, provided the needed water. These rains were torrential, causing erosion and constant maintenance on the numerous reservoirs used for irrigation. The soil was extremely fertile, and the people were industrious.

In the early days the greatness of these Semites (descendants of Noah's son Shem) was primarily in their traffic. They were the only navigators who dared cross the seas to India and to the East, and this commerce brought them immense wealth. The Indian Ocean trade was carried to Arabia by ships and transported from Aden overland to the markets of the western Mediterranean, Mesopotamia, and Egypt. Navigation on the northern part of the Red Sea was dangerous because of monsoon winds. This was probably how the ships built at Ezion Geber by Judah's King Jehoshaphat and Israel's King Ahaziah were wrecked.[111]

An unnamed Sabaean monarch, The Queen of Sheba, journeyed to Jerusalem to test Solomon's wisdom.[112] A major purpose of her long (1,600 miles) yet successful visit may have been to negotiate a trade agreement with Solomon, whose control of the trade routes jeopardized the income which the Sabaeans received from caravans crossing his territory. The spices, gold, and precious stones with which she sought Solomon's favor would have been typical of the luxurious cargoes of these caravans. These linked the resources of East Africa, India, and South Arabia to the markets of Damascus and Gaza by way of oases like Mecca, Medina, and Tema.[113]

All of this is evidence of trading conducted on the east coast of Africa 1,000 years before Christ. This territory was later known as Zinj, a Persian word meaning land of the black people. At first predominantly Persian in culture, Zinj gradually took on an Arab personality with a steady influx of immigrants from sheikdoms along the Red Sea, the Hadramant, and Oman. All these colonists, Persian and Arab alike, gave the African coast a remarkable face-lifting.

The northern region of Arabia between the Red Sea and the Euphrates River is arid. Deserts are regions having less than 10 inches of rain per year

---

[111] II Chronicles 20: 35-37.
[112] I Kings 10: 1-10.
[113] *The Illustrated Bible Dictionary*, (Wheaton, IL, Tyndale House Publishers, 1986), s.v. "Queen of Sheba."

and less than 10% vegetation coverage. There are moderately productive aquifers which can be reached by digging wells. This explains the frequent disputes over water in the Old Testament. The date palm is the most common plant which grows in the oases around water sources. In such harsh environments, continuous migration with herds of camel, sheep, and goats in search of grazing offers the best means of survival.

The people who have inhabited this region are Bedouins, the Arabic speaking nomads who have proudly maintained their pastoral way of life over thousands of years. According to Arab tradition, Arabians are descendant from two main stocks: pure Arabs from the line of Joktan, and naturalized or mixed Arabs descended from Ishmael. Even now every Bedouin tribe still claims descent from one or the other group and the rivalry between the two has caused many civil wars throughout history, not only in the Arabian Peninsula, but all over the Arab world.[114]

After Hagar ran away from Sarai's severe affliction, she was found near a spring by the Angel of the Lord. She was told to return to Sarai and submit to her.

"And the Angel of the Lord (continued), See now, you are with child and shall bear a son, and shall call his name Ishmael (that is, God hears); because the Lord has heard and paid attention to your affliction. And (Ishmael) shall be as a wild ass among men; his hand will be against every man and every man's hand against him; and he shall live to the east and on the borders of all his kinsmen."[115]

Ishmael was the first person in the Bible to be named before his birth. The others were: Isaac, (Genesis 17:19); Josiah, (I Kings 13:2); Solomon, (I Chronicles 22:9); Jesus, (Matthew 1:21); and John the Baptist, (Luke 1:13).[116]

A footnote in the Amplified Bible from Clark's Commentary says:

"Nothing can be more descriptive of the wandering, lawless, freebooting life of the Arabs than this. From the beginning to the present they have kept their independence, and God preserves them as a lasting monument of His providential care and incontestable argument of the truth of divine

---

[114] The Beduin of Arabia, Origins and History,
http://www.angelfire.com/az/rescon/mgcbedu.html. (accessed December 2, 2010).
[115] Amplified Bible, Genesis 16:11-12.
[116] Ibid., footnote on verse 11.

revelation. Had the books of Moses no other proof of their divine origin, the account of Ishmael and the prophecy concerning his descendants during a period of nearly 4,000 years, would be sufficient. To attempt to refute it would be most ridiculous presumption and folly."

The Jerusalem Bible note on Genesis 16:12e says: "Ishmael's descendants are the desert Arabs who are as intractable and vagrant as the wild ass (Job 39:5-8.)"[117] This reference is as follows:

"Who gave the wild donkey this freedom, and untied the rope from his proud neck? I (Yahweh) have given him the desert as a home and the salt plains as his own habitat. He scorns the turmoil of the town; there are no shouts from a driver for him to listen for. The mountains are the pastures that he ranges in quest of any type of green blade or leaf."[118]

"Traditional Bedouin culture reminds us of the Old Testament stories of the patriarchs. Through the Islamic conquests it has infiltrated the cultures of all Middle East groups and they and their lifestyle are regarded as a model by all Muslim people. Understanding the Bedouin therefore will help us in understanding most other communities in the wider area."[119]

Dr. Carroll Quigley in *Tragedy and Hope* stated the following:

Arabs, like other Semites who emerged from the Arabian Desert, infiltrating neighboring cultures of urban civilizations, were originally, nomadic tribal peoples. Their political structure was practically identical with their social structure and was based on blood relationships, not on territorial jurisdiction. They were warlike, patriarchal, extremist, violent, intolerant, and xenophobic.

In such traditional Arabic society, the extended family, not the individual, was the basic social unit. All property was controlled by the patriarch head. Accordingly, most decisions were in his hands. His control of the marriage of his male descendants was ensured by the price paid for a bride to her family. This would require the patriarch's consent.

This biological and patriarchal character of all significant social relationships in Arab life is reflected in the familiar feature of male

---

[117] Jerusalem Bible, Genesis 16:12.
[118] Ibid., Job 39:5-8.
[119] The Beduin of Arabia, Introduction,
http://www.angelfire.com/az/rescon/mgacbedu.html., (accessed December 2, 2010).

dominance. Only the male is important. The female is inferior, even sub-human. Females become significant only by producing males (the one thing, apparently, that the dominant male cannot do for himself). Sons are regarded as superior beings by their mothers and sisters, simply on the basis of their maleness. They are exposed to a dual standard of sexual morality in which any female is a legitimate target of their sexual desires. However, the girl they marry is expected to be a paragon of chaste virginity.

Another aspect of Arabic society is scorn of honest, steady manual labor, especially agricultural work. This resulted from the fusion of at least three ancient influences. First, the archaic bureaucratic structure of Asiatic despotism, where peasants supported warriors and scribes. Manual workers, especially tillers of the soil, were the lowest layer of society. The acquisition of literacy and military prowess were the chief roads to escape physical drudgery. Second, from Classical Antiquity the Islamic Civilization, based on slaves, came to regard agricultural (or other manual) work as fit only for slaves. Third, the Bedouin tradition of pastoral, warlike nomads, scorned tillers of the soil as weak, routine, persons, of no real spirit or character. These were fit to be conquered or walked on but not respected. The combination of these three formed the lack of respect for manual work that is so characteristic of Arab influence which has spread from Pakistan to Peru. [120]

World magazine published an interview with Darrow Miller, a 27 year veteran of *Food for the Hungry*. Mr. Miller was challenged with a statement by Dr. Francis Schaeffer at L'Abri in Switzerland. "If you want to understand why South America is relatively poor while North America is relatively wealthy, look at the ideas that came from Southern Europe and Northern Europe."

Here are excerpts from the interview:

Q: How did the ideas of Southern Europe and Northern Europe differ?
A: The ideas from Northern Europe were based on a biblical world view- for instance, that work is part of our dignity... Work existed before the fall. That should frame how we understand the concept of work.

---

[120] Carroll Quigley, *Tragedy and Hope*, (New York, NY, Macmillan Company, 1966), 1115-1121.

Q: Do many in developing countries see work as a curse?

A: Yes, and that mindset will create economic outcomes. If when you have "arrived" you don't work, and you're a second-class citizen if you have to work, then the goal of society is not to work. I was sharing that idea once in Venezuela and a woman said, "I have a song that describes the concept of work as a curse". We were in a group of about 20 or 30 people and within the first line of the song everybody who spoke Spanish from five different countries, started singing along. It talks about work being made for animals and human beings made to dance. So you have an ancient concept that is coming over into modern society through the arts and everybody in the Latin world can sing this song. [121]

Not only was contempt for manual labor spread by Islamic imperialism, other characteristics of traditional Arab life were also spread the length of the Pakistani-Peruvian Axis. The origin of these can be traced to the Bedouin outlook which reflected the attitudes of a relatively small group of the Islamic culture. Because the Bedouins were a superior, conquering group, they were copied by others in their sphere of influence, even the despised agricultural workers. Inasmuch as Arab influence in the Iberian Peninsula was spread to South America by the Spanish, these characteristics are evident today as far as Peru.

In *Tragedy and Hope*, Dr. Quigley states:

"To this day the Arab influence is evident in southern Italy, northern Africa, and above all, in Spain. It appears in the obvious things such as architecture, music, dance, and literature and value systems. Spain and Latin America, despite centuries of nominal Christianity, are Arabic areas.

No statement is more hateful to Spaniards and Latin Americans than that. But once it is made, and once the evidence on which it was based is examined in an objective way, it becomes almost irrefutable." [122]

Jonathan Cahn, president of Hope of the World in Lodi, NJ, is a Completed Jewish Rabbi. His commentary on Genesis 21 sums up the situation called: *World Peace and Ishmael's Rage.*

---

[121] Darrow Miller, "Godly Endeavors," *World Magazine*, December 5, 2009, 23-24.
[122] Carroll Quigley, Ibid., 1120.

Ishmael

The Arab – Israeli conflict goes back to the first book of the Bible as Abraham had a child by Hagar, his maid. The child is named "Ishmael." Later, Abraham has a son with Sarah; Isaac. Soon Ishmael fell out of favor; his relationship with his father was cut off. Can you imagine the resentment, the bitterness, the envy that Ishmael likely felt against Isaac for much of his life? From Ishmael came the Arabs, Mohammed, and Islam. From Isaac came Israel, the Jews, the Bible, and Messiah Yeshua, Jesus. And to this day, most of the children of Ishmael live in resentment and hatred against the children of Isaac. And it all goes back to the tents of Abraham. Ishmael teaches a valuable lesson. Without the blessing of God, you end up living with bitterness, restlessness, rage, and fear, always trying to prove yourself. But if you give all of that to God and receive the love He has to pour out onto your life, you find, it's more love than you could have ever known any other way. God has called you to live, a blessed life not to walk in the way of Ishmael.

Colonialism

The Kikuyu tribe from around Mount Kenya has played a key role in the politics of Kenya. One of the most notable characteristics of the Kikuyu culture was male dominance. The women did the gardening, carried firewood, cooked, bore children, and served the man of the household. At Kijabe, 140 pound women carried 100 pounds of firewood up the hill at 7,000 foot elevations. My father told of a pregnant woman carrying such a load, delivering her baby by the side of the path, putting her baby on top of the wood, and continuing up the hill.

Bride buying was a legacy of the Arab influence. In order to protect the pecuniary value of these transactions, female circumcision was practiced. It was assumed that this ritual reduced promiscuity and made the woman pure. The women were convinced that this practice would insure marriage to a wealthier man. It became a custom which precipitated a crisis in the AIM –related Africa Inland Church. This came to a head in 1921 when missionaries at their annual conference decided to 'condemn and forbid' it. Every church elder and every teacher was forced to sign repudiation. Many Christians rebelled, masses deserted the church. When my grandfather, Lee Downing, discovered that the elders at a village church refused to accept the official ruling, he immediately dismissed them. His secretary, Hulda Stumpf, wrote that on a day after Mr. Downing left Kijabe 'several daughters of our very best Christian elders were circumcised.' Miss Stumpf felt uneasy about the mission's rigid line. Privately she questioned if it was right to thrust upon African Christians rules of conduct that have not grown out of their own convictions.

This discord festered until January 1930. Grandmother Downing's diary has the following entries:

January 1, 1930 – Weekly prayer and business meeting in our house. Good meeting. All seemed happy.

January 2, 1930 – Miss Stumpf seemed happy and discussed 2 or 3 times the meeting of Wednesday night (Jan. 1, 1930)

January 3, 1930 – Was awakened at 7:10 with news that Miss Stumpf is dead. Found she had been murdered in her bed.

January 4, 1930 – Eight European Officers here yesterday and five today. Buried Miss S. at twilight last night. Fear is in every heart lest K.C.A. (Kikuyu Central Association) is planning to murder us all.

As if an angry abscess had burst, Hulda's murder marked a turning point. The government ruled that no girl could be forcibly circumcised against her will, and unrest "quietened." AIM backed away from the signed pledge, reserving it only for teachers. Slowly people trickled back into churches in the AIM heartland. Kikuyus working in the large white settled farms turned to Christ in large numbers.

Crown Colony

Two separate empires operated under the guise of the British Empire. One was the Crown Empire, the other the British Empire. All white colonial possessions were under the authority of the British government. The Union of South Africa, Australia, New Zealand, and Canada comprised only 13% of the inhabitants of the British Empire. All other people were owned and ruled by a private club in London known as **The Crown**. **The Crown's** representative held the absolute power of life and death over all the people under his jurisdiction. There were no courts, no method of appeal, or retribution against his decisions. Even a British citizen, who committed a crime in a <u>Crown</u> colony, was subject to the Crown law. He couldn't appeal to British law, as it didn't apply.[123]

"The City" of London is an irregular rectangle of 677 acres located in the heart of London. Often called the "wealthiest square mile on earth," it is ruled over by a Lord Mayor. Like the Vatican in Rome, it is a separate, independent state. It is the financial control agency of the British Empire. Consequently, a crown colony is an economic venture of the "City of London."[124]

Kenya was a British protectorate until 1920 when it became a crown colony. The Kenya highlands were seen as a great source of agricultural income, if they were property developed. The female work force in the male dominated society was hardly capable of developing this potential quickly enough. The demobilization of the British military after WW I provided a source of skilled leaders to make Kenya an economic success.

---

[123] Des Griffen, *Descent into Slavery,* (South Pasadena, CA, Emissary Publications, 1984), 44-45.
[124] Ibid., 41.

The Soldiers Settlers Scheme brought hundreds of ex-soldiers to Kenya as farmers.

Kenya was a uniquely self-ruling territory. For decades, Kenya had no political parties. It was just settlers vs. government with both Africans and Indians fighting for what they wanted. The vociferous minority of whites was so tough that it took the law into its own hands on several occasions. In 1923, Kenyans had a plan worked out to kidnap their own Governor. This was when London, to please India, tried to force ballot-box equality for the 46,000 Indians in Kenya, upon its 19,000 whites. Kenya was supposed to be a helpless pawn, so Whitehall (site of government officers in London) thought. When the British cabinet learned that settlers were being armed, and there were more ex-officers in Kenya's population in proportion than any other British possession, London backed down.[125]

People who have grown up in the United States are convinced that everyone should have their political system. It should be emphasized that the government that evolved in the United States could only work where there was a Judeo-Christian ethical base accepted by the majority. Absent this foundation, Nicola Machiavelli's form of government described in his book, *The Prince*, is the only effective means of control. His main theme was that all means may be used in order to maintain authority, and the worst acts of the ruler are justified by the treachery of the governed.[126] Again we see the Arab influence of Asiatic Despotism ruling with a 10% oligarchy controlling 90% slaves. A democratic middle class never developed.[127]

Literacy

Initially, African parents, elders, and headmen opposed the establishment of schools because missions required Africans to cast out the old traditions so that they became detribalized. Lee Downing tried hard to influence the leaders. In 1910 his secretary, Hulda Stumpf, told Charles Hurlburt, "Mr. Downing is in Nairobi since Tuesday attending a meeting of the governor with certain chiefs in regard to sending their sons to the different missions to be educated."

---

[125] Negley Farson, *The Last Chance in Africa*, (New York, NY, Harcourt, Brace and Company, 1950), 32.

[126] *Biographical Encyclopedia*, ed. David Crystal, (Cambridge, England: Cambridge University Press, 1994), s.v. "Machiavelli, Niccolo (di Bernardo del)."

[127] Negley Farson,, Ibid., 32-33.

Lee watched African attitudes change. By 1924 he wrote, "Fully 95 % of our church members have passed through our schools." The AIM home council, however, was opposed to education beyond learning to read the Bible. Other missions were sending their brighter students for further education. The young AIM Church, feeling themselves left behind, began to agitate. The government, short of money after WW I, looked to the missions to educate the masses, and was willing to subsidize their schools. In 1922 the American home council of AIM ruled against accepting government funds. The dispute between home and field continued for years. From this point on, the Arab belief that the acquisition of literacy was one of the chief roads to escape drudgery was a driving force among Africans.

Young men in the Kikuyu tribe went through a circumcision ceremony as a year group. They were then considered men, expected to become warriors as a unit. Belligerence against adjacent clans and tribes became their primary focus. Again this represented what they had observed in the dominating Arabs. WW I swept these young warriors from different tribes into military units in the Kings African Rifles (KAR). This provided the British Government a force to prevent tribal conflicts, but the reduced military training of young men in the native reserves created problems with the resultant undisciplined testosterone. They became easy prey to political rebel rabble-rousers. On the other hand, some whites feared that returning veteran KAR soldiers might continue killing.

Slavery

Within a few miles of Kijabe, a temporary cable incline was built in 1900 to raise and lower railroad cars 1,500 feet into and out of the Kedong Valley. This operated from May 1900 until November 1901, allowing the railhead to advance from mile 375 to mile 545, a distance of 170 miles. The permanent road was subsequently built down the escarpment using steel bridges built by the American Bridge Company of Ambridge, Pennsylvania. This passed just below the station at Kijabe. The scar of the incline was still visible in 1952. Also close by was the old Swahili slave trail that was still six feet wide, abandoned more than 50 years earlier. These were two relics from the war against slavery.

The Swahili people and language were the product of widespread intermarriage among Arab settlers and Africans. Swahili descendants were accepted on an equal footing in all walks of life with the Arab culture.

From Classical Antiquity, the Islamic civilization was based on slavery. Consequently the Swahilis were actively involved in this enterprise. The monsoon winds of the Indian Ocean were the dynamo for moving slave carrying Arab dhows to the empires around the Indian Ocean. The population of central Africa was markedly reduced by this traffic. Then William Wilberforce and William Pitt were instrumental in passing the Slavery Abolition Act in 1833 in England. The East African Railway was built to stop slave trading. The British presence effectively staunched this population drain.

Problems

Attempts to teach Africans improved agricultural practices fell on deaf ears.[128] Education was the focus for Africans, as their ticket to success. But success to them meant they didn't need to work. Work was for the lower classes, and the European leaders wrestling with the Africa mind-set never saw the connection with the permeating Arab influence. The Africans never developed a middle class of entrepreneurs, and ultimately drove out the white race that had been imported to develop the countries economic potential. Asiatic despotism became the de facto law of the land, and the people returned to the Arabic influence of tribalism and bovine submission.

Improvements

Hobbs was correct about human nature when he stated, "Life in the state of nature is nasty, brutish and short." Life in the land of Zinj before the British Empire was just that; nasty, brutish, and short. During WW I over 44,000 porters were killed or died of disease. The most common causes of death were malaria and dysentery. These killed three times as many men as were killed by the enemy, nearly 35,000. During WW I, except for the railroad, an infrastructure was non-existent. Everything was transported by porters. Those porters, conscripted from the higher elevations where there was no malaria, were especially vulnerable at lower altitudes.

But these two were not the only diseases threatening human and animal health. The tsetse fly, otherwise known as "The Fly," killed horses

---

[128] Negley Farson, *The Last Chance in Africa,* Ibid., 36.

and precluded their use. These flies also carried sleeping sickness to humans. Chiggers infected toes and feet while mosquitoes carried elephantiasis causing an enormous swelling of the lower legs. River blindness still causes hundreds of thousands of cases of blindness. Bilharziasis can be picked up by wading in water polluted by diseased snails.

Not only was disease an issue, droughts or locust invasions could cause starvation. Plagues were also a threat. When a famine ensued, the first group to be allowed to die was the elderly. Next would be the infants and children. The ones most protected were the women of child bearing age, who were necessary to repopulate the tribe in the shortest time.

So between diseases, natural disaster, tribal wars, and slavery, life in the state of nature in Africa was nasty, brutish, and short.

Negley Farson stated in his book, *The Last Chance in Africa*, England sent thousands of splendidly altruistic administrators over seas ("and no nation has sent better)." My father was of the same opinion. **The Crown** was able to employ the very best executives in its control of Crown Colonies: It was quite obvious in Kenya from 1920 until I left in 1952. It is significant that **The Crown** was virtually owned by the Rothschild family from the Battle of Waterloo in 1815 onward. It is also interesting to note the Disraeli observation that in effect holds that no country can be prosperous that does not offer prosperity to the Jews. In Genesis 12:3 God was speaking to Abram: "…those who bless you I shall bless; those who curse you, I shall curse. All the peoples on earth will wish to be blessed as you are blessed." (REB)

The Crown was instrumental in providing improved medical services and schools. The governments ruling on female circumcision helped to change the survival rates of small children. The first automobile arrived in 1914. Fourteen years later, Nairobi was a motorized town. Roads, water and sanitation improved the life of all races. Tribal wars no longer killed the young men and slavery was history. All of these efforts increased the population and friction evolved.

Despite the popularity of Colonial-bashing, the British Empire did have some redeeming qualities. Nigeria, on the west coast of Africa, was part of the Empire until gaining independence in 1960, three years before Kenya. After 50 years, one of its leaders, Harold Deppe-Biriye, had this to say:

Colonialism

"Colonialism was a positive thing. It brought its enlightenment, civilization and greater freedom and democracy than we had ever had. The English language and education united us. If the British had not intervened as they did, we would not have advanced as we have. Once they were in power, the British eradicated slavery, ended the Yoruba wars, and introduced Western education and medicine."[129]

Conclusions

The destruction of the Ottoman Empire was indeed accomplished in WW I. This was the end of the Islamic second Jihad. However, it is obvious from recent history that it was not the end of Islamic imperialism. As stated earlier, the roots of this conflict extend back to Abraham. It was obvious even before Ishmael's birth that he was not the son of promise. Not only did he alienate Sarai from her maid, he created a problem for Abraham who loved the boy Sarai detested. For generations, this has been an example of the fallacy of solving problems on the two dimensional plain of the flesh.

The character of the Ishmaelite was exemplified by their enslavement of Joseph in Egypt. Later the Bible reveals the animosity between the Ishmaelite and Israel during the time of the Judges. Everybody is aware of Gideon's great victory. Few are aware that the Midianites were allied with the Ishmaelites.

Today there are three monotheistic religions that trace their roots to Abraham. More than 30% of the world's population is Christian, 23% are Muslim, and the Jews in Israel are an enigma to all. Monotheism has always been more powerful than idolatry. Islam added this third dimension to Arab aggression. Mohammed was the prophet of Allah who forced monotheism upon idolaters with the sword. He gave three options to conquered people: (1) worship Allah through him, (2) pay extra taxes, or (3) become a "head shorter." The explosion of Islamic power in the last 1,400 years is without precedent, contending with the spread of Christianity for ascendancy.

---

[129] "Haunted by the Ghosts of a Happier Colonial Past," *The Washington Time,* December 6, 2010, 3.

AFRICA
Mombasa to New York – 1937

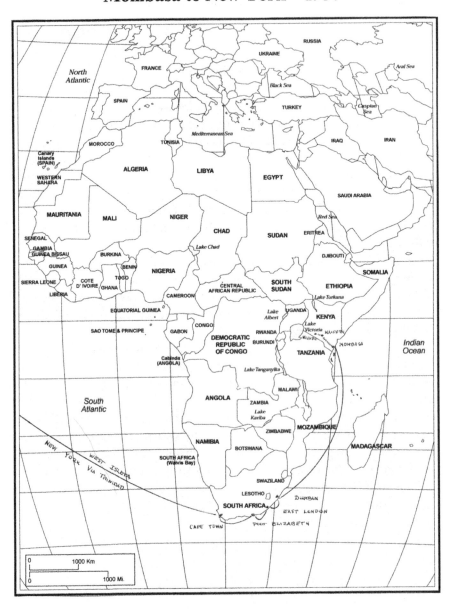

Fathers and Sons

From my grandfather:

For many weeks an old, lone buffalo bull, banished from the herd by his fellows, had been making periodic visits to the native gardens on the most distant part of our mission estate. It came only at night, and usually three or four nights in succession then was absent for perhaps a week. It had almost devastated one garden near the border in which was big corn almost ripe. The owner begged Herbert to come up at night and try to shoot it. He even constructed a platform in a tree in the garden where he would be safe and could make himself comfortable with blankets.

Herbert and Kenneth spent several hours one night in the tree with rifles and spot light from a car. They heard it feeding at a distance, and when it was doubtful whether it would come nearer, they turned the light on, and it immediately bolted. Sometime later the owner informed them that it was again frequenting the gardens so they spent an entire night in the tree, but it did not return.

After Kenneth went to Githumu, Herbert learned that it was again making nightly visits and consented to try once more. He and the owner of the garden had just taken their places on the platform about 7:30 PM when they heard it in the adjoining garden. They waited in hope of its coming nearer. An hour passed and it seemed to be moving farther away. Herbert told the native to turn on the light and they could just see it leaving the garden. He shot but missed it: he fired again and the ball struck it in the hip, but did not bring it down. They decided not to follow it in the dark, but to spend the night in a native hut nearby. Soon after daybreak they started on its track. In a little while they came to an area of dense bush in the forest, and near to the kraal of the chief of the Andorobo, who is an experienced big game hunter.

He and his son, also an experienced hunter, joined them, taking with them two trained dogs. Herbert said it was most interesting to watch these dogs work. One went ahead of the men and the other behind them very quietly with their heads uplifted and continually sniffing. They would go back and forth, a little to the right than a little to the left of the path broken through the bush by the buffalo. Herbert said he would have been afraid to enter that jungle without these keen scented dogs accompanying them. Presently they reached an area of bush isolated from the rest. All walked *around this and could find no tracks leading beyond, so they concluded it must be within that area.*

During the night Herbert had been committing the whole matter definitely to the Lord, and this text was brought repeatedly to his mind: "Commit they way unto the Lord: trust also in Him; and He shall bring it to pass". (Psalm 37:5)

With this promise in mind he was able to tell all the others to remain at the point where the buffalo entered the bush until he could go alone around to the opposite side, then for them to follow along the path, and he would be ready to shoot, if it should come out near him. In a little while, he heard the dogs bark and then a sound as of the animal coming slowly toward him. Presently he saw its back above the bushes and a moment later it emerged with its head close to the ground. He aimed at its neck and the shot brought it to the ground with a terrible groan. It lay there tossing its head vigorously but could not rise. He waited a few minutes then walked closer and gave it a finishing shot in the forehead.

It was an old animal and very large. The distance between the tips of its horns was 35 ½ inches. In the interval between two of Herbert's visits the natives had dug a pit eight feet deep in the path by which it usually came and covered it over. Into this it fell, but was able to horn sufficient dirt from the side and trample it under foot to get out.

There was great rejoicing over the death of this buffalo, as it was not only destroying the people's food, but they were in constant fear of being attacked on the paths. The Andorabo told the native foreman of our agricultural department that if "Bwana Herberti" would drink "njohi" (the intoxicating beer they make) they would give him all he wanted.

Herbert brought the skin, head (with horns in place), feet and rounds of meat to his house, and let the natives have the rest. Nothing remains, not even what we call "refuse", when they have access to a slaughtered animal.

The rifle he used was a Mauser, 9.3 millimeter, or .366". It was shot within 300 yards of the place where Mr. Devitt shot the elephant last June.

Shooting a Buffalo
By Lee H. Downing

In her autobiography, *My Childhood in Africa*, Aunt Lucile Downing Sawhill makes the following statement:

Many of the missionary men enjoyed hunting for relaxation. Father did not, and as far as I know, he never owned a gun. He used to laugh that the only animal he ever shot in Africa was a rabid dog.

Shortly after I was born, the RVA dorm supervisor had a nervous breakdown and Mother and Dad became dorm parents. One of Dad's responsibilities was shooting wild meat for more than 30 students. This was in addition to teaching with Mother and two others. Mother's comment after the Lehrer's came in 1936 was: "All I can say of this period: we *survived*." The Lehrers served as home-makers for almost 20 years.

After reading Lee Downing's tale of Dad's buffalo hunt, I was convinced my father would never have written this. Grandpa was obviously very proud of his son and rightly so. Herbert Downing was much too reticent to boast. In Africa, the big five game animals are: elephant, rhinoceros, lion, leopard, and the cape buffalo, also known as, "black death." Buffalo were widely regarded as very dangerous, goring and killing over 200 people every year. They are sometimes reported to kill more people in Africa than any other animal, although the same claim is made of hippos and crocodiles. Wounded buffalo are notorious among big game hunters for ambushing and attacking their assailants.

Chief game warden Captain Archie Richie once said: "…no man has the right   to press the trigger unless he is prepared to accept the possible obligations."[130] If a hunter wounds a lion and it doesn't immediately charge, it will "go to bush" and must be pursued. That's the unwritten law. No man (who wants to call himself a man after that) dare break it. More nerve-racking, yet tensely exciting, is following a wounded buffalo. By any standards, Dad's accomplishment was exemplary.

When asked to describe his father's characteristics, Dad said that his father was a great man of faith, with some wonderful answers to prayer. As a teenager, wondering what he could do in life, he had said: "If I could be the sort of man my father was, I wouldn't mind being a missionary."

Unlike a number of other missionary children, Dad never focused on going back to Africa. As he grew older his goal became engineering, and he saw no opportunity to serve in that capacity on the mission field.

He entered an engineering program at Muskingum College, New Concord, Ohio. In order to pay his way, he began to do mechanical

---

123 Negley Farson, *Last Chance in Africa*, (N.Y., N.Y. Harcourt, Brace and Co.; 1950), 137.

Father & Son – Herbert & Glennie

dentistry, making dentures, crowns, and bridges for Dr. Castor, father-in – law of astronaut John Glenn. During the school year, he was ill for several months, and got too far behind in the math and science courses. Dr. Castor suggested taking some teaching courses, regardless of what he would eventually do, and teach in a local school. After taking education training and passing the county examination, he got a job teaching that led on to becoming a teacher and eventually a school administrator. This qualified him to address the education problem his father had been wrestling with for decades.

— • —

Whenever Muskingum College is mentioned, reference is usually made of its favorite son, Astronaut John H. Glenn Jr., born on 18 July, 1921. There was an interesting story going around town when he tried to enlist. Upon checking on his birth certificate, he was told that he had died at birth. His mother told him to have them check 18 July 1921, not 18 July, 1920. He had apparently lost a baby brother with the same name exactly one year before he was born.

Mother's youngest brother Ed Houk and John Glenn Jr. grew up together in New Concord, and his family belonged to my maternal grandfather's church.

John graduated from New Concord High School in 1939, about 18 months after our return from Africa. He enrolled at Muskingum College studying chemistry, and received his private pilot's license in 1941 at New Philadelphia Airport.

After Pearl Harbor, he dropped out of college and enlisted in the U.S. Army Air Corps. The Army did not call him up, so he enlisted in the U.S. Navy as a Naval Aviation Cadet. I followed his path into the Navy about 13 years later. His first solo in a military aircraft was in 1943. He apparently applied for a commission in the Marine Corps, as I did. After finishing advanced training, he became a Marine 2nd Lieutenant.

In addition to being the first American to orbit the earth, he was the first to cross the United States in a supersonic aircraft in July 1957.

I was named for Mother's younger brother, Glenn Houk. Glenn was the family name of my maternal grandmother and though there was discussion of her relationship to John Glenn's family, nothing conclusive ever materialized.

— • —

A lady in New England was seeking to support missionaries in Africa with education experience. She agreed to fund Mother and Dad under AIM. When they accepted the responsibility of educating missionary children, her support was withdrawn. They were without regular finances for over four years.

When it came time for them to return to the States, Mother was pregnant with her third child. There was no doctor or midwife nurse at Kijabe. If they were leaving, they were advised to depart by the first of October; otherwise they would probably be delayed another year.

When Grandfather Downing's wife died shortly after returning from the U.S. in 1933, Mother arranged to serve him tea in our home at 4:00 every afternoon. Whenever a problem arose, he would say: "Let's just pray about it now." He made the need for furlough money a matter of prayer.

Dad remembers saying: "You have to know that we don't have anything in view at all. We don't even know anybody who could help."

Grandfather's response: "The Lord knows!"

One afternoon, he came over and said: "You're to get ready to go before the first of October."

Dad replied: "But Father, we don't have a cent we can spend that way."

Father said: "I know that, but you're to get ready. The Lord has given me the assurance that you are to get ready."

Dad's response, "Well, I have seen this happen before," so he began packing.

Grandfather kept checking on their progress. Shortly a telegram arrived from the shipping company that handled the American-South African freighter line. It said: "We have directions from our principals in New York to provide you with passage on the SS *West Isleta*-leaving Mombassa in October, 1937."

Father said, "Well, there's our answer!"

Dad's response: "Who is going to pay for this passage?"

He sent a telegram that said: "There must be some mistake in the directions that you have, we also have principals in New York ... and we have received no word from them authorizing this trip."

A quick telegraphic response said: "We're not interested in what your principals have said; we have our instructions to provide passage for you. You are to come to Mombasa and report to the captain that you have been told that accommodations are ready for you."

Thus began my first trans-oceanic journey. Although under three years old, I remember Grandfather Downing walking along the platform as our train departed Nairobi for Mombasa. It was the last time we saw him. Little did I know then, and I'm sure the man my parents called Father Downing didn't know, the impact he would have on my life. (See Appendix A)

Dad's memory of his meeting with the captain is amusing. In an interview with Robert A. Shuster at the Billy Graham Center he said:

I don't know if you have ever tried going on a ship and telling the captain that you had a space on his ship. I never felt sillier in my life, than when I walked up to the bridge of that ship. I hemmed and hawed and said: 'Do I understand correctly that there is passage here for a Mr. and Mrs. Downing and family?'

The captain said: "Oh, yes, Mr. Downing, we are quite prepared for you. I'll call the head steward and he'll show you to your cabin."

My memories of this voyage are sketchy. I recall watching freight being lowered into the hold at Mombasa. One of the deck hands castigated my mother for allowing me so close. Another memory was crossing railroad tracks near the ship after visiting Durban with Miss Zafke. She had given me a yellow rubber ball and a toy greyhound bus. I had the ball for years, but the bus was left in my bunk when we debarked. Dad took me back to look for it, but it was gone. And I will never forget falling away from the ladder in the improvised canvas swimming tank. Dad was there to rescue me. A movie on deck one evening showed men juggling Indian clubs. I don't know why this frightened me, but again Dad was there to make me feel safe. Lee Downing's son had truly become my father.

Swimming Pool – SS West Isletta

My older sister's memories of our voyage, much more vivid than mine, are worth repeating.

The dress was white organdie with blue narrow stripes, forming a geometric pattern of diamonds crisscrossing each other at wide intervals. A square collar, white, was also part of a yoke from which the gathered skirt fell; decorated with a single narrow black ribbon, streamers falling almost to the hem. I hated it! Because there was no waist, no belt.

We... Mom, Dad, Glenn and I... had been sailing from Mombasa around South Africa on the freighter, SS West Isleta. No five-year-old was ever more delighted with such an exotic adventure. The 12 passengers taken into the family of the ship's crew were treated more like royalty than passengers traveling first class on famous liners – at least this passenger and a younger brother enjoyed such attention.

Even with all the attention, including delightful goodies to eat and a sea-water swimming pool made of canvas, lining one of the holds, the days of confinement on shipboard grew tedious. As the first port-of-call drew nearer, it became the focus of anticipation and excitement, a break in the monotony of watery horizons and sloping decks... and the Number One topic of conversation.

The day finally dawned when land was sighted and cheered. But horror of horrors! Mother had chosen that awful blue-and-white dress for me to wear ashore! After much threatening and debate, the Head-Of-the-House handed down the final decision. Quickly and without apology, he simply said those awful words, many times recalled, "She's not going ashore!" And I didn't! No second chances.

When my parents returned from their tour of Port Elizabeth, they brought me my first "paper hankies" and tried to describe what "street cars" were like. I think all the passengers and sailors brought back gifts. Baskets of fruit and nuts, decorated with iridescent ribbons, pressed and worn in my hair for years, and nail polish, bright red, were the most appreciated. The sailor who brought the nail polish let me paint his nails each evening when he was off duty. It must have been at that point that I decided sailing the high seas was the ultimate adventure this world could offer. It still stands pretty high on my list.

I can still think mostly kind thoughts of that trip even though it lasted 43 days. Rounding the Cape of Good Hope, we ran into a storm that should have left me terrified for life.

Glenn and I soon learned how one can tell the difference between a passenger ship and a freighter. The ocean liner, designed to carry people as well as cargo, looks like one continuous big floating building shaped like a ship at each end. A freighter looks like two little houses, between which a long, flat connection rides close to the water. From the huge flat deck, the freight can be loaded and stored into huge holds below the water level.

Depending upon the amount of freight, the more freight, the lower the deck rides in the water. Our ship was well loaded.

Just little snatches of the big storm are etched in my memory. I do recall not being able to see the lower deck at all because of the fierceness of the waves crashing back and forth. The little deck at the back of the ship did not appear to be connected to our deck up front, so completely did the sea cover the ship between.

At supper, I remember all the chairs were hooked to the floor, and the table cloths had been dipped in water to prevent the dishes from sliding. Each person at the table was given something to hold on to as the ship rolled from side to side. Eventually the sea tossed us around so much we were thrown from our chairs, and food slithered back and forth on the floor as the ship dipped and rose, over and over. I can still see a little red blob of jelly sliding from side to side, looking like a little miniature sailboat on a pleasure cruise of its own. Only the adults were aware of the seriousness of the occasion. I've since heard that some did not expect to survive.

By the next morning, calm had settled over sea and ship. Very early, while walking on deck with my Daddy, we saw the cook, basket on his arm, gathering fish deposited by the huge waves only a few hours before on the lower decks. For breakfast that morning, we dined on the freshest of fresh fish.

Learning Adventure – First Voyage
By Gayle M. Downing Grass

As the SS *West Isleta*[131] approached New York she encountered three days of stormy weather. Cloud cover prevented accurate position fixes. However, Brooklyn Harbor was reached at dusk, on Thursday, 13 November, 1937. My Father was standing by the rail of the ship, watching it pull into the wharf, concerned about our future. Mother, my sister, and I debarked, and the steward carried our luggage ashore. Dad was the last to leave. The weather was foggy, rainy, and cold. At the foot of the gang plank was a figure in an overcoat who grabbed Dad's sleeve, pulled him toward her, and said: "I just wanted you to know, I am paying your way to

---

[131] It is interesting to note the fate of the SS *West Isleta*. In 1940, she became the SS *Empire Merlin*, ON 167595 for British Ministry of War Transport. On 25 August, 1940 she was the last ship on the port quarter of a 51 ship convoy to Hull, England. She was torpedoed by U.48 (Rosing) at 0153 and immediately broke in two. She sank within 35 seconds. There was only one survivor who was in the water for three hours before being picked up. Less than four years after we debarked from the SS *West Isleta*, she was gone!

any place in the United States that you've decided to go."   It was the lady who had cut off their support.

Mother's younger brothers met the ship and drove us to the home office. The streets were wet, and I remember being frightened by those old Marathon gas signs that flashed red and blue neon swastikas.

Later, Mr. Lanning, the AIM business manager, asked Dad who had authorized our trip. He said that he didn't.

Mothers comment later: "We eventually were able to pay for our passage; God does meet needs and answers prayers."

Mother's brothers drove our freight to New Concord, Ohio in her father's car. We traveled by train in a Pullman Car. The lady had seen mother's condition and insisted.

On 24 November, my younger brother, Edwin Lee, was born. My Father had his second son!

Reimbursement

The immediate obligation was to repay the mission for our travel expenses. We moved into a small house behind Professor Work's home, just north of New Concord. Ernest Work was professor of history at Muskingum College, formerly the advisor to the Ethiopian government. In 1935 he published the book *Ethiopia, a Pawn in European Diplomacy.* Dad was employed to design and build a large home on the Bloomfield Road across from their old house. I recall seeing the cardboard model he made for the professor and his wife's approval.

Professor Work was very interesting to me, because he had been in Europe during WW I. Among his war souvenirs were some "hangin' eggs." Dad corrected my misconception – they were hand grenades, inert, of course!

He had some beehives in his orchard, and gave Gayle and me each a drone in a small matchbox. Gayle's drone flew away, so I offered to go to the beehive and get a replacement. I used my little hoe to pull one off the bottom board and you can easily guess the results. That bee was no drone!

Since I was not in school, Dad would often take me to work with him. One day I was watching a man I only knew as Mr. Wilson grading around the house with a team of horses and a dam scoop. I was standing outside the house and got stuck in the mud. I couldn't move! Mr. Wilson had to pick me up and scrape the mud off my shoes.

My Uncle Ed told me, when I was older, that I used to walk the wall plates just like the carpenters. People were aghast at my temerity, but Dad told them not to scare me. I have always appreciated that kind of encouragement from him.

The record shows that the Work's house was completed in 1938. One realtor said he never had difficulty selling the house whenever it came on the market.

The next big project was finishing the interior of Uncle Tommy's house. Uncle Tommy was an older bachelor and no relation to anyone I knew. Dad was putting up dry wall on the second floor. He had bought me a good quality light hammer which I learned to use. He made x's on the boards as high as I could reach and had me drive nails.

We were in Cambridge one day when he bought a Stanley #3 wood plane for me. He had built a small portable workbench with an attached vise. My schooling in the use of a hand plan began. This became so satisfying that I now have 25 different planes in my shop.

John Glenn Sr., the astronaut's father, had a plumbing business in New Concord. Dad was employed to re-model his old building into an auto showroom. We bought our first automobile there. Our 1930 four door Chevrolet sedan cost $100, quite a step up from a one cylinder motorcycle.

It wasn't long before Dad began teaching mechanical drawing and shop at the college. Tool room control used personalized brass tags on hooks whenever a tool was checked out. I learned a lot just watching. Dad's hand printing was so perfect it looked like typing. I emulated his style and frustrated my first grade teacher because my writing was too small.

War Clouds

Adolph Hitler's threatened takeover of Czechoslovakia in September 1938 made the U.S. painfully aware of the danger in Europe. For the first time, America felt its isolationism threatened by a foreign war. A *Fortune* magazine survey indicated that 76.2% of the American people believed that the United States would become involved in a war in Europe, as happened 20 years earlier. William Manchester said: "The Czech crises had awakened America from its long slumber, and the country was anxious, biting its nails, drumming its fingers. Bombs, invasion, war-all that had been unthinkable as recently as last summer-were suddenly very real."[132]

Despite strong pockets of American isolationist and pacifist sentiment, President Franklin D. Roosevelt gave the green light to a military expansion. He was convinced that air power would win the next war and that the United States had to build up its air forces *and those of its European allies.*

In violation of the Versailles Treaty, Germany had been training pilots under the guise of sport and glider flying. Many of the members in these clubs were Nazi party members. All private and national flying organizations were absorbed into the German Air Sport Association in March 1933. This became the Reichs Luftfahrt Ministerium (RLM) or Reich Air Ministry. On 15 May, 1933, all other military aviation organizations were merged in the RLM. This was the official birthday of the *Luftwaffe.*

---

[132] Dominick A. Pisano, *To Fill the Skies with Pilots,* (Urbana, IL, University of Illinois Press, 1993), 28.

In October 1938 William Bullitt, the American ambassador to France, briefed Roosevelt on the situation in Europe. Bullitt stressed that the *Luftwaffe* was being used as diplomatic blackmail in the European crisis, and suggested that the United States needed to strengthen its defense by increasing aircraft production.

The Chief of the Air Corps, General Henry H. "Hap" Arnold reported that 1,499 aircraft would be needed if the United States were to mobilize for war. In November 1938 Roosevelt met with his council of war and shocked them all with the need for 20,000 aircraft in order to prevent an attack on the western hemisphere. That number was scaled down to 10,000, because the President believed that Congress would balk at the higher figure.

The obvious question was: who would fly all of these aircraft? Unlike many countries in Europe, the United States had only a small reserve of pilots, and no formal program of training. There were estimated 3,800 commercial and 3,600 private pilots between the ages of 18 and 30 in the United States in 1939. Many could not pass the stringent physical requirements necessary to be military aviators. Both the Army Air-Corps and the Navy were ill equipped to produce pilots in mass quantity.

Since the 1920's, college courses, influenced by John Dewey's pragmatic philosophy of education, had been introducing practical subjects that would prepare students for employment. In December 1938 President Roosevelt announced the establishment of a small scale experimental program. He had given approval to the Civil Aeronautics Administration (CAA), to promote the private aviation industry by giving flight instruction to 10,000 college students.

Under the able leadership of Robert H. Hinckley, the Civilian Pilot Training Program (CPTP), came into existence and ultimately trained thousands of military pilots during WW II. This was no mean feat since he had to overcome the objections of the military, colleges, fixed base operators, and Congress.

One of the factors that convinced all parties was the comparison of our posture with the German air program. It was estimated that Germany had 65,000 flight trainees between the ages of 18 and 35. The Nazis were turning out 25,000 pilots, mechanics, and aeronautical engineers annually. If the United States got involved in the European conflict, some drastic changes were necessary.

Hinckley's solution was to mobilize the civilian flight instructors and fixed base operators around the country, and merge them with various colleges to interest and train pilots. The program was to be funded by the government through the CAA. Politically this was opposed by those who were averse to Roosevelt's "New Deal" stimuli. The critical situation in Europe overcame this opposition.

It should be emphasized that not everyone is aviation qualifiable. Without a screening program, the pilot elimination rate was as high as 50%. In order to reduce this cost in time and effort, the input from Dean R. Brimhall was invaluable. Brimhall, professor of psychology at Brigham Young University, was instrumental in developing a research program to explore pilot selection and instructional methods.

The CPTP developed a battery of tests that the Navy used later to evaluate potential air cadets in the earliest phases of their training. These tests, which "previewed" a student's flying ability, enabled the Navy to eliminate 50% of those who would eventually washout of pilot training.

I recall being subjected to this rigorous testing, both on entering the Navy and when I began flying for the airlines. Believe me! They were demanding! After two days of testing it felt like I had a "charley horse" in my brain.

CPTP researchers at Purdue University, under the direction of E. Lowell Kelly developed a way to help standardize teaching methods. Two instructional guides were produced. The first, a manual of flight training called *Patter for Elementary Flight Maneuvers,* was widely used by the CPTP and the Navy. The second, *Fundamentals of Basic Flight Maneuvers,* was a standardized manual that allowed students to go through various aerial maneuvers on the ground before they did so in the cockpit. Twenty-five years later, I was subjected to the Navy's emphasis upon standardization both as a student and an instructor. It does work very efficiently.

The Army Air Corp (AAC), under General Arnold, considered the training of pilots as civilians of lower quality than that given to military recruits, even if the training was done by civilian instructors hired by the AAC. Military parochialism on the issue was a constant problem in the air corps' acceptance of the program. As the CPTP shifted into wartime high gear, the air corps' insistence on retaining its autonomy in matters of pilot training would have serious consequences. This attitude persisted and ultimately resulted in the Air Force being severed from the Army into a separate service in 1947.

Instructor

Dad taught at Muskingum College. The 1942-43 college catalog listed him as follows:

Herbert Caldwell Downing, B.A. Instructor in Physics and Mathematics (1940)

B.A. Muskingum College 1928, graduate study, Ohio State University summers 1929, 1930; University of Pittsburgh, 1931-32

Course description: Civil Pilot Training

Aviation theory and practice. Given jointly by Muskingum College and a nearby airport under supervision of the United States Civil Aeronautical Authority. Students must have attained at least sophomore standing; be of a prescribed age, pass a through physical examination, and present written consent of parents.

Dad's efforts to repay travel expenses gradually involved him in the war effort. He became more and more engaged in the Civil Pilot Training Program and was moved to the New Philadelphia Airport where Muskingum College flight training took place. On weekends he returned to New Concord to be with our family. With all this activity, however, all of our intentions were focused on returning to Kenya as soon as possible.

Zamzam

Just before sunrise on the 17th of April, 1941, Mrs. Lillian Danielson was in her bunk on the Egyptian passenger ship *Zamzam*. Suddenly, the morning calm was shattered by a "loud explosive rumble." Quietly she went out on deck, and was startled by a red spurt of fire from an ugly warship, three to four nautical miles away. Quickly she returned to her six sleepy children. As calmly as possible she directed them to get dressed and put on their life jackets.

The first salvo missed, but the second salvo destroyed the wireless room. Six seconds later the ship was hit below the water line. The ship trembled and began to list to port. A hit in a lower corridor caused screams from someone who had been badly hurt. A shell hit the cabin above, a steel beam crashed to the upper deck, and the lavatory broke away from the bulk head, in the Danielson's cabin. The air was filled with acrid smoke, and the floor was covered with broken glass.

Suddenly, the ship's purser urged them to their life boats as expeditiously as possible. Apparently, the ships whistle had been damaged by one of the first shells. By now, the 10 minute barrage was over. Their life boat was at deck level when they arrived. Seconds after Mrs. Danielson was seated with her two year old baby, they began their descent toward the ocean. Just before entering the water, the line from the davit came loose and Mrs. Danielson was struck in the head, causing a swollen lump. They entered the water with a splash and some of the panicked crew began to row feverishly away from the ship.

Shrapnel from enemy shells had perforated the boat's hull so that they were shipping water faster than they could bail. With a sudden lurch the lifeboat submerged pulling its passengers with it. Mrs. Danielson came to the surface with her baby in her arms. She was able to spot all but her fourth child. Suddenly, her son fought his way between crew and passengers and pulled her to the surface. She had been trapped under water.

The German Raider approached, and soon put out motorboats to rescue the helpless victims. By noon everyone was recovered. Two motorboats salvaged what they could from the stricken *Zamzam*. A roll call was made from the sinking ship's passenger list. A very tall officer looked down compassionately at Mrs. Danielson and asked, "Mother, how many of your children survived?"

Looking squarely into the German's eye, she replied, "I thank God, He saved us all."

The following is a quote from the book *Miracle at Sea* by Eleanor Anderson, the oldest daughter in the Danielson family.

Roll call was finally completed. But the officer was not yet satisfied. He whispered to his aide, and the two of them checked the records again, as if looking for an error. Finally, the officer was ready to speak. ' We have never had an experience like this," he began. "No one is missing. Not one life was lost today. Three men are very badly injured, but they are alive at this time. There are other injuries less serious. It is most unusual that nobody was drowned or killed by the shells.' He paused. 'We fired fifty five shells, but only nine hit your ship. Unbelievable,' he said. as if to himself, shaking his head.

Then clearing his throat and regaining military composure, the officer continued, 'Because no life was lost, we do not have to report this incident until we want to, and I do not think the captain intends to report it. We apologize for what has happened, but we surmised that your ship was aiding the Allies. You must remember, you were traveling blacked out,' he added emphatically. He paused and then continued, 'Ya, this is wartime, and this is a ship of war. The British are looking for us. It is not good to keep civilians on a warship. We will transfer you to another ship as soon as possible.'[133]

The *Zamzam*, built in 1910, was given the name *HMS Leistershire*. Originally a passenger liner, she served as a troop carrier during WW I. In 1933 she was sold to Egypt and re-named *Zamzam*, in honor of the sacred well near Mecca. She was crewed by Egyptian Muslims, but her captain was a British officer named William Smith. The German boarding party found evidence in Captain Smith's cabin supporting the assumption that the *Zamzam* was sailing under orders of the British Admiralty. This could be the reason that the *Zamzam* was traveling the South Atlantic toward Cape Town blacked out, showing no lights externally.

Because Egypt was a neutral country at the time of *Zamzam*'s sailing, several mission boards decided to send missionaries to Africa on her. To

---

[133] Eleanor Anderson, *Miracle at Sea*, (Molivar, MO, Quiet Waters Publications, 2001), 70-71.

avoid the war zone, she traveled by way of South America and South Africa. There were 201 passengers aboard on this voyage, including 35 children. Nearly three fourths of the total were missionaries from 20 Protestant denominations. In addition, there were 17 Roman Catholic priests and teaching brothers. There were 24 drivers from the British-American Ambulance Corps, and six tobacco buyers.

Inasmuch as this was wartime, none of the remaining passengers were traveling for pleasure. One of the passengers was David E. Scherman, a *Life* magazine photographer. The Germans allowed him to take pictures which were later seized. (He did manage to smuggle four rolls back to New York.) Charles J.V. Murphy, a *Fortune* magazine editor was also aboard. Murphy's account of the incident, as well as photos by Scherman, was in the 23 June, 1941 issue of *Life*.

Zamzam

Atlantis was built in 1937 as a freighter and given the name *Goldenfels*. She was owned and operated by the Honsa Line in Bremen. In late 1939, she was converted to a warship, and commissioned as the commerce raider *Atlantis* in November 1939. Having a length of 510 feet, displacing 7,862 gross registered tons, *Atlantis* had two six-cylinder diesel engines of 7600 horsepower each and a top speed of 16 knots. She was armed with six 155 mm guns, one 75 mm gun, two 37 mm guns, four 20 mm guns, four 533 mm torpedo tubes, 92 mines and two *Heinkel* HE-114B float planes. She was crewed by 349 officers and men, with one Scottish terrier, (Fevv), as a mascot. The Germans designated her *HSK II* or simply *Schiff* 16. She could alter her appearance into 26 different silhouettes. At the time of the *Zamzam* sinking, she appeared as the Norwegian ship *Tamesis*. Captain Bernard Rogge was in command from March 1940 until November 1941, when Atlantis was sunk by the British Cruiser *HMS Devonshire*. During that time she terrorized the British Navy and sank 22 ships for a total of more than 145,000 tons.

Capt. Rogge met with five men who represented the various passenger groups. V. Eugene Johnson, the father of one of my RVA schoolmates, was appointed the spokesman for the Protestant missionaries. Among other statements, he made the following report:

I was favorably impressed by the captain. He had been a full captain in the German navy. His name is Rogge, Captain Bernard Rogge. We can be thankful we are in the hands of such a decent man, folks. He apologized for what happened but pointed out we were traveling in blackout. Captain Rogge said he remembered having seen the Zamzam years ago, when she was an English troop ship during WW I. He did not know the Zamzam had been sold to Egypt.

'But why didn't he stop firing sooner? Didn't the <u>Zamzam</u> signal our identity?' someone said.

You know, that brings up a miraculous chain of events. Here's what happened: when the shelling began, the Zamzam's radioman had hurried to send out the SOS distress call to nearby ships. However, before the radioman could send the message, a piece of shrapnel grazed him, causing him to fall, slightly injured. Then another officer had rushed to send the SOS, but, as he was about to touch the machine, the next shell destroyed the radio antenna. Therefore, no message was sent, not even a blurb of one letter. Captain Rogge said that, had any message gone out, for his own safety, he would have torpedoed the Zamzam and not stayed around to pick up survivors. We were that close to death.

'Surely God was with us. That timing was more than an ordinary coincidence,' commented a passenger.

So you see why the shelling kept on as long as it did. Even the wire on the Morse blinker had been damaged. Finally Captain Smith found a flashlight and signaled our identity. Then the firing did stop immediately.

Captain Rogge says he was stunned to see all of us civilians, especially women and children. I believe his apology is sincere.[134]

True to his word, Capt. Rogge transferred the 330 *Zamzam* survivors onto the *Dresden*, a German freighter, which only had accommodations for 35 passengers. Women were assigned to cabins and lounges, but the men were directed toward one of two holds. The Egyptian crew was in one hold, and the more than 100 male passengers were in another 54 x 54 foot cargo hold. The *Dresden* became known as the prison ship. Twenty-six days after the *Zamzam* sank, the *Dresden*, which had been traveling northward, changed course to the east. This confirmed the rumor that Capt. Jaeger was going to take the Dresden through the British blockade into a German occupied French port. Big guns were moved into position on the bridge and hidden by bales of hemp and sand bags. A new name had been painted in place of *Dresden*. She was now the *Ognau*. Passengers were required to have their life jackets with them every minute.

One night a violent storm arose, protecting the ship from British attack. Another day an English convoy was spotted in the distance. The *Ognau* was turned toward the sun and engines stopped, waiting, waiting. Eventually the convoy disappeared over the horizon without incident.

Early on 20 May, the prison ship was piloted into the German occupied harbor of St. Jean-de-Luz. The German officers were amazed the *Dresden* had come through the blockade safely, a one in a hundred chance, some said. Two British missionaries from the Africa Inland Mission, Mr. Guilding and Mr. Mundy, were to be separated from the rest, and were incarcerated in a German concentration camp for the duration of the war. The Americans were returned to the United States, where most of them stayed until the war ended.

It should be noted that the reason the Danielson family was traveling without the head of their household was because Mr. Danielson had returned to Tanganyika in July 1940, because of a war shortage of missionaries there. The fixed gulf of the war torn Atlantic Ocean had kept this family separated for nearly four and a half years.

There are three reasons I have reiterated this poignant story. The first is to remind us that God can protect His people even under the most dangerous circumstances. Secondly, it emphasizes that there was a great gulf fixed between the United States and Africa during WW II. Finally, it

---

[134]Elenor Anderson, *Miracle at Sea*, Ibid., 76.

was a pivotal event that affected my father, Herbert Downing, and ultimately affected Rift Valley Academy, where he gave the best part of his life.

To illustrate how this great gulf affected peoples lives, let me give two examples. One was a *Zamzam* passenger. The other was a family that was very close to our family in later years.

Dr. Arthur Barnett was aboard the *Zamzam*, with his new bride, returning to his home in Africa. His parents had been missionaries in Kenya, and raised Arthur and his twin brother Eric, plus three other siblings in Africa, until they came to America for higher education. He was returning to Africa as a medical missionary with medical equipment and supplies in *Zamzam's* hold. Needless to say, all of this ended at the bottom of the Atlantic Ocean when his ship was sunk.

After he and his wife were returned to the United States, he became a doctor in the US Army Air Corps. He was subsequently flown across the Atlantic in one of the first flights of the *Douglas DC-6* to North Africa. It was interesting for me to learn that my mentor and friend for many years, Dr. J. H. Propst, was on that same flight. WW II detained both medical missionary doctors for the duration of the war.

Dr. Barnett has been an especially close friend of our family. I will be forever grateful to him for being my father's attendant physician during his terminal illness.

The second example concerns Mr. and Mrs. Harold Amstutz and their son David. The Amstutz family went to the Belgian Congo via Kenya, East Africa in 1937. They were assigned to a primitive mission station called Adja. The following is taken from Forty *Years as a Missionary in Africa, by Mrs. Jane Amstutz in Apr. 1998.*

This was a real challenge for us. But in 1939 when we were on "Safari" in "Kaliko" land (one of the four tribes), late one Sunday night we heard, from our little Zenith short wave radio, that the USA was at war with Japan. This came to us from the British Broadcasting Corporation. What a shock! For the next five years we were hostage missionaries at work in Congo. During one of those years, we did not receive a letter or any piece of mail from home. Our first term in Congo was supposed to be five years, but because of the war, it turned out to be eight years! In 1944 we thought it was time for us to try to get passage to USA. The war had not been declared finished as yet, so the passage pickings were very few. From Adja station, we drove south to Cape Town, South Africa, (about 3,000 miles) and contacted Cook and Sons Travel Agency.

After several weeks of roaming between Cape Town and Johannesburg, (about 800 miles) we finally had a call from the travel agency. We had with us a widowed missionary, Mrs. Grimshaw, and her daughter Mary, whom we were escorting back to the States. We needed six tickets. The agency offered us the six passages on a 78 year old three-mast sailing vessel, the Tijuca, sailing from Cape Town, South Africa to Buenos Aires, Argentina. There was one more passenger with us, a young girl from South Africa who was going to the United States to marry an American boy. The vessel only carried seven passengers. It wasn't until we were on the high seas that we learned that the main mast of the Tijuca had broken in high winds on the trip to Cape Town and the first mate had been lost overboard. The Tijuca had been commissioned in 1866 as a trainer for the French Navy by Napoleon III.

We were 45 days on the high seas; sometimes stormy weather, sometimes glassy seas with no wind! As we were arriving at Buenos Aires, on the River Plata channel, we could see the bow of the Graf Spee German war ship protruding above water where it had been destroyed during the war!

The hotels in Buenos Aires were full of Germans. After three weeks of waiting here, we managed to get plane tickets with over night stops at Rio de Janeiro and Belen, a short stop at Haiti, and finally Miami and New York. What a joy to set one's feet down again on American soil. Home at last – June 1944!

Following are two notes from World War II, 4,139 Strange and Fascinating Facts, by Don McCombs and Fred L. Worth.

Graf Spee – German pocket battleship that was scuttled outside Montevideo Harbor in December 1939, as a result of the first major naval engagement of WW II. She was engaged in the Battle of the Plate River by the cruiser HMS Exeter, light cruiser HMS Ajax, and the Royal New Zealand cruiser Achilles, all in Montevideo. Captain Hans Langsdorff of the Graf Spee believed he was opposed by a larger force and scuttled the ship after which he committed suicide.[135]

---

[135] Don McCombs & Fred L. Worth, *WW II 4,139 Strange and Fascinating Facts*, (New York, NY, Wings Books, 1983), 25.

D-Day - 6 June, 1944, a Tuesday marked the greatest invasion in history when the Allies assaulted Normandy. Involved in the initial assault were 185,000 troops, 18,000 paratroopers, 13,175 aircraft, 4,066 landing ships, 745 large ships, 20,000 vehicles, and 347 minesweepers...[136]

June 1944, the month the Amstutz' arrived back from Africa. June 1944, the greatest invasion in history, one of the "biggies" in Global Warring.

To bring this chapter to a close, let me include some family observations from this time period. My older sister Gayle was especially good at writing memorabilia vignettes. The following are from her sketches entitled: *I Remember When...*

World War II changed our lives.

We canned over 500 quarts of fruits and vegetables each summer, gleaned from commercial fields and our own gardens.

Mom was drafted to teach from the time Ruth Ann (our younger sister) was only a few months old until the war ended.

Mom never went out after supper during those war years. She knit our sweaters and mittens while we listened to radio drama, or she read to us, or played games.

She was my best friend...

---

[136] Ibid., 136.

Firsts and Seconds

The sinking of the *Zamzam* precluded children crossing the Atlantic Ocean. Our parents considered family a primary responsibility so we remained in the United States for the duration. What was intended as a one year furlough became nine years of war and mission-related activity. Five years were spent in New Concord, Ohio in seven different houses.

My father believed boys were not ready for school until they were six years old. Consequently I entered first grade in New Concord in the fall of 1941.

Pearl Harbor was bombed on 7 December. The Second World War had finally overtaken the United States and changed all of our lives. The first peacetime military draft had been approved more than a year earlier, but most people were not concerned until war was declared. In the evenings, our family remained quiet at the supper table while Lowell Thomas read the evening news. There was concern that Dad would be drafted and have to go off to war. Mother said he was too old at age 36, and had too many children to be drafted.

Although the Civilian Pilot Training Program (CPTP) had come increasingly under military influence from mid-1940 onward, the nature of the program changed entirely when we entered WW II. Five days after the Japanese attack, President Roosevelt in Executive Order 8974, officially transformed the civil pilot training into a wartime program. Henceforth, all Civil Aeronautics Administration pilot training efforts would be "exclusively devoted to the procurement and training of men for ultimate service as military pilots, or for correlated non-military activities."[137]

By early 1942, the program had lost much of its early flavor and character. The New Deal elements of interesting American youth in aviation and stimulating the light plane industry inherent in Hinckley's original plan gave way to the realities of war. In addition, the Army Air Force and Navy began pressing for changes to bring the program into line with their needs. To formalize the military aspects of training in wartime, the name of the program was changed one year after Pearl Harbor to the War Training Service (WTS). But its scope and direction had already been

---

[137] Dominick A. Pisano, *To Fill the Skies with Pilots,* (Urbana, IL, University of Illinois, 1993), 84.

altered drastically by the demands placed on it in the year following 7 December, 1941

At any rate, Dad found himself in a critical wartime position, and spent the rest of the war training pilots for military aviation assignments.

My maternal grandfather, Clarence Houk, was pastor of the Presbyterian Church in New Concord, and Dad was an elder. When I was five years old, I was baptized by grandfather Houk, and joined the church. After the war began, he became ill so Dad began to fill his pulpits in New Concord and Norwich on Sundays.

The fixed base operator at New Philadelphia was Harry Clever. Dad became his ground school instructor, rated to instruct Civil Air Regulations, Aerial Navigation, Radio, and Meteorology. In July 1942, Mr. Clever became Dad's flight instructor in a B model Taylorcraft. He soloed on 30 March, 1943. Flight training continued at New Philadelphia until May 1943.

One day Dad took me to the airport in our 1930 Chevrolet. He had made arrangements with one of the flight instructors for my first flight. This was the beginning of my career as an aviator. I remember how far I could see as we climbed high into the sky. Houses on the ground became smaller and smaller as we climbed higher. It was an exhilarating experience that has grown in intensity throughout my life. You could say I was "hooked" from my first flight.

Essential for every government program are the ever present inspectors. Dad's first experience created defensive irritation, which was quickly stifled by Mr. Clever. It was an important lesson in learning to function within a government bureaucracy. Basically, it means letting them find something that needs attention, and asking them how to fix the problem. The inspector feels he has done his job, and is flattered that his counsel is sought.

In April 1942, the sixth member of our family was born. Ruth Ann's arrival evened our family with 2 girls and 2 boys. Gayle said Ruth Ann was an answer to her prayers!

Second grade was better for me than first, if for no other reason than I liked my teacher better. Miss Noble was a member of the same church, and a friend of the family. Besides, she was attractive. I noticed things like that even then.

Gayle wrote that we began singing a cappella duets when she was in fifth grade and I in second. One of the first songs we sang at an evening service was: <u>This One Thing I Know.</u> This chorus told the story of the man, blind from birth, given sight by Jesus on the Sabbath. The lyrics say:

> This one thing I know,
> This one thing I know.
> God in great mercy pardoned me
> Snapped sins fetters and set me free.
> Once I was blind, but now I see
> This one thing I know.

This was the same message in a song I recently sang at my Air Force cousin's funeral: "I once was lost but now am found, was blind but now I see." Robert Sawhill had been a prisoner of war in North Vietnam for 5 1/2 years, a casualty of "global warring." <u>Amazing Grace</u> was requested by his widow and sister.

The requirement for thousands of new aircraft entailed the conservation of war materials. At the beginning of the war, cigarette companies wrapped their cigarettes in metal foil. People peeled the paper off the foil and rolled it into metal balls. Gasoline was rationed and highway speed limits were reduced to conserve fuel. I don't know why, but bubble gum became scarce. We found that by soaking scotch tape in warm water and combining the gum with regular chewing gum, we could blow satisfactory bubbles. Unlike subsequent wars, WW II was an all out effort that affected everyone.

New Concord was intersected by US 22 and US 40. One day the Army ran a large convoy through the center of town. This included trucks, jeeps, amphibious ducks, and amphibious jeeps with motorcycle military police. I have never forgotten the distinctive whine of the gears in four wheel drive army trucks. It was fascinating to watch the motorcycles stop and wait for the end of their unit. This convoy took a whole day to pass.

Training requirements for the army required facilities the peace time army did not have. Muskingum College was opened as an army school under the command of a colonel who drove a Lincoln. I know because I nicked his rear fender with my bicycle one day!

Another time, I was in our back yard when a B-17 flew over the center of town at an estimated 500 feet. Every detail was clearly visible. We had studied aircraft silhouettes and knew the type. I guessed it was one of our soldier boys showing his new office to the home folks!

Army Air Force vs. Civilian Pilot Training

At a carefully chosen site, in a small abandoned warehouse in Washington, DC, the trial of Brig. Gen. William Mitchell began on 28 October, 1928. Gen. Mitchell's offense was vociferously advocating a separate service Air Force. Testifying for Mitchell were Maj. Carl Spaatz, Maj. "Hap" Arnold, Maj. Gerald Brandt, and Eddie Rickenbacker. The president of the court, Maj. Gen. Summerall, was removed when defense counsel proved bias against the defendant. None of the 13 judges had aviation experience. Two other judges were challenged off the case for cause. The trial attracted significant interest, and public opinion supported Mitchell. The court found Mitchell guilty of insubordination, and suspended him from active duty for five years without pay. The significance of this trial is the awesome power of the military court martial system. It imposed arrogant ignorance on a non-traditional innovator, who was subsequently exonerated.

Billy Mitchell resigned, but Maj. Arnold used his assigned position in the information office to provide propaganda to airpower friendly journalists. This was in direct defiance of orders from the General Staff. Arnold was given the choice of resignation or a court martial. He chose the latter, and the Army backed down.

Henry Harley "Hap" Arnold, taught to fly by Orville Wright, was one of the first military pilots worldwide. Prior to WW II, he became the commander of the Army Air Force. He still persistently pursued his goal of a separate Air Force, ranking equally with the Army and the Navy.

Acknowledging the shortage of trained pilots, and recognizing their inability to train pilots quickly enough, both the AAC and Navy reluctantly waived certain "elimination" courses for CPTP graduates, and allowed them to proceed directly into pilot training.

The AAC deemed the situation to be so grave that it proposed that private aviation be suspended and all pilot training (most notably the CPTP) be brought under control of the military. The Army's proposal met stiff resistance from 83 general aviation companies organizing the National Aviation Training Association (NATA). The NATA and other aviation interests blunted the Army's bid with an effective lobbying campaign in congress. Their actions not only saved CPTP, they may have saved the entire general aviation industry in the United States.

The source of conflict between the CAA and the AAF on civilian versus military prerogatives, and the use of a civilian program in war time, was jurisdictional. The CAA felt that it had a legitimate right to continue its normal functions, including the training program, as long as they contributed to the war effort. The AAF on the other hand believed that the CAA was a civilian interloper in a military task.

The dispute was finally resolved in August 1942, when the Secretaries of War and Navy wrote to the Secretary of Commerce that the CAA would retain its independence. This meant that it could not be subsumed into the war department. Thus the CAA's program could not be taken over by the Air Force.

Though not provable, circumstantial evidence indicated that the AAF deliberately refused to cooperate with the CAA and congress in making full use of the approved program. Instead of using civilian fields, the AAF began constructing vast and ornate "Hollywood" air schools. By April 1942, six new schools were opened to the tune of more than $5 million each. Arnold was concerned that the CAA's efforts to legitimatize itself as a civilian agency necessary to the war effort, might draw attention away from the AAF, jeopardizing his separate service goal.

The resolution of the dispute revitalized the program, and expanded to an even larger segment of the nation's colleges and universities. This helped open the doors for the first African-American military pilots. The onset of WW II and political pressure combined to compel the US AAC to employ African-Americans as officers and pilots. The majority were graduates of the CPTP. Thus denizens of the land of Zinj were included in the largest, most powerful air force in the world, another first.

The Navy and the Civilian Pilot Training

It is curious that the Navy made full use of the CPTP graduates. Capt. Arthur Redford, director of training in the Bureau of Aeronautics, characterized the Navy's attitude toward civilian training. He admitted that the Navy had been skeptical about using civilians to train its pilots. This attitude changed, however, when the Navy realized that it could not turn out pilots in sufficient numbers to fight a two-ocean war without aid.

Program administrators in turn raised training standards and standardized training methods. Utilization of the <u>Patter for Elementary Flight Maneuvers</u>, and the screening test it developed to evaluate aeronautical adaptability, were both assets to the Navy. "Without question," Redford concluded, "the Navy is profiting greatly from the CPTP; it saves time in planes, saves time for instructors, and prevents loss of wastage by reducing the number of students eliminated."[138] The Navy's successful use of the CPTP as a screening device was obviously working. Its pilot elimination rate was 17 %, compared to the AAF's rate of 43 to 50%.

The Navy's V-5 Program

In September 1942, 28 young men assembled in Prescott, Arizona. This was the very first class of Navy V-5 aviator training cadets. The Navy desperately needed to correct deficiencies of previous flight training strategies. Despite rigorous physical testing, many of the young men accepted for flight training lacked the *innate* skills to become military pilots. For some of them, and their instructors, the discovery was fatal.[139]

A better way was needed to weed out the unsuited, without the loss of life and expensive military equipment. In May 1942, "the most effective and productive training program ever devised in the world history of military aviation" was developed by Rear Admiral (then commander) Thomas Hamilton USN, who designated the V-5 program.

The goal was to produce combat pilots to wage war in the Atlantic and Pacific theaters. However, its greatest side effect was the most thorough and complete unarmed combative training the Department of the Navy had ever seen. (Originally published in In Quartata as "Rough and Tumble" combatives.)

Hamilton, and other top Naval Officers, realized that efficient and effective close quarters fighting skills were needed by all Naval personnel. Most all were aviators who risked being shot down over enemy territory. The result was "catch as catch can" wrestling in its most no holds barred sense, employing every dirty trick, illegal hold, and bone breaking technique believed workable on the battlefield or the street. Unlike other famous WW II "hand-to-hand" combat programs, the V-5 system was a thorough and complete method of close quarters fighting.

V-5 Pre- Flight Training was dedicated to hardening the aviation cadets physically. Through sports, the men were indoctrinated with the group loyalty and psychological mind-set required in combat. The core of this program was physical contact, "controlled" violence: hand-to-hand combat and football. The former taught them to kill; the latter developed

---

[138] Dominick A. Pisano, *To Fill the Skies with Pilots*, Ibid., 88.
[139] Footnote from "Fledgling World War II Warbirds trained at Ernest Love Field", Al Bates, http://www.sharlot.org/archives/history/dayspast/text/2001-11-11shtml. (accessed July 16, 2010).

the teamwork used by V-5 graduates to amass considerably more air-to-air combat victories than pilots from other commissioning programs.

Every sport or athletic activity at the training center was altered in some fashion to better simulate combat. Boxing emphasized aggressiveness, and a hard core fighting spirit. Gymnastics, track, manual labor, and obstacle courses developed agility and stamina. Basketball and soccer operated under modified rules essentially allowing fouls and full body checks. The cadets were made painfully aware that they were being prepared for combat.

Hamilton wanted each graduate to be a fighting officer that "will be a hard bitten gentleman, extremely dangerous to the enemy and with the greatest chance of survival under all conditions that any fighting man could have."

Bowling Green State University (BGSU)

The 120-acre airport named Bricker Field was dedicated in 1942. It expanded the size of BGSU, and was its economic salvation during WW II. Enrollment in 1940-1941 was 1,600. By the fall of 1943 it had fallen to 842 due to military enlistments and the draft. Initially in 1939, the Findlay Airport was used for the CPTP. Bricker Field was used from 1942 on. By 1943, the Navy utilized the facilities at Bowling Green to train both V-5 cadets and V-12 officer candidates. The V-12 Navy College Training Program was designed to supplement the force of commissioned officers in the United States Navy during WW II. Between 1 July, 1943 and 30 June, 1946, more than 125,000 men were enrolled in the V-12 program nation wide.

In the summer of 1943, our family moved to Bowling Green where Dad became the coordinator of the V-5 program at the university. Some time later, Mother began teaching V-12 students.

Upon settling into our home in Bowling Green, Dad filled the pulpit of the Christian Church in Rudolph, Ohio. Rudolph was a small town in a farm community and many of the parishioners were farmers. Frequently, our family was invited to their homes for dinner after church.

After a year or so of no flying, Dad finished his qualifications and earned his private pilots license on 12 July, 1945. Fifteen days later Dad took me to the airport, and we took off in a Piper Cub. During that 30 minute flight, we circled one of those farmer's homes. Mother promptly received a phone call asking if she knew where her husband was. Of course she pleaded ignorance, but suspected we had been buzzing their farm. It was quite exciting. I was privileged to be Dad's first passenger on my second flight!

Jubilation

*(Bee Gee News: Student publication of Bowling Green State University –
21 July, 1943 :)*

I n meeting mild-mannered Herbert C. Downing, new coordinator of the
Navy V-5 program at Bowling Green, one never suspects that he has
hunted elephants and been chased by them.

However, he has spent 19 years in Kenya, East Africa. Born there of
American missionary parentage, he was 15 years old before he left Africa.
Several years later he returned there to serve four years as principal of an
academy for children of missionaries and white settlers.

Now he hopes to return to that position after the war. His younger
brother has been "filling in" as principal since 1937.

An enthusiastic amateur photographer, Mr. Downing was chased by an
elephant he was trying to snap in action 8.000 feet above sea level in Africa
several years ago.

Here are some excerpts from the interview:

Q. *Why were you taking a picture of the elephant?*

A. *I wanted to click the shutter just as he charged at me.*

Q. *Did he?*

A. *He certainly did.*

Q. *How was the picture?*

A. *I was so scared when I saw the elephant coming that I picked up the
camera, without snapping the shot, and ran faster than I ever did before or
since.*

Q. *How far was the elephant behind you?*

A. *About 150 feet when I turned on my heels.*

Q. *Did the animal get any closer?*

A. *I don't know. I didn't look back.*

Q. *How did you get away from the elephant?*

A. *I headed for some cattle. One cow ran in front of the elephant and
distracted him.*

Charge Account

After telling about the elephant; modest Mr. Downing inquired, "You're not going to use all that in the news story, are you?"

"Only the interesting part," he was assured.

Mr. Downing has had many interesting experiences in Africa, but none more exciting than being chased by the elephant.

With offices in room 202 of the Administration Building, he coordinates ground and flight work of naval aviation cadets at Bowling Green.

Herbert Downing
CPT Coordinator

Jubilation

Dad's office in room 202 had a large gyroscope used to demonstrate the mechanism that stabilized directional indicators in airplanes. He also had black models for teaching aircraft recognition. It was all very interesting to a nine year old boy.

Third grade was stressful for two reasons: (1) there is always tension until the pecking order of a new circle of acquaintances is sorted out; (2) my teacher was an older woman who seemed to be pushing me harder than other students. Later, I found out she was considering my advancement to fourth grade. After a parent-teacher conference, Dad persuaded her to keep me where I was. The decreased pressure was a relief.

Buying war bonds was encouraged throughout WW II. Two memorable military attractions encouraged this investment; (1) a Japanese two-man submarine that was trucked into town, like those used in the attack on Pearl Harbor; (2) an Army demonstration of military weapons and tactics on the high school football field, complete with smoke and loud explosions.

One of the benefits of Dad's affiliation with the university was access to it's in- door swimming pool. We spent many happy hours, splashing in chlorinated water. It was also interesting to watch the Navy men outside practicing close order drill.

Dad introduced us to our first symphony orchestra concert in the university auditorium. My wife and I have since become regular attendees at the Pittsburgh Symphony in Heinz Hall. Dad had been the concert violinist in his college orchestra, and transmitted his love of music to his family.

Miss Day was my fourth grade teacher and principal of Ridge Street School. She was an older, attractive lady and very encouraging. I was 10 and got my first job delivering the *Toledo Blade* newspaper. I bought a rebuilt blue and white bicycle and some school clothes with my earnings. Miss Day and Mother were impressed. Mother offered to knit a sweater and asked what wool I would like. Having always been a bit of a romantic, I requested one made out of steel wool. She never let me forget this!

Grandmother Houk came to live with us so mother could teach V-12 math at the university. I started a club with suitable initiations. One requirement was to walk the garage roof ridge, down each hip, around the edge, and jump off. Grandma was appalled and reported me. I think I was the only qualified member. Such antics were subsequently proscribed, forbidden, and prohibited!

We lived in a large house at Prospect Street and Evers Avenue. Just north of our house, a comfortable bicycle ride away, was Bricker Field. The hangar there had Piper Cub Aircraft and Waco Biplanes. Nearby were some old WW I trucks with solid rubber tires. Just south of the field was a large greenhouse that employed German prisoners of war. It was interesting to communicate with these men. They were the fortunate Germans.

27 July, 1943, Hamburg, the second largest city in Germany, was fire bombed. The attack started a fire storm that developed winds of 150 MPH and temperatures in excess of 1,000 degrees C. that seared or suffocated anyone in range. The bombing was part of <u>Operation Gomorrah,</u> which killed over 50,000 people. Thirteen percent of all German deaths due to bombing during WW II occurred during this attack. 14 February, 1945, the city of Dresden was bombed killing as many as 135,000 people. German prisoners of war in America were definitely more fortunate than their countrymen in Germany.

Dad told a memorable story about a serviceman entertaining the troops as a stand-up comedian. Included in his repertoire was a parody on President Roosevelt's "fireside chats." As I understand it, he was locked up in the "brig" for his indiscretion. Servicemen were not permitted to demean their Commander in Chief during war times.

I had just begun my paper route on Thursday, 12 April, 1945, when a boy ran out of his house and announced in a loud voice that President Roosevelt was dead. People were stunned! A nation engaged in a two ocean war lost its Commander in Chief. Granted, the war appeared to be winding down, but it was not over yet, and a costly battle for Japan was anticipated. What sort of a leader would Vice President Harry Truman be? Fortunately, his decisiveness ended the war, saving many lives.

Dad was working on a master's degree at the university. For years I believed his subject had been the caste system of the American Negro. A recently acquired copy corrected that misconception. His thesis was entitled: "A Case Study of Ground and Flight Training for Navy V-5."

Excerpts from his thesis:

The beginning of World War II in Europe aroused interest in education circles although in some localities, policies of banning from school classroom discussions all reference to war were considered. Upon this scene of relative indifference, the Pearl Harbor catastrophe came as a rude awakening. The immediate need for thousands of trained men was suddenly thrust upon the nation. President Roosevelt announced goals of 60,000 planes for 1942, and 125,000 for 1943. Flight crews, pilots, navigators, bombardiers, ground crews, and maintenance specialists would be needed to man them.

Every possible educational facility in the nation was needed. Training statistics before the war indicated that the "washouts" of military aviation trainees ran as high as 50 per cent at some stations. The waste of time and money in attempting to train the 50 per cent who eventually failed, could not continue...

The efforts of the military forces to meet their deadlines with trained personnel were met. High schools and colleges revised and accelerated their programs to cooperate and to assist in various phases of the war training effort.

The writer, associated with these programs for approximately three years was interested in the frequency with which cadets who were discontinued from training because of flight inaptitude, turned out to have above average reports in their ground school subjects...

The purpose of this study was to discover whether or not there was any criterion in achievement in ground school training which could be used to determine probable achievement in flight training...

In 1942 enlistees who successfully passed screening tests were given the V-5 classification. Flight Preparatory School served as an additional screening measure and the trainees entering CAA-WTS flight training became an even more select group. Those who failed to succeed in any of the strict standards of achievement were discontinued.

The third dimension of Aerial Navigation and Aerology presented concepts so unrelated to ordinary experiences that learning them was much more difficult.

Never in the history of mankind had there been such an opportunity for young men to receive training in a field which entailed so much expense, and at the same time, carried with it such an appeal...[140]

Excerpts from Conclusions:

1. In conclusion, it must first of all be admitted very frankly that the writer failed to find substantiating evidence that would support his opinion

---

[140] Herbert C. Downing, "A Case Study of Ground and Flight Training for Navy V-5," Master of Arts Thesis, Bowling Green State University, Bowling Green, OH, 1945.

that there is any degree of negative correlation in the association of ground school course grades with flight test grades...

2. With respect to the analysis of cases that were discontinued from training for flight inaptitude it would appear that flight ineptitude is no index of weakness in ability to master academic subject matter...

3. If any index is to be obtained which will be valid in picking pilot material it will have to be developed along some other line than that of measurements of achievement in scholastic work...[141]

One of the remarkable aspects of the unprecedented achievements in training was the cooperation between two mutually exclusive hierarchies: one the organized militia, the other academia. Each had its own distinctive rank structure, uniforms, and self esteem. One marched to the strains of John Philip Sousa, the other to the music of Sir Edward Elgar. One selected and trained qualified personnel for specific duties in the shortest period of time. The other stressed the development of latent faculties and powers by formal systematic teaching with few time constraints.

The implication that pilots need not be bright to fly airplanes has been a contention for decades. In other words, smart guys stay on the ground.

It is interesting to note that Dad's thesis found no statistical evidence to prove this opinion. Conversely the arrogant attitude pilots had, that non aviators had learning disabilities, was also unproven.

At the start of the war no one knew precisely what made a good combat pilot. Psychological tests developed for the CPT were initial attempts to identify those necessary innate skills. Commander Thomas Hamilton's effective and productive V-5 training program produced pilots with the most combat victories. This program was designed to weed out unqualified candidates without loss of life and expensive equipment. It used a series of sequential challenges which had to be accomplished in order to continue in the program. Essentially, it was a means of finding those rare innate rather than latent skills.

It is impossible to predict response to actual combat. The closest anyone comes is observing reactions to extreme training pressure. The V-5 challenges appeared to be the best means of finding qualified pilots.

---

[141] Herbert C. Downing Thesis, Ibid.

Renaissance Thinking

It is difficult to determine whether Dad's liaison between the Navy and academia broadened him into a renaissance mind set, or whether his third culture heritage developed this trait.

B. Forest Clayton in *Suppressed History* states:

Carver A. Mead is the greatest living physicist not only in theory but also in practice. "Silicon Valley knows him as the most influential physicist of the microelectronics revolution." Our computer speed is dependant upon his inventions. He won the 1999 MIT prize of invention and innovation. He is the inventor of the Foveon Camera, and invented color processing chips.

Few are aware of this man because of his opposition to the politically correct "Copenhagen School" of quantum physics. His view that there is only one reality is in opposition to Bohr's complementary and Heisenberg's uncertainty principle. He thinks "Bohr perpetuated one of those monstrous intellectual frauds that every now and then slips through the asylum gates and confuses people for decades.

Carver Mead is a renaissance man in an age of specialists. Like Leonardo Da Vinci and Ben Franklin, he is an inventor, scientist, artist, and philosopher all in one. Mead understands that all knowledge is interrelated and warns that too much specialization and fragmentation of knowledge in academia leads to the destruction of our ability to innovate. Specialization within one box does not lead one to think outside that box. Mead says that to give up on trying to be a well-read renaissance man and specialize in only one small area is a defeatist attitude and a cop-out.[142]

Probably Dad's character was formed by his father's sage advice in following God's plan for his life. The result was a man who was a musician, teacher, administrator, draftsman, builder, cabinet maker, designer, linguist, photographer, and hunter. He definitely was a perfectionist with broad interests. It is interesting to contemplate how a man raised under the influence of an altruistic missionary father, trained

[142] B. Forrest Clayton, *Censored- Suppressed History*, (Cincinnati, OH, Armistead Publishing, 2004), 95-97.

and experienced as an academician, would be involved in training three dimensional warriors.

Victory

Jacob Frank, a German Jew resurrected an older Messianic movement for the express purpose of destroying Orthodox Judaism, encouraged Jews to sin, reasoning that if salvation could be gotten through purity, it could also be achieved through sin. His "doctrine of reversal" permitted the prohibited, stating that "the subversion of the Torah can be its true fulfillment," and "great is a sin committed for its own sake," The Frankists, excommunicated by the Orthodoxy in 1756, became known as Reformed Jews in the 1850's.

Shortly following the French Revolution, the Reformed Jews, headquartered in Berlin, were causing such havoc in society that Orthodox rabbis prophesied a Jewish holocaust 150 years before Hitler and Nazi Germany. Just as Samson broke his Nazarite vows with a whore in Gaza, the place of his punishment, so would the holocaust come from Berlin.

According to Ann Coulter's book *Godless,* both Stalin and Hitler used Charles Darwin's *"Origin of Species..."* as the basis for their eugenics. Racial hygiene resulted in the first genocide in recorded history, both in Nazi Germany and Stalinist gulags. Few are aware of the full title of Darwin's book: "On the Origin of the Species by Means of Natural Selection or the Preservation of Favored Races in the Struggle for Life." (1859) From Marx to Hitler, the men responsible for the greatest mass murders of the 20th century were avid Darwinists.[143]

The nation of Israel refused to hear the voice of God at Mount Sinai. (Exodus 20:19) Disobedience, punishment, repentance, and deliverance were the cyclical history during the time of the Judges. Since then, there have been at least four instances when God's disciplinary wrath fell on His people: when Assyria deported Israel, when Babylon exiled Judah, when Rome destroyed Jerusalem, and when Hitler created the holocaust.

Isaiah 10:5: "The Assyrian! He is the rod I wield in my anger, the staff in the hand of my wrath."

Isaiah 10:12: "When the Lord has finished all that He means to do against Mount Zion and Jerusalem He will punish the King of Assyria..."

---

[143] Ann Coulter, *Godless,* (New York, NY, Crown Forum, 2006), 268-299.

Jubilation

It should be emphasized that Israel has never been assimilated into the nations. It has never lost its identity throughout its history of persecution...

On the 22nd of April, 1945, two days after his 56th birthday, Hitler experienced a complete mental breakdown. On the afternoon of 30 April, 1945, with Russian soldiers only a block away, his new wife, Eva Braun, took poison and Hitler shot himself through the mouth. One week later Admiral Karl Doenitz surrendered all German forces unconditionally. 8 May, 1945, V-E Day; war ended in Europe! Mystic Germanic tribalism brought death to 30 million human beings. That bestiality was over!

V-E Day

The elation among American troops in Europe was short lived. Instead of returning to their homeland with a job well done, they were deployed to the Far East. Japan was a totally different adversary. Unlike German soldiers, who surrendered when defeated, Japanese soldiers under the Bushido code preferred death to dishonor. Invading Japan would be a very bloody business. The battles of Tarawa, Iwo Jima, and Okinawa were foretastes of such slaughter.

David Bergamini's book, *Japan's Imperial Conspiracy*, is a very thick history of WW II Japan. It presents evidence that Emperor Hirohito fit the definition of an Asiatic despot. This term is applied to certain classes of rulers such as Byzantine emperors whose governments were characterized by complexity, deviousness, and intrigue. Bergamini describes in detail these machinations and plots.

The introduction was written by Sir William Flood Webb, an Australian jurist, president of the 11 judges who tried Japanese war criminals. He writes:

It may seem rather quaint for an alliance of democratic governments to wage war upon an autocratic government at great expense in life and material, and then leave the chief autocrats of that government in a position of leadership. But Hirohito was not only an individual, he was a symbol. However culpable he may have been individually, he was also the spiritual embodiment of his entire nation. In 1945 a majority of Japanese believed, as a matter of religious faith, that Japan and the Emperor were indivisible and must live or die together.

Mr. Bergamini presents a strong case for believing that Hirohito schemed and plotted to lead Japan to the conquest of Asia. Under the circumstances my feeling that the Emperor was worth saving may seem cynical and Machiavellian. But so may the author's evident admiration for Hirohito. And so may the decision to grant the Emperor immunity which was concurred in by statesmen of such disparate views as Truman, Churchill, Attlee, and Stalin.

Hirohito asserted his supreme authority as an absolute monarch to terminate hostilities which had escalated into nuclear warfare. It is true that he did so only as Japan reeled in the shock of the atomic blasts at Hiroshima and Nagasaki; but he did it at some personal risk as is revealed by Mr. Bergamini's account of the curious happenings (an abortive army insurrection) on the night of August 14-15, 1945.[144]

Mr. Bergamini writes: "…on the morning of August 14, when his ministers had debated the Allied reply to Japan's surrender note for two days, he cut off their deliberations and ordered them to accept the U.S. terms without further ado."

There is an interesting footnote on page 951: On the day General MacArthur left Corregidor on a PT boat for Australia, Hirohito had a liaison conference to formulate an explicit policy for dealing with the large numbers of Jews who had been brought into the Empire with the acquisition of Singapore and Java. "With special exceptions," no Jews would be allowed to immigrate into the Empire in the future.

Genesis 12:3a "Those who bless you, I shall bless: those who curse you, I shall curse."

This ended six years of world war in which 70 million men had been mobilized and 17 million killed in battle. At least 18 million civilians died with the Soviet Union and Germany losing the most heavily. Japan's armed forces had 1.9 million dead while America lost 294,000. VJ-Day was truly a cause for jubilation!

14 August, 1945 was Herbert Downing's 40th birthday. Three days later on Friday, 17 August, he received his Master of Arts degree. Coincidentally, the first party of AIM missionaries departed New York for East Africa, exactly 50 years prior to that date.

This concluded Dad's affiliation with the university, and freed him to participate with the AIM's jubilee team, including Harold and Jane Amstutz and five field directors.

[144] David Bergamini, *Japan's Imperial Conspiracy,* (New York, NY, Pocket Books, 1972), Introduction XI.

Just before leaving on the Jubilee trip, Dad preached his last sermon in the church at Rudolph. We were invited to dinner afterwards. The host's sons had a Cushman motor scooter which they allowed me to ride. I opened that machine up on an open country road until the front wheel shimmied so violently I was thrown over the handle- bars. I landed on my face and skidded down the road. The damages: chipped front teeth, stitches in my lip, and 14 bandages on arms and legs. When we got home from the doctor's office, Mother saw the big strawberry on my buttocks and asked why I didn't have that patched. Modestly I replied: "I wasn't that sick." Actually, I was out of school for several days.

California

"If I lift up my eyes to the hills, where shall I find help? My help comes only from the Lord, maker of heaven and earth."
"The guardian of Israel never slumbers, never sleeps. The Lord will guard you against all harm; he will guard your life. The Lord will guard you as you come and go now and for evermore." (Psalm 121: 1, 2, 4, 7, & 8 –REB)

Psalm 121, often called the *traveler's psalm*, was quoted collectively by our family at the beginning of each trip.

1946 found six of us in a newly acquired 1940 Chrysler Royal, en route to California. Dad had returned from his Jubilee itinerary, and was sent to work with Harold Amstutz on a deputation film strip.

I had started fifth grade in the fall of 1945 in Bowling Green. Student teachers from the university taught different classes, and one began to read a book about Plains Indians, by Ralph Hubbard. We left before the book was finished, and I wondered about it for years. Finally, 53 years later, my computer whiz of a son-in-law got me a copy of the book. Case closed. I had just missed the end!

There were limited travel accommodations after the war, so lodging had to be arranged by 4:30 P.M. It was a daylight adventure except for the last day.

Sunday found us in Haskell, Texas. The Baptist Church had friendly folks who welcomed us warmly. That was the Sunday they were having their afternoon "sangin service" and we were invited. Gayle and I sang and Dad spoke. It was a highlight of an otherwise uneventful trip.

We arrived at the Amstutz' residence in Manhattan Beach after dark. It was a beach cottage on a steep sand pile with two bedrooms. The three Amstutz slept in one, six Downings in the other! Despite crowded accommodations we had a pleasant time together. Saturday mornings were especially memorable. We would buy fresh glazed donuts at the bakery and listen to kids' programs on the radio.

One evening Mother and Dad went to a church in Hermosa Beach, the next town south. The four Downing kids were alone in the house. The two youngest were asleep when Gayle detected a strong odor of natural gas.

Eddie Lee and Ruth Ann were awakened, and clothed with warm wraps. Windows were opened and heads extended. The church was called, and our parents returned. The source of the aroma: the El Segundo oil field just north of us. An inversion layer with a north wind was the explanation. We never were allowed to forget.

Gayle and I attended Center Street School less than a mile away. One day, while walking home, two P-80 jet fighters flew low over the train tracks, the first jets I had seen. Little did I realize then, I would fly the two-seated version of that airplane as my first jet.

The Amstutz' owned another apartment a few blocks away, which we occupied when it became vacant. We kids slept in the garage, and got into the apartment through a small space made by removing a wooden wallboard. Everyone's sense of humor made this whole adventure a lot of fun!

The China Inland Mission (CIM) had a nice home we used when not otherwise occupied. Alternate accommodations were on Mission Road in Glendale, next to Forest Lawn Cemetery. It was much more convenient to be near the darkroom situated beneath the beach cottage, but this was not always possible.

The CIM Spanish style home had a red tile roof, set on a hill overlooking a municipal recreation park. There was a large patio in front of the house, with open rooms to one side. Around the sides of the house were ice plants with thick rubbery leaves and daisy-like flowers. School, a little closer, provided a much more interesting walk. Near our residence was an abandoned artillery bunker, with mine-like passageways and signs pointing to the powder magazines.

This was the site of temporary Battery Eubanks, constructed in 1942 and decommissioned in 1945. It consisted of two, eight inch MK V 1 M3A2 guns on an M1 railway mount. The railroad, ran just below our house, was later converted into a running trail.

The west coast was vulnerable to Japanese attacks. On 23 February, 1942, the Japanese submarine I-17 attacked the Elwood oil production facility at Goleta near Santa Barbara California. The submarine skipper radioed Tokyo that he had left Santa Barbara in flames. Actually, there were no casualties and the estimated damage was approximately $500. On the night of 24-25 February, 1942 several thousand anti-aircraft rounds were fired over Santa Monica. The target was officially determined to be a lost weather balloon, though it could have been an early Japanese fire balloon. These damages were minimal, but the attack at Pearl Harbor had created widespread fear. Shore defenses were necessary, and Manhattan Beach's artillery site was an intriguing relic of the second global war.

My parents became acquainted with an aeronautical engineer at the Hermosa Community Baptist Church. He and his wife were invited to the CIM home one evening. As an eleven year old boy, I will never forget his "wheels." He drove a 1937 black Buick Special with two-side mount spares, 'a la Al Capone'. The road below our house had no shoulder for parking so Mr. White parked down by the recreational field. I noticed that he left his parking lights on and reminded him. He replied that this was intentional. He wanted to avoid a mishap.

Charles White decided to acquire a 16mm movie camera for Dad. Such items were scarce close to war's end, but he managed to locate a Bell & Howell Filmo 70 DA in Los Angeles. This was the same type used by combat photographers during the war. There were no zoom lenses available, so three lenses of varying focal length were mounted on a revolving turret. It served him well for the next six years. This was the beginning of a close family friendship with the Whites that has lasted more than 60 years.

BIOLA

The Bible Institute of Los Angeles (BIOLA) came into existence under the leadership of Dr. R.A.Torrey in 1911. It was intended as a counterpart to Moody Bible Institute on the west coast. A large building was built in the center of Los Angeles with an auditorium seating more than 4,000. This was once the tallest building in Los Angeles and in 1935 two lighted "JESUS SAVES" signs were erected, making it a prominent part of the city's skyline. It had the largest auditorium on the west coast for several decades, and housed the Church of the Open Door (COD) from 1915.

Harold and Jane Amstutz graduated from BIOLA, and were supported by the COD. The AIM had a booth at the large mission conference at COD in1946. This lasted for several days and we kids were pressed into service to "man" the booth. My younger brother Ed was quite knowledgeable and articulate in response to questions. When asked if he had been born in Africa, he replied with deep disgust: "I was born a week after our family returned." He thought being conceived in the land of Zinj was not equal to being born there.

Clifton's Family Restaurant Near COD

Another BIOLA graduate was Irwin A. Moon. Dr. Moon was interested in science as a teenager, and was offered a scholarship to study physics at Yale. Instead he enrolled at Moody Bible Institute, transferring to BIOLA the next year. He completed his studies at Los Angeles Baptist Seminary, and became a Montecito Park Union Church pastor. In 1931 he designed scientific demonstrations to unfold a world of chemical, physical, and biological wonders to his congregation. His theme: "the marvels of science provide the visible evidence of a divine plan of creation."

Other churches began asking for his illustrated lectures, and in 1937 he resigned his pastorate to give full attention to *Sermons from Science*. He presented the programs in large civic auditoriums and on university campuses. Dr. Will H. Houghton, Moody Bible Institute president, observed one of his demonstrations and invited him to join the MBI extension department. In 1938, Dr. Moon began traveling full time as an MBI evangelist, and in 1939 he presented eight demonstrations a day, seven days a week, for nine months at the San Francisco World's Fair.

When war broke out in 1941, Dr. Moon began working among servicemen on military bases. This continued for five years, traveling from base to base under the auspices of the United Service Organizations (USO). During those days he saw the impact military training films had on soldiers. He broadened his ministry by filming platform demonstrations and other wonders of science too impractical for stage presentation.

In 1945 the Moody Institute of Science was founded. Dr. Moon and Dr. F. Alton Everest set up shop in a former lodge hall in Santa Monica. Dr. Everest, an electrical engineer with degrees from Oregon State and Stanford University, had been on the engineering faculty of Oregon State. Jane Amstutz's father, a builder before retirement, was engaged to remodel the building. This was the connection the Downings and Amstutz' had with Irwin Moon. Once a week or so, we were invited to the Institute for a get-together and courses on receiving Morse code, etc. Lapsed time photography used in the science films produced amazing effects. I still remember his film about time and speed. At least nine films are still relevant today.

In 1946, George Speake took over the live platform demonstrations, freeing Moon to concentrate on the film ministry. Speake and Charlie White were close friends from the same church in San Diego. Speake, a former fighter pilot and engineer, challenged audiences for 29 years with their need for Christ. He was especially effective with military audiences, and his Sermons from Science contributed significantly to spiritual awareness on military bases.

One of my last memories of the Moody Institute of Science was a trip on a 35 foot fishing boat out of San Pedro Harbor. Dr. Everest was steering back to port when we were passed by a convoy of Navy destroyers. Awesome!

Airports

World War II priorities caused southern California to become the hub of America's aircraft industry. What had been known as Mines Field before the war was officially changed to Los Angeles main airport in 1941. During the war, North American Aviation, Inc. had a factory at the airfield and would fly finished aircraft off. Charles White was involved in wing design of the B-25 bomber. According to him, North American produced 25 P-51's, 15 B-25's, and 15 AT-6's <u>per day</u>, at half the cost of other contractors. After VJ Day this production came to a screeching halt, and many employees were laid off.

Initially the airport was east of Sepulveda Boulevard. As runways were lengthened toward the ocean, Sepulveda was re-routed west. It was about this time we saw a military air show. An Army P-38 was doing acrobatics over the field. The diameter of the loop was almost a mile. The Navy had a multi-plane flyover, with the formation spelling NAVY. It is interesting to note that the aircraft were new Ryan Fireballs. This was the Navy's first jet fighter, with a propeller in the nose and a jet in the tail. The concern was the slow engine response for carrier landings with only a jet engine. The war ended before they were used in combat, but about 62 were delivered by wars end. Astronaut John Glenn told Dad he had been in that formation. He was a test pilot of Fireballs at Patuxent River at the time.

An amusing story is told about this aircraft. A P-38 pulled up along side a Fireball, and looked the newcomer over closely. P-38 pilots were proud of their single engine performance and feathered one prop. Imagine his surprise when the Fireball feathered his prop, but kept pace with the Army show-off!

On 8 July, 1946 the inaugural flight of helicopter airmail service in Los Angeles was flown. Six Sikorsky helicopters of the 62-11 detachment of the 62nd Army Air Force Base Unit at March Field were used. It was fascinating to watch these machines fly up the coast, low over the water, approaching the helicopter pad. The pilot hovered about two feet off the ground as the ground crewman exchanged mail bags. Then the aircraft nose dropped slightly and continued north to the next stop. Helicopters were very rare in 1946!

Memories

Manhattan Beach is a good memory. With two miles of beachfront and 40 acres of beach, it had sand dunes 50 to 70 feet high. In fact, there was so much sand that the Kuhn Bros. Construction Company supplied Waikiki Beach in Hawaii with Manhattan Beach sand for 10 years starting in 1920. There was the continuing sound of surf with waves as high as 12 feet in the winter. A beautiful round-ended pier extended 920 feet into the water, where fishermen were successful.

Things have changed since 1946. Manhattan Beach is a very affluent beach town, within commuting distance of Los Angeles. One of the most expensive coastal towns in America, the single family dwelling regularly exceeds the already high Los Angeles County median price by over 100%. Homes with an ocean view often exceed $3.25 million.

Yes, it is a good memory, and like all good memories you can never go back!

Mission

The filmstrip project developed slowly. The first order of business had been to build a darkroom in the sandbank under the cottage. The mission had requested photos from other missionaries for inclusion, but as I recall, the response was less than desired. Some photographs were tinted by hand and color pictures were included. Developing color slides required critical temperature control with crude equipment.

A presentation was planned, and a script written. The signal to change to the next slide was an African drum beat on the bottom of a metal waste basket! Gospel Recordings Inc. was used to cut the master record and make the records. Finally, the project was finished. It was time to pack up and head east.

Support

O ur return to Africa depended upon securing financial support for a five year term. The Radio Chapel in Mason City, Iowa had expressed interest in supporting part of our family, and invited us to a mission conference. With the film strip project complete, we bought a cargo trailer, loaded luggage, speakers, projectors and a screen, and headed towards Iowa. The Los Angeles basin is surrounded by mountains, so our first challenge was climbing the San Bernardino Mountains, towards El Cajon Pass.

As our loaded car labored up the steep grade, the water temperature began to rise. Upon reaching the pass, we realized our radiator had failed, and were happy to coast down the hill into the desert town of Victorville. The mechanic confirmed our worst fears, and said he knew of no radiators outside of Los Angeles. So Mother and four kids were put up in a motel, and Dad boarded the train for Los Angeles, 90 miles west. The proper radiator was located and bought just before closing time on Friday afternoon. Dad returned on the next train carrying the new unit with him.

Saturday morning saw the repaired vehicle ready to travel. The problem was the clock. We had started with just enough time to reach Mason City, so the delay entailed driving straight through. Mother didn't drive and we kids were too young, so Dad did all the driving. We stopped for breakfast after driving all night, got our thermos filled, and continued on our way. Apparently, we were sold some pretty vile coffee for when Dad became drowsy, Mother offered him a hot drink. Once was enough! After that the answer was always "no." The memory was enough to stimulate him. The distance from Victorville to Mason City was nearly 1,500 miles. He must have stopped for naps. We were all sleeping like a litter of puppies, in the back seat and never knew!

The conference was at the Baptist campground in Clear Lake State Park, and yes, we did arrive safely and in time. The church did support some of us for 5 1/2 years at Kijabe, and strong friendships have continued.

Radio Chapel was different from any church we had ever seen. The main auditorium was 96 feet long by 64 feet wide. There were no outside windows, light coming from recessed electric lights. The choir area was accented with stars and clouds seemingly floating across the ceiling. A "stereopticon" device flashed words on a screen, making hymnbooks unnecessary. This must have been one of the very first of now common "words on the wall" sanctuaries. There were 700 theater seats upholstered with blue material and a pulpit that rose up from the floor. And finally, the acoustics were superb.

This modernistic art deco inspired chapel was the result of a southern evangelist, who held six weeks of tent meetings in 1937. By July 1938, when the chapel was formally dedicated, he had raised pledges of $70.000 – almost $1 million in 2010 buying power. With the divorce from his first wife (mother of his two sons) finalized, this supposed bachelor married evangelist Kathryn Kuhlman in October of 1938. From this point on, both ministries came to a halt. His never recovered, and hers was on hold for eight years before the Lord gave her a remarkable ministry in Pittsburgh. They had lived together for six years, separated for two, and were finally divorced after eight years. They had left Mason City in May 1939 with the chapel $50,000 in debt.

It has been said that the four steps to reconciliation with our Holy God are (1) conviction, (2) contrition, (3) confession, and (4) cleansing. There is a fifth step which is part of the process and that is (5) consequences. Jamie Buckingham's authorized biography of Kathryn Kuhlman, *Daughter of Destiny,* provides insight into her life and ministry.

Kathryn's father was a wealthy indulgent man who openly opposed the severe punishment from her heavy handed mother. This could have conditioned her to believe the Lord would let her get away with open disobedience. After six years of married life, she realized she had been seeking God's blessing without living under God's precepts. She was finally brought to choosing between the man she loved and the God who had gifted her with a ministry and a mission. "I said it out loud, 'Dear Jesus, I surrender all. I give it all to you. Take my body. Take my heart. All I am is yours. I place it in your wonderful hands.'"[145] This was the turning point in her life. From then on, she was used by God to demonstrate the power of God's Spirit. Sick bodies were healed, lives were changed, and "goats" (seed of the serpent) were turned into "sheep" (seed of the woman).[146]

The consequences of Kathryn's sin followed her the rest of her life. For example: in 1970, newspaper columnist Lester Kinsolving (an ordained Episcopal priest) "exposed" that 32 years before, Kathryn Kuhlman had married, then divorced Burroughs A. Waltrip. The writer failed to realize,

---

[145] Jamie Buckingham, *Daughter of Destiny,* (Gainesville, FL, Bridge-Logos Publishers, 1999), 88.
[146] Genesis 3:15.

however, that while Kathryn had tried to keep that unhappy chapter of her life buried in the past, she was not ashamed of it.

"Once a mistake has been confessed, then it is under the blood of Jesus," she told Buckingham after the column came out. "But sadly, Mr. Kinsolving knows nothing of the forgiveness of Jesus."[147]

It is interesting to note David's status with God after his reconciliation. (Psalm 32 and 51) He was a man after God's own heart. (Acts 13:22)

Rev. Carl Sentman, a Baptist minister from Sheffield, Iowa, arranged for purchase of the chapel. The Midwest Evangelistic Association was formed and became the corporation that pulled the building out of financial ruin in 1940. A church was created which took the great commission of Acts 1:8 very seriously. This included financial support for some of the Downings. Rev. Sentman was a solid Bible teacher, a shrewd businessman, and an effective leader. The chapel was used for some 13 years, until the church needed more classroom space. In 1953 a new building was constructed at 804 North Tyler Avenue, with Dad's help, and became the Grace Baptist Church. The radio chapel became the home of KGLO Radio Studios in 1953. Later it was remodeled with studios for television broadcasting.

Chicago

Our next stop was Chicago. We visited Miss Bessie Stevenson, mother's midwife when I was born. Miss Stevenson lived with her father, a retired minister who was a widower. Mr. Stevenson was a fascinating man to an 11 year old boy. In his basement was a machine shop with a small metal lathe. His hobby was building model steam engines. Two things fascinated me: miniatures and machines that ran on their own power. These were more than two dimensional pictures in the catalogs I had pored over for years. These were three dimensional realities. They were unforgettable!

The Field Museum in Chicago has been a major attraction for our family for years. Dad especially wanted us to see the man-eating lions that were the scourge of the East African Railway in 1898. We had all seen lions in the Brookfield Zoo and were expecting spectacular specimens. You can image our disappointment when we saw two maneless, mangy lions that

---

[147] Ibid., 69.

were not very big. They grew in stature after reading Lt. Col. Patterson's book *The Man-Eaters of Tsavo*!

This book is one of the greatest man-eating sagas of all time. It gives a firsthand account of the Tsavo lions that brought the building of the East African Railroad to a halt. Their infamy reached as far as The House of Lords in England, and has been the basis for three films: *Bwana Devil (1958)*, *Killers of Kilimanjaro (1959)*, and *The Ghost and the Darkness (1996)*.

Theodore Roosevelt said: "I think that the incident of the Uganda man eating lion... is the most remarkable account of which we have any record."[148] It certainly was an absorbing read for me.

After speaking at the Field Museum in 1924, Col. Patterson agreed to sell the Tsavo lion skins and skulls for the then sizeable sum of $5,000. These lions spent the first 26 years of their afterlife as rugs. Much material was lost from converting the rugs back into mounts and more was lost repairing gunshot holes. Consequently, the mounted lions were much smaller than when they were shot. Actually the first one measured nine feet eight inches from nose to tail, and stood three feet nine inches high. It took eight men to carry him back to camp. The second lion measured nine feet six inches from nose to tail and stood almost four feet high.

There has been much speculation about what caused these two huge beasts to become man-eaters. One possibility was the abundance of dead bodies. Almost 2/3 of the Indian workers recruited for the project never lived to return home. Disease was the major killer.

Another source could have been the dead and dying slaves that littered the slave trail running through this area. A shortage of wild game due to the *rinderpest* plague of the 1890's could have reduced their prey. Both lions had dental problems, which could have limited their hunting ability. And their rejection from lion prides, where the females did most of the killing, could have driven them to their habits.

My copy of *The Man-eaters of Tsavo* has an editor's note by Peter Hathaway Capstick. In discussing the author he relates:

One of the best Patterson tales I know of took place during the Gallipoli Campaign, when the British were trying bloodily to take the Dardanelles Straits from the Turks. It fell to Patterson to organize the first Jewish battle

---

[148] Lt.Col. J.H.Patterson, *The Man-Eaters of Tsavo*, (New York, NY, St. Martin's Press, 1986), dust jacket.

units ever to take the field since the fall of Jerusalem in 70 A.D. These members of the Gallipoli Campaign, encompassed in battalions 38, 39, and 40, included such future leaders as Ben-Gurion, Jacob Epstein, Vladimir Jabotinsky, and Major James de Rothschild. Originally known as the Zion Mule Corps, they were now the Jewish Legion, 2,000 men strong. Unfortunately, as rough as they were, they arrived too late for the hairier fighting in Egypt but they did take part in Allenby's assault on Meggido (more commonly known as Armageddon).

After the action, Patterson's Brigade (he was now a full colonel) was to be inspected by a brigadier infamous for his hatred of Jews. Stalking the ranks, he finally found what he was looking for, some small infraction such as an unpolished button or an untied shoelace. Drawing the offending private up by the lapels, the brigadier screamed in his face: "You dirty little Jew!"

Instantly, Patterson-though he must have known his career was on the line-screeched the order to "fix bayonets." There was the screech and slither of oiled steel as the battalion obeyed to a man. Click! Patterson gave the order to about-face, and his men immediately formed the classic hollow square, leaving the brigadier mighty lonesome in a hostile forest of steel. Possibilities grew to probabilities, as the troops in an ugly mood; Patterson demanded a personal apology from the brigadier to the private. Swallowing his fear, the brigadier apologized, about-faced, and stalked from the square of steel.

Of course, it did not end there. Colonels simply do not "sic" their battalions on brigadiers and Patterson was in real trouble. Had he not had the reputation he enjoyed, he might well have been shot. At any rate, his case was partially upheld, although the Jewish Legion was disbanded, when the brigadier was immediately sent to the Middle East.[149]

This vignette is extremely interesting and significant in the overall scheme of global warring. The Jewish individuals mentioned have definitely been major players on the stage of life.

Back to Bowling Green

The Bowling Green Baptist Church had agreed to support the last members of our family. So it was time to return to Bowling Green, and

---

[149] Ibid., Editor's Notes.

begin the arduous task of packing our belongings for transoceanic shipping to Africa. This included knocking apart wooden living room furniture, and packing the pieces tightly in wooden boxes. Due to the pilferage of ocean freight, boxes had to be big, heavy, and banded with steel. Each box had to be weighed and marked. We only had bathroom scales, so the biggest box had to be weighed with the scales placed under each end and the two weights added together.

After our freight goods were picked up by moving vans, we finished cleaning the house and moved out. Grandma Houk, a widow since 1944, had lived with us for a couple of years. Uncle Glenn, Mother's bachelor brother, had assumed her teaching responsibilities at Rudolph while we were in California. He and Grandma then returned to New Concord.

We began moving towards New York for a December departure. We stopped in New Concord, OH, Slippery Rock, PA, Carnegie, PA, and Washington DC, saying good-bye to various family members. It was hard for me to believe that I was finally going home. For nine years it was always-someday. It had finally become a definite date, and I was more than ready to go!

AFRICA
From New York to Kijabe – 1946/1947

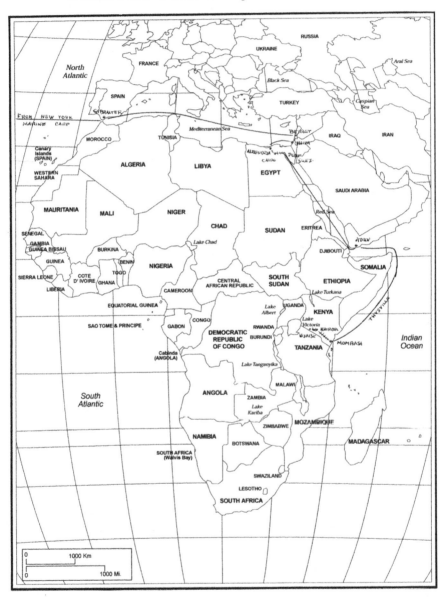

USNS Marine Carp (T-AP-199)

Atlantic Crossing Friday, 20 December, 1946 – New York, New York

USNS Marine Carp

It was a cold, wintry, overcast afternoon when our family boarded the *USNS Marine Carp* to return to our home in Africa. My first impression, stepping on the steel deck, was a lack of perceptible motion. I had thought that any ship afloat would have some wave motion, but the *Marine Carp* was as stable as the pier.

Our family was divided into two groups. Mother and my two sisters were ushered to their quarters with other women. Some were in junior officers' quarters with double-decker bunks. Mother and Ruth Ann had lower bunks. Due to last minute rearrangements, Gayle slept in a hospital bed in "sick bay." Dad, my brother Ed, and I were directed to a troop space with other men, near the bow. Four steel frames with canvas supports for thin mattresses were suspended by chains from the overhead. With two feet of separation between bunks, entry and exit required a horizontal rolling motion. The ship was recently built as a high speed troop transport for WW II to accommodate 3,451 passengers. Fortunately, with half that number aboard, only the two middle bunks were for sleeping, the top and bottom bunks for our luggage.

Access fore and aft was via two passageways on either side of the ship. Accommodations were strictly utilitarian, so these two corridors were no exception. Bundles of labeled, color-coded wires were visible in the overhead and water-tight hatches were encountered every so often. These were oval openings with the bottom some 14 inches above the deck. An exaggerated high step was required to pass, so they were called "knee-knockers." One of the ship's nurses was a serious, short, bowlegged lady who used a curious cross-legged maneuver to negotiate these obstacles, amusing enough to leave an indelible impression.

The evening meal was eaten from stainless steel trays on steel tables anchored to the deck. Steel lips around the table tops provided tray security during inclement weather. I went out after dark and was engrossed in the activities of getting underway. Tugboats pulled us from the pier and headed us toward the ocean.

As the hawsers were released, I was surprised by the farewell from the tug boat: "see you next year!" We hadn't even had Christmas, but it did make sense. They wouldn't see that ship again until 1947. There wasn't much to see once we were underway, so I "turned in."

Sometime during the night, the loud speaker ordered "all hands on deck." The ship that had been "stable as the pier" was now a bucking bronco. Shortly after leaving New York harbor, we encountered a vicious Atlantic winter storm. Being near the bow, we could feel it rise slowly, roll, shudder, and crash down into the next trough. Since we weren't crew members, we stayed in our bunks, but heard that a wave had dislodged one of the life-boats from its davits and broke an oil main.

Farther forward from our quarters was the "head" or communal toilet. As you might have guessed, there were no doors, so the sounds of sick passengers carried through our space. I don't recall being seasick, but trips to the toilet were challenging! Ruth Ann remembers a moaning Greek woman who thought she was going to die. Another passenger was kept awake by feet stamping on the deck above. Apparently displaced persons were quartered under canvas on the fantail and danced through the night to keep warm.

The next morning many passengers were still abed with Mal de mere (sea sickness), even though the ocean had calmed down a bit. One of the stewards came around with a tray of sliced fresh fruit. He was serving bravely until he too had to leave in haste! Finally, I was able to dress and go on deck. The fresh salt sea air was bracing and helped settle stomachs. Seeing a horizon also helped stabilize spatial disorientation.

The *Marine Carp* was laid down under Maritime Commission contract by Kaiser Co., Inc., in Vancouver, Washington, 6 December, 1944. She was 523 feet long, with a beam of 72 feet, a draft of 26 feet, and displaced 10,210 tons. She was less than two years old when we embarked. She had one steam turbine made by Joshua Hendy, driving one propeller with 13,750 horse power. Some considered welded ships not as reliable as riveted ships, but the records don't agree. She was a product of the most amazing ship building effort ever. The battle of The Atlantic was won by the mass of ships produced during the war.

Once past the storm, our voyage was quite pleasant. The food was typical Navy fare, with plenty of nutritious food and little preparation effort. Grapefruits were simply cut in half. It took a while to learn to extract the segments with a dessert spoon, but once learned, it worked quite well.

Salt sea air is very corrosive, and steel ships are vulnerable. Consequently, the condition of protective paint required constant attention. It was necessary to continuously chip away cracked areas and repaint, so the odor of paint blended with aromas from the galley below and sea air.

It was soothing to watch the bow wave roll away in an enlarging "V" as we plowed our way toward Africa. After a while, though, satiated with the new sights and smells, we looked for other interests.

Gayle's memories of this voyage are interesting:

We shared the troop ship, Marine Carp, with a huge entourage of missionaries representing several mission boards destined for several different African countries. Missionary families come in all shapes and sizes, holding as many various philosophies of life, educational, and spiritual. It didn't take me long to count my blessings. Heading the list was the kind of parents God had given me.

It seemed no other family upheld the genuine spirit of adventure comparable to ours. Other kids had to bring along schoolbooks! Another curious thing that seemed ridiculous at the time was that some parents brought along Christmas presents so their children wouldn't miss the all-important holiday. We had already learned that it wasn't gaily-wrapped packages that made any holiday – it was the warm security of a family together having fun.

To backtrack a bit... perhaps this major fact of togetherness was more sensitive for me than for the other kids in the family because the day before we were to sail, it was discovered there had been no reservations made for me to return to Africa with the family. Apparently the Home Office had assumed that a teenager as old as I was would remain in the United States to continue my education in boarding school. How relieved I was to be considered important enough to have so many last-minute adjustments made in order that I be included – even if my bunk was located in the former sick bay with my aunt and cousins, instead of with Mom and Ruth Ann. Since on the troop ship, we would have all been split up anyway, with the men in one place, women in another, I wasn't in such an unusual predicament.

A close call such as that sometimes helps us not to take things too much for granted.

Without making a big production over isolated incidents, our Mom and Dad seemed to put across the message that the spirit of adventure and the excitement of learning were one and the same. While books were always good and necessary tools, I cannot remember ever being forced to study. Learning included curiosity, awareness of our environment, an exchange of ideas and observations with others (with much emphasis upon being a good listener), and finally, the whole experience of living was to be greeted with excitement and enthusiasm.

We felt we led a rather charmed life at sea when we played "Flinch" while other kids had "to keep up with their lessons." We soon got the message; while one was living out one adventure, he didn't have to cram another into the same space. The kids who had to do school work in such a strange environment were learning two lessons their parents were unintentionally teaching: (1) all learning must come secondhand from textbooks, and (2) learning can basically be boring.

Several nationalities made up the passenger list: Greeks, French, an Egyptian antique dealer, and other Eastern Mediterranean people. We did engage a French man to teach French, but I absorbed very little.

Christmas and New Years were celebrated aboard ship, and the traditional dances were interesting. One of the holds was open for our recreation, and we spent hours there.

A chart was kept of our progress. The ships maximum speed was 18 knots, which would have been 432 knots in a 24 hour period. However, I don't believe we made more than 400 knots a day. Usually it was 350.

The distance from New York to Gibraltar was over 3,000 miles, so it was more than a week before we made landfall. Our first stop was Gibraltar, but only British citizens were allowed ashore. Seeing the huge rock and the coast of Africa was a pleasant change from endless empty horizons.

Gibraltar

We passed through the Strait of Gibraltar enroute to the British Crown colony. Gibraltar is situated on a small peninsula three miles long and three-quarters of a mile wide extending south from Spain. The Rock of Gibraltar, which was first sighted from the ocean, is 1,270 feet high and commands the western entrance to the Mediterranean Sea. It was named for the Arab conqueror who led the Moorish invasion of Spain in AD711. His name was Tariq ibn Ziyad. So it became Djebel Tariq (Mountain of Tariq), Anglicized to Gibraltar. It was annexed by Spain after the Arabs were driven off in 1492.

The Rock is limestone, honeycombed with concealed defensive positions and tunnels. It was captured from the Spanish in 1704 by an Anglo-Dutch force, ceded to Britain by the Treaty of Utrecht, became a British Crown Colony in 1830, and was an important port in WW I and II.

A runway was constructed across the neck of the peninsula. The road from Spain to the Colony crosses this runway. The population of the town, northwest of the Rock, is about 28,000. It is also known for Barbary monkeys, which occupy many of the Rock's caves. These are the only free-living monkeys in Europe.

Less than eight miles across the strait was the continent of Africa. But with Africa five times the size of the United States, we still had 5,000 miles to go.

Even though it was winter in the northern hemisphere, the temperature in the Mediterranean was much warmer than the cold Atlantic. Our quarters on the starboard side of the ship exposed us to the sun and caused hot sleeping conditions. We were below the main deck with no port holes, and there was one oscillating fan on the bulk-head.

The Egyptian antique dealer was closest to the fan. His bedtime routine included pajamas, a bath robe, and a scarf wrapped around his head, plus covers. This practice was the same even when the quarters were uncomfortably hot. This was amusing enough, but became personal when he insisted on turning off the fan. We tried to persuade him to leave the fan on, but it became a continuous ON/OFF game. He insisted that 'electric air' was bad for you!

Our next port of call was Beirut, 2,000 miles to the east. Not only was the weather more comfortable, the scenery was greatly improved. Other ships were seen more often, and the horizon was broken by islands and glimpses of Europe and Africa.

"The Turkish Empire is ruled by one man; all the others are his servants." – Machiavelli

The Ottoman Naval Battle was another war between a dictatorship and a coalition!

Just southwest of Greece, we passed the site of a most significant naval battle. On 7 October, 1571, in the Gulf of Lepanto in the Ionian Sea, the heavily manned fleets of the Ottoman Empire and the Holy Christendom clashed in one of the greatest turning battles of history. [150]

By the 16th century, the Ottomans through war and treaty had skillfully exploited the weaknesses of their enemies. They had gobbled up piecemeal, the Byzantine Empire and many other sovereign entities in the Mediterranean. When compelled to fight, their armies usually won, due to their superior tactics and discipline. The Ottoman Turks had arguably the best soldiers in the world.

The Janissaries formed one of the most formidable military corps of all time. A devsirme (collection) was decreed, and officials would visit Christian villages and select boys between 8 and 18. This was nothing less than enslavement of Christian subjects. These boys were sent to Constantinople, where they were inspected, circumcised, and selected for specific schools. They became slaves of the Porte, chief office of the Ottoman Empire. The new troops were educated for several years in Spartan conditions. They exercised with every type of infantry weapon and tactic. The years of hardship and training, enhanced by legally imposed celibacy and their religious commitment, contributed to the Janissaries' esprit de corps. Tough, disciplined, highly professional, and often brutal, the Janissaries were among the finest troops ever. They chose their own weapon, were superb marksmen, and were unbeatable man-to-man.

In contrast, the West was perfecting the musket and pike (a long heavy spear) system, allowing masses of men to be trained for battle in a relatively

---

[150] Nicclo' Capponi, *Victory of the West*, (Cambridge, MA, Macmillan, 2006), front jacket.

short time. Even more important, these men were easy to replace. Most Ottoman soldiers were not. The Ottoman Grand Vizier believed that troops should be few but excellent. In the end the Western system of warfare would emerge victorious.

For the Ottomans, war-fed expansionism was almost inevitable. The ideology of conquest developed by them was not fighting for gold or treasure, but for victory, glory, renown, and the increase of the empire. The Ottomans' ultimate objective was the conquest of the whole West. The Reformation had started in central Europe and the Ottomans had followed its progress with interest. However, the reality of the Turkish menace concerned both Catholics and Protestants.

The man most responsible for the outcome of this battle was 67 year old Pope Pius V. He formed a league of quarrelsome Christian Princes into a coalition to fight the Muslims. But, more importantly, this deeply religious pope had been fasting and praying for divine aid against the Islamic forces.

The key to victory was the use of six galleasses, unusually heavy vessels laden with six times the ordnance of a conventional galley. In a significant tactical shift, the Venetians relied on the overwhelming force of their artillery before resorting to hand to hand combat. The effect of the galleasses fire on the advancing Ottomans was devastating, as they lost over 200 warships. It is unclear how many men the Ottoman lost but their casualties were at least 35,000, including most of their senior officers.[151] Ottoman invincibility was broken forever.

In Rome there was much rejoicing. Pope Pius V had miraculously known about the outcome of the battle before receiving the official report. Some believed the galleasses were the key to victory, but ultimately many attributed this to God.

Beirut

As we approached the wharf in Beirut, I was conversing with one of the ship's crew. He told me of a previous visit of the *Marine Carp* to Lebanon, where there had been a serious brawl between the ship's crew and the Arabs. According to the sailor, it included hurling Coke bottles over the rail. I was advised to physically "deck" one of these people before engaging

---

[151] Ibid., 289.

in a conversation. I have since wondered how much was "sea story" and how much was truth.

I did however, run across an interesting editorial of Immanual Velikousky in the 8 June, 1948, edition of the *New York Post*:

A month ago the S.S. Marine Carp sailed from New York bound for Beirut, Lebanon, Haifa, Palestine and Alexandria, Egypt. This ship is operated by the American Export Line for the State Dept.; in other words, it is a government ship. On May 20, in Beirut the Lebanese military boarded the ship, ordered the passengers going to Palestine to leave the ship, and removed 69 passengers by force, 41 of whom were American citizens. The luggage of the passengers was split open with hatchets. The protest of the Captain was of no avail. The passengers were put in prison camps.

The American government meekly protested, received an arrogant reply, protested still more meekly, and was told to mind its own business. The Lebanese government refused to allow the 41 Americans to proceed to the country of their destination. The American government expended not a single word on behalf of the 28 passengers, not American citizens who had entrusted themselves to a ship flying the American flag and had paid the State Department for their transportation.

Did the American government at least cancel future calls of the S.S. Marine Carp at Beirut? No, indeed it canceled future calls at Haifa, Israel. But it will visit Beirut regularly.

Apparently there was "bad blood" between the Lebanese Arabs and the United States, especially after Israel became a nation in May 1948.

Several peddlers were selling their wares and some of the missionaries bought leather bags. My acquisition was a <u>Khanjar</u> knife, a curved dagger no fully dressed Arab would be without. It turned out to be only a souvenir made of painted brass.

Gayle was challenged by someone to use her newly acquired French. She leaned over the rail and asked if anyone spoke French. A handsome young policeman stepped forward, and answered in the affirmative. The only two words that came to mind were <u>les joujou et les animal</u>, i.e. toys and animals. We all got a chuckle out of this.

Haifa

Our next port of call was 68 miles south of Beirut, my first opportunity to go ashore and the only time I was in Palestine. Haifa a seaport in northwest Israel, has been the outlet for the Iraq Petroleum Company's pipeline from Kirkuk since before 1934.

In January 1947, Haifa was a dirty town, with rolls of concertina wire and sandbagged guard posts. It was patrolled by British soldiers, who were tasked with peace-keeping between Arabs and Jews.

The British Balfour Declaration of 1917 promised to seek a national home for the Jewish people in Palestine. Britain's promise to the Jews fulfilled a romantic notion among ruling circles that it would be "an act of historic and poetic justice to help the ill-used people of the Bible return to their ancient homeland." [152]

The Arabs believed that they would achieve the independent state their leaders desired, because they had responded to Britain's call to arms against their Turkish rulers. The provisions of the Balfour Declaration were incorporated into the terms of Britain's League of Nations mandate to rule postwar Palestine. It was not long before the "non-Jewish communities" concluded that these two objectives were irreconcilable. British attitudes with regard to the two Palestinian communities were, to say the least, ambivalent. [153] The result was a shooting war!

A 33 year old British Army Captain was posted to Haifa in September 1936. Capt. Orde Wingate was born in India to Col. George Wingate and his wife Ethel. He was raised in the fear of God and "the sincere milk of the Word." [154] Wingate was an Arabist by training, having mastered the language and absorbed much of the culture.

Britain's doors had been opened wide to Jewish refugees from Russian Pogroms of the late 19th century.[155] but British attitudes towards Jews were frequently frosty... The Jews were as "technological adept and culturally advanced as the British, or more so (which was quite intolerable) and, unlike the Arabs, altogether impossible to patronize." In short, "too clever by half," as the British officer class would say.[156] "The Jews at best were the

---

[152] John Bierman & Colin Smith, *Fire in the Night,* (Kent, Great Britain, Random House, 1999), 60.
[153] Ibid., 61.
[154] Ibid., 152.
[155] Pogrom- an organized persecution and massacre, often officially prompted, of a minority group, especially of Jews.
[156] John Bierman & Colin Smith, Ibid., 62-63.

recipients of grudging respect instead of the condescending affection accorded to the Arabs." Besides, the Arabs could be guided, and were sitting on vast reserves of oil, which the Jews were not[157].

Because of his third culture dissimilarities, Capt. Wingate never conformed to accepted customs and never followed the crowd. Shortly after arriving, Orde told a colleague: "Everyone's against the Jews, so I'm for them." As one who felt he had been persecuted in his youth for being "different," he had a natural affinity for the Jews. [158]

Without authorization from his superiors, and at the risk of severe condemnation if found out, Wingate began to take out small patrols at night. He wanted to break the Haganah volunteers of their defensive mentality, getting them to go "beyond the fence" to carry the fight to the enemy. This was highly controversial: it contradicted the Zionist's own policy of restraint, while flouting British determination to prevent the Jews from taking offensive action against the Arabs.

The patrols that Wingate led out of Hanita in the spring of 1938 were the forerunners of the officially sanctioned special night squads. General Sir Archibald Wavell, who became the general officer commanding Palestine in September 1937, soon recognized Wingate as a promising young officer. Wavell was first intrigued, and then convinced by Wingate's plan to defeat the Arab revolt by overcoming the rebel gangs with counter gangs.

According to Wingate's assessment: "There is only one way to deal with the situation: persuade the gangs that in their predatory raids there is every chance of them running into a government gang which is determined to destroy them, not by an exchange of shots in the distance but by bodily assault with bayonet and bomb."[159]

The most important lesson Wingate taught the Jewish settlers, as much psychological as tactical, was to form the basis of strategic doctrine in the future Israeli army. He taught them, not just to defend their settlements, but to confront the enemy in his lair.

The Israelis admired Wingate for his physical endurance, his capacity for hard organizational work, his casual bravery, and his uncanny ability to navigate in the dark. They also recognized a quality the Jews usually admire but the British often suspect: cleverness. His inventive mind seemed to devise an answer to every problem.

---

[157] Ibid., p. 62.
[158] Ibid.
[159] Ibid., 86-87.

Wingate's Special Night Squads, (SNS) played a crucial role in damaging the morale of the Palestinian Arab guerilla bands operating in the Galilee region of Israel during the last year of the Arab Revolt- a role far out of proportion to their numbers. But they were too few to crush the revolt. That was carried out by much larger and more widespread British forces and operations commanded by a tough new senior commander, Major General Bernard Law Montgomery. In 1939, British senior commanders, recognizing Wingate's passionate identification with the Jewish community, transferred him out of Palestine. There were standing orders that he never is allowed to serve there again.

But thankfully for Israel, it was too late. Wingate had already provided invaluable military education to a crucial number of the first defining generation of senior officers in what would become the Israel Defense Forces. His young soldiers and students included men who would become the greatest generals: Moshe Dayan, Yigael Allon, and Yitshak Rabin. [160]

Our last trip on the *Marine Carp* was 276 miles to Alexandria. Finally, at the age of 11, I was back in Africa, the land of my birth!

[160] Martin Sieff, *The Politically Incorrect Guide to the Middle East,* (Washington, DC, Regnery Publishing, Inc., 2008), 43-44.

Egypt

Egypt – the land that fed the Patriarchs when famine struck Canaan. Egypt - where Joseph as Egyptian Minister of State preserved a host of survivors during a seven year famine. Egypt - where a whole nation of Israelites was enslaved. Egypt – which sheltered young Jesus from Herod's wrath. Egypt – where Anti-Semitism was born in A.D.38, conducted by Hellenistic Egyptians.[161] Egypt – where doctrinal war[162] was started within the church. Egypt – the destination of the Herbert Downing family in January 1947.

Alexandria

Alexandria was founded in 332 B.C. by Alexander the Great. It was intended to be the capital of his new Egyptian dominion and a naval base that would control the Mediterranean. Without waiting for its development, he moved on to greater conquests. After his death, nine years later, Egypt came under Ptolomy I, one of his four generals. Under the Ptolomaic Dynasty, Alexandria became the center of government, power, and splendor in Egypt.

One of the seven wonders of the ancient world was the 440 foot light house on Pharos Island, inside the harbor at Alexandria. Built around 280 B.C., it was still standing in the 12th century. It was erected in three stages; the first was square, the second octagonal, and the third round. Each stage had walls that sloped in. A fire was built on top at night to guide ships to harbor.

Ptolomy I is usually given credit for founding the most famous library in the ancient world. The library at Alexandria possibly contained more than 500,000 works, and was expanded under Ptolomy II.[163]

School of Alexandria, the first Christian institution of higher learning, was founded in the mid-2nd century A.D.. Under its earliest known

---

[161] George Gilder, *The Israel Test*, (United States of America, Richard Vigilante Books, 2009), 31-32.
[162] Dr. Gary Hedrick, *Replacement Theology-It's Origins, Teachings, and Errors or"Supersessionism,"* http://www.shema.com/web2printer4.php. (accessed January 28, 2011).
[163] *Britannica Online Encyclopedia,* "School of Alexandria," http://www.britannica.com/EBchecked/topic/14441/School of Alexandria. (accessed December 12, 2011).

leaders, Pantaerus, Clement, and Origin, it espoused friendly relations between the Greek culture and the Christian faith.

Origin, one of the most influential theologians of the early Church, blended principles of Neo-Platonism, elements of mysticism, stoicism, some concepts of Judaism, and Christianity into theology. He created a system to interpret the Bible using allegory and spiritualization. "He was the originator of the concept that God had rejected the Jews and replaced them with the Church."[164]

Syncretism is a combination, reconciliation, or coalescence of varying, often mutually opposed beliefs. Principles, or practices, especially those of various religions are blended into a new conglomerate whole. Typically, syncretistic combinations are marked by internal inconsistencies.[165]

In the fourth and fifth centuries, a rival school arose in Antioch to challenge the Alexandrian insistence on allegorical interpretation of the Bible. Scholars of this school dismissed allegorical meanings as so much nonsense, and insisted on reading God's Word for the historical and grammatical meaning. What the text said was what it meant. It did not convey abstract philosophical concepts.[166]

It is interesting to note that Antioch was one of the first churches, sensitive enough to the Holy Spirit to send out Paul and Barnabas as missionaries.

Another syncretic theologian was Augustine from Algeria. He incorporated Plato's doctrines and New-Platonism into Christian Theology. "As a consequence, salvation was redefined. The Bible said, 'We believe in Jesus.' The Greek mindset said, 'We believe that...' Changing one word caused people to believe heaven was reserved for the doctrinally correct, which splintered the church into different groups supporting different theologies of salvation. This sparked more than 1,700 years of doctrinal war within the church, draining it of power."[167] Thus another form of global warring developed on the Zinjian continent.

The *Marine Carp* tied up at a long quay inside the Alexandria harbor for disembarkation. The train to Cairo was at the foot of the gang plank and droves of porters helped load the train. This operation had to be carefully supervised, for there were instances when articles were headed in the

---

[164] Michael L Galiga, *Win Every Battle*, (Minneapolis, MN, Bronze Bow Publishing, 2009), 128.
[165] Webster's College Dictionary, 4th ed., 142.
[166] The Bible: "The School of Antioch,"
http://www. gbgm-umc.org/umw/bible/Antioch.stm. (accessed December 12, 2011).
[167] Michael L.Galiga,, Ibid., 128.

wrong direction. We were informed that the porters considered our goods theirs, if they could get away with them. After everything was stowed, they would ask: "nice? nice?", and with hand outstretched demand <u>backshish</u> (a tip). A railroad, built in 1885, connected Alexandria with Cairo. So with all aboard, we left the northwest corner of the Nile Delta and traveled the 130 miles to the Egyptian capital. The Jolly Travel Agency had made arrangements for us at a pleasant hotel in downtown Cairo.

Cairo

The following morning, we enjoyed breakfast in a sunny dining room at the top of the hotel. The conversation included a discussion of the near proximity of the battle of El Alamein less than five years before. One of the unforgettable peculiarities was the butter served. Nicely formed little round balls, on iced trays, looked like the perfect spread for British hard toast. My first bite was a disappointment. <u>Salted</u> butter really does make a difference!

January mornings in Cairo can be chilly, so everyone put on warm clothes. I wore my two toned sport coat and a ball cap. A bus took us 10 miles toward the pyramids across the Nile River. We were met at the bus stop by a herd of camels and donkeys, with their Egyptian attendants. Mother and my younger sister, Ruth Ann, rode one camel. My older sister Gayle, my brother Ed, and I each rode a camel, but Dad rode a donkey. He was busy with his movie camera. (Mounting and dismounting a donkey was much easier than a camel!) There must have been at least 20 in our party, so we made quite a caravan. The first order of business was a photo opportunity in front of the Sphinx, which has a lion's body and a human head. Believed to be the largest stone sculpture in the round ever made by man, it is 238 feet long and 66 feet high. It spent much of its existence under sand. No one knows when it was made.

The Great Pyramid

From the Sphinx we continued up the hill toward the Great Pyramid. From a distance this largest building in the world looks like an organized rock pile. This was not true when it was built. The rough core blocks were completely hidden by a white marble-like limestone casing. These polished stones were so precisely fitted together that a razor blade could not enter the joints.

In 1201, a great earthquake destroyed Cairo and cracked some of the casing stones. The white limestone was then stripped from the exterior to rebuild the city leaving the denuded core exposed to the elements. As we drew closer, the stones became huge blocks laid in even courses, one upon another. These courses form a series of gigantic steps, sloping back from the base on all four sides, to a level platform at the top. One has to be there to comprehend the enormity of this almost solid mass of masonry.

We climbed a path to an entry in the north side of the pyramid. A descending passage led us about 100 feet to an ascending passage. The lower end of this new passage had been blocked by granite plugs which were tunneled around. About 125 feet up this passage we entered the Grand Gallery, a magnificent chamber that extended upward at the same angle more than 150 feet.

We finally came to a level area that led through two low passages and an ante-chamber to the King's Chamber, a spacious room 34 feet long, 17 feet wide and 19 feet high. It was empty except for an open stone coffer with a broken corner. Ventilator shafts on the north and south walls extend to the outer surfaces. The temperature inside the pyramid is a constant 68'F;[168] the average humidity level is 83 %.[169] Lighting was rather poor, so our guide lit a magnesium strip. This provided a bright light to see the beauty of the workmanship. I have since visited this site, and read many books about the marvels of this last remaining wonder of the ancient world.

In 1798, the French defeated the Ottoman Turks at the "Battle of the Pyramids" and Napoleon became master of Egypt.[170] Until August 1798, Bonaparte believed he would be back in France by winter, in time to invade England. But when Admiral Nelson destroyed the French fleet in the Mediterranean he found himself stranded there for 14 months during the French Revolution.[171] In addition to his 50,000 man army, he had 167 scientists and scholars. Their purpose was to survey the possibility of digging a canal from the Red Sea to the Mediterranean from Suez. These academicians produced the most impressive study ever of Egyptian monuments.

---

[168] E. Raymond Capt, *The Great Pyramid Decoded*, (United States of America, Artisan Sales, 1978), 62.

[169] Ibid., 69.

[170] Ibid., 7.

[171] Dr. Joseph Davidovits, *The Pyramids an Enigma Solved*, (New York, NY, Dorset Press, 1990), 26.

These eminent scholars surveyed the ground of the Great Pyramid, and determined the value of the location in trigonometrical relations. They found two of the corner sockets, peculiar to no other pyramid, and also the relationship of the Pyramid's structure and dimensions to astronomical science. Their observations, and mostly accurate measurements, with cuts, engravings, and descriptions of the Great Pyramid, were subsequently published in large and elegant form,[172] entitled <u>The Description of Egypt</u>. This sparked the birth of the science of Egyptology and, in particular, the study of the Great Pyramid.

An old and honest treatise on the subject is *The Great Pyramid: A Miracle in Stone* by Joseph A Seiss. The synopsis on the back cover gives a concise description of the significance of this largest of all archaeological monuments.

The Great Pyramid at Gizeh, the oldest and largest of the pyramids, is a time capsule from another age. Built before Moses even began writing the Old Testament, it was already ancient when the Greeks of Alexander's time called it one of the seven wonders of the world.

Like the time capsules our civilization has left upon the moon, the pyramid contains scientific information and clues to the knowledge that produced it. The information is contained in the measurements and proportions of the stone structure with its interior rooms and corridors, and in its orientation on the Earth and to the stars.

The silent stones at Gizeh contain many mysteries, as do the stones of Stonehenge, Chartres Cathedral, and the Mayan temples of the Yucatan. Many of their secrets have been uncovered; more are waiting.

<u>*The Great Pyramid; A Miracle in Stone*</u> *is a classic which has influenced all subsequent work on the subject. Published almost 100 years ago and long out of print, it is intriguing reading for those who seek clues to the wisdom of pre-historical times.*

When it came to descriptions of how the pyramids were made, most books are filled with speculation and, in my opinion, "pooled ignorance." The hardest metal available at construction time was copper, and there is no evidence of wheeled vehicles or pulleys. So how were they able to pile huge blocks weighing 15 or 20 tons over 400 feet high?

---

[172] Joseph A, Seiss, D.D., *The Great Pyramid: a Miracle in Stone*, (Blauvelt, NY, Rudolf Steiner Publications, -originally published in Philadelphia, 1877, 1976), 30.

In 1988, Joseph Davidovits and Margie Morris wrote <u>The Pyramids: An Enigma Solved</u>. Dr. Davidovits is a research chemist and founder of the new brand of chemistry named *geopolymerization*. By studying the ecology, ancient products, and documents of the Egyptians, he was able to trace the basic alchemical inventions that led to the development of pyramid stone. His conclusions: the pyramid blocks are not natural stone. They are actually exceptionally high-quality limestone concrete-synthetic stone – cast directly in place. They are imitations of natural limestone, made in the age-old religious tradition of alchemical stone making. His arguments are cogent and can only be confirmed or disputed by qualified scientists. Egyptologists as specialized historians are not qualified to approve or reject.[173]

The most obvious question is, why was it built?

There is an interesting passage in Isaiah 19:19-20. "In that day there will be an altar to the Lord in the midst of the land of Egypt and a pillar to the Lord at its border. And it shall be for a sign and for a witness to the Lord of Hosts in the land of Egypt…"[174]

The Great Pyramid stands at the geometric center of the Nile Delta quadrant, at its southern extremity. This satisfies its position in the "midst of Egypt." The official name is the Great Pyramid of Gizeh, which means in English, the *Great Pyramid of the Border*. The "border" refers to the point where cultivated land touched the desert.

The Great Pyramid may well be a witness in stone to the power, knowledge, pervasiveness and timelessness of a loving Heavenly Father. The Bible is a complete witness. The pyramid could be the second witness required by the Mosaic Law. [175]

King Tut

The next day we visited the Cairo Museum. The richest archeological find of the 20th century was there. It was later exhibited around the world as the "Treasures of Tutankhamen Exhibition."

In 1973, nearly a million people stood in enormously long lines stretching for several blocks in Great Russell Street, London. They waited four hours to enter the gates of the British Museum and see "Treasures of Tutankhamen Exhibition."

---

[173] Joseph A. Seiss, *The Great Pyramid: A Miracle in Stone*, Ibid., 68.
[174] Amplified Bible, Isaiah 19:19-20.
[175] Ibid., Deuteronomy 19:15.

Egypt

My older sister, Gayle's recollection of our Cairo visit in 1947 is interesting:

Twenty years later, on a flight to Chicago, a couple sitting in seats near mine made a point of advising me to be sure and see the "King Tut" exposition touring the United States, located at that time in Chicago. The realization of my own good fortune at being exposed to so many exciting adventures throughout my life swept over me afresh. I had visited the museum containing all the artifacts of King Tut's tomb... in the museum in Cairo! It was only one of many exciting exposures during that month en route to Africa: December 1946 to January 1947.

After days of observing ancient and post-war Egypt, we boarded another train for a trip to Port Suez on the Red Sea. Most Europeans traveled in first class coaches on British Empire railways. These were divided into cubicles that accommodated six day passengers and four at night. A narrow passageway ran the length of the car on one side.

The car just ahead was a second class coach with seats on either side of a center aisle. Passengers in typical Arab clothing filled this car. Two men with wooden fluteophone-like-instruments played lively dance music. Young boys danced in the aisle. My brother Ed's memory was the Arab vendor selling fresh eggs and salt. The idea was to poke holes in the eggs and suck the contents out for lunch. I asked if he had tried one, and he said not only "no" but "never!"

Suez

Port Tawfiq is the southern end of the Suez Canal. The link between the Mediterranean and Red Seas was surveyed by Napoleon's engineers in 1798, but due to a 16 foot miscalculation of relative water levels, the project was shelved for more than 50 years. Finally, a junior French consul, Ferdinand de Lesseps, planned and supervised its construction beginning in 1859. With a crew of 24 million Egyptian workers and at a cost of more than 125,000 lives, the canal was opened on 17 November, 1869. At more than 100 miles, it is the longest canal in the world without locks, which can accommodate all but the largest ships. It has been closed for periods of time during the 20th century due to the Arab/Israeli conflicts.[176]

The northern end of the canal is Port Said, named for the Egyptian viceroy Said Pasha, who died in 1863 before its completion. He was succeeded by his nephew Ismail Pasha, and the town near the port was named Ismailia.

Under Ismail Pasha, Egypt almost went bankrupt. His successor, Ishmael Pasha, in similar straits, decided to sell his canal shares for four million pounds sterling. When British P.M. Benjamin Disraeli heard that the French were negotiating for the shares, he sent his private secretary, Montagu Corry, to Lord Rothschild to float a loan. According to Corry, when told that the Prime Minister wanted four million pounds tomorrow, Rothschild ate a grape, and asked, "What is your security?"

"The British government," said Corry.

"You shall have it." said Rothschild.[177]

Today the canal is a major route for transport of crude oil from the Persian Gulf. Transit time is 15 hours, and 80 ships can transit per day.[178]

---

[176]Columbia Encyclopedia, "Suez Canal," http://www.answers.clm/topic/suez-canal. (accessed December 30, 2010).
[177]Margaret Penfold and Ami Isseroff, "The Suez Canal – A History,"
http://www.mideastweb.org/suez-canal-history. htm. (accessed December 30, 2010).
[178] Ibid.

SS Thysville

Wigon boarded the *SS Thysville* at Suez, bound for Mombasa. *SS Thysville* was built by J. Cockerill, at Hoboken, Belgium in 1922. She was a coal burning cargo liner of 8,300 gross registered tons. She was almost 2,000 GRT smaller than the *SS Marine Carp* but not nearly as utilitarian. She had wooden decks instead of steel, and most of the passenger cabins were on the main deck. The cabins had double-decker bunks and round portholes for light and ventilation. With fewer passenger accommodations and more spacious sleeping quarters, the *Thysville* was quite comfortable.

Gayle and Glenn on the SS Thysville

The dining facilities on a lower deck could not accommodate all the passengers at one sitting. As customary in European countries, children were fed earlier than adults. White table cloths and china dishes were a marked improvement over stainless steel trays and welded steel tables and benches! My only negative memory was creamed spinach, which was served far too frequently! (Once would have been too much!)

Thysville's Flock

Islam

Halfway down the Red Sea, we passed west of the Arabian port of Jiddah. Fifty miles inland is the old trading center of Mecca. Camel caravans moved cargo from the Far East over trails that paralleled the Red Sea through Mecca and Medina, farther north.

"The Arabs originally acknowledged the existence of one supreme God. This God, the creator of the universe, is called Allah Taala, the most high God. Their religion soon lost its earliest monotheism and degenerated into gross idolatry, fetishism, animal worship, and star worship."[179] The most celebrated and central object of Arab worship however was the <u>Blackstone</u> of Mecca, set in the corner of a square building called the Kaaba.[180]

---

[179] J.L. Menezes, *The Life and Religion of Mohammed,* (Harrison, NY, Roman Catholic Books, 1912), 5.
[180] Ibid., 6.

In A.D. 570 Mohammed was born to Abdullah, the chief of the Koreish tribe. At that time the Koreish, being the lineal descendants of Ishmael, had the privileges of the guardianship of the Kaaba. A short time before Mohammed's birth, his father died on a trading expedition to Medina.[181]

After his birth, Mohammed was given to a Bedouin wet nurse. Koreishite mothers believed that desert air was much more healthful than in Mecca. The foster family cared for him for five years. Approaching his fifth year, Mohammed appeared to be having epileptic fits. Bedouins attributed these to the influence of evil spirits and returned the boy to his mother.[182]

"Mohammed's mother, Amina, was of an excitable nature and often claimed that she was visited by spirits, or jinns. She also at times claimed to have visions and religious experiences. She was involved in what we call today the "occult arts," and this basic orientation is thought by some scholars to have been inherited by her son."[183]

At the age of six, Mohammed was taken to Medina by his mother. On the return journey Amina died, leaving her son an orphan. He was subsequently raised by his grandfather and an uncle, a man of great mercantile abilities. This "pet" boy learned what it was to be lordly and to exercise power and never forgot it.[184]

At 12 years old, Mohammed's uncle took him on a trading expedition with a caravan to Syria. Under his uncle's tutelage he grew into manhood. He was handsome and had an acute and piercing wit, was thoroughly versed in all the arts of insinuation, and was a man of excellent judgment. He had a good memory, was accomplished in business, and acquired wide experience and knowledge of men by continual observation in his travels.

At 25 years old, Mohammed entered the service of Khadija, a noble and wealthy widow of Mecca. He was in charge of her trading caravan to Bostra, 60 miles east of the Jordan. He doubled her venture capital, pleasing her greatly, and she became fascinated with his personal qualities. Mohammed accepted her offer of marriage though she was 15 years his senior. This raised him to equality with the richest in Mecca.[185]

---

[181] Ibid., 11-12.

[182] Ibid.

[183] Robert Morey, *Islamic Invasion*, (Eugene, OR, Harvest House Publishers, 1992), 71.

[184] J. L. Menezes, Ibid., 11-12.

[185] Ibid., 29.

During 25 years of married life, Khadija yielded her whole faith to Mohammed. She was the first to acknowledge him to be indeed the Apostle of God. Personally, Khadija was favorably disposed toward Hanifism, a monotheistic belief in Allah which rejected polytheism. It is probable that she exercised her commanding influence over her husband in formulating his belief.

After Khadija's death in A.D. 620, Mohammed, without her ascendancy, firmness, and wisdom, began to give way to lust and polygamy. Afterwards this became a conspicuous and characteristic feature of his life.[186]

In 623, Mohammed engaged in his first act of highway robbery. A Koreish caravan, traveling unarmed and without escort, under cover of the sacred month, was attacked. One man was killed; two were taken prisoner, and the whole booty taken to Mohammed at Medina.[187]

January 624, at a place called Badr, Mohammed with his band of fighting men engaged 1,000 Arabs from Mecca. Discipline and steadfastness of purpose under Mohammed's leadership defeated the larger force from Mecca. Thus was started that career of bloodshed and conquest, which has distinguished Islam more than any other religion.[188] For nearly 1,400 years, this global warfare has continued.

"Babylonianism," as understood from the Bible is the attempt to gain earthly honor by means of religious authority. "Babylonianism" has pervaded Hindu temples, Buddhist shrines, and Mohammedan mosques, and even influenced some Christian churches. This attempt to gain earthly power and prestige by means of religious authority is the element that characterizes a false religion. Nimrod began his rebellion in Babylon. God countered this by confusing human languages. "Babylonianism" will ultimately be destroyed in a single day by plagues.[189]

Ethiopia

About 1100 miles southeast of Suez are the Dahlak Archipelago Islands. West of these islands is the port of Massawa, in Eritrea, a country just north of Ethiopia. The opening of the Suez Canal in 1869 brought

---

[186] Ibid., 13.
[187] Ibid., 49.
[188] Ibid., 51-52.
[189] Revelations 18:8.

naval traffic into the Red Sea from Europe. Since Italy got into the colonial acquisition game later than other European nations, Ethiopia was one of the last independent African nations left. Massawa became the foothold for Italy's conquest of this last piece of her East African Colony.

The Italians invaded in 1935, shredding the Ethiopian's ragtag army with high explosives and mustard gas.[190] Emperor Haile Selassie was forced to flee. On 9 May, 1936, four days after Italian troops entered Addis Ababa, Mussolini proclaimed Italy's King Victor Emmanuel III emperor of the newly created Italian East Africa.[191]

General Wavell, Britain's farsighted commander in the Middle East, had been considering means of liberating Ethiopia from Italy's grasp. This was before the outbreak of war with Germany, 10 months before Mussolini had brought Italy into the war.

Though Emperor Haile Selassie's Ethiopian armies had been defeated in 1936, an insurgency using guerilla warfare was active in the highlands. These Patriots were doing their best to create physical and psychological danger for the occupation forces. The harsh Italian rule had intensified Ethiopian animosities. Instead of the planned reductions in Italian troop strength, augmentation was required for internal security.

General Wavell recalled Dan Sandford, a retired British army officer, and subsequently British vice consul in Addis Ababa. After retirement, Col. Sandford had returned to Ethiopia as a farmer. He became a friend and confidant of Haile Selassie, and was ultimately made a provincial governor in an African nation never colonized by the white man.[192]

When Orde Wingate was in Palestine between 1936 and 1939, he convinced Gen. Wavell of his plan to defeat the Arab revolt by taking back the night from rebel gangs with Special Night Squads.[193] Though Wavell's patience was often stretched by Wingate's abrasive zealotry, he never let him down. "...It was Wavell who would provide the opportunity for this maverick officer the loosest of all the Royal artillery's cannons to show his true mettle."[194]

---

[190] John Bierman & Colin Smith, *Fire in the Night*, (Chatham, Kent, Great Britain, Macmillan Publishers Ltd.,1999), 150-151.
[191] Vincent P. O'Hara & Enrico Cernuschi, "Red Sea Naval War," *WWII History Periodical*, March 2010, 55-59 & 73.
[192] John Bierman & Colin Smith, *Fire in the Night*, Ibid., 147-152.
[193] Ibid., 86-87.
[194] Ibid., 87.

Consequently, Major Orde Wingate was selected as a participant in Wavell's three pronged offense against Italian East Africa. He was appointed to organize and lead the training of the guerillas and act as a link between Emperor Selassie and Wavell's command. Wingate was responsible for increasing the effectiveness of the patriots in harassing Italian forces in the Ethiopian northwest. Wavell saw in Wingate "a much more virile and solidly balanced Lawrence (of Arabia) but with much the same sort of power of inspiring others."[195] Remembering him from Palestine, Wavell agreed to his appointment, but stipulated that Wingate was to be barred from entering Palestine.[196]

In 20 November, 1940, Wingate flew on a daring flight into Ethiopia to meet with Col. Sanford in the Gojjam Highlands. Both agreed that the Emperor should enter Ethiopia as a symbol of Ethiopian's lost independence and national unity. Disappointed by the lack of aid given to the Ethiopian revolt, and promoted to the temporary rank of lieutenant colonel, Wingate set about changing things immediately.

He expanded the mission from a holding action to one of liberation, from harassing to defeating the Italians in the northwest. He wrote: "First we must convince the Ethiopian that contrary to his previous experience, these white men with whom he has to treat will give him a fair deal. He must see us first not fighting by his side but in front of him... Example instead of precept is what we want."

The plan he formulated involved a trained core forming the mobile striking element. Wingate designated this his *Gideon Force*. They would penetrate into Gojjam, disrupt enemy communications, and seize areas in preparation for a drive on the capital, Addis Ababa. In support would be small detachments composed of British cadre, leading small groups of several hundred Patriots. They were to spread guerilla attacks around and in front of the main force, creating room for it, and acting as a rallying center for other Patriots. They would be without vehicles, to avoid being tied to the few roads; instead they would use pack animals. In union with local insurgents, their tools would be audacity, bluff, concentrated force, mobility, and surprise.

---

[195] Christopher Sykes, *Orde Wingate*, (New York, NY, New York World Publishing Co, 1959), 230.
[196] "Wingate in Ethiiopia,"
http://www.ordewingate.net/ethiopiaA.html, (accessed January 7, 2011).

Wingate was funded with credit for one million pounds in Maria Theresa silver coins from MI (R).[197] With these funds, 18,000 camels were bought, along with several thousand camel drivers plus weapons and supplies. A makeshift camp outside Khartoum was the assembly point. Two Battalions were organized as the main striking force, and Patriot training centers established. All told, the force numbered almost 1,700 men.

Gen. Wavell's three pronged offense included three divisions under Lt. Gen. Cunningham attacking in the south from Kenya, and two divisions from the north under Lt. Gen. Platt. On 19 January, 1941, Gen. Platt engaged the Italians in Eritrea. Five days later Lt. Gen. Cunningham attacked into Italian Somalia.

The regular forces and Wingate's force were assisting each other. Their advances and presence divided the enemy. Italian forces were prevented from massing and counterattacking. Nation-wide, actions by the Patriots and Gideon Force were tying down over 56 of the available Italian battalions, leaving only the equivalent of 71 battalions to face the main British force of five divisions.

Gen. Platt, military commander in Sudan, like most professional soldiers, did not think highly of unconventional warfare. He definitely did not like Wingate and his methods, but was stymied in dealing with this belligerent, determined lieutenant colonel. because of the high backing for his scheme. Capt. Tony Simonds, who led the back-up column to Wingate's Gideon Force, had this to say:

They didn't like Wingate, they didn't approve of his mission, and even more, they didn't believe it had any chance of success... Indifference, incompetence, apathy... it says volumes for Wingate's energy, determination, and relentless drive that he surmounted the obstacles and barriers put in his way.[198]

On 6 April, 1941 the leading armored cars of Lt. Gen. Cunningham's South Africans drove into Addis Ababa. Cunningham asked Wingate to

---

[197] Winston Churchill & Colin Gubbins, "Home Guard Auxiliary Units,"
http://www.aboutsociology.com/sociology/MI5, (accessed January 13, 2011).
(Military Intelligence responsible for the creation of the secret Home Guard Auxiliary Units during WW II. Initiated by Winston Churchill who appointed Major Colin Gubbins (an expert on guerrilla warfare) to found them.)
[198] John Bierman & Colin Smith, *Fire in the Night*, Ibid., 163.

delay Haile Selassie's arrival in Addis because of the possibility of Ethiopian citizens taking revenge on the Italian community.

Mounted on a gray charger, Wingate led the emperor into Addis Ababa on 5 May, 1941, exactly six years after the Italians' triumphal entry. The horse had originally been procured with the emperor in mind, but Haile Selassie was saddle weary and preferred to ride in a black Ford convertible.[199] The Gideon Force was disbanded, and Wingate came under Cunningham. Wingate knew that Haile Selassie, for domestic reasons, yearned for a famous victory where the victors were mostly Patriots and not British Imperial troops. The emperor placed 2,000 of his best Patriots under Wingate's command. Their task was to catch Italian Col. Saverio Maraventano.

Col. Maraventano commanded an unwieldy column of about 12,000 people, of whom some 8,000 were truly combatants, with 4,000 "pack animals." His goal was to get into rough country where he could hold out through the rainy season.

By his use of audacity, bluff, concentrated forces, mobility, surprise, and above all, tenacity, Wingate was able to force Maraventano to surrender.

After six months of hard and often dangerous campaigning, it was the kind of moment most professional soldiers only dream about. Years later Sir Wilfred Thesiger, one of the Gideon Force, told the authors of *Fire in the Night* Bierman and Smith: "Wingate deserved a knighthood for what he did in Ethiopia."

But Wingate was not even allowed to take his place at the victory banquet that the emperor hosted, or return to Addis Ababa to say his good-byes to the emperor. Officers around Cunningham's headquarters, men who would never march all night on an empty stomach to fight at dawn... who thought hardship was not changing their shirt for three days, expressed their distaste for "a bearded, scruffy, unimpressive figure."[200]

Karl von Clausewitz (1780-1831) has been acknowledged by traditional military professionals as the greatest military theoretician since before WWI. John Boyd is considered the greatest modern military theoretician since Sun Tzu (400 B.C.). Thanks to his influence, military casualties have been drastically reduced for the United States in the last two wars in the Middle East. Accepting a new philosophy of war has been very difficult for

---

[199] Ibid., 209.
[200] John Bierman & Colin Smith, *Fire in the* Night, Ibid., 216.

professional soldiers to accept. Orde Wingate was an early example of this traditional resistance.

Homeland

The southern end of the Red Sea ends at the Bab el Mandeb Strait. After passing through, we headed east toward Aden, a British port where we refueled. Refueling a coal burning ship was an interesting spectacle. Tugboats appeared pushing lighters.[201] The first to arrive was lashed to the starboard side of our ship. It had wooden steps that started at the lighter and reached the boat deck. A second lighter brought coal in gunny sacks. This was lashed to the first lighter, and pairs of men mounted the steps, two on each step. A second group of men came on board; each one had an empty gunny sack draped over his head. Men in the second lighter began carrying bags to the first step. The pairs of men on the steps lifted the bag to the next step until the coal reached the main deck. The bag was then put on a man's back and emptied into an open hatch. When the second lighter was empty, a third took its place. This process continued for several hours and left coal dust everywhere.

Leaving Aden with replenished coal bunkers, SS Thysville proceeded east and passed Somalia, the horn of Africa. Turning south, shipboard life fell into a pleasant routine. So many laps around the deck were a mile, and we all enjoyed the serenity of a smooth sea. Temperatures became warmer as we neared the equator, but there was a pleasant breeze. This leg of our journey was about 1,600 miles, so we were all ready to reach Mombasa.

Jane Amstutz recalled our arrival in a condolence letter after mother's death:

As we were entering the Channel to Port Mombasa, Herbert, Harold, and I were leaning on the ship-rail as we came nearer and nearer to the port, we were conversing with much excitement. We were all happy to be setting our feet on African soil again. Herb said that he was especially grateful that he could return with his family and with the most capable and the best teacher he had ever known! His Mildred! His statement was proven true to us, when our son, David, enlisted in the first 9th grade class at the Rift Valley Academy.[202]

---

[201] Lighters - a large, open barge used chiefly to load or unload ships anchored in a harbor.

[202] Jane Amstutz, *Precious in the Sight of the Lord is the Death of His Saints,* Psalm 116:15.

Many RVA High-School reunions have frequently re-affirmed this tribute. I must also add that Mother was *the best teacher I ever had!*

Mombasa – Island of War

After Thor Heyerdahl's balsa raft Kon Tiki crashed, on a 20-mile reef off the dangerous Raroia atoll of the Polynasian Islands, the hard charging waves deposited the wreckage on a rock inside the reef. Lounging on the white sand of the uninhabited islet, one of the crew commented, "Purgatory was a bit damp, but heaven is more or less as I'd imagined it." [203]

As we sailed into the broad inlet of the sheltered harbor of Mombasa, white sandy beaches, fringed with coconut palm trees, appeared on either side of the channel. Rainfall in January is minimal, and temperatures range from mid 70's to high 80's. The aqua colored water inside the coral reef was calm and inviting. Tourist brochures claim it is the "perfect place to help you fall into the naturally languid rhythm of Swahili life while enjoying the modern comforts of home." [204] It looked like heaven to me!

The town of Mombasa is on a flat island, three miles long by two wide. It is separated from the mainland by two creeks. On the north is Tudor Creek, which forms the old harbor still used by Arab dhows. Reitz Creek is on the south.

After passing the harbor inlet, our ship turned left and proceeded to Kilindini harbor. This natural deep water port is considered the finest harbor anywhere on the African east coast, from the Red Sea to southern Mozambique. Seafarers from the Persian Gulf, the Indian sub-continent, Cape of Good Hope, and denizens from darkest Africa met at Mombasa Island to enjoy the calm beauty once described by Winston Churchill, (1908) as alluring and delicious. [205]

History

As we approached our wharf, nothing would indicate why the Swahilis called Mombasa "the island of war." However, history provided proof enough.

---

[203] Thor Heyerdahl, *Kon Tiki*, (New York, NY, Washington Square Press, 1984), 198.
[204] Mombasa Kenya, "Lifestyle, Culture, People,"
 http://www.buzzle.com/articles/131432.html. (accessed February 8, 2011).
[205] "Indicator Loop Stations and Harbour Defenses, Mombasa, Royal Navy,"
 http://www.visitKenya.com/guide/10162cities-towns-visitKenya.com-keny-. (accessed January 27, 2011).

The merchants from Sheba had been trading at ports of the East African coast since the time of Solomon. The wealth of Southern Arabia was no secret. Not only were they the first to navigate the Indian Ocean, they had developed agricultural methods to grow a large number of rare, high value plants. Conservation of water was crucial. A large dam was built in the seventh century B.C. at Marib in southwest Arabia. This dam broke in A.D. 450 and in A.D. 542. It was repaired twice, but broke for the third and last time in A.D. 570, creating a lengthy depression. This, coupled with a prolonged period of warlike raids from the African interior, caused economic stagnation in Africa.[206] The Koran refers to the Marib Dam failure as a punishment on the Sabeans for their ungratefulness to God.[207]

The farmers at Marib began to migrate; some whole tribes moved north to Syria. Others joined the victorious armies of Islam, and scattered. The Bedouins were not the only ones to find Islamic expansionism a lucrative business. Gaining earthly power by means of religious authority financed an unprecedented global war.

The birth of the prophet Mohammad in Mecca changed the world. By the time he died in 632, the message of Islam, revealed to him, had united all Arabia under one rule for the first time. Less than 100 years later, the new Empire of Islam extended from the borders of France as far as China.[208]

What awakened the African coast from its slumber was Islam? The death of the Prophet in 632 created splinter groups asserting rightful succession to Mohammed's spiritual stewardship. Persia and Arabia in particular did not seem big enough to hold the two main sects known as Shias and Sunnis. Bitter conflicts resulted in a wave of Sunni migrations to East Africa. All these were responsible for the first foreign-ruled dominion in East Africa.[209]

Known as Zinj (a Persian word meaning land of the black people) this developed into a loosely knit confederation of some dozen cities scattered

---

[206] Charles Miller, *The Lunatic Express,* (New York, NY, Ballantine Books, 1971), 15,

[207] Ibid.

[208] Rhea Talley Stewart, Saudi Aramco World, "A Dam at Marib,"
   http://www.saudiaramcoworld.com/issue/197802/adam.at.marib.hitm. (accessed September 29, 2010).

[209] Charles Miller, Ibid., 15.

along 2,000 miles of coastline. Initially Persian in character, a steady influx of Arab immigrants changed its culture.[210]

Zinjians were... unique in that they made no real effort to impose their ways on the original inhabitants. Islam and Arab customs did come to shape the character of the coast, but the process was not one of decree; it came instead from absorption through widespread intermarriage among settlers and Africans, producing the people and the lingua franca called Swahili. Here, too, the Zinjians showed a striking aspect of their imperial personality; an indifference to social immaculacy; their Swahili descendants were accepted on an equal footing in all walks of life. Certainly repression and inhumanity existed, mainly in the form of slavery, but this was not a Zinj or even an Arab innovation. Nor did the sale of slaves run into large numbers. (That would come under a different rule.) If Zinj could not be called a Utopia, it nonetheless gave a respectable account of itself as empires go.[211]

The decline and fall of this favorable state came abruptly. On the other side of the continent a major upheaval was taking place.

The Inquisition

In A.D. 711 the Moors of northern Africa conquered the Iberian Peninsula (the region known as Spain and Portugal). These Muslim rulers chose to coexist with Jews and Christians as long as they paid a special tax. Jews, who had lived there for generations, gladly agreed. Jewish art, music, medicine, education, and religious study flourished. The Jewish population increased greatly and prospered. Many Jews became fabulously wealthy.

Jews and Crypto Jews (those forced to become Catholics in previous persecutions) flourished in relative peace and plenty. This was known as the Golden Age and lasted 300 years.

"Although the Jews coexisted peacefully with the Muslims, Catholics bitterly resented the loss of Christian control of the peninsula since 711 and

---

[210] Ibid., 16.
[211] Ibid., 19-20.

had perpetuated unrest and uprisings, and by 1212, outright rebellion."[212] Catholic control gradually won out, however, Jews suffered.[213]

The bubonic plague ravaged the Iberian peninsula in the mid 14th century killing as many as one in every four people. Relatively few Jews died from the plague, probably because of better hygiene. Catholics hated the Jews for their apparent immunity to the plague, and widely believed the canard that the Jews were the source of the "black death" by poisoning the wells.[214]

The "supersessionism" initiated by Origen, the concept that God had rejected the Jews and replaced them with the Church, came into full bloom with the Spanish Inquisition. For 500 years scholars almost unanimously believed its purpose was to eliminate small heretical factions that threatened the union and integrity of the Church at that time. [215] In 2001, Benzion Netanyahu produced a meticulously researched, exhaustive book: *The Origins of the Inquisition in Fifteenth Century Spain.* His book shows that the Inquisition in Spain was not hostility to Jewish religion, but rage against the superior effectiveness and ascendancy of Jews out-performing established clerics as <u>Christians</u>. "New Christians," mostly Jewish, were taking over the Spanish church by being more learned, eloquent, devout, resourceful, and charismatic than Christian leaders. As Bezion Netanyahu wrote, "The struggle against the Jews was essentially motivated by social and economic, rather than religious considerations…"[216]

One of the persistent characteristics of the Jewish people is the acquisition of wealth. Another is the prevention, whether by law or by choice, of amalgamating with Gentiles. A frequent motivation for Jewish discrimination is separating them from their wealth. This appears to be a primary reason for King Ferdinand and Queen Isabella to sign the edict of expulsion on 31 March, 1492. The Jews were allowed four months to prepare for departure. They could take out of the country only their personal effects and were forbidden to have with them any gold, silver, or jewels. [217]

---

[212]Yvibbe Garaia, "A Brief History of Cryto Jews and Portuguese Descent," http://www.cryptojew.org/the-history-of-the-beni-anusim.html, (accessed February 11, 2011).
[213] Ibid.
[214] Ibid.
[215] Ibid.
[216] George Gilder, *The Israel Test,* (United State of America, Richard Vigilante Books, 2009), 32.
[217] Nathan Ausubel, *Pictorial History of the Jewish People,* (New York, NY, Crown Publishers, Inc.), 32.

In his diary Columbus noted: "In the same month in which their Majesties issued the edict that all Jews should be driven out of the kingdom and its territories, in the same month they gave me the order to undertake with sufficient men my expedition of discovery to the Indies."

About one hundred thousand of those expelled sought a haven in neighboring Portugal. But these were merely leaping from the frying pan into the fire. Thousands were forced into baptism. Many were sold into slavery. Others out of a despair that could no longer be endured sought escape in death.

In this manner, the great Jewish community that had wrought a wondrous Golden Age of Jewish civilization in Spain came to a disastrous end.[218]

It is interesting to note that the ascendancy of the British Empire followed Cromwell's readmitting Jews into England. It is also significant that both Spain and Portugal, who had been in an intense trade competition with England, waned from the Jewish exodus onward.

Canons and Cannibals

The strategic position of Portugal on the Atlantic coast gave her an advantage when European nations began seeking new sea routes to the Orient. The Age of Discovery began with expeditions under the patronage of Prince Henry (Henry the Navigator). Among the navigators who sailed under the Portuguese flag were Bartholomew Diaz (1450-1500), who discovered the Cape of Good Hope in South Africa; Vasco de Gama (1460 - 1524), who discovered the sea route from Portugal around the continent of Africa to India, and Christopher Columbus.[219]

The Treaty of Tordesillas (1494) partitioned the non-Christian world into two areas by an imaginary latitude line 1,300 miles west of the Cape Verde Islands. Portugal could claim and occupy everything to the east of the line, and Spain everything to the west. Portuguese rule in the Indian Ocean and Brazil rested on this treaty. It was sanctioned by Pope Leo X in a papal Bull of 1514.[220]

---

[218] Ibid., 110.

[219] John Daniel, *Scarlet and the Beast,* (Longview, TX, Day Publishing, 2007), 774.

[220] Encyclopedia Britannica's Guide to Black History, "Western Colonialism," http://www.britannica.com/black history/article-25869. (accessed February 13, 2011).

In 1497, Vasco de Gama made his famous voyage around South Africa to the East. Traveling up the east coast of Africa, he viewed the land of Zinj as a source of convenient provisioning for his ships. Little more was asked of Kilwa, Mombasa, Lamu, and other Zinjian cities than the supply of fresh water and stores for transient ships. The "little more" was an annual tribute payment of about $1,000. These requirements were enforced with energy so cruel that it was not long before the Portuguese won the most offensive reputation ever achieved by a conqueror of East Africa.[221]

By their own accounts the Portuguese appeared to find sanctimonious enjoyment in mutilating the coast. In 1505 Dom Francisco d'Almeida's forces took Kilwa without opposition. "…the Vicar-General and some of the Franciscan Fathers came ashore carrying two crosses and singing the Te Deum. They went to the palace, and there the cross was put down and the Grand-Captain prayed. Then everyone started to plunder the town…"[222]

Perhaps the most pleasure was taken in the sack of Mombasa, whose residents had resisted the Portuguese. One of Dom Francisco d'Almeida's agents wrote: "The king of this city refused to obey the commands of the King our Lord, and through this arrogance he lost it, and our Portuguese took it from him by force… They slew many of his people and also took captives many, both men and women… and the town was left in ruins."[223]

Malindi was the only coastal city to accept Portuguese conquest without opposition. Within 10 years the new rulers had sacked, looted, burned, raped, tortured, and beheaded until the entire coast became a seething volcano.

In 1586 a Turkish admiral, named Ali Bey, arrived at Mombasa. With voluntary donations of manpower from the Zinjians, he blasted the Portuguese from their settlements. The Portuguese retaliated by sending a squadron from India to level these rebellious cities.

Three years later, Ali Bey returned for a repeat performance, but was bottled up in Mombasa harbor by 20 Portuguese war ships. About this time a large Bantu tribe, known as the Zimbas, showed up on the mainland and offered their services as anti-white mercenaries. The catch was, the Zimbas were known to be celebrated cannibals, and had been previously denied entry. But with several hundred Portuguese canons trained on Mombasa, the inhabitants had little choice and threw their gates open.

---

[221] Charles Miller, *The Lunatic Express*, Ibid., 20.

[222] Ibid.,

[223] Ibid., 21.

The Zimbas promptly devoured everyone in sight. Sophisticated European weaponry prevailed. The Zimbas were wiped out shortly afterwards.[224]

Mombasa's behavior remained so rebellious that the Portuguese built an enormous fort in 1593. Fort Jesus, still standing, changed hands nine times between 1631 and 1875.[225] (The Portuguese gave up their claim to the coast in 1729.)[226]

Fort Jesus is the only remnant of Portuguese occupation. In their 200 years in East Africa, the only significant impression the Portuguese left was the introduction of some crops like pineapple, banana, maize, and cassava, plus a few words now used in Swahili. [227] Their claim to be Christians was totally contradicted by their conduct.

British Ascendancy

The Portuguese were driven south to what is now Mozambique, and their place taken by Omani "liberators." The Omani considered Zinj theirs by right of conquest, and for the most part ruled in absentia.

This system of proxy government was not a success, for despite their religious and cultural bonds with Zinj, the Omani Arabs were foreigners. The coast people might welcome deliverance from Portugal, but subjection was subjection even if the overlord happened to be a fellow Muslim, and the imams of Muscat soon discovered that in their new colonies they held "a tiger by the tail."

In keeping with its Swahili name Mvita, island of war, Mombasa became the first city of dissent. Here the Omani had committed a prodigious blunder in selecting as administrators a ferociously aristocratic family named Mazrui, whose members considering themselves the rightful

---

[224] Ibid., 22.
[225] "Fortjesus, Mombasa, a Historical Monument," http://fortjesus.wordpress.com/2006/01/31/fortjesus-au-introduction. (accessed January 31, 2011).
[226] Mombasa Kenya, "Lifestyle, Culture, People," http://www.buzzle.com/articles/131432.html. (accessed February 8, 2011).
[227] Fortjesus, Mombasa, a Historical Monument," http://fortjesus.wordpress.com/2006/01/31/fortjesus-au-introduction. (accessed January 31, 2011).

rulers of Mombasa, had no more intention of genuflecting to Muscat than they had to Lisbon.[228]

Meanwhile, the Marquis of Wellesley, Governor General of India, was cultivating friendships with countries on the exposed flanks of Britain's land, and sea routes to the East. In 1799, Wellesley concluded a treaty with the reigning Imam of Muscat, by which Oman was pledged to British interests in India. The Imam thus consented to a full time British agent in Muscat. "Whether or not the Imam realized it, Oman had become a client state of England."[229]

Thanks to Oman's own satellites in Mombasa and the other descendant-cities of Zinj, the treaty gave Britain her first foothold in East Africa.

In 1824, England established her first East African colony without knowing she had done so. The British Royal Navy's Captain, William F. W. Owen, commanded two ships charting the East African coast for the Admiralty. On 14 December 1823, Owen's junior ship *HMS Baraconta* put into Mombasa for stores.

The port was under an Omani blockade in preparation for a siege. The Mazrui Sheiks begged the ship's captain to give them British protection against Oman. The Mazrui request was denied, but as soon as the *Baracouta* departed, they raised their own inventive version of the Union Jack.

On 7 February, 1824, Capt. Owen entered Mombasa harbor in *HMS Levin* and was puzzled by the flag flying over Fort Jesus. Capt. Owen was not impressed by the Mazrui, who admitted raising the flag without authorization. Owen, a devout man, saw an opportunity to strike a blow for freedom in Britain's recently declared war against slavery. He stated: "It is to me as clear as the sun that God had prepared the dominion of East Africa for the only nation on earth that has public virtue enough to govern it for its own benefit and for the only people who take the revealed word for their moral law."[230]

Capt. Owens' only problem was that he was born 75 years too soon. His granting pro tem protection to the Marzrui was a breathtaking act of insubordination. "It amounted to open defiance of the Imam, the Governor General of India, the Directors of the East India Company, the

[228] Charles Miller, Ibid., 25.
[229] Ibid., 28.
[230] Ibid., 31.

Lords of the Admiralty, and the Foreign Office."[231] The mad scramble to put out the political fires ended, when Oman dislodged the Mazrui from Mombasa. Britain's awkward moment in East Africa was happily forgotten.

Or so it seemed at the time. As events were to prove, England might have saved herself infinitely greater embarrassment - and tribulations multiplied a hundredfold – had she simply allowed the Union Jack to keep flying over the Old Harbor.[232]

The Sultan of Oman, Seyyid Said, moved his capital from Oman at the toe of the Arabian Peninsula, to lush Zanzibar. Said died in 1856, and was succeeded by his son Barghash ibu Said in 1870. Barghash granted to the British East Africa Association a 50 year concession in 1887. This became the Imperial British Africa Company in 1888, with Sir William MacKinnon as its founder.[233] Mombasa thus came under the umbrella of Pax Britannica for 75 years, and was affected by war only during World War II.

World War II

Bletchly[234] Park cipher experts were initially monitoring Japanese signals traffic from small units at Singapore and Colombo.[235] Singapore was the Malaysian capital and a key British base called "the Gibraltar of the Far East." It was captured in February 1942 by the Japanese, after a 70 day siege in the greatest debacle of British history.[236]

Japanese Admiral Nagumo, with his five Pearl Harbor aircraft carriers, four battleships, and three cruisers, attacked Colombo in Ceylon (now Sri Lanka) on the 5th of April. The British lost one aircraft carrier, two heavy cruisers, two destroyers, one armed merchant cruiser, and a corvette.[237]

---

[231] Ibid.

[232] Ibid., 33.

[233] M.F. Hill, *Permanent Way*, (England, Hazell Watson & Viney Ltd Aylesbury & Slough, 1961), 3, 11-12.

[234] Bletchly-English country town where a team of British intellectuals set up their team to decipher intercepted German secret messages.

[235] "Mombasa was Base for High-Level U.K. Espionage Operation," http://www.coastweek.com/cldes.htm. (accessed February 2, 2011).

[236] Don McCombs & Fred L. Worth, *World War II*, (Avenel, NJ, Wings Books, 1983), 544.

[237] http://www.navel-history.net/WW2CampaignsJapConquests.htm. (accessed February 14, 2011).

On 25 April, 1942 the British Royal Navy's commander, Admiral Somerville, sailed for Mombasa, taking the code breakers with him. From April 1942 through August 1943, the Mombasa outpost named 'Kilindini' formed a vital link in the radio eavesdropping chain which blanketed the Indian and Pacific Oceans. Reports were sent to London, Washington, New Delhi, Melbourne, and Hawaii. While London read the now celebrated 'Enigma' codes from Berlin, and Washington perused Tokyo's 'Purple' cipher, it was in Mombasa that code-breakers helped interpret the all-important Japanese JN40 code.

This later allowed the Allies to keep an hour-by-hour track of all movements by the imperial Japanese Navy.

So successful were subsequent breakthroughs that the Japanese merchant marine suffered 90 percent losses by August 1945 – victim to Allied submarines and bombers alerted to their presence by this unique and deadly intelligence.[238]

— • —

One final note: 17 November, 1943 a GLEN from Japanese submarine I-37 piloted by W/O. Imaziumi conducted a reconnaissance flight over Kilindini Harbor. The Yokosuka E14Y (GLEN in allied code) was designed to be carried on submarines. The aircraft could be easily dismantled and stowed inside a watertight stowage compartment on the deck of the larger submarines.[239]

In retaliation for the Doolittle raid, on 9 September, 1942, the I-25 launched a specially configured "GLEN" with four incendiary bombs and no rear observer. It bombed a forested hill near Brookings, Oregon, and started a small forest fire.[240] The blaze was quickly extinguished by local authorities. Though the results were minimal, the Japanese exploited this mission for its propaganda value. This was the only time the Japanese ever bombed Continental American soil.[241]

— • —

---

[238] "Mombasa was Base for High-Level U.K. Espionage Operation," http://www.coastweek.com/codes.htm, (accessed February 2, 2011).

[239] Enzo Angelucci, *Military Aircraft-1941-1980*, (New York, NY, The Military Press, 1983), 328.

[240] "War Plan Orange," http://www.globalsecurtiy.org/military/ops/war-plan-orange.htm., (accessed February 15, 2011).

[241] Enzo Angelucci, Ibid., 328.

Kenya & Uganda Railways and Harbors

The railroad station was a short bus ride from the *Thysville's* berth at Kilindini. The shops along the road had continuous covered walkways between the street and the store fronts. One of Dad's first orders of business was acquiring protection from the tropical sun for our heads. He chose double felt hats for my brother and me, instead of the "cool" sun helmets we had hoped for. This was a difference of opinion, which Dad naturally won, although it was not finally resolved until we arrived at Kijabe.

The train from Mombasa to Nairobi was scheduled to leave at 4:30 P.M. Our luggage was piled in a heap on the train platform. I was posted as a guard, while Dad went to get a porter. Dad's familiarity with languages added to the enthusiasm of the African who ran towards me. At first I didn't see Dad, and vigorously motioned the African away. Dad appeared with a big grin, and clarified the whole affair.

The train platform was filled with passengers and vendors, loudly hawking their wares. The tropical fruits looked inviting, but we passed. Our carry-on loads were already excessive. Besides, there were dining facilities on the train.

Passenger trains in Kenya had accommodations for three classes. First class coaches had separate cubicles on one side of the car, with a passageway the length of the car on the other. The facing seats were quite long and the backs could be rotated upward to form bunk beds. First class passengers were usually Europeans.

Second class coaches had center aisles, with seats for two on either side. Passengers in these cars were usually Asians. The grouping in Kenya was essentially racial discrimination. Eventually it boiled over, as population pressures increased. It is interesting that in my travels there has always been discrimination. Even in the United States, "the land of the free," there is economic discrimination.

Third class coaches were usually more than filled with Africans who usually traveled with bulky bundles which could even include live chickens.

Luggage was stowed under the seats and in overhead bins in our first class cubicles. Finally, our train rolled out of the station on a 320 mile trip to Nairobi. We were not scheduled to arrive until 8:00 A.M. It would be quite an adventure sleeping on a rocking and rolling train!

When railroad construction was started in May 1896, a wooden bridge connected Mombasa Island with the mainland. A permanent steel bridge was built in 1898. By 1947, a causeway had been constructed, which carried both railroad tracks and a motor roadway. As the railroad curved its way on the long climb to mile high Nairobi, you could occasionally glimpse the wood-fired steam engine puffing up the grade.

Due to the voracious appetite of tropical termites, the useful life of wooden ties made them economically unsuitable. Consequently, steel rails were anchored to formed steel ties laid on a gravel bed.

Fifty miles from Mombasa, we passed the station of MacKinnon Road, named for Sir William MacKinnon, who founded the Imperial British Africa Company.[242] It was his long dreamed-of idea to deal a death blow to slavery.[243] He died before it was completed, but the railroad effectively accomplished his purpose.

MacKinnon Road is on the eastern edge of the Taru Desert. This 37-mile stretch was a major barrier to caravans traveling from the coast to the interior. Joseph Thompson, an early explorer in 1883, described it as a skeleton forest, weird and ghostly. A dreary cracking wind said: 'Here all is death and desolation!' "To become lost and to die in the Taru was simply a matter of straying a hundred yards or so from one's party."[244] It presented an almost unsurpassable obstacle to railway construction in 1896.[245]

Between 1947 and 1950 MacKinnon Road was the site of a large British engineering and Ordnance Depot, designed to hold 200,000 tons of military stores. The British had anticipated the loss of military bases in Egypt due to a rising nationalism. They decided to create another base that could serve their military needs in the western Indian Ocean. The plan was abandoned, and the base became a detention camp for Mau Mau suspects until 1955.[246]

Our bunks were already made up for the night, when we returned from the dining car. Mother's description of her train ride in 1933 is interesting:

---

[242] M.F. Hill, *Permanent Way*, (England, Hazell Watson & Viney Ltd Aylesbury & Slough, 1961), 12.
[243] Charles Miller, *The Lunatic Express*, (New York, NY, Ballantine Books, 1971), 195.
[244] Ibid., 109.
[245] Ibid.
[246] http://en.wilipedia.org/wiki/MacKinnon-Road, (accessed February 2, 2011).

Herbert, Gayle, and I had a private train car. The train wound its way up to Nairobi, stopping for twenty minutes at every station, all through the night. Those selling vegetables and other items were loud in their demands that we buy their produce. We didn't get much sleep but it was exciting to finally see all these new scenes and to hear the African languages.

I slept well. My one memorable impression was that we were not to flush the toilets while the train was stopped at the stations.

Next morning we rolled smoothly over a broad plain. In the distance, flat-topped acacia trees dotted the landscape. Frequently, small herds of gazelles and an occasional giraffe were seen, just like the pictures I'd poured over for the previous nine years.

We arrived at the same station grandfather Downing was last seen nine and a half years before. He was no longer alive, having died in 1942. He and grandmother were buried at Kijabe, where they had spent the last years of their lives.

The train to Kijabe did not leave Nairobi until later in the day, so we spent some time at Mayfield, the mission rest home. Nairobi, capital of Kenya, is more than 5,400 feet above sea level, and just south of the equator. The altitude, however, makes the temperature pleasant. Most of the streets were paved, and filled with automobiles and bicycles. It was quite cosmopolitan, with European, Asian, and African residents. Nairobi was a very stimulating community under British control in 1947.

When the railroad was first built, a broad plain was selected for maintenance facilities, switching yards, and storage buildings. Some objected to this decision, because it was on swampland. The swamp was drained, and the mild climate and railroad caused a large city to grow. Nairobi became the administrative center of Kenya, and is now a large metropolis.

Leaving Nairobi, the railroad entered hilly terrain which required tortuous turns and fairly steep grades. In order to pull heavy loads, a special locomotive was built by the Beyer-Peacock Company in England. The Garret-articulated engine had a peculiar conformation. There was a tender in front of the boiler as well as one behind. One tender carried water, the other fuel. Under each of these were eight driving wheels. The boiler for both sets of drivers was suspended between pivots on the tenders. It enabled the engine to negotiate tight radius turns and steep grades. Northwest of Kijabe was the highest point of any railroad in the

British Empire, Mau Summit, 9,136 feet above sea level. The Kenya & Uganda Railroad was truly a remarkable feat of engineering.

Limuru at 7,349 feet was near the edge of the Rift Valley, higher than Kijabe. There were many coffee and tea plantations in this area. Kenya coffee and tea are known around the world for their high quality. Interestingly, the best grades were not exported. We were spoiled!

Kikuyu was on the edge of the Rift, the site of the old 1,450 foot cable incline into the Kedong Valley. The subsequent permanent way was a gradual descent down the escarpment using three steel bridges, built by the American Bridge Company in Ambridge, Pennsylvania, to cross the steep ravines. In order to reduce the danger of bridge sabotage during WW II, a survey developed a much more gradual descent using deep cuts and fills instead of bridges. These were completed by the time we arrived in 1947, but had not settled sufficiently for active use.

As our train began the descent to Kijabe the posted speed, according to brother Ed, was 25 miles per hour due to curves and grade. Ed was deeply impressed with Dad's excitement. Our speed was slow enough for Dad to engage Africans along the way in verbal exchanges. It was the first time Ed had heard how fluent our father was in the Kikuyu language.

We arrived at the old Kijabe station in the afternoon. It was fascinating to walk along the dusty road in front of several Indian dukas (shops). Right next to the post office was the shop of Sunderjee Nathoo. He was still there after nine and a half years, and was obviously pleased to see our father again.

That evening we had supper at the Charles Teasdales. Mother and Dad had traveled to Africa with them in 1933, and worked with them at Kijabe during their first term. Their son Paul, "Junky," and I have been best friends ever since.

The following morning was 22 January, 1947, my 12th birthday. I considered this the finest gift I'd ever received! I was finally home, beginning the most memorable five and a half years of my life!

Ocean Freight

A few weeks later the shipping company announced the arrival of our freight in Mombasa. This included the heavy boxes we had carefully packed, and our 1940 Chrysler. Dad, Uncle Kenneth, and Harold Amstutz proceeded to the coast to clear customs and arrange transportation. Ocean freight from New York to the east coast of Africa usually came via South

Africa. Due to the multiple stops en-route, it could take six, eight, or more weeks. Surface mail also encountered such delays, resulting in Christmas celebrations in February or March!

It must have been the rainy season when their caravan started up the dirt road paralleling the railroad to Nairobi. Only the railroad had bridges over the rivers. The auto road crossed through these rivers on concrete spill ways. About halfway to Nairobi, they came to a river in flood state due to torrential rains. As they waited for the river to subside, Harold Amstutz suffered a severe case of appendicitis, so boarded the train for Nairobi. Dad was left with the vehicles.

While waiting, Dad had two experiences I have never forgotten. He spoke both Swahili and Kikuyu fluently. (President Jomo Kenyatta once remarked that Dad's Kikuyu was better than his own.) He became acquainted with an African working at the railroad station, who invited him to dinner one night. When he arrived at his host's humble dwelling, he was seated at a table in the middle of the room. The African proceeded to serve a meal he had prepared, which included a whole chicken with all the trimmings. When Dad invited him to dine with him, he declined, and served his honored guest with great deference. My Father was a quiet man, respected wherever he went.

The second experience was indicative of fallacious thinking regarding the British Empire. Britain had implied Arabs would gain independence if they would help defeat the Ottoman Empire in WW I. The Balfour agreement, on the other hand, had promised the Jews a land of their own in Palestine. When the Arabs realized these two promises were incompatible they began to agitate. Since the British were responsible for Palestine, they had to choose sides. Because the Arabs were more controllable, and were sitting on oil, they became the favored party. The Jews became the enemy. One night a whole trainload of captured Palestinian Jews was shipped from Mombasa to a prison at Gilgil northwest of Kijabe. Dad's comment: "They were certainly a tough looking bunch!" A year or two later the Jews successfully defended themselves against at least five British armed and British officered Arab armies. Within a few years, the wheels came off the British Empire, which is no longer the empire it was when I lived in Kenya. Britain ascended because of its attitude towards the Jews under Cromwell's leadership. Its demise came quickly after making the Jews its enemy.

After several days, Dad put the vehicles on the train to Nairobi. Shortly after our arrival at Kijabe the new alignment of the railroad opened. The trains ran just above Grandfather Downing's two story brick house, within 100 yards of the hospital where I was born. The track bed provided a convenient hiking path to the new train station that was a mile or so from the old station. A ravine just short of the station had a small dam up the hill that held water for trains. The valley on either side of the dam had steep sides extending several hundred feet high. This precluded the sun warming the water except for a short time around noon. Despite the frigid water temperature, we hiked four or five miles to swim. As you might imagine, we didn't "lounge" in the water long.

Years later Mother, Ruth Ann, and I traveled by train to the end of the line at Lira in Uganda. Again sleeping accommodations were used. Before arriving at Lira, the steward brought a wake-up cup of <u>strong</u> black tea, with plenty of milk and sugar. It really tasted good, so I drank it all.

Harold and Jane Amstutz met us with their Ford station wagon for the drive to Congo. There were seven of us in the car with the Amstutz, their son David, Mother, Ruth Ann, a single missionary lady from Memphis, and me. The car was crowded! Fortunately the weather was warm enough to have the windows open. I had odoriferous gastric reactions from the morning tea. Everyone noticed and commented accordingly. I was never allowed to forget!

To this day the sights and sounds of steam engines produce a nostalgia for that period of my life. My wife and I enjoyed a delightful diesel train ride from Toronto, Canada to Vancouver. Diesels, however, cannot match the excitement of steam engines.

Rift Valley Academy

"From whence come wars and fighting among you... Ye lust and have not: ye kill and desire to have, and cannot obtain: ye fight and war, yet ye have not, because ye ask not." James 4:1a & 2 – KJV

Peter Cameron Scott, the young man who first had the vision for the Africa Inland Mission, saw a line of mission stations stretching 2,000 miles from Mombasa to Lake Chad in the Sahara Desert. In December 1896 he died of malaria at age 29 after little more than a year in Kenya.

Charles Hurlburt helped establish three organizations: Africa Inland Mission (AIM,) Pennsylvania Bible Institute (PBI,) and Central American Industrial Mission (CAIM.) Upon Scott's death, Hurlburt "stepped up to the plate" and was appointed General Director of the Africa Inland Mission in 1897.

His first step was a two month survey tour of British East Africa in 1900. The next year he left the United States with his wife and five children, ages 4 to 12. Some questioned the audacity of exposing his family to such an unhealthy environment. But Charles Hurlburt was a man of prayer; he not only spoke to his Father in heaven, but listened carefully to God's voice. He was successful because his priorities were in line with Scripture.[247] His first priority was his family. Too frequently, men consider "their ministry" preeminent. Fortunately for me, Charles Hurlburt, Lee Downing, and my father were not so inclined.

Things were at their lowest ebb when Mr. Hurlburt and Grandfather Downing arrived. Working together they brought new life to the AIM, producing growth and fruit.[248]

Both were educated men. Charles Hurlburt attended Oberlin College (1881-1883,)[249] and became State Secretary in the YMCA. Disappointed by its secular trend he resigned to undertake door-to-door evangelism. Appalled by ignorance among Christians, he set up Pennsylvania Bible

---

[247] Mark 7:10-13.

[248] Kenneth Richardson, *Garden of Miracles*, (Great Britain, Africa Inland Mission, 1976), 53.

[249] Oberlin College Archives – Recent Accessions – "Accession 2009/036," http://www.oberlin.edu/archive/recent-accessories, html. (accessed March 8, 2011).

Institute in 1895.[250] "On his first journey to Africa he took with him 1,000 volumes, being a deep thinker and omnivorous reader… "[251] He later co-authored the book *Names of Christ* with T.C. Horton.[252]

Lee Harper Downing graduated from Jefferson College in 1892 and was appointed lecturer in New Testament Greek at PBI by Hurlburt in 1896. "Lee Downing had a prodigious memory. He could recite large portions of the New Testament by heart, as well as extracts from other writings which had impressed him."[253]

Both men were hampered by rear echelon insistence on emphasizing Christ's gift of evangelism to the exclusion of His gift of teaching.[254]

Despite the Home Council's disavowing responsibility for the education of missionary children, Hurlburt recognized the need for a school. The future of the mission depended upon it. On furlough in 1905, a wealthy friend asked him what the pressing needs of the mission were. Among other things, Hurlburt mentioned a school for missionary children. Nothing more was said, but in 1908 that gentleman donated a large sum of money for that school in the name of his stepmother, Mrs. Butterworth.

Josephine Hope was in the missionary party aboard ship when Hulburt returned in 1906. One day he drew up a deck chair, and talked to her about Kenya. Knowing that she was an experienced Montessori teacher, he asked "Would you be willing to teach the children of missionaries?"

"Sure," she replied. "I'd be glad to."

Missionaries going to Africa were focused on black Africans. This was one of the first qualified missionaries to refocus previous expectations to missionary children.

Montessori

The Montessori Method of education was developed by Maria Montessori, the first woman to practice medicine in Italy. Caring for young children, she observed specific phases that children went through, and developed three dimensional materials that enhanced learning. One

---

[250] Dick Anderson, *We felt like Grasshoppers*, (Great Britain, Crossway Books, 1994), 30.

[251] Kenneth Richardson, *Garden of Miracles*, Ibid., 47.

[252] T.C.Horton & Charles E. Hurlburt, " Names of God – Victory in Purity," http://www.logos.com/product/7702/names-of-christ-coched. (accessed March 8, 2011).

[253] Kenneth Richardson, Ibid., 54.

[254] Ephesians 4: 8-13.

goal was to interest children in the process of learning, which would continue throughout their lives. Her methods produced measurable improvement in the education process. It was a cutting edge concept in the early part of the 20th century, and Rift Valley Academy (RVA) was fortunate to have a teacher with these skills.

Romans chapter one emphasizes the disparity between the seed of the serpent (goats) and the seed of the woman (sheep). The former suppressed the truth, refused to honor God or give Him thanks. Therefore God gave them up to vile desires, sinful passions, and depraved reasoning. They are incapable of thinking clearly, though they worship at their shrine of reason which they call "science." This provides a fundamental motive for the seed of the woman to awaken them to God's passion for restoring men to His design specifications, which includes a renewed spirit. Restoration can be claimed by a heartfelt acceptance of Jesus Christ as their shepherd, transferring from the "goat" culture to one of His sheep. Then, and only then, can they learn truth.

This goal of evangelism is just the beginning. God intends for His children, "the seed of the woman," to grow. His most effective means is to send a personal tutor to guide them into all truth.[255] It has occurred to me that this tutor, the Holy Spirit, frequently uses methods similar to Montessori. Grandfather Downing's tract: *How May I Know God's Plan for My Life,"* (Appendix A) exemplifies this concept.

It should be emphasized that Marie Montessori's method was for the purpose of cultivating innate God-given learning abilities. This is diametrically opposed to John Dewey's goal of separating children from the influence of Christian parents, and leveling them into an egalitarian mass that is easily manipulated by society, with political correctness.

In *John Dewey & the Decline of American Education:*

Thanks in no small part to Dewey, much of what characterizes contemporary education is a revolt against various expressions of authority: a revolt against a canon of learning, a revolt against tradition, a revolt against religious values, a revolt against moral standards, a revolt against logic-even a revolt against grammar and spelling. In many classrooms, the concern is whether sufficient authority exists simply to guarantee physical safety and survival. Dewey's revolt has carried American education to the place where he himself admitted he had arrived late in life: "I seem to be

---

[255] John 16:13.

unstable, chameleon-like, yielding one after another too many diverse and even incompatible influences; struggling to assimilate something from each and yet striving to carry it forward."[256]

Genesis

Rift Valley Academy (RVA), though it had a grand title, began with few resources apart from an enthusiastic person who possessed boundless confidence in a benevolent God. Miss Hope prayed about the curriculum, and received advice from her former American schools. She prayed for teachers, books, and desks, which arrived the following year. She prayed for a building to accommodate 50 pupils.

Shortly after the Butterworth funds arrived, Hurlburt selected a flat site called Kiambogo, a Kikuyu name meaning the "Place of the Buffalo." The site was a plot of scrub brush and small trees frequented by African Cape Buffalo, with a spectacular view of the longest fracture in the earth's surface. Rising from the floor of the valley below, two extinct volcanoes form focal points in the panorama at Kijabe.

Hulburt agreed to supervise the construction of the building designed by Miss Hope and him. It was 150 feet long and about 36 feet wide, having two stories with accommodations for 40 students. Fifteen thousand bricks were formed from local clay, and fired in three kilns. When the largest kiln burst into flames and was destroyed, an alternative was found in the local lava ash. This was a soft stone, which could be cut with hatchets and chisels. The sandstone/tuff cornerstone was laid in brick, but the walls were lava ash. The building is still used by the school after more than 100 years.[257]

Josephine Hope was surprised when former U.S. President Theodore Roosevelt came to lay the cornerstone. Charles Hurlburt had previously been invited by the president to advise him on plans for a post-presidential African hunting trip. Years later, ex-President Roosevelt remembered Hurlburt as "the greatest man he had met in Africa."[258] With the former president a drawing card, settlers from Britain and South Africa converged on the mission station. Some came on foot from as far as 40 miles away. They saw RVA as the only source of quality education for their children.

---

[256] Henry T. Edmondson III, *John Dewey & the Decline of American Education,* (Wilmington, DE, ISI Books, 2006), 56.

[257] Phil Dow, *School in the Clouds,* (Pasadena, CA, William Cary Library, 2003), 23-25.

[258] Quoted from Stephen Morad's unpublished PhD dissertation, 145.

Initially Kiambogo housed only a dozen missionary kids (MK's) and a handful of settler's children in a large building with sparse furnishings. A few months after President Roosevelt's visit, Miss Hope visited the United States in search of supplies. Upon her return she married Theodore Westervelt and moved into Kiambogo.

Josephine established a firm Christian foundation for RVA, stressing Bible study and prayer. To settlers and officials, who asked her to educate their children, she carefully explained that she and her staff aimed to lead each student into a Christian commitment. They rarely failed.

Just before the outbreak of war (WW I) Josephine became ill. Doctors diagnosed a heart disorder and warned her that Kijabe's altitude would make it worse. Under the best conditions in USA, they reckoned, she might survive two years. Sadly the Westervelts handed the work over to others.

The doctor's prognosis for Josephine Westervelt proved wrong. Although her heart condition prevented her return to Kenya she never lost her love for MK's. The Westervelts developed a ministry to MK's attending college in America, eventually moving to Columbia, South Carolina where a university and a Bible college offered all the education the young men needed.

Josephine trained her family vigorously: the fellows cooked, cleaned, washed, and ironed; they turned out their lights at 10:00 and rose early; for breakfast they ate oatmeal porridge with lashings of milk, but no sugar or salt. She forbade dating. 'You must get your education first,' she insisted, 'then you will be mature enough to know the kind of girl you need.' [259]

Mrs. Westervelt a large, imposing woman, was able to prepare young men for leadership roles. She went on to run an establishment (still Westervelt Home) in Batesburg, SC, which was school and home for MKs, with an enrollment over 100. Beneath her severe, matronly bearing was a smart, caring soul.[260] Ten of her first 11 students returned to long ministries in Africa. RVA produced one of its first groups of strong, second generation missionaries.

---

[259] Dick Anderson, *We Felt like Grasshoppers*, Ibid.,206-208.
[260] Note from Roy Shaffer, http://us.1117mail.yahoo.com/mc/showMessage, (accessed April 12, 2011).

The Founding Father Fired

Charles Hurlburt never lost sight of Scott's vision for the AIM. As mission stations were established westward toward Chad, he persisted in focusing on that goal. In 1919 he moved from Kijabe to the mission station at Aba, in the Belgian Congo, to be close to the front lines.

For whatever reason, lines of responsibility became blurred about this time. Rear echelon support for the General Director in the field began to diminish. Hurlburt chose to lead from the front, and by 1919 had come remarkably close to his goal. From a military point of view, the rear echelon exists to support the forces in the field. Inasmuch as they are not in the combat zone, they must rely on observations of the General, who is. The Director and his Lieutenant (Grandfather Downing) both saw the need for schools to train leaders for a strong church. In the end, evangelism took precedence resulting in immature converts incapable of leadership needed for a self-sustaining church.

Both Charles Hurlburt and Lee Downing had remarkable track records of hearing God's voice. Their responsibility was to obey the Head of the Body,[261] and their obedience is bearing fruit to this day. In contrast, Israel refused to listen to God's voice[262] and was given 613 rules to obey. Their choice prevented living on the level of the Spirit, and produced a checkered history of disobedience.

A whispering campaign resulted in Charles Hurlburt's forced resignation on 31 July, 1925. One of the stated factors was failing health. His health improved dramatically as soon as he left AIM. He became Superintendent of the Bible Institute of Los Angeles (BIOLA), and founded a new society, the Unevangelized Africa Mission.

He was still actively serving in his 77th year, when he suddenly collapsed. He died a week later on 27 January, 1936 from complications of tropical diseases.[263] RVA lost its founding father.

The attitude of a mission whose new leader wrote emphatically that, "Undue stress (was) being laid on education," resulted in a drop of RVA students from 50 in the early 1920's to 18 in 1928.[264] "…without the outstanding efforts of the academically- minded British missionary, Muriel

---

[261] Ephesians 4:15-16.
[262] Exodus 20:19
[263] Dick Anderson, *We Felt like Grasshoppers*, Ibid., 37.
[264] Phil Dow, *School in the Clouds*, 56.

Perrott, it is difficult to imagine what the school would have evolved or devolved into."[265]

Miss Perrott was the first teacher after Miss Hope to come specifically to RVA. Tiny and slightly hunchbacked, she was not an imposing figure. Yet her love for the students and teaching made a lasting impression on those who knew her. In four critical years she established a standard of excellence that began to permeate RVA's value system. She was head teacher from 1924 to 1927, and left RVA in 1931, never to return. Her legacy, however, included relics of Old Britannia which persisted for many years.[266]

Downing Dynasty

When my parents were assigned to RVA in 1933, no one wanted the job. Granted, Dad was best qualified with his education and experience. He was also better qualified than most to work with Africans. He had mastered both the local Kikuyu language and the Swahili trade language as a young boy. His indigenous experience, with Kikuyu acquaintances, made him aware of their culture and mores. He was considered by some Africans as almost a member of their social year group.[267] When Kenya was experiencing the throes of independence, they visited late at night, trusting Dad's counsel.

People who saw Dad in his role as principal at RVA could not be aware of his stature as an educator. I was unaware of this until after leaving home. I visited my Mother's older brother in New York City, on a cross country flight from Texas, while instructing in advanced jets. Uncle Dale was a Dean at New York University at the time. He had been president of Slippery Rock State College, and had been with the United States Overseas Mission in Bangkok, Thailand. Uncle Dale said he was deeply disappointed when Dad went to Africa. Educators of his stature were badly needed in the United States. Few people at Kijabe were ever aware of this.

In 1933, the Field Council gave Mother and Dad the mandate to organize a first-rate high school. There were 34 students at the time, in grades one to eight, with three teachers temporarily assigned. The

---

[265] Ibid., 59.

[266] Ibid., 42-43.

[267] Social precedence in African society is determined by a man's birth-year. Men are grouped accordingly.

headmistress left immediately. The other teacher was studying language for further assignment, and the student teacher stayed on for a while. So Mother and Dad were immediately involved in full time teaching. School development had to wait.[268]

After I was born, Mr. McKenrick, the school homemaker, became ill. Mother and Dad moved into Kiambogo with Gayle and me until Paul Leherer and his wife became dorm parents in 1937. Dad's comment was: "We had a rather heavy go of it…" Mother wrote: "All I can say of this period is: "We survived…""

When our family departed on furlough in 1937, Dad's younger brother, Kenneth, accepted "temporary" responsibility while Dad was gone. Little did he know his "tour" would last nine years.

Dad's return in 1947 marked the beginning of his high school mandate. Gayle was in the first class of four to graduate in 1950. I graduated two years later. By 1974 the school was fully accredited by the Middle States Association of Colleges and Secondary Schools. Seventy-two graduated that year.

By the early 70's, the effects of secular education in the United States began showing up at RVA. One of the first steps in the establishment of this system was consolidation. In the U. S. 259,000 parent-controlled school districts were consolidated into 1,600 government-controlled districts.[269] After consolidation, parents were no longer intimate with teachers. They were alienated by the large National Education Association (Teacher's Union,) which gradually became adversarial towards parents. Secular textbooks were placed in schools and the 1962/1963 Supreme Court decision outlawing Bible reading and prayers in public schools completed the plan. Compulsory education was becoming completely atheistic.[270]

Unaware of the revolutionary causes of the degradation of education in their homeland, defensive missionary parents and legalists blamed RVA. With no formal means of adjudicating differences in the mission, a whispering campaign began, and Dad was forced to resign.

Dad was 69 years old, but much younger than the president of Kenya. Age was not a valid reason for dismissal. For years he had been grooming a replacement, and was fully prepared to step aside. But the hysteria of the opposition demanded an immediate solution with stringent rules, regulations, and mandatory penalties for violations. Both Dad and his

[268] Mildred Houk Downing, *Short Autobiography*, (unpublished), in my files.
[269] *Word of Life Quarterly*, Winter 1990, 24.
[270] John Daniels, *Scarlet and the Beast*, (Longview, TX, Day Publishing, 2007), 230-233.

preferred successor were unwilling to implement such counter-productive procedures. Time-consuming investigations and careful corrective exercises were necessary. Training students to effectively enter an atheistic environment and maintain spiritual equilibrium was their goal.

Imbedded in my files of related correspondence, Dad noted: "...I'm quite sure that before I came to the mission field I had had a more comprehensive indoctrination in politics, particularly school politics, than most of you men... and I feel your letter is not in keeping with the dignity of your office."

Previously Dad had countered special interest moves by school boards, with political skill. He was able to keep the school on a steady course. In order for the opposition to be successful, Dad had to go.

The opposition's solution was an older, respected evangelical, but educationally, unqualified missionary. His mission was to reverse the 'permissive broadmindedness' that had created the problem. Dad's qualified replacement was made vice principal. Predictably, this myopic solution proved unworkable. Ironically, in two years the vice principal was promoted, and the older man unceremoniously dismissed. This was hardly the smooth transition Dad had intended.

This appears to be another case of the "Head of the Kingdom" not being properly consulted. If you refuse to hear the voice of the Lord, rules and regulations are the only alternative: Israel's mistake was apparently repeated!

One of the top three requested quotes of Theodore Roosevelt is the "Man in the arena."

It is not the critic who counts: not the man who points out how the strong man stumbles or where the doer of deeds could have done better. The credit belongs to the man who is actually in the arena, whose face is marred by dust and sweat and blood, who strives valiantly, who errs and comes up short again and again, because there is no effort without error or shortcoming, but who knows the great enthusiasm, the great devotions, who spends himself for a worthy cause; who, at the best, knows, in the end, the triumph of high achievement, and who, at the worst, if he fails, at least he fails while daring greatly, so that his place shall never be with those cold and timid souls who knew neither victory nor defeat.[271]

---

[271] The Theodore Roosevelt Association, "Quotations of Theodore Roosevelt," http://www.theodoreroosevelt.org/life/quotes.htm. (accessed March 17, 2011).

After being born at Kijabe, spending more that 50 years of his life living there, and 'spending himself for a worthy cause,' Dad could say: "Driving down the hill from Kijabe, I had no desire to look back!"

Blessed (content) are you when people insult you and persecute you, and falsely say all kinds of evil against you because of Me. Rejoice and be glad, for your reward in heaven is great; for in the same way they persecuted the prophets who were before you.
Matthew 5: 11-12 (NASB)

My wife and I attended the RVA Centennial celebration at Kijabe in 2006. Kiambogo was still a well-maintained center piece on a large campus. Flags from nations represented homes of students. Surprisingly, 20% of the students were from South Korea. The Korean War was considered by some to be a waste of American service personnel, but today it is a Christian nation sending missionaries all over the world.

Our God is all-powerful, all-knowing, all-present, and timeless. In His sovereign love, He is worthy of our allegiance and our obedience. God's brand of multiculturalism has no internal inconsistencies. The Holy Spirit is building us all into one perfect body to be bonded into the Godhead by Love!

Zinjians in War

A used bookstore in San Diego had an old book entitled *Pondoro-Last of the Ivory Hunters*. The author, John Taylor, published his auto-biography in 1956. Having read of Karamoja Bell, one of the greatest ivory hunters of all time, I was drawn to this tale.

In 1904 John was born in Dublin to Sir William Taylor, a great surgeon, and Lady Taylor, an American from Louisiana. Properly educated in one of "the big five" English public schools, his ambition was to hunt elephants and collect ivory.

John Taylor sailed to South Africa, bought a motorcycle, and rode north into Central Africa. He sold his "wheels," bought a rifle, and engaged an African to teach him how to hunt. For more than 30 years, John hunted in remote sections of the continent, naked like the tribes around him. He lived entirely by hunting and bartering what he shot. Since the 1930's, he was the only professional ivory hunter left in Africa.

In the Prologue to *Pondoro*, Taylor tells one of the most fascinating leopard stories I've ever heard. He and his gun bearer had been canoeing up the Zambezi River, landing early one evening to scout the surrounding country. As he returned about sundown, along a small game trail, a leopard dropped from a tree, knocking John to the ground. He was able to draw his revolver and shoot the leopard in the chest. But the dying leopard's claws exposed all the ribs on the right side of his chest, and left his left thigh in ribbons. Joro, his African companion, ran forward, broke the stock of his rifle on the leopard's head, ending the struggle.

Any wound from a leopard's claws almost always becomes septic. The only water available was from the muddy river, hardly suitable for the occasion. Joro immediately solved the problem with urine from the source. Medical research on urine indicates that it is completely sterile, antibacterial, antifungal, antiviral, (anticancer), anticonvulsive, and antispasmodic.[272]

Joro then disappeared, returning 10 to 15 minutes later with various leaves, roots, and the soft inner bark from some tree. He pounded the roots until they bled thick, white milk. This was smeared on and into the wounds. It felt most soothing. A nest of white ants was stirred up, and the

---

[272] Steven C Denk, *How you Rot and Rust*, (Des Plaines, IL, Biomedx, 2001), 136.

big warriors among them were used to suture the wounds after drawing the lips of the deep gashes together.

White ants were a source of entertainment when we were growing up. After a heavy rain, they would emerge from their nests with four, translucent wings. Their wings were about two inches long, their bodies about ¾ of an inch, and they flew slowly through the air like small helicopters. We would snatch them from the air, pull off their wings, and eat them raw. They tasted like black walnut meat. One bit my tongue before I learned to pinch off their heads. They tasted even better fried in butter. Thankfully the Lord protected us from the botulism that took several lives in 1980.

The big warrior ants had large heads with strong jaws. They never grew wings, and when allowed to lock their jaws on our shirts, with their thoraxes pinched off, looked like little pad locks. We never thought to use them as sutures, but they must have worked perfectly for Pondoro.

The leaves were used as a dressing; with the soft inner bark serving as bandages. The next morning the bandages were removed, and the wounds pressed, and probed until Joro was satisfied there was no pus. Fresh bandages were then applied, and left for three or four days. The bandages were then discarded, the ant-jaw stitches removed, and he was given a clean bill of health.

John Taylor was out of touch with civilization for as long as four years at a time. "I did not learn of World War II until some of my men went in for provisions and brought back tea and salt, wrapped in old newspapers. Where I am, there is no radio and I never see another white man."[273]

Suspects

Edith Holman was the RVA teacher, studying language, when my parents arrived at Kijabe in 1933.[274] She married Wellesly Devitt in April 1938, and served with him there for 28 years. The Devitts became close friends of our family. The Ford Ferguson tractor Wells brought to Kijabe in 1948 was my first tractor driving experience. Their daughter, Helen, and my younger sister, Ruth Ann, were close buddies for years. After Welles's death in 1978, Edith wrote *On the Edge of the Rift*. Her experiences at

---

[273] John Taylor, *Pondoro-Last of the Ivory Hunters,* (London, England, Frederick Muller Ltd., 1956), "About the Author."
[274] Mildred Houk Downing, *Short Autobiography,* (unpublished), in my files.

Kijabe during WW II provide information that we missed while in the States.

A drama of pre-war intrigue was enacted within sight of Kijabe Mission station at a high jutting point of land overlooking this section of the Rift Valley, (including the mission station), which had a 360 degree view in all directions. This point with its residence and grounds came into the possession of a German gentleman and his attractive, blonde, English wife. On one occasion they visited the mission station and were our guests for lunch. They became suspect by the Intelligence Department, but in spite of considerable surveillance, remained impeccably clear of any proven violation. Among other things, they were suspected of possessing firearms, signaling devices, explosives, and other articles useful in the event of war.

Eventually two officers were dispatched with a warrant to search their entire premises. The search failed to turn up a single clue. Reluctantly the officers drove away a short distance, over and down a slight rise out of sight of the house, where they stopped to discuss their frustration and failure. Suddenly one of them exclaimed,

"Say! What kind of a roof has that house?"

"You've struck it, man. That house has a flat roof," the other answered excitedly.

"Let's go back and have a look."

With that they returned to find that the roof had walls extending upwards, concealing a large cache of war materials of many kinds. Authorities gave the couple three days to leave the country.[275]

The Devitts and Lehrers were rudely notified of the outbreak of WW II, when returning from a camping trip near the Tanganyika border. Setting up a bivouac near a clean stream, they noticed a camp on the other side. When Welles approached to investigate, he and the rest of the party were arrested by a European in an army uniform with a tommy gun.

Several white officers and African soldiers rounded up the party and assigned them to two tents, men in one, and women in the other. The detachment had been hastily dispatched to capture some prominent German escapees from Tanganyika. Men with 10 day old beards, one having the German name of Lehrer, seemed like their obvious quarry. In

---

[275] Edith Devitt, *On the Edge of the Rift,* (Langle, Canada, University Printers Ltd., 1992), 122-123.

their haste, they had been sent out without rations, expecting to shoot meat on the go.

The missionaries were allowed to fix supper and breakfast for captors and captives alike! After breakfast, a truck was sent to Narok to check on the hunting party's story. The truck returned that afternoon with orders to release their captives. In their haste, the detachment had failed to find their names in their book, missing them by one page. With military apologies and good humor all around, no time was lost in returning to Kijabe.

A Missionary Goes to War

In January 1943, Welles Devitt was appointed Chaplain with the 11th Kings African Rifles, East Africa Command. He was in Ceylon by June, and was moved to India a year later. By July 1944, he was in Burma.

When on leave, he related the following amusing story: An officer friend had gone ahead with his men. Welles decided to follow alone to join him. Coming around a bend, he saw two Japanese soldiers sitting by the roadside. They obeyed when he ordered them to drop their weapons and march ahead with hands up. He stopped their conversation by hitting them in the back of their heads with thrown pebbles. He arrived at the company location with his two captives, providing live prisoners for interrogation[276]

September 1944, Maj. Devitt was at the front when forward companies needed supplies. The Indian muleteers said their mules could not carry supplies up such a steep mountain. When Wells learned that there was grass on the hill, his experience with mules convinced him that they could climb with light loads. Loading 12 mules with rations for 96 men, Welles took the lead mule and led them up the hill. The moon was up by the time he got back to camp, covered with mud and sweat. The missionary had become a veritable Yankee "muleskinner" in the British Army!

On 27 November, 1944, Rev. Devitt won the Military Cross. The citation reads in part: "The Rev. Devitt, immediately and without thought for his own safety, exposed himself for a considerable period to attend to the wounded and administer to the dying. By his magnificent example and Christian bearing, he was an inspiration to all ranks in the vicinity."[277]

---

[276] Edith Devitt, *On the Edge of the Rift*, Ibid., 252.
[277] Ibid., 270.

HQ FOURTEENTH ARMY
S.E.A.C.
Dated 31 Jan. 45

Dear Rev. William Wellesley Devitt,

I am very pleased to hear that your distinguished conduct has been rewarded, and send you my warmest congratulations on a well deserved honor.

Yours Sincerely,

[Signed] W. J. Slim
General Officer Commanding in Chief
Fourteenth Army[278]

Burma

After Pearl Harbor, the Japanese had inflicted one humiliation after another on the British. In about 100 days, they had overrun most of Britain's Far Eastern Empire, including Hong Kong, Singapore, Malaya, and half of Burma. Gen. Sir Alan Brooks, the new chief of the Imperial General Staff, noted in his diary: "If the army cannot fight better than it is doing at present we shall deserve to lose our Empire."[279]

Granted, the defense of Burma was left largely to a conglomeration of half-trained Indian troops – the best having been sent to the Middle East. The leadership seemed unable to mobilize an effective force. This could have been the result of the Law of Entropy[280], with the Peter Principle[281] and Parkinson's Law[282] contributing. However, it's possible that the

---

[278] Ibid., 279.

[279] John Bierman & Colin Smith, *Fire in the Night*, (Oxford, England, Macmillan Publishers Ltd., 1999), 241.

[280] Law of Entropy - A process of degeneration marked variously by increasing degrees of uncertainty, disorder, fragmentation, chaos, etc: specifically, such a process regarded as the inevitable, terminal stage in the life of a social system or structure. Webster's New College Dictionary, 4th Edition, 475.

[281] Peter Principal-The facetious proposition that each employee in an organization tends to be promoted until reaching his or her level of incompetence. Ibid., 1077.

[282] Parkinson's Law-Propounded by C. Northcote Parkinson (1909-93), [Brit economist] any of several satirical statements expressed as economic laws, as one to the effect that work expands to fill the time allotted to it. Ibid., 1048.

undercurrent of Jewish antipathy in the British Officer Corps could also have been a factor. The man who provided the first victory in that theater was an expert in unconventional warfare, and never lost his interest in leading a Jewish force into battle.

Shortly before the fall of Singapore, Gen. Archibold Wavell, overall commander of British forces in the Far East, had written to Gen. Sir John Kennedy, planning chief at the War Office, deploring the lack of fighting spirit, and the general softness of Britain's increasingly conscript army. Wavell needed a tough-minded leader with imagination, who could mobilize an effective solution to the Japanese Juggernaut. Maj. Orde Wingate, who had successfully solved problems in Palestine and Ethiopia for Wavell, was summoned to the Far East.

After studying the situation, Wingate assembled, trained, and led a brigade deep into enemy territory. His conclusion was that the enemy was most vulnerable far behind his lines, where a small force could wreak havoc. Supply was to be by air, communication by radio, two weapons not properly exploited before.

After crossing the first river on 16 February, 1943, Wingate began to play undreamed-of remote control games with his doggedly mobile foot columns, sending some to attack and some to distract. He generally used tactics the Japanese had never encountered before, not even against Chinese guerillas.[283]

By the end of April, when the remnants of his brigade had returned, Britain's propaganda machine finally had an achievement to trumpet. A large scale raid behind Japanese lines had finally confounded the Japanese forces. It was obvious, however, that losses were high. Only 2,182 returned of the original force of approximately 3,000 men. Only 600 of the survivors would be fit for future active service. This was the price of a turn around.[284]

Churchill was excited by the report that Wingate finished on 17 June, 1943, and invited him to travel with him to Canada on the SS *Queen Mary*. On 18 August, 1943, Wingate delivered a crisp, concise, brilliantly persuasive plan to Roosevelt and American service chiefs. It called for 26,500 men, divided into three groups, each of eight columns. This force was to be inserted deep behind Japanese lines to soften up the enemy before a three-pronged, frontal attack by the British in the west, the Chinese

---

[283] John Bierman & Colin Smith, *Fire in the Night,* Ibid., 307.
[284] Ibid.

in the east, and Gen. Joseph Stilwell's Sino-American force in the north. The Kings African Rifles from Zinj were to be part of the British force. Everyone liked the plan except Gen. Claude Auchinleck, the Commander-in-Chief in India. Auchinleck and his staff of "curry colonels"[285] were offended by an upstart substantive Major, now a Major General.

A British general in New Delhi said Wingate was unfit to command a brigade. When Wingate heard about this, he said: "The personal attacks cannot be answered by argument. But they can be, and are, answered by the facts. It is because I am what I am, objectionable though that appears to my critics, that I win battles."[286]

Gen. "Hap" Arnold of the U.S. Army Air Force assigned Lt. Col. Philip Cochran to command a miniature air force (which included helicopters) for Wingate's operation. After his second meeting with Wingate, Cochran had this to say:

I saw it as an adaptation of air to jungle, an application of air-war tactics to a walking war in the trees and the weeds. Wingate had hit upon the idea independently... In his own tough element he was thinking along the same radio lines that an airman would about tactics among the clouds. I realized that there was something very deep about him... He was a thinker and a philosopher... When I left him I was beginning to assimilate some of the flame about this guy Wingate.[287]

5 March, 1944, the initial fly-in began. By 7 March, Wingate flew into "Broadway" landing site. His operation was finally coming to fruition. Nineteen days later, the B-25 he was traveling back to his operational headquarters at Hailikandi Airport, after a brief visit at "Broadway," crashed killing all on board.

History is written by the victor, and in 1956 many detractors in high military places began to castigate the first British Officer to successfully oppose the Japanese ground forces. The official history of World War II in Asia, *The War Against Japan,* published in 1961, devoted six pages in assessing Maj. Gen. Wingate. No other commander received such a lengthy assessment, not even Mountbatten or Gen. Slim. This would be

---

[285] Ibid., 329. "curry colonels" as they were contemptuously called by those in the field, who viewed them as motivated mainly by sloth and selfish ambition.
[286] Orde Charles Wingate, "Hayedid,"
http://www.zionism-israel.com/bio/Charles-Orde_Wingate.htm. (accessed March 21, 2011).
[287] Ibid., 325.

remarkable testimony to Wingate's significance but for the fact that the assessment was almost entirely negative.[288]

One of Wingate's subordinates subsequently stumbled across a possible explanation, turning up an Army Council minute that stated in summary: Wingate was a divisive influence and "we don't want any more Wingates in the British Army. Therefore we must write down Wingate and the 'Chindits'."[289]

I believe the "wheels finally came off" the British Empire shortly after their failed attempt to keep the nation of Israel from coming into existence in 1948. "The one who curses you: I will curse."[290]

But perhaps the most effective witnesses to Wingate's prowess at arms are the Japanese commanders. The official Japanese view, based on statements taken from more than 30 commanders in the Burma Theater, states unequivocally that "the raiding force (Chindits) greatly affected Army operations, and eventually led to the total abandonment of Northern Burma."[291]

Japanese Lt.Gen.Renya Mutaguchi asserted that "General Wingate's airborne tactics put a great obstacle in the way of our Imphal plan, and were an important reason for its failure."[292]

In the final analysis, the success of the British forces in Burma, which included the Kings Africa Rifles from Zinj, was the result of a Christian warrior who wrote in Hebrew script: "If I forget thee, O Jerusalem..."[293]

Governor Mitchell

Canton Atoll, the largest of the Phoenix Islands in the South Pacific, is about half-way between Hawaii and Fiji. In April 1939, it came under joint control of the United Kingdom and the United States. It became significant as an aircraft refueling point for Pan American World Airways in 1939.

After war broke out, a British civilian radio operator persisted in sending messages which, though innocent, threatened U.S. Navel Security. Warned twice, the operator continued a third time, and a detachment of

---

[288] Orde Charles Wingate, "Hayedid," Ibid., 385.
[289] John Bierman & Colin Smith, *Fire in the Night*, Ibid., 386.
Chindits - The name of Wingate's forces in Burma.
[290] Genesis 12:3 (NASB)
[291] John Bierman & Colin Smith, *Fire in the Night*, Ibid., 386.
[292] Ibid.
[293] Ibid., 331.

U.S. Marines closed him down. This molehill became a political mountain. Standing on his dignity, the British High Commissioner in the Western Pacific threatened Anglo-American cooperation in the entire western Pacific Ocean.

The British, acting quickly, replaced their High Commissioner with Sir Philip Mitchell. Mitchell had been Governor of Uganda from 1935-1940, and a Maj. Gen. under Gen. Wavell in North Africa. After reading the relevant documents given him by Lord Halifax in Washington, Mitchell concluded that the "Brits" were wrong, visited Admiral Nimitz in Hawaii, and said so.

'Nimitz asked if he meant what he said about Canton.' Mitchell's response: "Admiral, when I talk to you I will always mean what I say. You are the Commander-in-Chief. I will do what you say. If you tell me to burn down Suva, (the capital of Fiji) I will do it... but I'd like to have that one in writing."[294] The final agreement between the two men was: 'No politics west of Hawaii.'

Governor Mitchell told Negley Farson later: "Nimitz was the Commander-in-Chief, and what a great, brilliant commander and delightful personality he was! No better introduction could have been had to a great-hearted man like Nimitz than that Canton rumpus. I was lucky to begin my relations with him on such a foot."[295] When Mitchell arrived in Fiji, he said: "I came out here not to govern but to wage war."[296]

Mitchell also told Negley Farson: "It was in the Pacific, with the Americans, that I first fully realized that the distressing color conflict, which disfigures so much of our life in Africa, is totally unnecessary. There is no color bar, and no color feeling in the Pacific. Each race respects the other and they get on very well together. It made a deep impression on me, and has colored a great deal of my thinking ever since."[297]

Sir Philip Mitchell was Governor of Kenya from 1944 until 1952, the year I left for the United States. Most people agree he was the best Governor East Africa ever had. [298]From Edith Devitt's book, *On the Edge of the Rift*:

---

[294] Negley Farson, *The Last Chance in Africa*, (New York, NY, Harcourt, Brace & Co., 1950), 30.
[295] Ibid., 51
[296] "Sir Harry Charles Luke, KCMG (1884-1969),"
   http://tighar,org/wiki/Sir-Harry-Charles-Luke,-KCMG-(1884-1969), (accessed March 24, 2011).
[297] Negley Farson, *The Last Chance in Africa*, Ibid., 51.
[298] Ibid., 52.

Our thirty-three years of work in Kenya coincided with the emergence of this undeveloped country of many tribes, each with a different language and customs, into a democratic republic. Two forces in the process were the churches and schools introduced by missionaries of several societies. Sir Philip Mitchell, G.C.M.G., M.C.,[299] former governor of Kenya and a resident there many years, in the book <u>Africa Today</u>:

(Edited by C. Grove Haines and published in Baltimore by Johns Hopkins Press, second printing in 1956, on pages 15 and 16) wrote,

"Well, I believe that, fundamentally, it was the Bible, the Bible and the brave, determined, merciful men and women who carried it and its message of hope – hope to the end of the slave-trade, of prevention of epidemics and relief of famine, of protection from the savage whims of tyrants or the obscene orgies of sorcerers – to a people who were living in a brutish lethargy induced by continuous danger, horrors, and sufferings... few men and women could roll themselves in their sleeping hides or mats in their smoky huts at night with any certainty that tribal enemies, slave raiders, marauding elephants, or lurking lions or leopards, would not strike them down in the night, that sorcerers or evil spirits would not slip through between the eaves and the walls and the dangerous darkness and destroy them by magic, that small pox or sleeping sickness would not break out among them, or drought, locusts or flood wipe out the crops so that famine, which could not be relieved, would destroy maybe half a tribe."[300]

---

[299] G.C.M.G. - Knight's Grand Cross of St. Michael & St. George
  M.C. - Military Cross
[300] Edith Devitt, *On the Edge of the Rfit,* Ibid., 10-11.

"Doc"

The transition from life in the United States to Kijabe in 1947 was like stepping through a time warp. The chill in the morning air was invigorating, so a fire in the living room was necessary and cheering. There were no electric lights and no refrigeration. The one luxury in our home was an extra long bathtub with hot and cold running water. The wash basin was a pan, and other bathroom needs were met in "the little gray house in the weeds."

Lighting was from kerosene pressure lights and Aladdin lamps. Water was piped to the house from springs above the station, but drinking water was collected from the metal roof over the kitchen. The phone system was a party line with crank telephones. Vegetables and fruit were delivered to our door in bamboo baskets and dirty wooden boxes, carried by African women using tump lines.[301] Rice and other staples were bought from the Asians near the railroad station, three miles away. Other needs were purchased in Nairobi, 40 miles distant. Some of the roads were paved, but most could be quite exciting, especially in the rainy season.

Kijabe mission station was 2,000 acres on the east side of the Rift Valley. There were schools, a printing press, a hospital, and homes for the staff. Our neighbor, to the north was Grandma Propst. Clo Alice Myers and her mother, Mrs. Jane Huey Myers, arrived at Kijabe with a large contingent of new AIM missionaries on 5 December, 1907. Clo Meyers was a trained teacher, who planned to assist Josephine Hope at the fledgling RVA.

Included in the party of new missionaries was a young man from North Carolina, named Lawson Propst. This man was skillful and self sufficient in making such items as saddles and leather shoes from tanned bushbuck[302] hides. Lawson became involved in brick making, building, maintenance, and working closely with Charles Hurlburt in the construction of Kiambago.

In 1909, romance developed between Lawson and Clo and they were married on 29 June, 1909, three weeks after the Roosevelt fete at Kijabe. Lawson was responsible for managing various construction projects.

---

[301] Tump lines - a broad strap passed across the forehead and over the shoulders for carrying a load on the back. (New World College Dictionary, 4th ed.), 1541.
[302] Bushbucks are 30 – 36 inches high and weigh 100 – 120 pounds.

Three children were born, Charles, James, and Roxanne. The two boys started school at RVA in 1916, staying with their grandmother, Mrs. Myers at Kijabe.

In 1920, Lawson and Clo were called back to Kijabe to develop an agriculture program for raising vegetables. On a plot of land, granted to the mission for that purpose, Lawson raised cabbage, carrots, beets, corn, potatoes, and other things. At 8,000 feet, with rich soil, mists and rains, he was able to raise two crops a year. He developed a system for sending vegetables from Kijabe to other mission stations and merchants as far away as Mombasa. This became a great cash crop, as well as a supply of otherwise scarce produce.

Africans were trained to manage the operation, and young boys were employed, helping them earn school fees. Vegetables were packed in bamboo baskets, and covered with moss. The baskets were then moved to the railroad station by an ox cart with four yoke of oxen, or a mule cart with a team of mules.

By 1931, the three Propst children had been in school in the United States. Before going on furlough, Lawson suffered a head injury from a recalcitrant horse, and was sent to the United States for specialized treatment. His wife Clo, and Grandfather Downing, accompanied him. Unfortunately, he passed away two days after arriving in New York, a casualty in the warfare against darkness in Africa. The effects of his efforts continued for generations in the land of Zinj.

After her husband's death, Grandma Propst returned to Africa, and with the help of an African, trained by her husband, continued the business. In 1947, the mule cart would frequently pass our house on the way to the railroad station. With larger shipments, the two wheeled ox cart was used. The lead yoke of oxen was really a strange pair. The one on the left was a huge animal, yoked with a little runt on the right. The drivers said the little ox was the only one that could make the big one work.

Sunday mornings, we kids occasionally attended the African church service. We sat on benches without a back, men on the left, women on the right. The service was in Kikuyu, which we understood very little. Words in the song books were written phonetically, and we could follow along. The sermon, however, was beyond understanding. The only entertainment was watching blackbirds, we called "stinkies", hop around the rafters. We mentally lined them up with imaginary air rifle sights. The African kids would bring their families' tithe to church: eggs, corn, etc. One boy brought a chicken, and tried to sit on it to keep it quiet!

The Sunday afternoon service, for missionaries and RVA students, was held in the auditorium at Kiambogo, known as the "big swat room." The missionaries would take turns preaching. The most interesting preacher was Grandma Propst's older son, Charles. Shortly before we arrived, he had apparently preached a sermon about King Agag, the Amalekite king Samuel killed when King Saul refused. Apparently, it must have been a rousing presentation! From that time on, Charles was known by capricious brats as Agag. His "graduation" (passing) while on furlough was my first experience with death. I vividly recall the experience, like a wooden box around my head slammed with a huge sledge hammer. I was stunned!

The Africans held prayer meeting on Wednesday evening. A young, African boy brought a Petromax pressure lantern to our house before dark. It was my job to fill and light it. I have a copy of one of these neat German lights in my museum room.

Hunting was a necessary part of our subsistence. Once every two weeks, Paul Lehrer drove down into the valley to shoot meat for RVA. The road to the game area was dirt, so we students could watch his progress by a cloud of dust. A kongoni or hartebeest is about four feet high at the shoulder, and weighs 320-450 pounds. It has a very long face, higher shoulders, low hind quarters, and horns shaped like racing bike handlebars. This was the most common quarry, and two or three would serve the whole station's needs. A hind leg could be hung in the shade and last a week or two in the cool mountain air. Cooked properly, the meat was delicious.

The Lehrers invited me to hunt lions with them on a camping trip behind Mount Suswa. Mr. Lehrer had a 1946 International pick-up with a heavy steel cover over the bed. It had a four-speed transmission, useful for negotiating dry river beds. Two Africans rode on a removable steel seat in the bed. One was Shindo, the cook, the other his helper/skinner. Tents were set up, and a fire started with sage brush roots, dug up by a heavy hoe called a jembi. The camp site was under yellow barked acacia trees, and sage brush leaves perfumed the air. Days were hot and dry, nights were cool. The enchantment of Kenya camp sites still brings fond memories.

A zebra was shot for bait, dragged to a spot away from camp, a pup tent erected near the bait and camouflaged. After supper we crawled into our bivouac and waited, and waited, and waited. The excitement of seeing a wild lion live and up close diminished as drowsiness overpowered me. Mr. Lehrer said it was a lion no-show.

One afternoon, we were joined by "Doc" Propst in his brother's Ford Model A. It had a wooden body with a full length top. A canvas curtain was supposed to keep the dust out, but it was seldom tied down, and jauntily flapped in the breeze. This was the vehicle Charles used to visit the stations that needed his maintenance skills. Once a year he would completely disassemble the car, wash each part with kerosene, and pile all the pieces in a heap. Worn parts were built up with an acetylene torch and reshaped with a file. A neat car! I loved driving it!

I will never forget two other things Doc brought with him: a .22 pistol and the latest copy of the *American Rifleman*. I was hooked, and he was just the man to reel me in.

The two Propst brothers were Westervelt boys. Doc finished high school at John Brown University in Arkansas, attended Colombia Bible College, University of South Carolina, and graduated from the University of Pennsylvania Medical School. He was an army doctor in WW II, and crossed the Atlantic to North Africa on one of the first flights of the Douglas DC-6. Dr. Arthur Barnett, a *Zamzam* survivor and close friend of our family, was on the same flight.

Doc returned to Kijabe a few months before us with WW II surplus gear, such as a Chevrolet 4 x 4 truck, Witte Diesel generators, and machine shop tools. Dad said he had a lot of engineering schooling before finally deciding on medicine. He definitely was a clever engineer.

The 30:06 Springfield rifle he built for himself was a work of art, and the gunsmith work on a Model 52 Winchester .22 rifle was flawless. When Dad shot meat for RVA on his first term, he used a Mannlicher Schoenauer .256 Rifle. He acquired a 9.3 Manser in 1947 but was really too busy to do much hunting. Both Dad and Doc inspired my interest in firearms. I pored over the *East African Sportsman Guide*, memorizing the ballistics of many of the recommended cartridges.

Doc volunteered to upgrade the hot water system at RVA. An old railroad boiler had been used, but was too small. I was his "gofer" on that job. The boiler had a water jacket around the firebox, and heat tubes through the tank. Doc cut the heat tubes out and welded plates over the ends. I still recall the beauty of his welds. It's been more than 60 years now, but I will never forget his words: "Come on, let's get on with it, we're dickin' around!"

Doc acquired three big war surplus diesel generators and with Roy Shaffer Jr's help, set up a central power station at Kijabe. I was hired to wire a single missionary's house. I still remember my satisfaction when

Doc inspected and passed my work. My pay was a 1917 Enfield 30:06 rifle from his collection. That weapon is still in the family.

Safari

Dad was busy building at RVA, and employed me on various projects, such as plumbing a girls' bathroom and maintenance jobs. Consequently, there was little opportunity for hunting and camping. So it was a really big deal when we did go across the valley towards Tanganyika on a big safari.

Our destination was in the Masai reserve in south western Kenya. The Masai are a nomadic tribe with Nilotic[303] features distinct from the Bantu.[304] They are tall and lean, herding cattle on vast grazing lands. Their warriors carried distinctive heavy spears with a broad blade in the front, extending back to the wooden handle between blade and tail piece. If a Masai warrior intended to use his seven foot spear on human beings, he greased it so that it would pass completely through a man.[305] The Masai always had a "standing army" of warriors with proven fighting ability.[306]

There was perpetual war between the Masai and the Kikuyu prior to British Colonialism. The Kikuyu occupying the forests around Mount Kenya were able to hold their own with bows and arrows. In open areas, Masai training and discipline were formidable.

There were 10 people in our party: Doc and his wife, Lila, Gordon Johansen, a huge Norwegian settler and his wife Ruth, two single ladies, Dad, Mom, Ed, and myself. Three rode in the cab of the army truck, six rode in our 1946 Dodge pick-up, and the rest of us rode on top of the gear in the truck with the African help.

The road to the government post at Narok was reasonably smooth, but very dusty. The road beyond was much more rugged, occasionally requiring four-wheel drive. Our Dodge pick-up had a four speed, crash gear box for crossing steep river banks.

Doc had chosen a camp site inside a big loop on the Talek River. As we drove in, a crusty old cape buffalo gave us the eye and departed. The river, with standing pools of water, was flanked by tall acacia trees, and our

---

[303] Nilotic - *Webster's New World College Dictionary*, Peoples living in the valley of the White Nile, including the Dinkas, 975.
[304] Bantu- A group of more than 200 languages belonging to the Niger-Congo language sub-family, including Swahili, Xhosa, and Zulu, Ibid., 114.
[305] Negley Farson, *Last Chance in Africa*, (New York, NY, Harcourt, Brace and Company, 1950), 165.
[306] Ibid., 160.

tents were soon set up. One tent was for the ladies, one for the men, and a third for the food and Africans. Doc left to shoot some bait for lions, and dragged a dead zebra in front of our tent.

It was dark by the time we finished supper, and lions roared around us. We moved hastily from the net dining tent to the men's tent and realized the grass was too high around the bait. Quickly, we stamped it flat, Gordon shining his torch (flashlight) around, quickly headed for the tent, whispering excitedly about several lions out there.

We settled on camp cots with lights out waiting quietly. Then, we heard swishing in the grass, and saw a darker shape move from stage left to the bait. Soon the same thing happened from the right. The sound of voracious lions tearing into a dead zebra, 20 yards away is indescribable and unforgettable. Suddenly, with a loud roar, a third lion bounded in from the rear, cuffed the first two out of the way, and appropriated the feast exclusively. The first lion rolled toward the front of our tent, less than 10 yards away.

Turning on the spotlight, a huge blond maned lion stared back at us with two maneless lions waiting on either side. Wandering around in the background were other lions that made up the pride.

We must have enjoyed this exceptional performance for an hour or so, when our long days travel began taking its toll. The blond maned lion (which we called "Fuzzy Face") showed no sign of being satisfied any time soon, and there were several other hungry lions in the vicinity. The question was: how do you bring down the curtain on such a show? The consensus was: drag the zebra down the road. The next question: how do you do that with a 400 pound lion in the way? A lion can break every bone in an ox's face with one blow of his forepaw. The truck was parked to the left of the bait and the pick-up to the right. Dad decided he would creep out to the truck and run "Fuzzy Face" off while Doc hooked onto the zebra with the pick-up. Dad crawled under the back of the tent on his way to the truck. We waited to hear the truck start and nothing happened. Presently, Dad re-appeared, changed his light shirt for a darker one, and disappeared a second time. We waited again, for what seemed like a long time. We heard the pick-up truck door slam, the engine start and saw the headlights come on. "Fuzzy Face" merely glanced toward the pick-up and continued eating. Dad drove toward the lion with engine racing, horn honking, and lights flashing. "Fuzzy Face" finally stood up but continued eating. The 1946 Dodge pick-up had headlights in round containers mounted on top of the fenders. Dad was concerned he might knock a headlight off and backed off. He rushed the lion a second time, stopped out of reach, and imitated the bark of a male baboon. This unnerved the "King of beasts" and started him on his way.

Dragging the zebra away was anti-climactic. We finally got to sleep, but we had to feed that pride of lions every night until we left. One night the Africans had some meat in their tent, and one of the prides' lesser lights jumped over a row of metal boxes, lay down, and proceeded to dine. One of the Africans woke up, beat on the side of the tent, and called: "Bwana, the lion is here in the tent... I'm the only son of my mother and she's too old to have another!" The lion finally left, but that man spent every night in the metal cab of the truck until we returned to Kijabe. Mother also expressed the desire for something more substantial than a canvas tent under similar circumstances.

Lioness at Lunch

Kapsowar

"Kapsowar commands one of the most magnificent views of any station in the AIM. It looks east across the Great Rift Valley to hills on the opposite side. There is a drop of about 4,000 feet to the floor of the valley below, where the air is hot and the earth arid."[307] At the station, the climate is pleasant and the nights cold.

At 7,000 feet, Kapsowar was selected, in keeping with Peter Scott's vision of establishing mission stations in the hills, and training Africans to evangelize people on the plains.

While attending an inter-field medical meeting at Kapsowar, Doc noticed three donkeys with four gasoline cans, each passing by one evening. This was the local water works in action. Water from the river, at 600-700 feet lower elevation, was hauled by donkeys to the station. Water was so scarce that all missionaries had to bathe in one tub of water, dirtiest one last. Table talk at supper decided bathing order.

Doc heard a waterfall from the station, and determined there was enough power to pump water up hill. A firm of hydraulic engineers, previously consulted, advised that this was impossible.[308] Doc went back home, searched his engineering books, and developed a "water scheme." In his shop at Kijabe, he fabricated a six foot water wheel from steel. The mission gave him leave of absence from medical responsibilities to install the system. He camped for six weeks by the project, and finally got it to work temporarily. After returning from medical meetings at Kijabe, he completed the installation. It pumped 500-600 gallons a day into a large storage tank, through 2,600 feet of pipe. Sixteen years later, another missionary engineer, Herbert Andersen, upgraded the system.

Available water allowed a community to develop around the mission station, increasing its witness and producing a positive impact among the Africans. Pumps were changed from time to time, but the water wheel pumped water for at least 40 years.[309]

Zappers

Doc was fascinated by a story that came from a missionary in Tanganyika. An African was stung by a scorpion, and an old Model T coil

---

[307] Kenneth Richardson, *Garden of Miracles,* (London, Great Britain. Billing & Sons Ltd., 1976), 82 -83.
[308] Ibid., 84.
[309] Information from Doc's oldest daughter, Lila Balisky, April 4, 2011.

was used to neutralize the poison. This started the "little gray cells" in Doc's brain, and he began experimenting with high voltage, low amperage electricity to counteract insect and snake poison. He experimented with piezo-electric igniters to stop the itching of mosquito bites. This progressed to bigger and stronger electrical sources. His final solution was a Chrysler windshield wiper motor that he geared to be cranked by hand. A DC motor, when cranked in reverse, produces DC electricity. The 12-volt was increased by using an auto coil, points, and condenser. The whole unit was installed in a steel 50-caliber ammunition storage box with a wire probe and grounding plate. I assembled one from parts he gave me, and it did indeed work.

He assembled hundreds of these units, and had them used by Wycliffe Bible Translators around the world. They proved effective in both hemo-toxic and neuro-toxic snake venom. The big advantage over anti-venin was unlimited shelf life, and no need for refrigeration.

Today special forces personnel use stun guns for the same purpose. Doc developed the idea, and provided empirical proof that it worked.

Unsung Heroes

"See, I have called by name Bezalel, the son of Uri the son of Hur of the tribe of Judah. I have filled him with the Spirit of God in wisdom, in understanding, in knowledge, and in all kinds of craftsmanship." Exodus 31: 2 & 3 NASB Updated

Bezalel has long been one of my heroes. Moses had a special relationship with his God, but was unqualified to make the tabernacle. It took a specially gifted man to accomplish this project exactly as God ordered. And it is interesting to note that the tabernacle was around for 400 years after both Moses and Bezalel were gone.

The work of Christian Missions in Africa could not have succeeded without the gifted men God sent to the land of Zinj. People without these gifts take the results of craftsmanship for granted. In addition to Doc Propst, here is a short list of some of these unsung heroes:

Herbert Downing: My father was one of the most meticulous craftsmen I know. Every project was a work of art. When he constructed the building that housed the big generators, a piece of paper could not be slipped between the tricky joints of that building's hipped roof. In 1955, the Church at Kijabe was not large enough for the increased attendance induced by the Mau Mau Emergency. He planned and supervised a new church building, which still stands more than 50 years later.

Lawson Propst: The building he helped build is still standing, used for its designed purpose after more than 100 years. The business he started was productive 20 years without his supervision.

Andrew Andersen: An expert carpenter from Denmark. In the early years in Kenya, he built houses, saw-mills, bridges, and dams. He and his wife sequentially established six successful mission stations. Criticized for doing so much manual work, he literally drove himself to an early grave. But in every place he started work, the gospel is being preached today.[310] His legacy continued through his son and grandson, making a difference in the land of Zinj.

Fred Hoyt: In 1928 he installed a water turbine saw-mill and started a school to train Africans to make bricks, saw lumber, and build roads and houses. He enabled Africans in western Kenya to become economically successful. His spiritual leadership produced a much stronger mature church than ministries that over-emphasized evangelism and under-emphasized spiritual maturity.

Wellsley Devitt: This man ran the industrial department at Kijabe. The first building he built was the hospital where I was born. His school-trained craftsmen were able to become successful businessmen. The buildings he constructed still stand.

Aunt Lucile Downing Sawhill, who grew up at Kijabe, wrote: "When the white man first came to Africa, he was admired and respected, not because he was white, but because he had so many possessions and so many skills."[311]

Doc was my friend for more than 50 years. He inspired me to make a difference in every circumstance. His work ethic helped me get on with important things and "quit dickin' around." His life was a consistent example of godly living. He was obedient to God's original orders: "Be fruitful, multiply, spread throughout the earth, dominate, and subdue."[312] Doc definitely made a difference wherever he went, and I'm a better man for having known him.

---

[310] Mary Andersen Honer, *Missy Fundi*, (Lincoln, NE., iUniverse, Inc., 2003), 81 & 84.
[311] Lucile Downing Sawhill, *My Childhood in Africa*, (unpublished), 13.
[312] Genesis 1:28.

"Doc"

Doc Propst

Congo

After spending several hours discussing climate and essential paraphernalia for a proposed hunting trip, President Theodore Roosevelt said to Charles Hurlburt: "Now I want you to know that I am very grateful for the help you have given me in planning my trip to British East Africa. Is there anything, by the way, that I could do while I am still at my position as President that would be of help to your work?" Thinking rapidly of the impasse the protestant Africa Inland Mission was having with a Roman Catholic Belgian government, he said, "If there was any way that you could help us get a permit to continue our work westward toward Lake Chad, it would be very much appreciated…"

The President said: "I think I can do something about that." Within weeks, written permission from the Belgian government was received.[313],[314]

Propitious Poacher

Charles Hulburt had hoped to make the first trip to Congo with John Stauffacher, but urgent business necessitated his visit to America. Mr. Gribble was appointed in his place. This two man reconnaissance team departed Kijabe in May 1910, traveling by train to Kampala with five porters. After 10 days of hard safari, they reached the Church Missionary Society (CMS) station at Hoima in Uganda. Rev. Lloyd, (later Achdeacon) as head of the station, informed them that the British had taken over the West Nile District (on both sides of the Albert Nile) and had placed the whole area under quarantine for sleeping sickness. All access was forbidden. The two men were invited to stay with the Lloyds for a few days.

Several days later, Rev. Lloyd recalled a fishing trip on Lake Albert, and suggested entering Congo from the south. Stauffacher and Gribble were off the next morning, arriving at the Semliki River four days later. The porters reported that local natives warned that all seven would be killed if they crossed the river. The porters were sent back to Hoima, and the two missionaries hired a man with a canoe to take them across.

---

[313] Collection 251, TI. Interview of Herbert Downing by Robert D. Schuster on June 14, 1983.
[314] Lucile Downing Sawhill, My Childhood in Africa, (unpublished), 38.

The crowd of natives on the west bank appeared ominous, but seeing only two unarmed men, allowed them to land. The people in a nearby village appeared even more bellicose, when two armed men in a sort of uniform appeared and asked who they were. "Missionaries," they replied. The soldiers laughed and pacified the crowd. To their astonishment, the visitors were informed that their "Bwana" was waiting up the hill to see them. The two men followed their escorts up a tortuous path until they met a figure seated on a rock. He had red hair, red whiskers all over his face, and spoke with an Irish brogue. Ironically, the first to welcome the AIM's emissaries to the Congo was an Irish ivory poacher.

This burly Irishman led Stauffacher and Gribble to his camp, and invited them to stay as long as they wished. His African wife, Annie, spoke English well, and was an excellent cook. Their host admitted that the Belgian authorities were after him, so he was planning to leave for good. All his possessions were offered to them, if they wished to remain. His camp was within a few miles of the site where the Bogoro mission station was established.

The proposed escape plan was to go down the west side of Lake Albert in dugout canoes, cross over into Uganda, and evade both Belgian and British police. The missionaries were welcomed to accompany him, if prepared to run the risk of being arrested as elephant poachers. With a letter from King Albert of Belgium in their possession, the surveyors decided to go with him.

'Imagine our feelings,' recorded John, 'as we were traveling in perfect comfort with a man who knew the country perfectly, and who could give us information concerning both the natives and the land beyond us, which could not then have been obtained in any other way…'[315]

After several days, they saw the buildings of Mahagi Port and decided, against the advice of their host, to pay their respects to the Belgian officials there. Graciously received by the officials, they ultimately located the hidden canoe left for them, and were re-united with their benefactor. Some distance down the Albert Nile, they embarked on a small tug which took them to Butiaba on the east side of Lake Albert. They returned to Kijabe three months and one day after they set out. Today, almost within sight of the course taken by these two pioneers, there are 10 AIM mission stations in Congo.

---

[315] Kenneth Richardson, *Garden of Miracles*, (London, Great Britain, Billing & Sons Ltd., 1976), 130-137.

Train Trip to Congo

By 1946, there were at least 20 AIM stations in the northeast corner of Congo. After Harold Amstutz' appendicitis attack on the road from Mombasa in 1947, the Amstutz family continued on to Congo to their mission station at Adja. Their son Dave returned, and was enrolled at RVA for ninth grade.

School calendars in Kenya had three-month semesters, with a month' vacation between. Since most schools were boarding schools, this system was designed to enhance family unity. Even though students traveled two to four days en route, family ties were reinforced more frequently and effectively than one three-month vacation at home with busy parents. Students from Tanganyika and the Congo area usually traveled on the Kenya & Uganda Railway and the ships on Lake Victoria. 1 May, 1948, the addition of Tanganyika railroads changed the name to the East African Railroads and Harbours. (EAR & H)

Roger Whittaker, the famous singer, was a student at the Prince of Wales School in Nairobi from 1950 to 1954. Since Cambria is the old poetic name for Wales, the Old Cambrian Society referred to the 'Old Boys' of this school. Under Whittaker's alumnus entry, he is referred to as "arguably the most famous and well known Old Cambrian."

Trains made a big impression on Roger, the schoolboy. In 1982, he recalled train memories in a song entitled *The Good Old E A R & H.* The song was introduced with the following monologues.

When I was a boy, the railway meant so much more to me than the abolition of the slave trade or the opening up of the country, because it was the train that took us up the hills to school and brought us home again or down the hills to the coast and then brought us home again. They were the East African Railways and Harbours or for short the good old E A R & H. No boy ever had a railway quite as fine as mine.[316]

One vacation, instead of watching all the RVA students leave Kijabe, Mother, Ruth Ann, and I boarded the train with Dave Amstutz for a visit to Congo. The train platform at the new Kijabe station was filled with RVA students and the rear echelon of our family. Dad, busy with RVA

---

[316] To School Behind a Garratt – School Trains and the Locomotive That Hauled Them, "Roger Whittaker & 'The Good Old Ear&H'," http://www.oldcambrians.com/Train4.html, (accessed April 11, 2011).

construction projects, couldn't get away. Dave's parents were to meet us in Uganda, and drive us to their home at Adja. They didn't have room for more of our family in their station wagon. Getting away from Kijabe and seeing different parts of Africa was an anticipated adventure. After the customary station delay, we were on our way.

The train stopped at every station, and every platform had its share of vendors and entertainers. In Uganda there were thumb pianos for sale. These were hollow wooden boxes with steel blades of various lengths that vibrated at different frequencies when thumb plucked. A man at another station was beating a big djembe drum. These drums were first made in West Africa with a single goatskin drum head. The body, hand carved from a single piece of hard wood, was shaped like a large goblet. The rounded cup, with the extended tube of the body, forms a device known in physics as a Helmholtz resonator. This structure gives the djembe drum its exceptionally deep bass note. That sound is memorable nearly 60 years later!

Since our train had three classes of coach, the station platforms were usually crowded with Europeans, Asians, and Africans, as meeters or passengers. It was about midday when we arrived at Lira, the end of the line. As planned, we were met by ebullient Jane and her jovial husband, Harold Amstutz.

Our journey continued on a fairly smooth dirt road, northwest to the town of Gulu. Uganda had a much denser population than Kenya, and the roads were crowded with thousands of bicycles. That evening we stopped at a comfortable government rest house. This was one of my first experiences sleeping under a mosquito net, our routine for the next few weeks.

After breakfast, we headed WSW toward the Albert Nile. The head waters of the Nile River flow into Lake Victoria. The Victoria Nile begins at Jinja, flows through shallow Lake Kyoga, and wanders around to the northern end of Lake Albert. Lake Albert and the Victoria Nile then form the Albert Nile, and flow northward. In 15 miles, the river narrowed enough for a ferry to move cars across at Pakwach. This operation was primitive, and the operators took their time. Still, it was a new and interesting experience. The AIM station of Arua, near the western border of Uganda, was about 60 miles northwest of the ferry. We stopped for a short visit, and were served a proper cup of tea by very British missionaries.

Fifteen miles further, we crossed into Congo and arrived at the AIM station at Aru. The missionaries there were close friends of the Amstutz', and we had met their oldest son Paul Pontier, a sailor in the Navy, in 1946.

Accommodations at Adja that night were very comfortable. Harold built a beautiful brick home for his family, and across a small yard, a brick guest house. Traveling with us was Josephine Reed, a single missionary from Kijabe. Miss Reed hailed from Memphis, Tennessee, and brought her accent with her. She had a delightful sense of humor.

Mother and Jane Amstutz were close friends, spending time together in California, and traveling halfway around the world together. In the eulogy written after Mother's death, Jane wrote: "1946 was a fun year for us all! We lived on rationed food and gasoline rations, but we lacked nothing! Mildred and I had fun shopping together. We even bought 'look alike' jackets." With time to relax from their busy schedules, the humor between three witty women was infectious.

Gayle, my sister, wrote a paragraph about Mother that describes why she needed this vacation:

The day was rainy and dark... Suddenly the door opened, and with the gust of wind that made the busy students shiver, came a more pleasant "breath of fresh air" ...my mother, the teacher. On time, as always. Few people realized how much had already been accomplished by this whirlwind of an organizer. Before arriving at school, the family wash might have been done... or an ironing... or letters written to faithful supporters who never wanted for a prompt acknowledgement for their help in missionary work she and Dad had done faithfully for so many years. It is impossible to itemize everything, but she did balance home and school responsibilities with expertise characteristic of a good conductor directing a fine symphony orchestra.

In writing this, I am reminded of my role in Mother's tight schedule. We had to generate our own electricity at the time, and I was responsible for fueling and starting the "put-put" generator for her washing machine. One morning I emptied the jerry can into the generator, and the tank was almost, but not quite full. Getting more fuel entailed siphoning with a rubber hose from a 55 gallon drum. That always meant going to school with the taste of gasoline in my mouth all morning. I decided the tank level was "close enough" and went off to school. Needless to say, I guessed wrong and earned my last "hiding!" Mother arrived at school on time, but she was in a foul mood. She had to leave half a tub of wet clothes in her machine. It must have been grace that allowed me to go on this vacation with her!

Adja Church

Harold trained his African workers in the art of building, by constructing his home and a guest house. His goal was a beautiful brick church that seated 2,000 people. He used pit sawyers to cut tropical hardwood for interior furnishings. The result was the Adja Church, a stately brick cathedral, built to last.

I must admit, church attendance was a bit distracting for a teenage boy. As at Kijabe, males sat on one side of the church and females on the other. The distraction, the female attire! All the women wore was a grass bustle at the back, and fresh green leaves below the waist in the front. That was the extent of their wardrobe. I was glad convention in my culture included better coverage. Guessing was better than knowing!

My first motorcycle experience was with Amstutz' old *Indian*, with a foot clutch and a stick shift. My Honda *Dream* in Japan was much more convenient, but the Indian was still an adventure. I was older and wiser after my previous motor scooter mishap!

We had fun hunting guinea fowl, making knives from old files, and pole vaulting with bamboo poles. Good food, good humor, and pleasant weather all left an indelible memory.

Rethy

The Amstutz' planned a return trip, visiting three more mission stations. Seventy-five miles south of Adja was the lovely station of Rethy. Located in the line of hills on the west side of Lake Albert, Rethy became the headquarters for AIM's Congo field. At 7,000 feet above sea level, it was higher, healthier, and cooler than Aba, Charles Hurlburt's headquarters. Higher elevations of mission stations were in keeping with Peter Scott's original vision for the AIM.

Rethy Academy, a school for Congo missionary children, was started in about 1928. Encountering similar difficulties to RVA's early years, it was not properly organized until Wheaton College Professor, Earl Winsor, became headmaster after 1949.[317] Well established, it took scholars through junior high, in preparation for high school at RVA.[318]

Oicha

Two hundred miles south of Rethy is Oicha, the southern-most AIM station in Congo. Oicha is located in the Ituri Jungle, a dense tropical rain forest on the northeast lip of the Congo River basin. It covers about 24,000 square miles, of which 20% is set aside as Okapi Wildlife Reserve.

Unknown to science until about 1900, the okapi are the only mammals alive related to the giraffe. They are found only in the Ituri Rain Forest. With a reddish brown coat, legs and rear end striped like a zebra, they are considered to be a short necked forest giraffe. Like a giraffe, they have a long velvety tongue to eat leaves off branches. In some cases, their tongues are 12 inches long. Illusive and solitary, Okapi communicate with infrasound vocalizations in the 14 Hz range. Inaudible to the human ear,

---

[317] Gerald Hugh Haddock, *Mine is a Missionary Family*, (unpublished), 14-15.
[318] Kenneth Richardson, *Garden of Miracles*, Ibid., 251.

these sounds are distinguishable at great distances by Okapi. Since 1960, the Dallas Zoo in Texas has been successful in breeding these endangered animals, producing more than 30 calves.[319]

The Ituri Forest is also populated by traditional nomadic tribes like the Mbuti and Efe Pygmy hunters. They are considered some of the few remaining "forest people" of the world.[320] Mbuti pygmies are almost exclusively hunter-gathers, and do not exceed four feet ten inches in height. In my museum is a very broad metal-tipped spear, designed by these little men for killing elephants. My spear was given to me by Fred Hoyt on his last visit to Kijabe. Pygmy poison can even bring down elephants.

In 1934, Dr. Carl Becker, a successful medical practitioner from Pennsylvania, founded a medical center at Oicha. His purpose was to serve the needs of pygmies, establishing a leprosarium in a 1,100 acre village, the largest leper community, save one in that province.[321] Specialists and medical missionaries from all over the world came to observe his work, and borrow from his research. Serving as the only resident medical doctor at the hospital, Dr. Becker performed more than 3,000 operations, and delivered hundreds of babies each year.

Dr. Becker practiced the maxim: 'Never do anything which an African can be trained to do.' He put a great deal of faith in, and reliance upon African workers, and trained many for very responsible positions. "As a teacher, Dr. Becker was a strange amalgam of infinite patience, inveterate optimism and nearly impossible standards."[322]

Patient with his students' shortcomings, he expected high standards from his staff, and they usually measured up. The effectiveness of his methods was tested by the fire of Communist-inspired Simbas, driving Europeans from the country. Returning at the first opportunity, Dr. Becker found his hospital effectively run by his trained Africans. [323]

---

[319] All About Okapi – Fun Facts, Questions, Answers, Information, http://www.funtrivia.com/en/subtopics/All-About-Okapi-228170.html. (accessed April 20, 2011).
[320] Ibid.
[321] GFA Missions, "Dr. Carl Becker – (1884 -?)," http://www.gfamissions.org/missionary-biographies/becker-dr-car/-1884.html. (accessed April 20, 2011).
[322] Dick Anderson, We felt like Grasshoppers, (Nottingham, Great Britain, Cox & Wyman Ltd, 1994), 123.
[323] Ibid., 126.

As with most successful servants of God, Dr. Becker was a man of prayer. Beginning at 5:00A.M., he spent an hour getting his 'directions' for that day, listening carefully to the voice of his Heavenly Father.[324] One of the main purposes of Christ's resurrection was to open the way for every one of the Father's children to converse directly with Him. No longer are rules and regulations sufficient for His purpose in our lives. Each needs specific guidance for effective combat against the kingdom of darkness. As John Piper has said: "Until we know that life is war, you cannot know what prayer is for."[325] No two cells in the human body are identical, and no two people in the body of Christ are the same. Each needs to be specifically directed by the Head, and prayer is a primary means of guidance.

In 1948 the AIM in Congo was confronted with the issue of accepting or rejecting government subsides for schools. This was similar to the issues in Kenya decades before. A deep division of opinion was revealed at field conferences. The only solution was collectively submitting the impasse to the Father through prayer. The result was a decisive vote in favor of accepting government appropriations.[326] Every church dilemma is quickly resolved when the voice of the Head is heard and obeyed.

Our purpose at Oicha was to attend a missionary wedding. Dave Amstutz, a gifted pianist, had been invited to play for this ceremony. After the celebration, we were invited to hunt monkeys in the forest with the pygmies. We were successful!

Ruwenzori

When John and Florence Stauffacher decided to retire from active missionary service, they went to Congo, where their two sons were serving. Raymond and Claudon had both attended RVA and the Westervelt Home, as two of Josephine Hope Westervelt's first 11 young men. The older Stauffachers settled at Ruwenzori (Mevenda) on the foothills of the Mountains of the Moon. This was close to the spot where John crossed the Semlika River into Congo in 1910. There they dedicated themselves to serving missionaries who would enjoy cool, restful, quiet holidays at that delightful station. This was our final stop in Congo on our return to Kijabe.

---

[324] Ibid., 123.

[325] Prayer, :"Prayer and the Christian,"
   http://www.inplainsite.org/htm/prayer.html. (accessed November 23, 2011).

[326] Kenneth Richardson, Garden of Miracles, Ibid., 162.

The Ruwenzori Mountains rise along the border of Uganda and Congo. Apart from being one of the main sources of the Nile, they are among the strangest and most mysterious mountains in the world.[327] The highest peak, Mount Stanley, is 16,761 feet above sea level, almost a 1,000 feet higher than Mount Blanc, the highest Alp. They are some of the biggest block mountains in Africa.[328] Block mountains are produced by faulting and the uplifting of large blocks of rock.[329] Both, the two higher mountains in Africa, Mount Kilimanjaro (19,340 feet) and Mount Kenya (17,058 feet), were volcanic eruptions.

According to local native language, "Ruwenzori" means "The King of Mists" or the "Rain Maker." These mysterious mountains are frequently obscured by clouds. Though they are located on the equator, they are capped with snow year round. When Ptolemaeus made his famous world map in the 2nd century A.D., he put a huge mountain in the middle of Africa and described it as "the Mountain of the Moon, feeding the source lakes of the Nile with its snow." Both the description and the position on the map are astonishingly correct in view of the geographic knowledge of his day.

Snow, glaciers, tropical rain forests, sinister mists, and violent thunderstorms, coupled with clouds, hid these mountains from non-African eyes until 1888. These contribute to the mystery of the Mountains of the Moon.

Most memorable was the fruit served at Ruwenzori. Papayas were at least 10 inches long, and sweeter than I have ever eaten. Bananas were huge, and red plantain fruit was a foot long. The variety, size, and sweetness of fruit at our departing breakfast made a lasting impression.

Our journey back to the railroad in Uganda took us along a river that had hundreds of hippos. We crossed Lake Kyoga on another ferry, and boarded the train for Kijabe.

Dad's big surprise for Mother was a built-in closet in their bedroom. Recounting the adventures and exploits of our time apart, provided interesting conversations at mealtime. Incidentally, supper was more formal in our home than others. We always ate together, and I was expected to wear a jacket. Table talk was always lively, and our

---

[327] Erik Pontoppidan, Ruwenzori, "Trekking Back to the Age of the Dinosaurs," http://www.poity.dk/ruwe-eng.htm. (accessed April 27, 2011).

[328] Magelah Peter, "The Ruwenzori Mountains, Africa," http://www.eoearth.org/article/The-Ruwenzori-Mountains,-Africa. (accessed April 27, 2011).

[329] Webster's New World College Dictionary, 157.

recollections were stimulating enough to interest the whole family in a second trip to Adja.

Congo by Camper

Our 1946 Dodge pickup was brought into Kenya by Welles Devitt. He had removed the rear fenders and installed side boxes. When he replaced the truck, he kept the boxes for his new vehicle. Dad built some flat wooden fenders, an aluminum covered plywood top, and a comfortable removable seat for three in the back. Wooden frames, with expanded metal, protected things in the back from pilferage on trips to Nairobi.

Camper

For the trip to Congo, Dad neatly altered the truck to provide sleeping accommodations for six people. Our last family vacation in Africa was a safari to Congo. I had gotten my drivers license in Nairobi, and shared the driving with Dad. It really was a well earned respite for Mother and Dad, and we always enjoyed a special camaraderie with Jane and Harold.

One of the highlights was a visit to the AIM station at Aba. This station was opened in 1918, and Charles Hurlburt transferred the office of the Central Executive Council from Kijabe to Aba in 1919. Aba is situated on a rise which dominates the surrounding country. On top of the hill is a huge rock used by Mr. Hurlburt and others as a quiet, secluded place of prayer.

Most memorable was our visit to the Elephant Domestication Center at Gangala-na-Bodio, 75 miles west of Aba. In 1900, King Leopold II sent to India for several mahouts (elephant drivers or keepers) and their elephants to be shipped to Congo. The Indian elephants soon died of African diseases, but the mahouts stayed. The king started the African Domestication Program in 1906 with hopes of using elephants to haul freight from the Congo River to the Nile.

It is economically far more sensible to catch elephants wild and train them, than to breed them in captivity like horses. It is not merely that a female elephant's pregnancy lasts 22 months, and that she would be practically useless for work for more than a year on the occasion of each pregnancy. More important than this is the fact that, once her baby is born, the mother elephant can think of nothing else, and thereafter, for a period of years again, is always dropping whatever she is doing at the moment to go trumpeting off in rage or anxiety to discover what has happened to her offspring. [330]

The camp was managed by a Belgian major, who trained his men to capture young bulls. The capture party included 30 to 40 men, and 8 to 10 big elephants. Carts carrying heavy ropes, chains, and supplies were pulled by pairs of elephants.

Working downwind of the elephants herd, a camp was set up just before dawn. The men were armed with guns and blank cartridges to scare the elephants. Dressed in rough clothes, heavy puttees to protect their legs, and carrying ropes, the men moved into position without being seen. At a given signal, the men rushed toward the large herd and the hunt was on.

For hours, men would run with the herd, and lasso hind feet with ropes, anchoring them around trees. When immobilized, two big monitor elephants were maneuvered along side and roped to the captive. The touch of these monitors calmed the prisoner, and the long march back to

---

[330] Gangala-na-Bodio Elephant Domesfication Center in Congo, http://www.elepahnt.se/location2.php?location-id-=703&show=1. (accessed May 3, 2011).

camp began. Elephants are probably, of all animals, the most difficult to train. Training methods developed by the Zande tribesmen are very different from anything seen in India. Their methods were extremely painstaking, requiring day-long patience month after month.

We watched as the trainers took their elephants to the river for baths. These elephants seemed much smaller than the Aberdere elephants near Kijabe. At one time, there were more than 80 elephants working near the Center in Congo, maintaining roads and plowing fields. As of last report, only four remain.

Domestic Elephants

The return trip to Kijabe was uneventful; we were soon engrossed in the routine of another semester at school. Gayle had finished high school and was working in the store at RVA. I had skipped sixth grade in 1947, and with extra effort, was able to graduate in 1952 to attend college in the fall with her. Five and a half of the best years of my life were drawing to a close! It was time to leave home, and hopefully grow into manhood.

Ready for College

Barrington College

Shortly after Bethel Bible Training School moved from Spencer to Dudley, Massachusetts in 1923, its founder, E.W. Kenyon, resigned as president. The position was offered to Paul Rader, evangelist and pastor of the Chicago Gospel Tabernacle (CGT), who chose to stay in Chicago. Twenty-five year old Howard W. Ferrin, one of his co-workers, became president of Dudley Bible Institute in 1924.

President Ferrin was born in Auburn, New Hampshire in 1898. He attended Concord High School, excelling in football and track. His record for most touchdowns stood for more than 80 years. Initially, he was inclined towards coaching, but after graduating from Northwestern University in Chicago in 1921, he began working with Paul Rader.

In the 1920's, Paul Rader was one of the most dynamic evangelists in North America. He was a pioneer in the use of new media (such as radio) to evangelize. His CGT was one of the most active churches in Chicago, with an outreach to all parts of the city. His ministry impacted a multitude of lives, many of whom became evangelists, pastors, and missionaries. His influence affected Howard Ferrin, who became the superintendent of CGT.[331]

President Ferrin moved Dudley Bible Institute to Capitol Hill in Providence, Rhode Island in 1929, renaming it Providence Bible Institute (PBI). Dr. Ferrin was also president of the North American Home Council of AIM from 1947-1957. In 1948, he toured the AIM mission field with Dr. F. Carlton Booth, the head of the PBI music department. Dad was the photographer for their tour through Kenya. This was Gayle's and my first exposure to PBI as a possible school option after RVA.

Using Grandfather Downing's recommended procedure for determining God's direction, I was convinced that PBI was the next undertaking in His plan for me. My thinking was to return home, and a Bible College credential was a pre-requisite. With aspirations toward engineering, like Dad and "Doc," I hoped to proceed with a degree in that field. God has never revealed the whole plan, just the next step. Little did I suspect what was in store for me!

---

[331] http://www.wheaton.edu/bgc/archives/does/rader./a.html, Box J. Folder 52, (accessed May 14, 2011).

Freshman Year

Dad gave Gayle and me each $100 to start school, which meant we both had to work. Gayle served in the dining room, and I was janitor in the radio station on campus. Mine was actually a neat job. I was able to read the news as it came from the Associated Press on the teletype machine. Imagine my interest when news of the Mau Mau outbreak came. My RVA schoolmates at Kijabe found themselves involved in a hot war.

We were informed that our house at Kijabe was destroyed by fire. A kerosene stove flared up in the bathroom and ignited curtains. The adults were at a prayer meeting, and refused to be disturbed by school children. Little could have been done, however, since there was no fire fighting equipment on the station. Cedar shingles soon ignited and burned rapidly. Attempts were made to rescue some of the furnishings until my ammunition collection began to "cook off!" Most of our keepsakes were destroyed, including Grandfather Downing's diaries. Fortunately, fires cannot destroy memories!

House on Fire

Christian service was part of the curriculum at PBI, so Gayle and I sang in the Presbyterian Church Choir. Music was a major emphasis, and all freshmen were in the Oratorio Chorus, singing parts of *Handel's Messiah*. Dr. Booth joined us, and stood next to me in the tenor section. Whether I needed remedial help, or whether he heard potential, he offered to help pay for voice lessons. I will always be grateful for the influence this great man had on my life. Music has provided many travel opportunities both in college and in the Navy.

Most of the freshman courses were unexciting, with one exception. Oral communication was taught by Dr. Richard K. Curtis, a WW II P-51 fighter pilot. I have used *Monroe's Motivated Sequence Outline* for speeches, reports, and military communications ever since: (1) Attention, (2) Need, (3) Satisfaction, (4) Visualization, and (5) Action. This has been useful for more than 50 years.[332]

Depressing city life in a northern climate, with a gloomy winter approaching, induced a melancholy countered by long lonely walks. Realizing that my carefree, exciting life was history, I escaped the PBI campus by strolling the Rhode Island capitol grounds. This unfamiliar cold reduced my resistance, resulting in a malaria attack. Once exposed, malaria stays in the bloodstream seemingly forever. I ended up in the school health center.

Malaria attacks usually result in a series of sweats and chills. One minute you perspire profusely; the next, your teeth are chattering with cold. I told the doctor what my problem was, he said that was impossible. After he left, I asked the nurse to get some quinine from the drugstore. That night my bed was soaked with perspiration! After they replaced the sheets, the fever was gone, and I was "limp as lettuce." I had brought some of Africa to America with me.

Ours was a close knit family. Separation from the others strengthened the ties between Gayle and me. Initially, we were a puzzle to our classmates. Their first assumption was that we were married. Next, they concluded we were twins. There were advantages to our relationship, especially for Gayle. Gayle was a cute, vivacious 20 year-old. Typically, there were young males engaged in the mating game, so I was a suitable date when Gayle was not interested. This was a two-way street, when one girl considered Gayle an "obstacle." Personally, I was not interested, just busy, broke, and bored! I had two dates in three years!

---

[332] http://changingminds.org/techniques/overall/monroe-sequence.htm, (accessed May 14, 2011).

Christmas vacation was our first family reunion. This involved an 800-mile drive. Special student, Phil Petersen, had a Ford convertible heading for Chicago. He planned to drive straight through, and drove the first day. My stint was driving all night to eastern Ohio, where Dad met us. Driving the Pennsylvania Turnpike, in snow at night, was a new experience. Home was a welcome respite from travel and school.

Though the courses were less than thrilling, and there were no absorbing math courses, I did study and barely made the honor roll. Summer vacation was spent with the family in Ohio. Brother John Martin was born 20 March, 1953, when Mother was 45 years old. The whole family was pleased with his arrival. With the new baby, the folks planned to extend their one year furlough to two.

A trip to the west coast, to visit friends and supporters, required a 21-foot house-trailer towed by our 1948 Chevrolet. The Downing family of seven set out from Coshocton, three in front, three in back, and a three month old baby suspended in a hammock, over the knees of the rear passengers. There were neither seatbelts nor child-car seats in 1953.

The two college students found it a welcome family adventure. One of the siblings considered the inconveniences, difficulties, and close quarters unbearable. It was our last family adventure, less stressful than our previous west coast trip. There was no time constraint, and I enjoyed being an assistant driver.

Sophomore Year
(Providence Barrington Bible College)

By 1950, PBI was outgrowing its campus. Dr. Ferrin and the Board of Trustees bid $331,001 for Belton Court, a 150 acre estate in Barrington, RI. Their bid was one dollar higher than the closest competitor! The property became known as the "Miracle Dollar Campus," and the mortgage was burned 30 May, 1953. Both campuses were used, with the Barrington campus accommodating sophomore students. So the ambience of my second year was a vast improvement.

Originally built as the Peck Mansion in 1905 by Martin & Hall, it was a residence until PBI bought it. Its architectural style was colonial revival, Queen Anne, Stick/Eastlake. The buildings had ivy-covered natural stone walls and red slate roofs. Interior walls were paneled with dark wood and carved accents. It was the only time in my life I lived in a wealthy man's mansion.

I shared a bedroom with three other men. Our large black and white tiled bathroom even included a sitz bath. The view from our room overlooked broad lawns, stone walls, and green shrubbery. Down the hill was an arm of Narragansett Bay. Across a lawn, on the other side of our buildings, was a wooded area with a delightful running trail. It really was elegant!

Barrington Second Year Dorm

My jobs included kitchen clean-up and dishwashing. Dr. Ferrin's oldest son began working on a black and white movie entitled *Revolt in Berlin*. I was employed as an assistant carpenter. The film was a fictional story of a communist-minded German girl who finally realized Christianity was the only answer. It was an interesting learning experience. Part of the film was shot along the bay, which was very cold. There is nothing more bone chilling than the damp cold in New England! African temperatures did not prepare me for such misery.

Dad was the principal speaker at the annual missionary conference. His emphasis was: Our God, who is powerful "to the pulling down of strongholds." Dad's delivery was low key, conversational style. He definitely commanded attention. The folks were planning their return to Africa, so this was one of the last times spent together. Dad took this opportunity to give me a copy of F.B. Meyer's *The Consecrated Life*. This helped take the <u>effort</u> out of Christian obedience, and is included as Appendix B.

Five members of our family departed New York on the *SS African Planet* on 19 March, 1954. Gayle and I were graciously allowed to go and see them off. It was now just Gayle and I as family. This was a time when PBI was the 'providence' of God to help keep spiritual equilibrium.

Christian service responsibilities were fulfilled in vocal quartets. Gayle was in a mixed quartet, singing soprano. She had a sweet soprano voice. She struck up a friendship with the baritone, Kendall Grass, which ultimately ended in matrimony.

Melodymen

My quartet was known as the "Melodymen." Don Goodhart was 1st tenor, Warren Whitney 2nd tenor; I sang baritone, and George Huber bass. Bill Maxim was a gifted pianist. I have never forgotten his arrangement of the western song; *You Laid Your Hand Mighty Lord on the Range*. Our signature song was:

Good bye, our God is watching o'er you
Good bye, His mercies go before you,

Good bye, and we'll be praying for you.

So goodbye, may God bless you.

The harmony was euphonic and fun. We were away from school on engagements almost every weekend, traveling the east coast from Maine to Pennsylvania. This was my most satisfying college experience.

Summer vacation was spent in Coshocton. Uncle Merrel made arrangements for us to stay in an apartment over the garage of M.D. Custer, a wealthy banker from his church. (These were our years to stay in the "digs" of the affluent.) Judge Ross helped us get summer jobs. I worked a swing shift at the Buckeye Fabric and Finishing Company, and Gayle worked in the office of Surveyor Aston Stewart, a family friend.

Our apartment was in the upper end of town, and transportation was a black bicycle brother Ed had fixed up. I recall riding home during a summer storm one afternoon. The street was shaded by large trees, when suddenly I heard a sharp crack over head. I kept peddling and glanced over my shoulder. A long branch, six inches in diameter, had fallen completely across the street where I had just been. It was a most stimulating experience. I whooped in triumph over my narrow escape!

Mrs. Custer was one of the sweetest women I ever knew. I never heard her say anything unkind about anyone. They couldn't have been more cordial to Gayle and me. We worked with a young people's group in the church, and the Custers opened their home to these kids for a party. They let us use one of their two cars, when not needed, and the apartment was commodious and comfortable.

The second year of college was definitely an improvement over the first, even to the point of willingly returning to the Providence campus.

Third Year

On the morning of 31 August, 1954, Hurricane Carol crashed ashore in southern New England. This was the most destructive hurricane since the Great New England Hurricane of 1938, leaving 65 people dead in her wake. Sustained winds of 80 to 100 MPH roared across Rhode Island. Homes along the shore had roofs blown off by high winds, which gusted to over 125 mph. The strongest wind ever recorded on Block Island occurred during Carol, when winds gusted to 135 MPH. The storm arrived shortly after high tide, causing widespread tidal flooding. As in the 1938 hurricane, downtown Providence was flooded under 12 feet of water. Rainfall amounts ranged from two to five inches. Nearly 4,000 homes,

3,500 automobiles, and 3,000 boats were destroyed. This all took place just before we returned from Ohio. Clean-up continued after school started.[333]

Residents of Providence appeared aloof to the transients of PBI. At first, I believed it was the effect of the big Catholic Church, between the campus and the capitol. It could have been typical New England reticence. This all changed with Hurricane Carol. Everyone pitched in to clean up the mess, and was much more willing to chat. Natural disasters have a way of uniting people.

My room was on the second floor, shared with one roommate. We acquired an FM radio, and were quite compatible. I worked at the Food Basket Grocery Store, a 20 minute walk downtown. This involved stocking shelves, sweeping, running a cash register, and taking inventories.

By this time, I had given up on seeing practical value in Greek philosophy. I learned much later, 'Zeno's Paradox of Motion' was quite easily solved with calculus. The blending of Greek philosophy with the Bible appeared to solve no problems. On the contrary, division and contention ensued. My attitude resulted in less than stellar grades. All I wanted was to get my diploma and move on.

The one bright light was music. I had two semesters of voice. The first semester Eunice Thompson, a 1953 graduate, was my teacher. The second, William Hoyt, one of the leading male vocalists, instructed me. As usual for music students, a recital was required. Halfway through the program, I realized I had forgotten my music. I ran back to my room to retrieve it, but was too late for my programmed time. Everyone was informed and amused. I was to sing two songs; the first a tedious Italian song, which I dutifully got through. The second was *The Hills of Home* by Oscar J. Fox. This has a very difficult piano accompaniment which Faculty School of Music, Frank Converse, easily read. This really was <u>my</u> song, for I still missed Kijabe. So I gave it my best shot. Gayle commented in her book: "I was so proud... when Glenn got a standing ovation at a college recital for singing, *The Hills of Home.*"[334] I don't remember; I was just glad to have finished.

Three of the previous quartet made up the "King's Choraleers." Additionally, we had Ron Devries singing bass, soloist Lois Harding, from the film department, and faculty member Mary Alice Goodridge, at the

---

[333] National Weather Service Forecast Office, Boston, MA, "Hurricane Carol (CAT 2 – August 31, 1954),"

http://www.eth.noaa.gov/box/hurricane/hurricaneCarol.shtml, (accessed May 18, 2011).

[334] G.D. Grass, *A Christian Family, Lessons Learned,* (unpublished), 1-2 & 1-4.

piano. Our itinerary again took us up and down the east coast from Maine to Pennsylvania. We were a "big time quartet," with charcoal gray suits and matching ties.

Gayle was in a quintet with a ladies trio, a male tenor and bass. For some reason, Gayle was spending more and more time with Kendall Grass. She finally decided to take his last name towards the end of the summer.

The Torch

Gayle and I worked on the staff of the college yearbook known as *The Torch*. Gayle was make-up editor, and I was an assistant. J. Herbert Kane, the faculty advisor, was a graduate of Moody Bible Institute. He and his wife served as missionaries in China from 1935-1950. This was during the Sino-Japanese War, WW II, and the Communist Nationalist China Civil War. Dr. Kane was professor of Missions and New Testament at Providence. He went on to write texts on biblical contextualization and cross cultural ministry for seminaries and mission training schools.[335]

A man of principle, Dean Kane was defending his conservative position in a debate against progressives, when he was accused of dragging his feet against progress. I will never forget his response: "I only wish I were a centipede, so I could drag more feet!" I am beholden to this man for taking my older daughter, Ann, 'under his wing' when she was a student at Miami University in Oxford, Ohio.

My responsibilities were photographing Barrington campus and sports. This was the first year our school was able to defeat arch rival Gordon College in basketball. It was such a big deal; I recorded the event with eight pages of pictures. The pictures taken of Barrington campus cover six pages, a pleasant reminder of my most memorable year in college. It wasn't until now that I realized an informal *Torch* staff picture shows me behind the only two girls I dated in college: Sylvia Mitchell and Bethia Reoch. Gayle was busy with her fiancé, and didn't need my escort services.

---

[335] Christian Courses, "J. Herbert Kane, L.H.D.," http://www.christiancourses.com/professors/dr-j-herbert-kane, (accessed May 4, 2011).

Torch Yearbook Staff

In light of what followed, it was prescient that the 1955 *Torch* was dedicated to Marine Staff Sergeant and Professor Gordon J. Eaton; that the members of the basketball team were called Warriors; and that Dr. Ferrin's hand-written charge, in the 1953 *Torch,* encouraged men to be "Strong hearted Davids" conquering Goliaths, and women "Valiant Deborahs" leading the people of God on to victory.[336]

Reflections

For years, my frustrations in college colored my memories. Considering my conviction that this was God's plan, it seems appropriate to consider the advantages. <u>Most important</u> was finishing the course. On 31 May, 1955, I received a three year diploma in Bible, Theology, and Christian Education.

A nother advantage was reaffirmation of the authenticity, accuracy, and reliability of the Bible, as a divine document. The only proscribed book in the United States public schools since 1963 is the Bible.[337] By any measure, *

---

[336] *The Torch*-1953. Vol 15, 11.
[337] John Daniel, *Scarlet and the Beast,* (Longview, TX, Day Publishing, 2007), 234. ". . .the 1962/1963 Supreme Court decision outlawing Bible reading and prayers in pubic schools."

Yearbook Picture

the United States has demonstrated the law of entropy[338] in a rapid decline. The Bible must be dangerously inimical[339] to the designs of the seed of the serpent. The Bible reveals a God who is all-powerful, all-knowing, pervasive throughout the universe, eternal, and loving. Should every human on earth band together in opposition to this God, they would lose, for every human is mortal. Banning the Bible is proof of Romans. 1:18 (R.E.B.). Since men have a choice, it seems only reasonable to side with the strongest force.

Most enjoyable was learning to sing properly. Most useful was learning to organize thought for speeches and writing. I also learned that I am not, nor do I aspire, to ever be a philosopher or theologian.

Lois Teuscher, one of Gayle's roommates, lived in Illinois, traveling with us on vacations. Years later, Lois was instrumental in introducing me to her younger sister, Thelma, known as "Tweet." Tweet became my greatest asset and the greatest advantage of my college experience, and throughout my life.

My grandchildren believe learning to "hambone" was my greatest accomplishment, and "Tweet" insists I explain its acquisition. My freshman room was on the third floor of dorm 59. Just down the hall was Reggie Winbush from East Orange, New Jersey, a third year student studying to be a pastor. He could beat out the most fascinating rhythm with a limp wrist slapping thigh and chest. The key was the limp wrist. After a while, I got the 'hang of it' and we entertained ourselves frequently. He had this little poem he chanted with the beat: Hambone walk, Hambone talk,

---

[338] Entropy - a process of degeneration marked by increasing degrees of uncertainty, disorder, chaos specifically a process regarded as the inevitable terminal stage in the life of a social system or structure. (*Webster's New World College Dictionary*), 475.
[339] Inimical - like an enemy, hostile, unfriendly; in opposition; adverse. Ibid., 735.

Hambone eatin', with a knife and fork.
Some people say, that the preacher don't steal,
I caught the preacher in the watermelon field.
Eatin' the watermelon, down to the rind,
Shoutin' "Hallelujah," havin' a mighty fine time!

And that's the story of how this *American African* learned to hambone from an *African American*!

The Next Step

The Korean War started on 25 June, 1950, and ended on 27 July, 1953. It was an indirect war between Truman and Stalin, between Capitalism and Communism,[340] between the seed of the woman and the seed of the serpent. According to History channel estimates, it took the lives of more than five million people.[341] All the fighting occurred around the 38th parallel in Korea, not in Washington or Moscow.

Norman Podoretz contends that the "Cold War" was more precisely WW III, beginning in 1947 and ending in 1989.[342] A segment of that war which destroyed more than five million people in three years can hardly be called a "Cold War."

Shortly after taking office in 1953, President Eisenhower lifted the naval blockade around Taiwan. This had been in place to prevent conflict between Nationalist Chinese Chiang Kai-shek, and mainland China. In August 1954, Chiang moved his troops to the Nationalist stronghold islands of Quemoy and Matsu. One month later, Mao Tse-tung ordered the bombing of these offshore islands. Mao had lost a million people in Korea[343] with no territorial gain. He believed that an international crisis could benefit China. Mao also wanted to manipulate the Taiwan situation to demonstrate China's independence from the Soviet Union.

Taiwan and the Quemoy, Matsu islands became the focal point of one of the most contentious episodes of WW III. Gordon H. Chang, professor of history at Stanford University, persuasively demonstrated 'on the basis of newly available documentary evidence', that *Eisenhower actually brought the country to the 'nuclear brink', far closer to war than a distraught public feared in 1955, closer than Eisenhower acknowledged in his own memoirs, and closer than most historians have heretofore even suspected. "He" was*

---

[340] "How Many People Died in the Korean War," http://www.howmanypeopledied.net/2010/10/how-many-peopledied-in-the-Korean-war.htm. (accessed May 23, 2011).

[341] Ibid., 6 of 11.

[342] Norman Podhoretz, *World War IV*, (New York, NY, Doubleday, 2007), 5.

[343] "How Many People Died in the Korean War," http://www.howmanypeopledied.net/2010/10how-many-people-died-in-the-Korean-war, (accessed May 22, 2011).

privately determined to defend the islands and to use nuclear weapons if necessary."[344]

On 31 March, 1955 General Curtis LeMay, commander of the Strategic Air Command, provided eerie details in a cable to General Nathan Twining, the head of the Air Force. One wing of B-36 bombers was in position in Guam, with other wings on alert in the United States. A bombing plan was ready for immediate execution. Target selections had been made and coordinated with responsible commanders.[345]

After Chang's study, the Associated Press asked "a former senior counselor to President Eisenhower" for comment. His response confirmed that "the President was definitely considering" the use of atomic weapons. The plan was to drop several "small" (Hiroshima-size) atomic bombs on coastal Chinese air bases in the vicinity of Queymoy and Matsu. The CIA estimated this would cause a total of 12 to 14 million civilian casualties. Anticipated public reaction to such horrific collateral damage proved to be a delaying caution.

Secretary of State, John Foster Dulles, admitted: "Of course we were brought to the verge of war… If you run away from it, if you are scared to go to the brink, you are lost." The Peoples Republic of China changed course, proposing negotiations rather than war, effectively ending the crises. "The reasons for this historic decision are unknown."[346]

What Next?

During my last semester at Barrington much thought was given about the next step. As required by law, I registered with the Selective Service System on 26 January, 1953, just four days after my 18th birthday, and by 4 March, 1953 was classified 4D. This was a divinity deferment based on affiliation with a Bible college. Upon graduation in May 1955, that would change. With the crises in the Far East, chances of being drafted were dramatically increased. The desire to study engineering was financially impossible. The only options: the draft or enlist. A second year roommate joined the Air Force Cadets in 1954. His girlfriend, in Gayle's quartet, reported his progress. It sounded better than "splinterville."

---

[344] Gordon H. Chang, *To the Nuclear Brink: Eisenhower, Dulles, and the Queymoy Matsu Crises,* (International Security Magazine 2, No. 4, Spring 1988), 99.
[345] Ibid., 112.
[346] Ibid., 116 – 118.

Three magazines' articles enhanced the flight training option. *Life* had a full spread on jet fighter pilots. *Readers Digest* described the rigors of Air Force Flight Training, and a third magazine listed the several skills required of a fighter pilot: flying, navigation, radio operation, aerology, and gunnery. Any one of those sounded more interesting than theology or philosophy!

Grandfather Downing's recommended procedure for learning God's plan was carefully followed. I was so convinced that Air Force flight training was the next step that the Air Force recruiter in Providence was notified of my availability!

Every military applicant must go through a battery of tests and a physical examination. The testing facility was some distance from downtown Providence. Since one of the applicants had a car, five of us rode to the site with him. His radio was playing *The Elephant Tango*, a jazzy reminder of home, and an exhilarating time for the "Kenya Kid."

One of the first steps in a military physical is filling out a form that asks if you have had mumps, measles etc. One of the boxes was hay fever. About the middle of August, I frequently got a runny nose. Dad said it was hay fever, so I checked the box "Yes." After finishing the rest of the tests, one of the doctors said they couldn't accept anyone with hay fever and stamped my papers with a big rubber "REJECTED" stamp. The trip back to Providence wasn't nearly as exciting.

We arrived downtown about noon, and "chicken in a basket" was cheap. The pros and cons of God's plan were reviewed. They still seemed valid, but not to the United States Air Force.

Next morning a second review of the work sheet revealed no significant changes. One reason to fly was the continuing hope of an engineering degree. Upon completion of military obligations, seasonal crop dusting could finance this. Obviously, Dad's WW II work with Navy Pilot Training made me aware of another military flight program. It seemed much more dignified to gracefully touch down on a long smooth runway than to slam into a cable on a moving carrier deck. Pictures of aircraft carrier operations looked really "hairy." The dignified option, however was not available.

The closest Navy recruiter was in Boston. A long distance phone call produced a travel voucher to the Navy testing site at South Weymouth, Massachusetts.

Friday, 25 March, 1955 found me on a train to Boston, and that evening quartered in the Bachelor Officers Quarters (BOQ) at NAS South

Weymouth. My roommate was a Marine Captain, an insurance man in civilian life. This particular weekend he was maintaining flying proficiency in a gull wing Corsair, a single engine WW II fighter.

Somehow, my attitude on this trip was totally different. No longer was the 'Cocky Kenya Kid' waltzing off to a lucky Navy just waiting to sign him up. My prayer was: 'God if you want me as a military pilot you're going to have to pull some strings!'

My Marine roommate that night was one of the first strings. He asked if a doctor had diagnosed my hay fever. When I replied in the negative, he stated the box should be marked "No." This was encouragement enough to allow a good nights' sleep, important for the next days' tests.

Five tests were administered on Saturday. Sunday was physical examination day, a relief from brain strain. A discussion with the doctor about hay fever revealed I was aeronautically acceptable. Remarks on the application:

DOWNING: *Good bearing and dress. Very neat in appearance. Sincere in his desire to be a naval aviator. Good officer potential. Highly recommended for selection and activation on or after 7 June, 1955.*

Apparently God's plan had been revealed. The significance of divine intervention that weekend was brought to mind two years later at NAAS Barin Field in Foley, Alabama. I was waiting in an SNJ aircraft for the rest of the gunnery flight to check in on the radio. Sometime earlier, two flights had collided, causing aircraft pieces to rain down on the Florida panhandle. Suddenly I thought, "What am I doing here?" Almost immediately, I was reminded that God had pulled strings to put me in that cockpit. Never again did I question my calling.

Twenty year olds were considered minors in 1955, and enlisting as a Naval Aviation Cadet required parental consent. You can imagine the process with parents on the other side of the globe. First, the consent form had to be mailed to them in Africa then they had to appear before an officer of the American Consul in Nairobi, sign the form, have it notarized, and mail it back. This was further complicated by Mother's reluctance to approve a dangerous occupation. Dad would never sign without her consent, so he must have reminded her of their trust in the "Commander in Chief of the Universe". The form was signed on 11 May, 1955.

After graduation, Gayle and I returned to the apartment over Custer's garage in Coshocton. Gayle resumed her work in the surveyor's office, and I worked at the grain elevator. This involved weighing farmer's shelled corn and checking moisture content. An additional job was scraping and painting the Stewart's house. Aston Stewart, Gayle's boss, also employed me on surveying and construction jobs. Gayle was working until her wedding to Kendall Grass. I was taking temporary jobs until the Navy called me to active duty, sometime after 7 June. Gayle was hoping I would be around for her wedding on the 1st of September. The summer passed with working and waiting, and working and waiting…

The wedding was planned with Mother's youngest brother, Rev. C. Edwin Houk, officiating. He was the minister of the Presbyterian Church in Uniontown, Pennsylvania, where the ceremony took place. On 1 September, 1955 Gayle's brother Glenn sang in the front of the church, ran through the basement, escorted his sister to the altar, and gave her away as a proxy for her father. Gayle's hopes for my presence on that special day were met by a gracious heavenly Father.

With the matrimonial dust settled, I contacted Lt. J.G. Bush, the Naval procurement officer at Naval Air Station, Columbus, Ohio. He was able to retrieve my application from South Weymouth. I believe the papers had fallen behind a file cabinet. For some reason the process was delayed in answer to Gayle's prayers.

After taking a physical at Columbus, I was sworn in to the Navy, and shortly after was on my way to Pensacola, Florida. There were no direct flights from Columbus to Pensacola, so the itinerary included about five flights on regional airlines.

Pensacola

On 14 August, 1559, 11 ships from Vera Cruz, Mexico brought 1,400 frontiersmen to the panhandle of Florida. This was the first attempt to place a permanent European settlement in the area, and the second attempt to put such a colony on the land mass that would one day become the United States. The Indians who greeted them were the Penzacolas, giving their name to Pensacola Bay. About a month later, a hurricane destroyed several ships and killed hundreds. The survivors were hard pressed by famine and attacks, and the effort was abandoned in 1561. Northwest Florida was considered too dangerous for white men. No further attempt was made for 135 years. Had this been successful, Pensacola would have

Swearing In

been the oldest city in America, six years older than St. Augustine.[347] [348]

In 1698, Pensacola was again settled by the Spaniards, and the community grew and prospered. Over the next century and a half, possession changed eight times. Spain, France, Britain, the Confederacy, and the United States all flew flags over the port of Pensacola. In the final analysis, the most significant change was the Battle of Pensacola, when Spain recaptured the city from the British in 1781. This is considered one of the turning points in the American Revolution. After the war, the British officially ceded both West Florida and East Florida to Spain. In 1819, Spain sold the Florida's to the United States for five million US dollars. In 1821 Pensacola, with Andrew Jackson as provisional governor, became part of the United States.

Pensacola Bay is 13 miles long and three miles wide, with depths from 20 to 30 feet. Santa Rosa Island, a long narrow strip of white sand beach and dunes, separates it from the Gulf of Mexico. The bay is entered

---

[347] Florida Seafood and Aquaculture, "Pensacola,"
http://www.fl-seafood.com/pensacola.htm, (accessed May 29, 2011).
[348] http://www.wikipedia.org/wik/Pensacola, Florida, (accessed May 29, 2011).

between Fort Pickens on the western tip of Santa Rosa, and Fort McRae on the eastern end of Perdido Key. Opposite the entrance is a 160-foot lighthouse. On the bluff, near the lighthouse, is Fort Barrancas built between 1839 and 1844 intended, with Fort Pickens and Fort McRae, to defend the Bay entrance.

No matter what flag flew over the city, beautiful Pensacola Bay continued to share the bounty of its waters with any who took the time to harvest it.

In addition to the Christian majority, Pensacola was home to a small but significant Jewish community, whose roots stretch back to the mid-to-late 19th century. The first Florida chapter of B'nai Brith was founded downtown in 1874, as well as the first temple, Beth-El in 1876.[349] Of note is the fact that Pensacola became the center of the red snapper fishery in the gulf in 1872, and by 1880 red snapper landings are recorded at 1.5 million pounds.

A Federal Navy Yard, authorized by Congress in 1824, was established on the northwest shore of Pensacola Bay. It became one of the best equipped naval stations in the country. In the early years, the base dealt mainly with the suppression of slave trade and piracy in the Gulf and Caribbean.[350] With ships made of steel, the need for the forests around Pensacola diminished, and the Naval Station was closed in 1910.

By 1911, the Wright brothers, and especially Glenn Curtis, successfully convinced the Navy of the value of airplanes. In 1914, the Navy established the U.S. Naval Aeronautical Station at Pensacola. Most of the pilot candidates were graduates of the Naval Academy at Annapolis, Maryland. Pensacola became known as the "Annapolis of the Air" and the "Cradle of Naval Aviation." Almost 2,000 pilots were trained at Pensacola during WW I.

The cadet training program was inaugurated in 1935, and training facilities at Pensacola were augmented by two more naval air stations, one at Jacksonville, Florida, and the other at Corpus Christi, Texas. An auxiliary base, known as Saufley Field, was established as part of the Pensacola complex in 1940. During WW II some 28,000 received their training in the area.[351]

---

[349] Florida Seafood and Aquaculture, "Pensacola," Ibid.
[350] Ibid.
[351] *The Flight Jacket Classes,* Cadets 30-43, 1955, Officers 38-47, 1955.

The Next Step

Historic Pensacola, *Western Gateway to the Sunshine State*, *Red Snapper Capital of the World*, and the *Cradle of Naval Aviation*, became "home" for the next 20 months. The purpose was to become a Naval Aviator and live up to a Naval Flyer's Creed:

I am a United States Navy flyer. My countrymen built the best airplane in the world and entrusted it to me. They trained me to fly it; I will use it to the absolute limit of my power. With my fellow pilots, air crews, and deck crews, my plane and I will do anything necessary to carry out our tremendous responsibilities. I will always remember we are part of an unbeatable combat team-the United States Navy. When the going is fast and rough, I will not falter. I will be uncompromising in every blow I strike. I will be humble in victory. I am a United States Navy flyer. I have dedicated myself to my country, with its many millions of all races, colors, and creeds. They and their way of life are worthy of my greatest protective effort. I ask the help of God in making that effort great enough.

So what was next in God's plan for my life? I believe it was to step into the ranks of three dimensional warriors in the United States Navy.

Pre-Flight

I don't want to be a tiger! I refuse to vote for the tiger! I'm tired of tiger emulation, and I think it's high time the tiger image is exposed for the hoax it is.

From the day I set foot in the Indoctrination Battalion at Pensacola, I had the tiger jammed down my throat sideways, and I'm full up to here. Oh, I'll admit I was fooled for a long time. I was right there with the other skinheads, quavering under the malevolent gaze of arrogant BSOOD's (Battalion Student Officer of the Day) who were all of three months ahead of us in the flight program.

"Are you TIGERS" they'd shriek as they strutted up and down the ranks.

"Yes, Sir!" whooped me and 37 other suckers.

"Then growl!"

And 38 full grown men strained their sing strings to imitate a beastly bellow.

Stupid? Sure! But there was method to this madness. This, my friend, was an image in the making. The image of a goer. An aggressive guy who feared nothing - - so what if he brought the bird back with permanently increased dihedral, (over-stressed wings), he shot the other blighter down, didn't he? And so, we became TIGERS the image of aggressiveness.

But with the inflation of bird costs, it was found that this breed of beast was no bargain. So in 1957, the pressure was on to eliminate wild recklessness. The emphasis changed. It was no longer in vogue to be just a tiger. They began discriminating even among tigers. Now they wanted smart tigers. And through this emphasis the TIGER talk turned to TIGER tutelage, and a big campaign ensued to stamp out the species that was all claws, and no brains.

Bye and bye, some of these brainwashed beasts began to escape to Madison Avenue. And wouldn't you know it, the proliferation of tiger imagery invaded every aspect of our culture. It got on our tires, in our gas tanks, even in our toilet kits. And I think it's high time to halt this harassment... <u>an excerpt from one of my last editorials</u> written before leaving active duty.

As a graduate of the University of Southern California Aviation Safety School, I was the editor of *The Hot Dope Sheet,* a safety publication of the 2nd Marine Aircraft Wing. The excerpt above is included for two reasons: first, it gives a picture of techniques used in 1955 to develop aggressiveness in the minds of combat pilots: second, it indicates the trend that was economically necessary to preserve astronomically expensive equipment. Disciplined, dedicated, deliberate masters of weapons systems were needed. Instead of "devil-may-care" aerial dualists, men who rose above two dimensional predators were becoming "snake eating eagles."

The Navy's V-5 program (Chapter 14) developed by Rear Admiral Thomas Hamilton, produced pilots amassing more air-to-air combat victories than pilots from other commissioning programs. Located at five universities, scattered throughout the country, these schools were consolidated into one pre-flight school at Iowa City, Iowa at the end of the WW II.

In December 1945, Naval Pre Flight moved to NAS Ottumwa, Iowa, and remained there until July 1947, when it was transferred to NAS Pensacola.

Indoctrination

The final leg of the flights from Columbus, Ohio landed at Hagler Field, Pensacola's municipal airport northeast of town. Navy vehicles transported cadets across town, and deposited them outside the indoctrination battalion at the Naval Air Station (NAS). There stood a long, red brick, two-story building, faced with a white portico and screened porches. A major improvement over the college in Rhode Island!

Broad concrete steps led up to a screened entry way. Passing through those doors ended the civilian life of Glenn Downing, and began 13 years of active duty. A new beginning! Was I "man" enough?

Major Sommerville, a Marine Naval Aviator, commanded the indoctrination battalion. Gunnery Sergeant Riefle, with other staff sergeants, were his drill instructors (DI). His job was to conform a heterogeneous gaggle of civilians into uniformity in the shortest time. Every detail was carefully instructed. Beds had to be made just so, towels folded in a uniform manner. Undisciplined individuals learned to suppress their resentment and comply. Creativity was discouraged. In reality, life was simple. The only requirement: *obey orders.* My father's discipline made the transition an interesting game.

Unlike civilian education, military instruction holds the instructor responsible for results. Military trainers have three responsibilities: (1) train to specified performance standards, (2) motivate recalcitrant individuals, (3) eliminate incompetent trainees. If anyone found the program unacceptable he was encouraged to "Drop on Request" (DOR) at any time. He would then be transferred to an enlisted status, and fulfill his obligation wearing a "white hat" colloquially known as a "Dixie cup."

Pre-dawn calisthenics started the day, followed by cleanup and the march to the chow hall. Food was plentiful and of good quality, though not *haute cuisine*. DI's marched us to various places for haircuts, a quarter of an inch all around, disbursing for pay records, small stores for uniforms, and the "grinder" for marching and rifle drills. Civilian clothes were packed and shipped home, since these were proscribed until advanced training.

Battalion Student Officers of the Day, known as BSOOD, took over from the DI's during the evening hours. They were cadet officers from the senior class in Pre-Flight. Their job was to keep us busy until "Taps" at bed time. Most of the evening was spent polishing brass on our uniforms and spit-shining our shoes. Occasionally, the class was called to "muster" on the quarter deck for competive games or to "field day" the building. This involved dusting, sweeping, and swabbing "decks" that had been cleaned several times previously - BUSYWORK!

Occasionally, we were given "base liberty" for toiletries and sundries at the Post Exchange. One time, when liberty was expected, the Basood found the barracks "filthy." "Liberty" canceled! One smart aleck in the last rank yelled, "Give me liberty or give me death!" The strutting Basood whipped around and said, "Who said that: Who said that?" Aleck replied, "Patrick Henry, Sir." Everyone paid with push-ups!

After two weeks we had learned to call floors *decks*, walls *bulkheads*, stairs *ladders*, and ceilings *overheads*. With a few exceptions, we could march in step without bouncing up and down. Spit-shined shoes, polished brass, starched khaki shirt, trousers, and overseas caps, with black ties tucked into shirt fronts, presented a smart military outfit. We were ready to transfer to one of four battalions for the next phase.

Our class was transferred to Battalion I in an adjacent brick building. Battalions II, III, and IV were temporary frame structures along the "grinder," a macadam, covered drill area. Wooden structures were referred to as *splinter-ville*. We were fortunate to have terrazzo decks to swab instead of wood.

NavCad G. H. Downing

Battalion I

High ceiling rooms were divided into squad bays by two lines of four steel lockers with a doorway between. Eight cadets were quartered in each squad bay. While settling in, I overheard a classmate in the next bay say: "I hate that Downing, he's a *clean liver!*" Being such a loner, I laughed it off. However, this was the beginning of an interesting story, evolving over the next few months.

The mission of Pre-Flight was two-fold. First, it served as an officer candidate school for Naval Cadets (NavCads) to equip them for future duties as Naval and Marine Officers. Second, it provided potential flight students with a thorough mental and physical background needed when flight training began. It was a 16-week course for cadets with 531.5 scheduled hours of training.

The Academic Department provided formal classroom instruction in aeronautical and naval subjects. Included were Aerology, Engineering, Naval Orientation, Navigation, Principles of Flight, and Study Skills.

The Physical Fitness-Survival Department stressed muscular coordination and survival at sea, in order to develop the keen minds and agile bodies essential for alert, competent aviators.

Routine administration, discipline, military proficiency in the manual of arms, sword handling, etc. came under the Military Department.

Navigation in 1955 emphasized dead reckoning, using a rather large plotting board. During WW II, single engine fighter pilots carried these cumbersome contrivances in their cockpits to return to a carrier which had subsequently moved. It emphasized all the variables inherent in aerial navigation, such as wind drift and instrument errors. It would have been impractical at speeds of jet aircraft, but it did provide basic orientation with instrument and radio failures. Radar, Automatic Direction Finding (ADF) and Tactical Air Navigation (TACAN) with Distance Measuring Equipment (DME) made navigation at high speeds manageable.

The speed reading course was one of the most beneficial exercises of the whole program. The basic premise: the human mind works at high speed, so if reading speed is not fast enough, the mind wanders. This exercise definitely improved my learning ability.

Aerology, Engineering, Naval Orientation, and Principles of Flight were much more absorbing than theology or philosophy. My academic performance improved dramatically.

Survival involved a thorough course in water survival. Learning to swim proficiently was the first order of business. Bobbing was the first exercise. This allowed people to stay afloat for long periods of time without any flotation devices. After filling lungs with air, the body relaxed and settled to a buoyancy level. When more oxygen was needed, air was expelled through the nose, and languid strokes to the surface provided a fresh lung full of air. One sailor was rescued after spending a whole night using this technique.

The swimming instructor was a small German, whose command to enter the water was: "Peel Off!" Four strokes were taught: breast, side, back, and crawl. The final test was swimming two miles around the pool. My legs became useless towards the end. Push-ups and pull-ups gave me the strength to finish with my arms.

Swimming under surface fires, protecting ones self from under water explosions, dropping into the water from a parachute, and jumping from a high platform that simulated a ship's deck… all were part of the course.

The mst intimidating exercise was the "Dilbert Dunker." This was an airplane cockpit on rails at the deep end of the pool. Wearing flight suits and helmets, we were strapped into the cockpit at the top of the rails. When ready, the cockpit was released and rolled swiftly into the water. After the initial splash, the cockpit rotated forward and settled to the bottom upside down. We were required to wait until all motion stopped, un-strap, pull ourselves down, and swim to the surface. A scuba diver was positioned at the bottom of the rails in case someone had difficulties. If he was not satisfied with the egress, repetition was required.

Land survival was taught in the woods. We learned to use parachutes and nylon lines to survive. This was the first of on-going survival training that continued throughout my military career.

Physical fitness was conducted in one of the old flying boat hangers along the waterfront. Two fitness tests were used to measure progress. The step test required stepping up and down on a 20-inch bench to an audible cadence for a specified time period. Pulse rates were taken before and after. The difference determined physical conditioning. The second was a timed speed agility course. This required changing direction, picking up blocks, and dropping them in a box at the end, etc. Push-ups and pull-ups strengthened the upper body. Trampoline training conditioned spatial orientation, and parachute landings techniques were taught with harnesses suspended from the overhead. Hand-to-hand combat and boxing conditioned us not to panic when blows were aimed at us.

The second episode of the *clean liver* story occurred during boxing. The guy who hated *clean livers* was my size, and we were paired as sparring partners. In the course of the exercise, I caught him with a right cross that knocked him on his butt. He gamely got up and continued, but had tears in his eyes.

The 1982 film *An Officer and a Gentleman* graphically showed the obstacle course we were required to run weekly. I found it stimulating, but not interesting enough to practice several times a week as an "afternoon sport."

Physical conditioning continued during the afternoon with elective sports. Some chose the obstacle course, some football. My choice was soccer. This was the part of Admiral Hamilton's program designed to harden cadets physically through sports.

We were indoctrinated with the group loyalty and psychological mind-set required in combat. The core of this program was physical contact, "controlled" violence, and hand-to-hand combat. Basketball and soccer operated under modified rules, allowing fouls and full body checks. Cadets were made painfully aware that they were being prepared for combat. Several years later I walked out of the Officers Club at Atsugi, Japan. A navy pilot said, "Hi, Downing, you don't remember me, do you?" I really didn't. "You put me in the hospital with a broken leg, playing soccer in Pre-Flight."

I apologized!

Sundays were more relaxed than the rest of the week. Everyone marched to church in the big auditorium. If the Naval Aviation Cadet Choir was in town, they sang.

After church, the chow hall was open for brunch. Later on we were given liberty, and several went to church in Pensacola. Before long, an entourage of cadets followed along, hoping to meet some of the young ladies.

The Naval Aviation Cadet Choir, under Lt. Howie, a Pre-Flight instructor, held auditions for new members. I became a part of the baritone section. We traveled from Florida to Seattle, Boston to Los Angeles, Minneapolis to Corpus Christi, and many places in between. Remember Dr. Booth, my music mentor at Barrington? His investment was making a big difference in my life!

The Military Department of Pre-Flight really came into focus during the last four weeks. Battalion Cadet Officers were selected and made responsible for running the routine affairs of the day. The cadet with the highest academic, physical fitness/survival, and military scores became the battalion commander and wore four bars on his collar. To the outrage of my *clean living* critic, I was that man. "That means victory for the *clean livers*," he groaned. This was episode three of the *clean livers* story. The first day of command, the graduating class was still in ranks. As I shouted, "Battalion, attention!" the whole class chanted: "Big Man." I had to grin.

Friday afternoon was regimental parade day. All four battalions assembled on the large parade ground to the strains of the Naval Air Station Band. Each battalion was led by the Cadet Battalion Commander and his three staff members. Once the battalions were in position at the back of the field, the commanders and staff marched toward the reviewing stand, and saluted with swords. The first time I came across the field, one of the DI's was all over me like *gravy on rice*. "Mister, when you come across that field, you'd better act like you know where you're going, and mean it. Next time you'd better strut!" I didn't have to be told twice!

The 15th week the Battalion Commander and his assistant moved up to regiment, and became part of the four man regimental staff. The 16th week, the Battalion Commander became the Regimental Commander, and wore five bars on each collar. Thus, Glenn Downing became Cadet Regimental Commander of the Pre-Flight Regiment in Pensacola, Florida on 10 February, 1956.

Things would have run routinely, had not the Secretary of the Navy chosen to come to Pensacola that week. It was amusing to observe the gyrations of those responsible for planning the parade. I memorized several different routines. There really wasn't much to decide. The battalions marched on, staffs approached the reviewing stand and saluted, the battalions exercised their manual of arms sequentially, the band played, and the regiment passed in review. The sequence was changed several times before we finally assembled.

It was chilly in February, so we wore green field jackets with long sleeves. Our swords were old navy weapons with the dragon's head broken off the hilt. All four staff members saluted simultaneously with their swords. When we approached the reviewing stand, my assistant commander, Doyle Fife, caught the broken hilt in his jacket sleeve, and the sword flipped out of his hand. Without taking a step, he reached up and grabbed the handle in mid-air and completed the salute. After the salute, the staff moved to the back of the commander as he turned to give the regiment the next orders. The routine was supposed to have been to exercise the battalions. This consisted of banging M-1 rifles through a manual of arms.

Before I could give the order, the band began "sound off." I heard the DI's jumping up and down saying, "No, no, no!" Out of the corner of my mouth I said: "What do we do now, Fife?" He replied: "I don't know." To end the charade, I ordered the regiment to "pass in review." Few knew the difference!

Later that day I received my certificate of completion and the outstanding student award by Charles Thomas, the Secretary of the Navy. He commented that he hoped I'd make the Navy my career. I didn't tell him I was thinking of joining the Marine Corps!

Pre-Flight was finished! It was time to get into the third dimension and fly!

Conclusion

When I raised my right hand and was sworn into the Navy, I was in essence offering my body as a *living sacrifice*. At that time, military pilots were one of 10 most dangerous groups to get life insurance. No one expected me to live this long. Through obedience to God's will, Romans 12: 1-2[352] was proving true: God's plan was good, acceptable, and perfect. I had found my niche as a warrior!

---

[352] Romans 12:1-2. 1 "Therefore, my friends, I implore you by God's mercy to offer your very selves to him; a living sacrifice, dedicated and fit for his acceptance, the worship offered by mind and heart. 2 Conform no longer to the pattern of this present world, but be transformed by the renewal of your minds. Then you will be able to discern the will of God, and to know what is good, acceptable, and perfect." The Revised English Bible.

Graduation from Pre-Flight

Basic Training

In January 1956 the NavCad Choir was flown from Pensacola to Los Alamitos, California in a four engine R5D transport. This was my first trip with the choir. The itinerary included singing at Disneyland and the Tennessee Ernie Ford TV show. Brand new Disneyland was enchanting and the TV show enlightening. Mr. Ford was a genuine gentleman, unlike many Hollywood-type phonies. As soon as the red light winked out on the front of the TV cameras, their animated faces became gloomy. Each cadet was given an autographed record of Mr. Ford's hit song, *Sixteen Tons*, and his picture taken with the celebrity.

Sixteen Tons

We returned to Pensacola on Sunday, 22 January, 1956, my 21st birthday. Had I been in a British possession that day, I could have claimed dual citizenship. Since the British Empire was unraveling, there was little advantage to be gained.

Flight orders were signed on 18 February, transferring me to NAAS Whiting Field near Milton, Florida. Whiting had two airfields, North and South. The cadet barracks was a wooden building midway between. North Field was primary training field using old North American SNJ, WW II advanced trainers. I was looking forward to flying that big noisy machine!

Primary

SNJ ground school was completed and procedures memorized. The engine failure mnemonic is still in my memory bank: Glide, Gas, Gear, Grass, Prop, Top, Trim, and Hymn. The procedure was: (1) establish the best engine out glide speed, (2) switch gas tanks, (3) extend the landing gear, (4) identify landing field, (5) set the prop in low pitch, (6) open canopy, (7) trim aircraft to fly desired glide speed, and (8) sing for help with a "May Day" call.

Winter weather created a training backlog. After breakfast we marched to the hangar and waited. We fueled airplanes when they returned, but most of the time just waited. Steel tables in one corner of the hangar were converted into checker boards with masking tape. Bottle caps were our checkers. This passed the time of day.

Once a week we were required to run around South Field, about four miles. I ordered a pair of dumbbells just to keep in shape. This lasted about five weeks. One afternoon I was walking from the hangar to the barracks. Just as I passed the chapel, who should step out but the *clean liver* hater? He called, "Hey, Downing, wait up."

I said, "What's up?"

He replied, "I just did something I should have done a long time ago."

"What was that?" I replied.

"I just went to confession." I learned later that he had come from a Catholic university up north. Sometimes the Lord lets you know He has used you as a witness in the "courtroom of life." That was the last episode of the *clean liver* story.

The week before our instructors were assigned, plans were changed. Instead of the SNJ, we were to be trained in the new Beechcraft T-34B. Doyle Fife and I considered this a "revolting development." Not only did it mean going through another ground school, the airplane was a joke. The engine was half as big as the SNJ, and adding insult to injury, it had two mufflers. The SNJ was more than twice as heavy and could go 25 miles an hour faster. The T-34 had tricycle landing gear which took the challenge out of taxiing. We should have been happy with a newer, better airplane, but we wanted the more demanding, noisier one. The ultimate indignity was wearing a green back-pack parachute that made you look like a two legged beetle. Our attitude made absolutely no difference... we learned to fly in the Beechcraft T34 Mentor.

Ensign Goetz was my instructor. Usually Ensigns are young commissioned officers, but Goetz had been one of those rare enlisted pilots. He had been a Chief Petty Officer, with many hours as a multi-engine driver. My first flight was an hour and half long on Monday, 26 March, 1956. After 23 hours of flight instruction, I soloed 52 days later. I will never forget the feeling of three dimensional freedom, taking off at Pace Field, a big mile square grass airdrome. The customary rite of passage was to cut off your black necktie. I was now authorized to wear a solo bar above my left breast pocket.

One of the program's requirements was learning Morse code. Once a week, for choir practice, a bus took the NavCad Choir members into Pensacola. Spending this travel time spelling out the road signs in code actually worked.

The flight syllabus of simulated engine failure, slow flight, precision landings, acrobatics, wingovers, inmelmans loops, and half Cuban eights were introduced. This was all fun.

That summer a young lady from my Uncle Ed's church drove from Uniontown, Pennsylvania to Pensacola with two girlfriends. Two cadets I'd met at the Officers Christian Union (OCU) and I spent a pleasant week-end with these young ladies. NavCad Choir trips slowed my progress through the program, so these two men moved to another base where they were involved in a multi-plane mid air collision. One of these guys died. Flying can be dangerous.

My last primary flight was on 9 July, 1956, and Ensign Goetz put me up for "student of the week." My certificate stated: *"In recognition of his outstanding performance of duty in flight, academic, and military areas of training as a Student Naval Aviation, Primary Stage, Basic Training, NAVCAD G. H. Downing having been selected from a group of 1,032 candidates, is hereby named Student of the Week for the week of 9 July, 1956."* God's plan was definitely good.

Basic Instruments

Corry Field, within a few miles of Mainside, Pensacola was the next base. Ground school on a new airplane was the first order of business. The Navy's T-28 with 1,425 hp. was much more powerful than the Air Force version with only 800 horsepower. It was over six times more powerful than the T-34. This would to be a handful! I should have been pleased to have flown the T-34, since the T-28 was so much more 'airplane.'

Before flying this new machine, the NacCad Choir was sent to Long Beach, California to perform at the Miss Universe Beauty Pageant. Friday afternoon, 20 July, 1956, we attended a rehearsal at the three million dollar Long Beach Municipal Auditorium. Later, with time to kill, I bought a ticket for a roller coaster ride. Before leaving the gate, the attendant suggested I take off my frame cap. Nonchalantly, I complied and enjoyed the ride. The only problem: my hat was squeezed so tightly it was never again quite right!

The choir sang that evening. The program introduced us with a half page ad stating:

This acappella group of... male voices will be featured on the stage at the Miss Universe Beauty Pageant on Friday, July 20th. It is difficult to realize that most of these young men have had no professional vocal training. Singing is a voluntary, off-duty pastime and is not their primary goal. Each is mastering a much different job... each is a future flying officer of the United States Navy.

These cadets are a cross-section of American youth. They come to Pensacola, Florida from colleges and universities throughout the United States to participate in a seventy-thousand dollar aviation education. They leave Pensacola wearing Navy Wings of Gold, ready to take their places aboard the aircraft of our fleet.

Saturday evening we were scheduled to escort the contestants to the Coronation Ball and banquet. NavCad Al Weslesky and I were strolling along the golden strand waiting for 7:30 P.M., the time of the banquet. Dressed in our white uniforms we neared one of those wedding chapels by the sea. A gentlemen approached us from the door, and asked a favor. A sailor, with a time constraint, was to be married that evening, and his wedding party was delayed. Would we witness the wedding and sign the license? Al, always ready for new adventure, agreed with me, and in we went. Al was the "bridesmaid" and I was the "best man." The minister reached behind, and turned on a record player with the wedding march.

Shari Lewis – Miss Nebraska

The service was read, we handed over the rings at the appropriate time, and the couple was married. Al and I signed as witnesses and were on our way again. Our good deed couldn't have taken more than 15 or 20 minutes!

It is customary to dance at a ball, which had been <u>verboten</u> on the mission field. Al tried to show me a few steps, but I had to muddle through with what Fred Astaire instructors call "the penguin waddle." Fortunately my date, Shari Lewis (*Miss Nebraska,*) was very gracious and understanding. Actually cadets were just uniformed stage props for a feminine spectacle. This was an exhilarating moment for this callow cadet from Kenya.

Flight training continued after returning to Corry Field. My first flight was 6 August, 1956. The most vulnerable part of any flight is on take-off. The aircraft is heavy, and must accelerate to take-off speed. When airborne, an immediate climb is required to clear the traffic pattern. In order to accomplish this maneuver, all 1,425 horse power was used. Unlike the T-34, the T-28 had no mufflers and the snarl of all that power was intimidating. Things happened much faster than any previous flight. In fact, the aircraft was 1,000 feet in the air, and my mind was still *back on the runway.* It didn't take long to get used to that power. Ten days later, with 10 hours of experience, I soloed.

Basic instrument flights began two weeks later. This involved flying the aircraft from the back seat with a tent over your head. There were six basic instruments that had to be cross-checked systematically to control the aircraft three dimensionally. When things began to go wrong it was easy to "lock up" on one instrument and ignore the other five. The key was trimming the pressures off the controls with trim tabs, so you could supervise the flight rather than physically drive the airplane. The "yoke" pattern was an exercise that required frequent changes in heading, with constant rate turns and altitude changes at constant rates of climb and descent. It was very demanding, requiring memorizing power settings and keeping oriented in the pattern. One nice thing, the T-28: when trimmed properly, was very stable. The big bugaboo was vertigo, when your inner ear was telling you a different story than the instruments. You ignore your sensations and believe the instruments. Crossing the eyes and shaking the head occasionally helped.

Training was interrupted by another choir trip to Atlantic City on 5 September, 1956 for the Miss America Pageant. The brochure of this pageant read:

The nationally famous Naval Aviation Cadet Choir from Pensacola, Florida... will appear nightly at the Miss America Pageant, and escort the Miss America contestants to the ball at The Claridge on Saturday night.

...the Miss America contestants, who will be escorted by these young men to the glamorous ball following the coronation of Miss America, will have to await that night before they are introduced to each other. The ball, as in the past five years, will be held in Trimble Hall of the Claridge Hotel.

Parenthetically, did you know that the Miss America contestants are not permitted to talk to any man – not even father, brother, or fiancé' – from the time of their arrival Monday evening until the ball on Saturday night? The only exception is made when the Atlantic City hostess gives her permission and the conversation takes place in her presence.

At midnight on Saturday, these restrictions are lifted. Then Miss America of 1957, the four runners-up, and all the other lovely contestants spend a few happy, thrilling hours dancing in the arms of the afore mentioned singers, smartly groomed in their traditional formal whites. By the way, the young couples will be paired with height as a factor and geographical background as a consideration.

I was paired with Dorothy Moreau, *Miss Canada*. She was the oldest contestant, a point she made at the banquet. She attended Carol University of Quebec – <u>cours superieur</u> in singing. The Miss America pageant was more than "cheesecake." Character and real talent were also in the mix. Once again, this *African rustic* was out of his element.

Formation and Tactics

The basic instrument phase was completed by mid-September, and I was transferred to Saufley Field for Formation and Tactics.

Saufley, about eight miles north of Mainside, Pensacola, and about six miles from Corry Field, was opened in August of 1940. Since that time Pensacola has been known as the "Cradle of Naval Aviation." The emphasis at Saufley was formation flying in the T-28, which required a keen perception of relative motion. There were cues taught which could only be learned by seeing the real thing. Initially an instructor showed the student, who watched, and then was coached through his own attempts. Later on, the solo student was coached by the instructor from the lead aircraft. Soon this became second nature, since most tactics used two plane sections as the operating elements.

Formation was the most interesting and satisfying phase. I thoroughly enjoyed flying close formation! Two sections made a division of four planes. In normal flight the flight leader's wingman was on one wing, the section leader on the opposite wing, and the section leader's wingman on the wing away from the formation. The flight leader positioned the flight with hand signals. On landing, the flight flew over the runway at 1,000 feet. When over the landing end, the leader broke away smartly from the echelon with a sharp turn, and began slowing to landing speed. The second, third, and fourth aircraft broke sequentially at pre-determined intervals. The goal was to have the same interval between each aircraft. This was really interesting and challenging.

Once, on a cross-country flight, my friend was flying the lead, and I was on his wing. He signaled a cross over into echelon. There wasn't much room between the division leader and the section leader, so I stayed in close. As I passed behind and below, my big prop sucked his elevator down slightly and caused his nose to drop. The young instructor, a "plowback"[353] from flight training, had never seen that before and was convinced I was going to clip a tail someday. I never did!

Al Weslesky was certain that I needed a girl friend. He had gone to a military academy in Pennsylvania and courted a girl for some time before becoming a NavCad. Though marriage was forbidden, Al figured the Navy had enough invested in him, that they would look the other way. So they had an open wedding in a Pensacola church and yes, he did get away with it. He was so satisfied that he thought I should have female companionship. He arranged a double date with a girl in his church; and the four of us drove to New Orleans. Being away from Pensacola, I bought a sport shirt to wear with my uniform trousers. We stopped at an amusement park and rode the roller coaster, because pilots like motion excitement. Al and his wife were in the seat ahead. Just as we topped the first elevation, my date turned and grabbed a mouthful of my new shirt. She clamped down on that shirt for the entire ride. Roller coasters were hard on my attire!

Two significant events occurred during my time at Saufley. The first happened at a movie at Mainside Pensacola. While eating popcorn, an incisor that had a root canal performed in Nairobi, broke off. My two front teeth were broken during a motor scooter mishap, so were unusable for a bridge. A Navy dentist pulled all four incisors to bridge between the

[353] Plowback - A recently graduated pilot whose first duty is a flight instructor.

canines. I looked like a hockey player and vividly remember my diet that day: strawberries and cottage cheese. I could sing, but didn't do much smiling!

Navy dentists have the reputation of being the best trained dentists of any service. My gold bridge with porcelain *steeles* facings has lasted for 55 years. Dentists all over the world have admired this bridge.

The second event was a hurricane. The instructors flew the aircraft inland, and the cadets spent the day in the chow hall. The cadet barrack was a frame building and considered vulnerable. The chow hall, a one story masonry building, was our refuge in the time of storm.

Gunnery and Carrier Qualification

The T-28C, used for carrier qualification, was just being built in late 1947. So the old SNJ would to be my aircraft for that phase. Finally, I was going to fly that venerable old workhorse. My last flight at Saufley was on Thursday, 8 November, 1956. The next duty station was Barin Field, just across the border in Foley, Alabama.

A McIlwain Church party was held at the pre-flight gym on a weekend. One of the church members, an instructor, made the arrangements. It was fun playing with the equipment without being graded. During the course of the evening, I was doing a full dismount from the high bar. Seated on the bar, you swing backwards with arms extended, when under the bar you straighten your legs, releasing the bar and land on your feet. I had done this many times. That night my sweat pants wrapped around the bar preventing leg release at the right time. I attempted to break my fall with my hands, and broke bones in both wrists. Suddenly flight training came to a screeching halt. I was grounded for two months!

It didn't take long to decide why this happened. My bitterness about not flying the SNJ in primary was a mistake. The Father used this accident to correct my misconception about what was best for me. God is a Father who can be approached with any request. However, He is Sovereign. There are no buttons to push to manipulate Him. He filters everything that touches His children. Since He is a good and loving Father, everything we experience is for our good and He deserves our thanks. It was a tough lesson, but I haven't repeated that mistake. "My son, do not think lightly of the Lord's discipline, or be discouraged when He corrects you; for whom the Lord loves He disciplines; He chastises every son whom He acknowledges." (Hebrews 12:5&6 - REB)

Gunnery Training Pattern

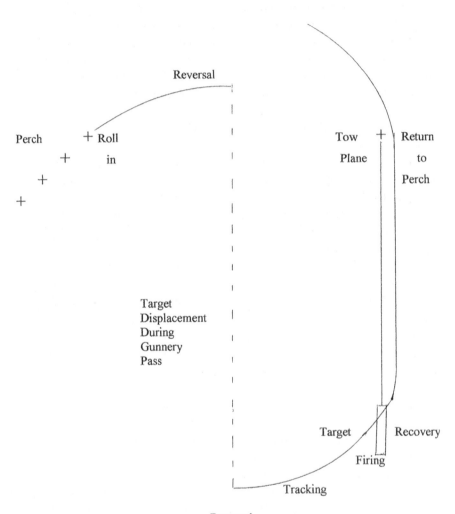

On 8 February, 1957, I flew the SNJ for the first time. It was everything I had hoped. It had been three months since my last flight in the T-28. The most significant difference was conventional landing gear. The low tail wheel elevated the engine restricting forward visibility on the ground. S-turns, left and right, were required in order to see what was ahead. I flew 11 hours of dual training in four days, and soloed on the fifth.

Weather must have restricted flight training from February through March. Three gunnery flights were flown between 21 February and 9 April. Flight operations picked up the last half of April, and I finished Aerial Gunnery on the 25th.

Gunnery was really interesting. The instructor took off dragging a target sleeve on a long cable. A four plane flight of students then got airborne. One of the students flew escort on the target. The other three followed at a higher altitude. The whole flight proceeded out over the Gulf of Mexico. When well over the water, the chase student joined the other students in the perch position abeam[354] and above the tow plane.

Reversal

When cleared by the instructor, the student would manually arm his gun, which was mounted just below the canopy on the right side of the cockpit. This was a 30 caliber machine gun that had a timing mechanism, allowing it to fire through the prop arc. Occasionally the timing mechanism would malfunction, and a round would penetrate the prop. Mechanics smoothed the hole and sent it out again. These props made a distinctive whistling sound taxiing on the ground.

When cleared in "hot," the first airplane on the perch rocked his wings, added full power, dropped his nose, and turned toward the tow plane, accelerating to firing speed. After turning 90 degrees towards the target, the turn was reversed and tracking began. A gun sight compensated for the required lead, and when in range, the trigger on the stick fired the gun. The pursuit arc required a "G" load[355] to track the target. Now things were happening quickly. At just the right moment, the wings were leveled to fly over the target sleeve and an immediate turn to parallel the tow cable. When abeam the tow plane, the nose was raised to climb back up to the perch. This was really quite exciting!

---

[354] Abeam - abreast of the tow plane on a parallel course.
[355] G-Force - Pulling back on the stick.

Multiple passes were made sequentially throughout the flight. When firing was complete, the instructor returned to the field, one student flying escort on the target. The cable was released parallel to the runway, and the whole flight landed. Ground personnel retrieved the target, and holes were counted. Each student had different colored paint on his bullets so scores could be kept. There weren't many holes!

Gunnery was completed after 10 flights. The last phase of Basic Training was aircraft carrier qualification shortened to "carquals." This began on 9 May, 1957, and six landings on the *USS Antietam* completed 19 days later. In that period, more than 80 Field Carrier Landings were made. The Navy was very particular about who was qualified to land on their ships. The precision required for carrier landings demanded concentrated, repetitive practice. A Field Carrier Landing (FCL) was much different than a normal approach. A normal landing began at 1,000 feet at the 180 degree position[356] descending, and slowing to approach speed throughout the turn. The FCL began at 500 feet in the landing configuration, with approach speed at the 180 degree position. Approach speed was 60 knots and the airplane stalled at 58 knots. Ground thermals required constant power adjustment throughout a level turn.

With 45 degrees of turn to final, the Landing Signal Officer (LSO) could be seen. This was the man who controlled the landing with two fluorescent pink paddles. If the paddles were extended at shoulder height the plane was where it was supposed to be. If the paddles were low, the plane was low. High paddles meant the plane was high.

The *Antietam* was the first U.S. carrier with an angled deck. This was a British innovation that permitted simultaneous landings and take-offs. The landing deck was angled to the left of the ship's axis.

On 17 May, 1957, flying my third FCL flight, as I was approaching the 45 degree position, the windshield was suddenly covered with oil. I could see the LSO out the side, since all carrier operations landed with open canopies. I was given appropriate signals, and continued. When the LSO gave me the "cut" signal, I was told to stay on the ground. After touch down, I was told my airplane was on fire! I stopped, set the parking brake, and went through the stopping litany: gas, battery, and switch-Off. I unlatched shoulder harness, seat belt, and stood up. The SNJ had a seat pack parachute which hit you behind the knees when walking. I slipped on the oil-covered wing, but was able to step off the trailing edge. Fire trucks

---

[356] 180 Degree Position - Heading down wind 180 degrees from the landing runway.

surrounded the airplane, but the fire was extinguished when the engine shut down. An oil seal on the prop governor failed, but nobody seemed too excited. I rode back to the hangar in a ground vehicle, and since it was Friday afternoon, had the weekend off. There was no aircraft damage so no accident report was necessary. Monday FCL training continued as usual.

When a carrier is first sighted from the air, it appears much too small to land an airplane. Our flight of four was led by an instructor. At 500 feet we flew parallel to the ships course, just right of the island. After passing in front of the ship, the flight leader broke left and began slowing. At pre-determined internals the rest of the flight broke and ended in a straight line with proper spacing down wind.

The major difference from field landings was the ships movement. Consequently, to compensate, the 180 degree turn began abeam the bow of the ship. Things became more familiar from the 45 degree position when the LSO was sighted. At the proper cut point and with the signal from the LSO, power was cut and the nose dropped momentarily, then rotated up. The aircraft banged the deck, and I was suddenly restrained by seat belt and straps as I decelerated.

With relative movement stopped, a man in a yellow shirt rapidly signaled me to stay off brakes. As I was rolled back, wire was disengaged, brakes applied, and hook raised. I was vigorously directed across the foul line to clear the deck for the following aircraft. Another director had me hold brakes and power up my engine. When satisfied that I was ready for take-off, I was cleared and rolled toward the bow. The wind across the deck made a short take-off roll, and I was airborne for my second approach. After six traps, I was released back to Barin Field for my final basic landing, a qualified "hook" pilot!

SNJ on Carrier

Advanced Training

It was a good party, but time to retire. Older RVA students had been invited from Kiambogo to a mixed party in Grandfather Downing's old house. RVA had grown, and the old homestead had become a dormitory for grade school boys, with Roy and Betty Shaffer as home-makers. Since it was a bright moonlit night, romantic couples wanted to walk the mile back to school. Of course, this was frowned upon by bluenose[357] residents, and Roy had planned transportation in his Chevy panel delivery van. To avoid dampening the festive mood, Roy began walking with us. It was a magnificent night, moonlight shining through trees in speckled patterns on the road. In about a quarter of a mile, a leopard walked slowly into a moonlight patch. Everyone stopped, and retreated slowly. Roy whispered for me to run. With a whoop, I began a stampede back to the van. All of a sudden, walking was "out" and the van quickly filled. Three of us stood on the rear bumper hanging on the rain gutter around the rear door.

As we passed the danger point, grade school boys were lying in a ditch, laughing with their feet in the air, holding a leopard skin. Later, one of the culprits said it was not a leopard but a lion. He was the masquerader, named Elliot Lyon. Roy Shaffer had beautifully anticipated a sticky situation, and won my admiration.

Roy attended RVA, had been at Westervelts, was in the Army for WW II, and attended Wheaton College. Our family had been in the Lane home in Wheaton, when I was quite young. The Lanes had the reputation of entertaining Wheaton College students, including many MKs. Roy met Betty Lane there, and married her.

Betty, one of the most attractive women at Kijabe, was my French teacher at RVA. Her parents (the Lanes) moved from Wheaton to Long Beach, Mississippi, and entertained another cadet and me on our way to Corpus Christi, Texas. My visit with the Lanes brought a flood of memories.

---

[357] Bluenose - A puritanical person who tries to impose a strict moral code on others. *Webster's New World College Dictionary*, 4th ed., 160.

Transition

Advanced training was a huge change from the first 18 months of the flight program. I bought my first car in January 1957. For the first time in my life, my horizon blue Volkswagen gave me mobility and independence. We were now allowed civilian clothes when off duty. I had clothes given to me most of my life, so it was a new experience to choose my own wardrobe.

NavCad Choir

I sang with the NavCad Choir for the last time before leaving Pensacola. The big decision was which *service* to choose. If I did nothing, it would be the Navy. I could be flying multi-engine transports, patrol planes, submarine hunters, sea planes, helicopters, or even blimps, (which we called "poopey bags"). With such a wide variety of cockpits to be filled, flying fighters in the Marine Corps seemed a much better prospect. Grandfather Downing's counsel convinced me of God's plan. I applied, was accepted, and now wore a double bar with a Marine Eagle, Globe, and Anchor above my left breast pocket. I was an Advanced Cadet, Marine selectee.

Another change was meal payment. An enlisted man is guaranteed "three hots and a cot" (three hot meals a day and a bed). Cadets were not commissioned officers, so meals and beds were provided. I was required to sign a statement that I understood that "...upon reporting to activities of the Naval Air Advanced training command, Naval Customs ashore require payment of one month's mess bill in advance at the time of joining an officer's mess." Advanced training treated its students with more respect, and expected the same.

The 750 mile trip from Pensacola to Corpus Christi took a couple of days. Upon checking in at the Naval Air Station, we were assigned to Advanced Training Unit (ATU) 213 at Beeville, Texas, 70 miles north.

Beeville Naval Air Station was open from 1943 to 1946 for WW II flight training. It was re-opened in 1952 for the Korean War, re-named Chase Field. Beeville, the county seat for Bee County, really wasn't much of a town. Fortunately, I had my VW!

Beeville Pool

Instead of being assigned to a training squadron, I found myself in another back-log. My official status was "pool," and I was encouraged to take leave. Fifteen days were approved with Coshocton as my leave address. Driving to Kelly AFB in San Antonio, I caught a space available flight to Ohio, and visited family and friends. A young lady from Coshocton was studying at Ohio State University. We had a few dates before returning to Beeville. I was interested, but concluded that she was not enamored with my choice of professions. She couldn't have objected to my "suave personality."

Heading back to Texas with what should have been ample travel time, I got as far as Scott Air Force Base near St. Louis. I waited a couple of days for another flight. Leave expired at midnight on Saturday, 29 June. At 6:40 that evening, I checked in with Air Police Operations, and received a standard leave request DD Form 460 to avoid being Absent Without Leave (AWOL).

I boarded a train in St. Louis for San Antonio, Texas. After departure, the train returned to St. Louis. Heavy rains along the Mississippi River made a bridge impassable. Eventually we were again on our way and arrived in San Antonio on Monday, the 1st of July. My leave papers were signed in at 9:37 P.M. that evening. Apparently, I hadn't been needed, for nothing was ever said about the delay.

TV-2

TV-2 Instruments and Formation

ATU-213 ground school began later in July, with my first TV-2 flight on the 25th. This aircraft was the two seated version of the P-80's I first saw in California more than 10 years earlier.

The P-80 had an interesting history. The United States was far behind Germany and England in jet aircraft during WW II. America's first jet, built by Bell, first flew on 1 October, 1942. Its basic airframe was totally inadequate for a fighter. The 50 that were built were relegated to trainer status.[358]

Lockheed hired Nathan Price, an expert in turbo-superchargers, who was well into the design of an extremely advanced jet engine in 1941. Kelly Johnson and three other Lockheed engineers designed an aircraft using

---

[358] Walter J. Boyne, *Beyond the Horizons, The Lockheed Story,* (New York, NY, St. Martin's Press, 1998), 150 - 151.

two of Price's engines. The aircraft, known as the L-133 fighter design, was largely of stainless steel, with refinements reminiscent of a current F-16. The United States Army Air Force (USAAF) at Wright Field showed no interest. It was considered too advanced to be realized in time to help the war effort.[359]

The growing evidence of Germany's developing jet aircraft forced the USAAF to seek counter measures. Recalling Lockheed's proposal, an opportunity to build a jet fighter of its own design around the British H.1 Goblin jet engine was tendered on 17 May, 1943. Lockheed accepted the challenge to build an airframe immediately and in less than a month submitted a proposal which Wright Field designated the XP80. Official approval was given 17 June, 1943. In 143 days, the aircraft was delivered!

Johnson, the designer of the P-38, was responsible for this feat. He assembled a select group of designers and expert workmen into a team under his direct control. His goal was to translate drawings into metal by the close cooperation of designers and workers, with a minimum of interference from the company or the USAAF. With no room at the Burbank plant for his project, a circus tent was set up near an odoriferous[360] manufacturing plant. Security was the key to his success, and all 123 members of his team were sworn to secrecy..

Cartoonist Al Capp's *Lil Abner* comic strip invented Dogpatch, where the main industry was the Skunks Works, headed by inside man, Big Barnsmell. One day with the strong odor permeating the tent, an engineer named Irv Culver answered the phone with, "Shunk Works, inside man Culver." Fellow employees quickly adopted the name for their mysterious division. When the comic strip objected, the official name was changed to the registered trademark SKUNK WORKS R. Products of the Skunk Works R included the F-80, F-94C, SR-71A, U-2, F-104, and the F-17A.[361]

The P-80's first flight was 8 January, 1944. Inevitably, accidents marred the flight test program. In October the chief pilot who made that first flight was killed when a fuel pump failed on take-off. A turbine failed in March 1945, cutting off the tail of the beautiful "Gray Ghost." The pilot bailed out, but broke his back when he hit the ground. Major Richard Bong, the leading P-38 ace with 40 victories, was killed in a P-80 in August 1945.

---

[359] Ibid., 151 - 152.
[360] Skunk Works – Lockheed Martin, http://www.lockheedmartin.com/aeronautics/skunkworks. (accessed July 11, 2011).
[361] Walter J. Boyne, *Beyond the Horizons*, Ibid., pictures between 226 - 227.

The trend was alarming! With Major Bong's death, eight aircraft had been destroyed, seven more damaged, and six pilots killed. By September 1946, more than 60 accidents had occurred, primarily due to pilot factors. The new aircraft was deceptively simple to fly when all was going well, but it was a challenge on take off and landing, and when malfunctions occurred. The obvious answer was a transition trainer. The TP-80C first flew on 22 March, 1948. It became the immortal T-33, navy designation TV-2, my first jet.[362]

On 1 August, 1957, I soloed in the TV-2. Three days later, jet instrument training began. Like basic, this was flying from the back seat with a tent over your head. The big difference was aircraft speed. Things happened faster. The other big differences were approaches for landing. Jet efficiency improves with altitude. The object was to stay high as long as possible. When over the destination a penetration was performed, a high speed dive to descend as quickly as possible.

Distance Measuring Equipment (DME) was just coming to the fleet, and was not in our aircraft. We practiced using Automatic Direction Finding (ADF) needle drift to determine distances to the station. Two exercises were used: (1) a fade 90, when you put the tail of the needle on your wing tip and timed a three degree shift, (2) offsetting the needle from your nose, and flying until the angle doubled.

One of the most difficult exercises was an instrument take-off. The compass card was fixed with north on the nose of the aircraft. The heading needle for runway 13 was about the four o'clock position on the card. You had to imagine standing on your head to figure which way to make proper corrections. All of this was superseded when Radio Magnetic Indicators (RMI) and DME were installed.

Radio range stations, while still in use, were difficult at the speeds we traveled. A range station had four legs, with an A Morse Code signal transmitted in opposite quadrants. An N signal was transmitted in the other two. On course you were supposed to hear a steady tone. Fortunately, the instructor demonstrated this. We were not required to become proficient.

Formation in the TV-2 was really fun for me. The main difference was a lack of torque, and corollary rudder corrections with power changes. The big surprise was slowing down. Reducing power in a prop decelerates the airplane immediately, the propeller acting as a fan in reverse. The jet

---

[362] Ibid., 155 - 156.

was so slick that it kept going. There were speed brakes on the belly that increased drag, but they took some getting used to.

On 26 September, 1957 I finished the TV-2 syllabus and was issued a standard instrument card authorizing me to fly in instrument weather to specified limits. This was considered a major accomplishment!

Beeville experienced a periodic cicada infestation in 1957. They were everywhere with their incessant cacophony. You could rarely walk across the street without stepping on the crunchy things every step. Their dead bodies were everywhere. The hangers had bays to stow open hangar doors. Wind blew them into these enclosures several inches deep, and the smell was terrible!

When not scheduled for a specific activity, we were free to leave. Since Beeville was pretty boring, I headed to Corpus Christi on the week-ends. Many of the Officers' Christian Union (now the Armed Forces C U) friends from Pensacola were gathering at a big Baptist church in Corpus. One family in that church invited many of us into their home. Jack and Gina Morrison, with young twin boys, provided a home away from home for many lonely aviators. No one could have been more hospitable. They provided a cheerful haven for a man whose close kinfolk were on the other side of the world.

Upon completion of Instruments and Formation, I was commissioned. It was especially meaningful to have Jack Morrison drive an hour from Corpus Christi to honor me with his presence. Although not a big ceremony, it was a big day! On Friday, 4 October, 1957, 2/Lt. Glenn Downing became a full fledged Marine!

Advanced Tactics and Gunnery

The advanced training command had been using straight wing F-9 Panthers for jet training until late 1957. Chase Field had just received swept wing F9F-8 Cougars, and I was one of the first students to fly one. One of the prettiest airplanes Grumman Aircraft built was the F-9, used by the Blue Angels demonstration team from 1955-1958.[363]

The F-9 Panther was the first US Navy jet fighter to be used in combat. Introduced into the Korean War in July 1950, it recorded a victory against an enemy MIG-15 the following November.[364] The swept wing F-86 and

[363] Bert Kinzey, *F9F Cougar*, (Fallbrook, CA, Aero Publishers, 1983), 47.
[364] J.H. Taylor, *Jane's Encyclopedia of Aviation*, (New York, NY, Portland House, 1989), 447.

MIG-15 clearly outclassed the straight wing Panther and other straight wing aircraft in Korea.

The U.S. Navy was concerned about compatibility of swept wing aircraft with shipboard requirements. Chance Vought's F7U Cutless and North American's Fury were the first operational Navy jets, but Grumman proposed a wing change for their F-9. It was low risk, low cost, and faster than developing a new aircraft.[365] The F9F-8 Cougar was the result. The first production F9F-8 was flown on 18 January, 1954. More than 600 were built, the last phased out in the early 1970's almost 20 years later. It really was a rugged, durable and dependable airplane,[366] colloquially attributed to the Grumman "Iron Works."

Flight Physiology

The F9F-8 had a 50,000 foot maximum ceiling, well into altitudes where human beings need supplemental oxygen to survive. The "school solution" to the question of the maximum altitude for survival was 22,000 feet. We were regularly operating at dangerously hostile elevations. In order to acquaint jet pilots with the insidious effects of hypoxia, a low pressure chamber was used. An adjacent chamber with decreased pressure was suddenly opened demonstrating explosive decompression. This was like losing a canopy from a pressurized aircraft.

After the chamber was stabilized at a higher altitude, oxygen masks were removed. Individuals were given different tasks to perform. An instructor watched until performance obviously deteriorated, and oxygen masks re-fitted. The purpose was to recognize symptoms of hypoxia, and take corrective action. The low pressure chamber was a "must" in high altitude flight.

The F-9 cockpit was pressurized, but oxygen masks were used from take-off to landing. One day, riding in the back seat on a long cross country back to Texas, my overseas cap was caught in the outflow valve preventing cabin pressurization. We were well above 40,000 feet. The oxygen regulator is programmed to go to a pressure breathing mode at specified altitudes. Oxygen is forced into your lungs under pressure and you must forcibly exhale. It is normal breathing in reverse. While providing useful consciousness, it is uncomfortable.

---

[365] Bert Kinzey, Ibid., 5.
[366] Ibid., 47.

The real problem was a case of the bends. Nitrogen comes out of solution from the body and collects in joints. I began to feel pain in my elbows. We were taught that exercise only exacerbates the problem. So I sat quietly for the rest of the flight, eager to get home as soon as possible!

Bailing out of a jet aircraft was not the same as escape from slower airplanes. The F-9 was equipped with an ejection seat which used an explosive charge to separate the seat from the aircraft. In addition, it automatically separated the pilot from the seat and deployed a parachute. Training in the use of this system utilized an ejection seat trainer on the ground. The pilot was strapped into a seat, with hard-hat and oxygen mask on. When ready, both hands pulled a handle attached to a curtain over head. As the curtain was pulled over the face for protection, an explosive charge propelled the seat up a pair of rails about eight feet in the air. The seat then slowly descended back into the cockpit, the pilot unstrapped, and was issued his ejection seat training card. I still have mine, dated 12 October, 1957.

High speed turns in jet aircraft exposed pilots to high "G" loads. Everyone is exposed to one G, or one-gravity. When you stand on a scale, one gravity is indicated in pounds on the dial. If you were exposed to four G's, a scale would indicate four times your body weight. In order to prevent blood from pooling in lower extremities and reducing vision, a G-suit is worn. Rubber bladders across the lower abdomen down the thighs and calves are filled with pressurized air, as the aircraft is exposed to "G" forces. Everyone wore G-suits in flight.

Tactics

The final phase of flight training was in Squadron 203, the new swept wing F-9 squadron. The first two flights were in two seated F9F-8Bs. I was on my own in single seated F9F-8B's for the next two flights for landing practice. Swept wing aircraft had an insidious habit of getting into a high sink rate on approach, if not enough power was used. Unlike a propeller, a jet is much slower to accelerate and produce thrust. The solution was to carry power all the way to touch-down. Our training emphasized this, but practice without a coach was the only way to really learn.

Formation tactics were the next step. Single piloted aircraft required teamwork to prevent attacks from the rear. The best tactic was spreading two aircraft abeam of each other to eliminate blind spots. The basic element was a section of two airplanes, with the wingman protecting the leader. The spread formation was used enroute to a target or on patrol. The wingman's responsibility was to close in on the leader's tail when an enemy was encountered. Staying with a leader, maneuvering in combat required vigorous response from the wingman.

A flight was composed of two sections. The flight leader and his wingman were lower than the second section. Maintaining flight integrity to eliminate blind spots required practice. There wasn't enough time to perfect it, but we understood the concept.

Gunnery

F-9 gunnery used the same training pattern as in basic, but a vertical banner was used instead of a sleeve. The visual presentation was larger, but higher speeds made hitting the target very difficult. The F-9's guns were 20 mm cannons in the nose which gave a much more satisfying chatter. The problem was correctly judging the firing range. A gun sight presented the correct lead when tracking smoothly, but compensation for bullet drop was determined by range judgment. The closure rates were much faster, and tracking, firing, and recovery required split-second timing.

On one of the early flights, the guy ahead of me must have gotten target fixation for he hit the cable, tearing it from the tow plane. The loose cable lodged between the boundary layer splitter plate and the fuselage, just forward of the left intake. With no way to release the cable, he had to land with this whole mess dragging behind. The instructor flew wing on the student coaching him. I was assigned target escort until we got back to the field. Everyone landed safely, but it was harrowing!

Finale

The few requirements after gunnery included night flying and a formation cross-country. Night flying was fairly routine. The major differences were the cues for landing. The F-9 did not have landing lights. Jet landings were predicated on a stabilized sink rate, so "grease job" (smooth) landings were not encouraged. The cues for landing were colored edge lights, white for runways, blue for taxi ways, green for runway ends. Parking was directed by plane captains with lighted wands.

A night flying accident killed one of the students at Chase Field. The road from Beeville passed the approach end of the landing runway. The student on a left hand approach apparently mistook diverging auto lights for an approaching aircraft, and flew into the ground trying to avoid a mid-air collision.

A four plane cross-country was part of the syllabus. On Saturday, 16 November, 1957 an instructor and three students set out from Chase Field for El Toro, California. The lady I dated in Coshocton was teaching school there, and I was hoping to wow her with my prowess. I don't remember the details, but we ended up at Walker AFB in Roswell, New Mexico. We were quite a curiosity as we taxied around an Air Force facility with our wings folded. The Coshocton lady married a preacher. The wife I married was much better suited to my profession, thanks to a Heavenly Father who knew better.

Ten days later, I flew my last training flight, qualifying to wear the gold wings of a Naval Aviator. The training requirements of the previous two years had been rigorous, but very rewarding. This was the best qualification available for my profession as a pilot.

AFRICA
Home for Christmas – 1957
Corpus Christi, Texas to Nairobi via Norfolk, Virginia

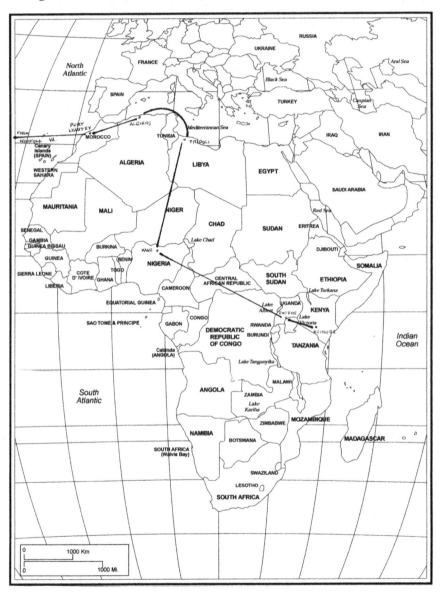

Home for Christmas

From Texas to California, 30 days leave plus 11 days travel time was authorized. Leave options included visiting brother Ed in Chicago, or sister Gayle in Maine. One evening the sudden thought of traveling to Kenya excited me. After more than five and a half years, how nice it would be to celebrate Christmas at home..

This was a wild idea, but the more I thought about it, the more intriguing it became. The possibility was worth investigating. Out of curiosity, a visit to sick bay was made to learn of necessary inoculations. A Corpsman went to a map on the wall, turned, and said, "Roll up your sleeve." He quickly gave me two shots and wrote a request for a yellow fever shot only given at Corpus Christi. A Department of Defense immunization certificate was filled out even before deciding.

The next challenge was finance. The disbursing office computed leave and travel pay. Just before departure, they said, "With permanent change of station orders, you know you can take out a dead horse, don't you?" A "dead horse" was three months advanced pay, reimbursed by six months half pay. Funds were available for return, if hitchhiking home worked.

With orders in hand, and my luggage in the VW, Corpus was the next stop. The Morrisons provided a place to stay, while travel arrangements were finalized. A passport had to come by mail from New Orleans. Meanwhile, space available travel on Navy planes to the east coast was requested.

Shortly after the passport arrived, Navy operations called. An R4D (DC-3) going to Norfolk, Virginia, had room. Leaving the car at the Morrisons, friends took me to the base for the first leg of a most memorable pilgrimage. Would the turn around point be home or Timbuktu?[367]

After warm Texas, Virginia was quite chilly the evening we arrived. A visa for Kenya could be obtained in Norfolk. Early the next morning, a bus took me downtown to the consulate. Mr. Henshaw, the British Consul, signed the visa in my passport, as he was leaving the city early for the weekend. It was Friday the 13th of December, my Mother's 50th birthday. Later that day, two pilot acquaintances offered to fly me to the Naval Air Station at Glenview near Chicago or NAS Brunswick, Maine. They offered

---

[367] Timbuktu - Another name for Tombouctou, a town in central Mali near the Niger River.

Photograph of bearer

Renewal, extensions, amendments, limitations, and restrictions

This passport, properly visaed, is valid for travel in all countries unless OTHERWISE RESTRICTED. It is not valid for travel to or in any foreign state for the purpose of entering or serving in the armed forces of such a state.

This passport is not valid for travel to the following areas under control of authorities with which the United States does not have diplomatic relations: Albania, Bulgaria, and those portions of China, Korea and Viet-Nam under Communist control.

See Stamp on Page 6

> **THIS PASSPORT IS NOT VALID FOR TRAVEL IN HUNGARY.**

4   5

1957 Passport

two safe and easy alternatives to my audacious escapade. Their proposals were declined in favor of the rewards of home.

Saturday morning the passenger manifest to the Naval Air Station at Port Lyautey, Morocco included me. Just before boarding the plane, a Naval Officer asked me to be a Courier Officer for official documents or pouches exempted from examination by customs and censorship officials. This involved checking the list of articles, seals, and signing for them. A qualified official received the articles at the destination and signed for them again. It provided continuous custody for sensitive materials. Later, this proved very important!

Morocco was dark when we arrived. Saturday was typically quiet. The Bachelor Officers Quarters provided sleeping accommodations that night and breakfast Sunday morning. Operations said there was nothing scheduled that day. However, the Air Force at Sidi Slamane was moving several airplanes to Tripoli on Monday. Sidi Slamane was 40 miles west of the Naval Air Station, so arrangements were made for the Navy shore patrol to take me to the small town of Sidi, when they changed the guard that night. The air police then drove me on to Sidi Slamane.

Monday morning found me enroute to Libya in an Air Force C-119. The distance to Wheelus AFB in Libya was at least 1,200 miles. A stop at Algiers revealed parked AT-6's and bullet holes in hangar windows, evidence of the war of independence raging from 1954 to 1962.[368]

Wheelus Air Base was located on the Mediterranean coast, just east of Tripoli, Libya. With its 4,600 Americans, the U.S. Ambassador to Libya once called it "a little America... on the sparkling shores of the Mediterranean." Originally built by the Italian Air Force in 1923, it was captured by the British 8th Army in January 1943. The USAAF began using it as a bomber base in the spring of 1943.[369] It was taken over by the AAF and renamed Wheelus Army Airfield in honor of USAAF Lt. Richard Wheelus, who had died earlier in a plane crash in Iran.[370]

Wheelus operations said that traffic east bound went to Saudi Arabia, and it took a week to get a visa. Supper that night in the commissioned officers open mess was bleak. Somehow, the RAF base south of Tripoli was mentioned. A telephone call revealed a flight leaving for Kano, Nigeria in a day or so, with space available. Again the air police came to my aid, and provided a pick-up truck and driver to take me the 10 miles to the Idris RAF Base.

The airplane, a Handley Page H.P. 67 'Hastings,' looked like a "DC-3 on steroids." It was a tail dragger with four engines, a crew of five, and carried 50 passengers. The distance from Tripoli to Kano was roughly 1,400 miles. Accommodations were Spartan, but comfortable. The steward dispensed hot tea with milk from a large aluminium (al you min e am) tea kettle. Definitely British!

The airplane, scheduled to continue on to Nairobi the following day, was weight limited. The captain, hoping to make Nairobi nonstop, needed extra fuel. Now close enough to buy a commercial ticket, I was inquiring on the telephone at the hotel front desk. Commercial air traffic went only north and south in Africa. One course went down the eastern side; Kano

[368] Algeria Independence France 1954-1962, "Wars of the World, Armed Conflict Events Data," http://www.onwar.com/aded/data/alpha/algeria1954.htm. (accessed July 16, 2011).
[369] Wheelus Air Base – United States Nuclear Forces, "Weapons of Mass Destruction (WMD)," http://www.globalsecurity.org/wmd/facility/wheelus.htm. (accessed July 16, 2011).
[370] Wheelus Air Base – Wikipedia, The Free Encyclopedia, "World War II," http://en.wikipedia.org/wiki/wheelusairbase. (accessed July 16, 2011).

was on the western route. There were no flights east and west, and Nairobi was still 1,330 miles away. The possibility that this might be my turn-around point must have shown on my face, for the captain, standing next to me at the counter, asked, "What's the problem, Leftenant?" When he heard I was trying to get home near Nairobi for Christmas he said, "Oh, we'll make room for you. We thought you were just jollying about." It meant stopping for fuel at Entebbe, Uganda but the captain was as good as his word. I was on the airplane with him the next day.

Uganda was a land locked country in dire need of air travel facilities. Entebbe Airport, 23 miles southwest of Kampala the capital, served that purpose. It was the airport from which Queen Elizabeth II departed Africa to return to England after her father's death in 1952.

In December 1957, an RAF HP 67 'Hastings' arrived from Kano, Nigeria with 2nd Lt. Downing aboard. While the aircraft was being refueled, a telephone call to Dad at Kijabe went something like this:

"Hello, Dad, this is Glenn in Entebbe."

"Oh?"

"Can you meet me in Nairobi in an hour or so?"

"How long can we see you?"

"I plan to be home for a week or two."

"Where shall we meet?"

"We will be arriving on an RAF transport plane at Eastleigh Airport."

"We'll be there!"

When they arrived, I was wearing my winter service, green uniform with a frame hat. My younger brother, four year old Martin, had been a baby when last seen on the ship in 1954. He looked up at my hat and asked, "Why is Glennie wearing a policeman's hat?"

As we left the operations room, the man behind the counter said. "When you're ready to return, Leftenant, give us a call. We'll see what we can do." This statement allowed me to relax and enjoy my visit.

What a treat it was to be home again! The panorama of the valley below, with its familiar volcanic craters jutting up from its floor; the wooded hills behind the house with their noisy colobus monkeys and hyraxes; the smell of wood smoke in the chilly mornings; all reminded me of my life five and a half years earlier.

"MY house" was gone. The garden, yard, and trees were still there but the house had burned when Gayle and I were in college. My parents' house was designed and built by Dad 100 yards north of the old one. The living room window framed a view of Mt. Suswa, a double cratered extinct

Glennie and his "Policemen's Hat"

volcano. The walls were cut lava ash, the windows steel sash, and the roof corrugated metal. It was bigger and better, but it wasn't my old house.

School was out for a month long Christmas holiday, but Dad was busy every day with administrative duties. After supper we talked late into the evening. It was amazing how much smarter Dad had become! One of the main reasons for my visit apparently, was to see my parents from a more mature perspective. They really were amazing people! Dad was in charge in a quiet but firm manner. He was able to evaluate staff members assigned to the school, give them appropriate responsibilities, and motivate them with just the right words. He was an adroit manager.

Mother was not only the best teacher I had, she was an efficient homemaker and hostess. In the years attending RVA reunions, other alumni have frequently said that they hold her in that same regard. She was an amazing woman!

My Mother

Christmas and Boxing Day

Both Christmas and Boxing Day were celebrated in Kenya in 1957. Boxing Day began in Britain during the Middle Ages. Details are sketchy, but it is supposed that Christmas was a festive day for the well-to-do, so servants were needed for the parties. Boxing Day was the first week-day after Christmas, a day off for the servants, when the well-to-do gave them gifts. In 1871 it became a bank holiday. Another event that coincides with Boxing Day is St. Steven's Day, when the church authorities opened their alms boxes and distributed the collected money among the poor. At present, Boxing Day is the time for post-Christmas shopping bargains.[371]

Christmas was on Wednesday, and Boxing Day on Thursday. By Friday, return travel arrangements were needed. Dressed in my natty uniform, Dad and I drove to Nairobi. When we approached the RAF desk at Eastleigh Airport, we were very disappointed that no traffic was expected for several days. The airman behind the counter did say that Hunting-Clan, a freight carrier across the field, had accommodated service men in the past. So off we went to the Hunting-Clan godown.[372] There were only warehouse men there, but they directed us to the manager in downtown Nairobi.

We were ushered into the office of a pleasant English gentleman. After listening to my predicament, he put both elbows on his desk with fingertips touching and said, "Well, you have a problem. I have two problems." After a few moments deliberation he said, "I'll tell you what; I'll authorize travel on one of our airplanes to Malta or wherever you want to go. By the

---

[371] Christmas Traditions, "Boxing Day,"
   http://www.buzzle.com/articles/christmas-traditions-boxing-day.html., (accessed July 18, 2011).
[372] Godown - In the Far East, a warehouse, (*Webster's New World College Dictionary*.)

My Dad

time the rocket hits here, you'll be where you need to be." We both thanked the man profusely, and finished other business in Nairobi.

Nairobi was as I remembered: wide streets, well-regulated traffic, pleasant temperatures, and a cosmopolitan population that meshed smoothly. It was still the British Empire, civilization at its finest in the heart of Africa. The drive back to Kijabe was on macadam roads until within a few miles of the mission station. The view of the Rift Valley from the top of the escarpment was still breathtaking. It was nice to be home, even for a short while!

The following week, an Avro Lancaster converted bomber was airborne with piles of rolled rugs, boxes of butter, bananas, dogs, and me. The first landing was at Entebbe, where the cordial crew invited me into the terminal for tea. New Years Eve was spent winging our way from central Africa to the Island of Malta. The drone of four Rolls Royce, Merlin engines throughout the night was reassuring.

We arrived on New Years Day, 1958. Approaching the U.S. Naval base, a flight training acquaintance recognized me and said, "What are you doing here, Downing?" I told him I needed to get to Wheelus. This guy was a new pilot in the Lockheed P2V Neptune Squadron based there. (The P2V was a maritime-reconnaissance bomber flown by the U.S. Navy.) The Commanding Officer's plane was not being used, and some of the crew needed flight time. He'd see what he could do. The third leg of my trip was aboard a Navy bomber that could really scoot.

Wheelus was the first stop of the embassy flight from Dhahran, Saudi Arabia, to Charleston, South Carolina. It would be nice to be on that flight. After my Navy buddies dropped me off, the operations desk was approached about space available. A rather snotty airman shook a handful of requests at me and said, "All these people go before you, Lieutenant!" Having passed the courier's office on a previous visit, the agent there was asked if they needed a courier officer. "Man, we sure could have used you this morning but let me check and see if more mail has come in." He soon returned and told me they would have me on the flight that night.

At 10:00 P.M. aboard one of the most beautiful airplanes ever built, a triple tailed Lockheed Constellation, we headed west with eight articles weighing a total of 144 pounds. It was nice to know nobody was going to bump the Courier Officer off the flight!

Cruising at roughly 320 miles per hour, we arrived at Lajes Airport in the Azores seven hours later. Lajes Field is on the northeast tip of Terceira, an oval island roughly 8 x 15 miles bordered by high cliffs, located 2,290 miles east of New York City and 990 miles west of Lisbon. Lajes was used as a refueling field for trans-Atlantic American flights since 1943.

While the aircraft was being refueled, passengers were transported to a mess hall on a ridge overlooking the runway. Heavy waves were crashing against the cliffs below. A large rock away from the cliffs was sending spray three times its height into the air. A man next to me asked, "Do you know how high that rock is?" My guess, it was 30 feet. He informed me it was 100 feet high, sending water 300 feet in the air.

Just before re-boarding that evening, I was asked if human remains aboard the aircraft bothered me. When I realized what they meant, I said, "Of course not." So off we went on the last leg to Charleston. Looking out the windows you could see and feel four big radial, piston engines, pounding away hour after hour without missing a beat.

After the courier mail was signed for, a query to operations about flights to the west indicated there were none. By the steps, outside the terminal, was a Greyhound bus. The operations officer informed me that bus was headed for Jacksonville, Florida. That was my next conveyance.

A transfer in Jacksonville put me on a bus for Pensacola which arrived Saturday night, 4 January, 1958. Sunday morning I was in church with old friends at McIlwain Presbyterian Church, and that evening was asked to sing a solo. Before singing, I briefly outlined my FAITH quest, a 'Fantastic Adventure In Trusting Him'. The song that best expressed my gratitude was; *No One Ever Cared for Me like Jesus*. Apparently, the message got through. The pastor had tears in his eyes.

Monday morning aboard a CH-46 twin rotor helicopter from Sherman Field, I was headed for Barksdale Air Force Base in Shreveport, Louisiana. There was one major deficiency - no heat! A cold snap in the south made the trip extremely uncomfortable. With every piece of clothing I could put on, shoes off, feet in my bag, and head phones on my ears, Barksdale was most welcome. The final leg to Corpus was by ground transportation. I still had time to drive to the west coast.

The taxi driver to the Morrisons was quite talkative and was interested in my travel yarn. When told of the drive to California, he asked about my 'wheels.' When told it was a VW, he said, "I had you figured for a Corvette or a Thunderbird." I didn't know a Porsche would be my next vehicle!

Recounting the details to the Morrisons highlighted the efficacy of my Heavenly Travel Agent, God. The best description of my experience is summed up in F.B. Meyer's essay *The Consecrated Life*. He writes:

When a man is right with God, God will freely use him. There will rise up within him impulses, inspirations, strong strivings, strange resolves. These must be tested by Scripture and prayer; and if evidently of God, they must be obeyed.

But there is this perennial source of comfort: God's commands are God's enablings. He will never give us a work to do without showing exactly how and when to do it, and giving us the precise strength and wisdom we need.

Do not dread to enter this life because you fear that God will ask you to do something you cannot do. He will never do that. If He lays aught on your heart, He will do so irresistibly; and as you pray about it, the impression will continue to grow, so that presently, as you look up to know what He wills you to say or do, the way will suddenly open; and you will probably have said the word or done the deed almost unconsciously. Rely on the Holy Ghost to go before you, to make the crooked places straight and the rough places smooth.

Do not bring the legal spirit of "must" into God's free service. "Consider the lilies of the field, how they <u>grow</u>." Let your life be as effortless as theirs, because your faith will constantly hand over all difficulties and responsibilities to your ever-present Lord. There is no effort to the branch in putting forth the swelling clusters of grapes; the effort would be to keep them back.[373]

With belongings in the VW, and profuse thanks to the Morrisons, the journey continued to my next duty station. El Toro was 1,500 miles away, requiring at least 24 hours of driving. Driving my *bug* was enjoyable, but in west Texas, in heavy cross winds, the little car had to be continuously driven, and cruise control was not available on a '57 VW. Tumble weeds were being blown by strong winds. One huge one hit the front of the car and stuck. It had to be removed to see through the windshield!

Fortunately the January weather was cool, and the southern route had no high mountain passes. Still, eight hours of driving made me ready for a good sleep in a motel.

Sunday afternoon returning, weekend traffic in LA slowed progress, but the Hermosa Beach Church was reached in time for the evening service. This had been the church of Charles White and family, when we met in 1946. There were no familiar faces, and it was not a typical Baptist

---

[373] F. B. Meyer, *The Consecrated Life.* See Appendix B.

service. Afterwards, a telephone call to the Whites resulted in an invitation to spend the night. The two teen-age girls went into gales of laughter when I described my evening. The Baptist church had built a new building in Manhattan Beach, and sold the old one to another group. The new occupants were very different!

The Whites were very cordial, inviting me back after checking in at El Toro. Thus began a friendship that has grown stronger over the past 53 years. With the passing of my own good father in 1986, Charles White, age 96, has become my surrogate father.

My journey in summary:

10 legs in eight different aircraft –

54D, RGD, C-119, HP67 Hastings, Lancaster Bomber, P2V-Neptune, C-121 Constellation, CH-46 Helicopter

Three pick up trucks, Three buses, One taxi (only the buses and taxi cost money) It was really nice to be home with my own family. Home for Christmas!

AFRICA
Return to Corpus Christi, Texas from Nairobi-
January 1958

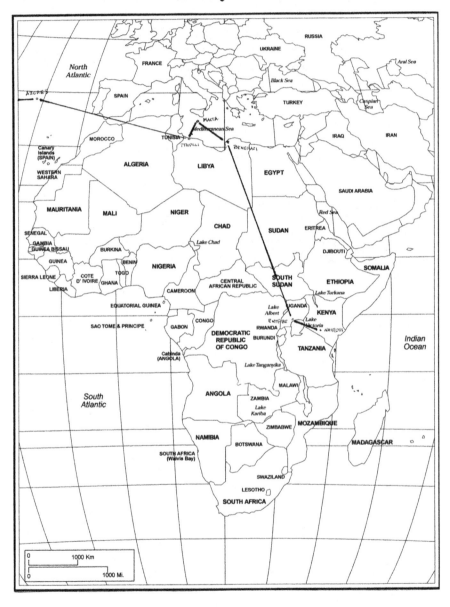

Eagle, Globe, and Anchor

Captain John W. Thomas, Jr., in his book *Fix Bayonets!* gives the accepted version of the original *Tell it to the Marines*!

They relate of Charles II that at Whitehall a certain sea-captain, newly returned from the Western Ocean, told the King of flying fish, a thing never heard in old England. The King and court were vastly amused. But, the naval fellow persisting, the Merry Monarch beckoned to a lean, dry colonel of the sea regiment, with seamed mahogany face, and said, in effect: "Colonel, this tarry-breeks here makes sport with us stay-at-homes. He tells of a miraculous fish that forsakes its element and flies like a bird over the water." "Sire," said the colonel of Marines, "he tells a true thing. I myself have often seen those fish in your Majesty's seas around Barbados--" "Well," decided Charles, "such evidence cannot be disputed. And hereafter, when we hear a strange thing, we will tell it to the Marines, for the Marines go everywhere and see everything, and if they say it is so, we will believe it."[374]

This 22 year old hadn't gone everywhere nor seen everything, but he had surely seen a lot. He was about to see a whole lot more in the Marine Corps!

El Toro

The White's residence in Rolling Hills was about 40 miles from El Toro. The weather was cool under an overcast sky. Orange groves were on either side of the road near the field. The long straight road to the base was lined with tall eucalyptus trees, and the terrain was flat.

The main gate was manned by sharp Marines, who directed me to the check-in office. Streets were wide and lined with semi-tropical trees. Buildings were Spanish-style with beige stucco. El Toro was the headquarters of the 3rd Marine Aircraft Wing (MAW), where I was assigned to Marine Air Group (MAG) 15. The Group placed me in Marine

---

[374] Col. Robert D. Heinl, Jr., *The Marine Officer's Guide*, (Annapolis, Maryland, United States Naval Institute, 1964), 156.

Attack Squadron VMA-311, flying the same aircraft last flown in advanced training.

The Navy doctors found me physically qualified for duty involving flying on 14 January, 1958. The next day rooms 223 and 224 were assigned in a new brick Bachelor Officers Quarters (BOQ). After the building was completed, the rooms did not meet government minimum floor area standards, so each officer had two rooms with a private bath. Those were pretty neat "diggings" for a displaced Zinjian! Meals were served in the Officer's Closed Mess, across from the Officer's Club.

VMA–311, billeted in one story buildings near a 1942 vintage medium sized hangar, was shaded by eucalyptus trees. Flying began on 24 January, and 10 hours were logged in before the 2nd of February.

January weather brought mostly overcast skies. So it was an eye opener one morning when clear skies revealed a 5,600 foot plus mountain 13 miles east of the field. Several Corsairs had attempted penetrating that "cumulogranite" cloud during the war – all had failed! They were still there!

Many pilots came into the Marine Corps directly from the Navy, so Air Fleet Marine Force Pacific (AIRFMFPAC) Leadership School set up an Indoctrination Course to "eliminate ignorance." Students colloquially called it "charm school." My only memorable recollection was the commanding officer's introduction. A Major, bald as a cue ball, said the only problem with his "hairdo" was noise when it rained.

Every Marine is considered a rifleman, and must qualify annually with the weapon issued to each recruit. In 1958, that firearm was the MI Garand. In 1936, the Department of War adopted it as the basic service rifle. That bold step placed the Army far ahead of its rivals around the globe. The Marine Corps normally desired uniformity with Army weapons, but was not convinced it was rugged enough for landing operations. The Corps also hesitated in part, due to tremendous confidence in the accuracy and reliability of the 1903 30:06 Springfield.[375]

The Springfield replaced the 30-40 KRAG after the 1898 Spanish American War. Springfield Armory, which had been manufacturing the best rifles in the world for over 100 years,[376] copied features from the 93 and 98 German Mauser actions. A royalty on each rifle was paid to Mauser amounting to $200,000 for patent infringement rights.[377]

---

[375] *U S M C - A Complete History*, (Hong Kong, Hugh Lauter Levin Associates, Inc., 2002), 252.
[376] Col. T. Whelen, "Days of the Springfield, Part II," *Gun Digest* – 1961, 107.
[377] Ibid.

Production at the Springfield Armory of the 1903 firearm was discontinued in 1937. The Corps established a formal competition for a new weapon in November 1940, comparing three semi-automatic rifles with the Springfield. The results: the Marine Corps formally adopted the Garand.[378]

One of the best purchases I made was one of the million and a half surplus1903 Springfield rifles. It has one of the smoothest actions of any bolt action rifle, and cost 40 (1950's) dollars. It is still in my gun safe.

Army Col. Townsend Whelen, closely involved in its manufacture and performance, had this to say in 1963:

The superb record that the Springfield rifle has made in our service for dependability and durability is well-known, as is its remarkable record for accuracy at the National Matches and other competitions where it was used. At the National Matches in the last two years the MI (Garand) rifles, also manufactured at Springfield Armory, are said to have shot as accurately and scored as high as the Springfield 1903 rifle ever did. Our army has won two World Wars with Springfield rifles.[379]

The Marine Rifle "A" Course consisted of several hours of lectures and practice. This included disassembly, cleaning, assembly, and lubrication. Firing positions, sight picture, and trigger squeeze were taught, shooting jackets issued, and use of the sling demonstrated. Dry firing practice followed. Safety was emphasized from start to finish.

Finally, we went to the Rifle Range. That was where the fun began. There were three levels of performance; Marksman, Sharp Shooter, and Expert. Doc's coaching bore fruit in my expert score. The only inconvenience; with my thumb on the universal-fits-all stock, rifle recoil gave me a fat lip!

Pilots were armed and expected to shoot the .38 caliber revolver. The short sight radius made this more challenging, but with practice, an expert score was achieved.

El Toro, the first Marine Corps installation ever visited, was the nicest base of my military career!

[378] *U S M C - A Complete History*, Ibid., 252 – 253.
[379] Col. T. Whelen, Ibid.,107.

VMA–311

Amphibious assault doctrines developed in WW II included Marine Close Air Support.[380] *The Functions Paper* of 1948, a Defense Department directive, required the Marine Corps to provide forces of <u>combined arms</u>, including supporting air components.

The idea was to have an autonomous force in readiness that could be moved into action quickly. The peculiarity of Marine doctrine was the full spectrum of support provided the infantry man on the ground. Close air support provided readily available aid from ground attack aircraft capable of putting ordinance within 50 yards of supported troops. This was integrated with artillery and naval gunfire. The biggest advantage was the short response time for infantry to receive requested air strikes. It was a three dimensional air/ground team.

VMA–311 used F9F8 Cougar aircraft, originally designed as air superiority fighters. The role of fighters was to isolate the battle field from enemy air. Being one of the first Navy jet fighters, it had a centrifugal flow compressor which required a larger frontal area than axial flows. The J–48 engines had a 48 inch compressor diameter, much larger than the axial flow engines of the F–86 and MIG–15. Outclassed as a fighter, the Cougar became an air-to-ground attack aircraft.

During my seven months in this squadron, my log book shows lots of bombing flights. Getting accurate hits on the ground was tricky. The first consideration was wind direction and speed. Bomb sight adjustments were predicated on dive angle. The roll-in point was the determining factor, so ground observers had a "harp" to measure this critical component. Once established on the dive, tracking to the target was essential, but could not become exclusive because target fixation could be fatal! Release airspeed was critical, and had to be reached at the pre-determined release altitude. Four things had to coincide for accurate hits: dive angle, correct air speed, release altitude, and sight pipper on the target.

Three dive angles were practiced; 30 degrees, 45 degrees, and a high dive which was as close to 90 degrees as possible. This delivery started about 10,000 feet above the target. When over head, you rolled on your back, pulled the nose sharply down, and tracked to the target. As the aircraft accelerated, it pulled the aircraft horizontally towards the vertical.

---

[380] Col. Robert D. Heinl, Jr., *The Marine Officer's Guide*, Ibid., 131.

The practice bombs were heavier than the glide bombing ordinance, so better hits were possible.

There were two squadron deployments during this period. The first was 95 miles north to Mojaive, near Edwards Air Force Base. The purpose was to operate closer to bombing targets. The second was 105 miles west of El Toro, on San Nicholas Island. This was an exercise in operating from a captured island. In 1958, the helicopter was used in developing vertical envelopment. Consequently, my transportation to the field was an H – 34 helicopter. Cots and tents were our accommodations.

There were two Cougar squadrons deployed, and one of the other unit's aircraft flamed out over the approach end of the runway. It landed short, and damage appeared minimal. The impact, however, drove the seat up the ejection track, releasing seat belt and shoulder harness. The pilot didn't survive.

One of the pilots in my squadron had rented a house in Laguna Beach in preparation for his upcoming marriage. The dead pilot was supposed to have shared the place until the wedding. The situation was offered to me. Moving out of the BOQ put me in a delightful community on the Pacific Ocean near the church I had been attending. An apartment right on the beach was subsequently taken. My situation for the next year couldn't have been more enjoyable. It is still a pleasant memory!

The Cold War emphasis in 1958 was nuclear deterrence. There were nuclear weapons that could be delivered by single engine aircraft. The problem was escaping the blast of your own weapon. The stipulated technique was a loft maneuver that tossed the bomb in the air, giving time for egress prior to detonation. An atomic weapons course was given in San Diego in preparation for such tactics.

Another school in San Diego was a five day survival course. One day's rations were issued to each student for the duration. The first two days were in San Diego, where water survival was reviewed. Easily caught crabs became tiresome! One little fish was cooked for me by the Filipino sailor in my group. What a treat! The second segment was in the hills away from the ocean. The idea was to become hungry enough to eat anything. (Black snake was like gnawing a chicken neck.) The final phase was escape and evasion, which included prisoner of war survival. I promised myself a big steak that Friday night. I could only eat half. My stomach had shrunk!

Section tactics frequently involved two aircraft, contending with each for a firing advantage on the loser's tail. This used to be called "dog-fighting," but our term was "hassling." There were two factors that improved aircraft performance, getting lighter by burning off fuel and descending into denser air. The rule was that the game was over when the minimum altitude was penetrated, or when a minimum fuel was reached. One day a more experienced pilot in our squadron wiped a new man off his tail on the ground, when they both violated the minimum altitude restriction. Breaking that rule was fatal for the new guy.

Douglas Aircraft developed a small, but powerful airplane specifically designed for the ground attack mission. It had long, awkward-looking landing gear, allowing nuclear shapes to be carried on a centerline rack. It first came into service in 1955, and was scheduled to replace the F–9 in VMA-311. We attended ground school on the new aircraft, and visited the factory to observe construction. I was slightly disappointed in its sub-sonic top speed, but knew better than to argue with the Lord. The F–9 was at least transonic if you climbed as high as possible and pointed the nose straight down with full power. The mach needle might barely pass the mach one index before you were slowed by denser air. But that was faster than the A – 4s were allowed to fly. What would really be nice would be flying one of those bat winged Douglas F4D Skyrays with its noisy afterburner!

VMF–251

Whether the Lord built the desire for speed and noise in me, or whether He was reading the deep desires of my heart, is probably debatable. The end result was change of squadron orders. My last flight in VMA-311 was a glide bomb sortie[381] on Wednesday, 30 July, 1958. Exactly three weeks later, I had my first flight in the newest, fastest, noisiest, most expensive jet fighter the Navy had ever bought. A junior pilot in VMF (Marine Fighter Squadron) 251 was one of the most prestigious positions in Marine Corps Aviation. Who would have thought skinny, knobby-kneed Glennie would ever have such an opportunity?

VMF-251 was just forming across the field in MAG–33. It was the second F-8 squadron on the base, scheduled to rotate to the Far East in a year or so. A lot of training had to take place in that time. After ground school, the squadron deployed to El Centro, Arizona, where there was less traffic and better weather.

---

[381] Sortie - One mission by a single military plane. (Webster's New World College Dictionary), 1369.

My first flight was 20 August, 1958 in Bureau Number 145365. The weather was clear, and the familiarization flight went as briefed until the first touchdown. After burning fuel down to a landing weight, touch and go landings were scheduled. The first approach was monitored by a qualified LSO (Landing Signal Officer) and was normal until touch down. A sharp jolt caused me to add power immediately for a go-around. When airborne again the cock-pit was lit up with warning lights and the LSO said my right landing gear had separated from the aircraft.

The chase airplane confirmed the damage, and the decision to burn down to minimum landing weight was made. Yuma was a WW II practice airfield with three runways in a triangular pattern. The east/west runway on the north was extended to the west for jet landings. The nose gear and left main were safely down and locked. The approach and touch down was made to the east on the runway extension. After touch down, the right wing was held up as long as possible. When the wing tip touched, directional control was lost. The aircraft slid to the right at the northwest end of the old triangular runway, slewed 180 degrees, and stopped on the runway. Fire equipment was on the scene immediately but no time was wasted in shutting the engine down and jumping to the ground, survival equipment and all. Needless to say, my pulse rate had been elevated for some time! My log book recorded two landings.

The cause of the accident was determined to be the failure of an alloy gland nut that held two barrels of the shock strut together. The shock strut acted as a hydraulic accumulator for one of two aircraft control systems. A third hydraulic system controlled the landing gear, wing slats, and flaps. The third system was lost when the gear extension cylinder was torn loose. All that was working was one of three 3,000 psi hydraulic systems to control the aircraft. Later, the aircraft was fixed and flew again.

Much later, I was invited to the home of the Personnel Officer of VMA–311. This man was instrumental in my transfer to the new squadron. He related a phone conversation with my new CO (Commanding Officer) that went something like this: "Colonel, I'm sending you a pilot that doesn't drink."

"Well, we'll just open him up and pour it down."

"Not this one!"

"Then we'll get rid of him."

"If you do, you'll be making a big mistake, and I personally will do everything I can to make you look bad."

My first flight was apparently what was needed for the new colonel to give me a chance. We got along just fine. He required his officers to show up at happy hour on Fridays after work. My solution was to belly up to the bar next to the skipper, order a grapefruit juice, and drink it down. Setting the empty glass on the bar, I would say: "By your leave, Sir, that's my one for the road."

His response, with a grin was, "See you on Monday, Lieutenant."

F8U–Crusader

Supersonic flight in the Crusader was a neat experience. The syllabus called for a normal take-off and climb above 30,000 feet. In level flight the afterburner was lit. This was simply dumping raw fuel in the exhaust gases creating a rocket-like explosion. As the aircraft accelerated towards mach, the pitch controls became more sensitive, requiring a delicate touch. Once the aircraft was supersonic the noise level diminished, so that the only sound was from spinning gyros. Response again became normal, giving a solid feeling of control. This was the first Navy aircraft to fly 1,000 miles an hour. We wore special pins on civilian clothes proclaiming our prowess. It was embarrassing to the Air Force that the Crusader out-performed the contemporary F–100 Super Sebre by a handsome margin, powered by the same Pratt & Whitney J–57 afterburning engines. It also had more internal fuel. Carrier-based fighters were not supposed to be superior to the land-based variety.[382]

50,000 feet was the max altitude pilots could fly without full pressure suits. Our squadron hoped to fly our aircraft to Japan, across the Pacific Ocean. This was known as a "transpac." Since the F-8 could exceed 50,000 feet, and a water immersion suit was needed over the ocean, a full pressure suit met both requirements. We were sent to the U.S. Navy S.P.A.C.E. School in San Diego. S.P.A.C.E. stood for "Society of Pioneering Astronauts and Celestial Exploration." We underwent low pressure chamber exercises, and were fitted with very expensive suits. They were difficult to don, very hard to cool, and cumbersome to fly in. Worn in the aircraft only once, above 50,000 feet, it was difficult flying without aural cues. The fish bowl helmet blocked out all cockpit sounds. At 50,000 feet, the deep purple color of the sky above with light blue around the horizon

---

[382] Peter Mersky, *Vought F-8 Crusader*, (London, England, Osprey Publishing Limited, 1989), Back Cover.

was memorable. Fortunately, the transpac was cancelled, so we didn't have to spend uncomfortable hours in those "Moon Bags."

In July 1960 we began preparing for carrier qualification. This required extremely precise speed control down a stabilized narrow beam of light (glide path.) Speed control was important because of the almost 55 foot length of the aircraft. If the speed was too slow, an in-flight engagement slammed the aircraft to the deck. If too fast, the aircraft floated over the wires, resulting in a bolter and a go around. After 110 practiced passes on the field we were scheduled to qualify on the *USS Oriskany* (CVA 34) off San Diego.

There was very little wind on the 25th of July, so the ship had to sail fast enough for wires to stay below the aircraft's maximum engagement speed. A squadron of A-4s was qualifying, with a lower speed, so they began. We were spectators, high above the flight deck in vulture's row. One of the A-4's got a cold catapult shot when the bridle parted. The pilot almost got stopped but dribbled over the bow. The cockpit was severed by the ship and bounced down the port (left) side. The fuselage went down the starboard (right) side. The helicopter followed the larger part until the pilot popped a flare. The rescued pilot was brought back to the ship, put in a dry flight suit, launched in another aircraft, and deprived of time to ponder.

Later some of us got a few landings until the engineering officer came to the bridge with a double handful of Babbitt metal. The propeller shafts melted their bearings, putting a squadron of disgruntled Marines back on the beach.

One day, one of our pilots aborted a take-off requiring heavy breaking. The cause for the rejected take-off was apparently resolved, and he taxied back for a second attempt. The gear was retracted soon after liftoff, without giving hot brakes a chance to cool. The tires cooked off in the wheel wells where fuel lines were routed. The pilot died in the wreckage – our first fatality.

Japan

Our aircraft were transported to Japan aboard ship, and the pilots were flown by commercial aircraft. My first impression of this Asian civilization was that the Japanese people were culturally refined in contrast to many Americans. Though never exposed to those of the higher castes, the people were a pleasant surprise.

After our aircraft were restored to flying condition, we began standing the Japanese self defense hot pad. This entailed two armed aircraft on 15 minute alert during daylight hours. Our mission was to fly BARCAP (Barrier Combat Air Patrol) between Russian aircraft and Japan.

Two-wheel Approach

By November, Field Mirror Landing Practice (FMLP) was resumed in preparation for "carquals." Sunday, 29 November, 1959, on my sixth FMLP pass, the left wheel rims came apart, leaving a stub axle. An attempt to engage arresting wires from the Morest,[383] gear at the center of the field failed when the stub axle caught the wire before the hook engaged. The aircraft was cocked to the left, and slowed too much to take-off even with afterburner. The stub axle came off the wire and the airplane skittered in a wide curve to the left, headed towards an ammo bunker. Spectators on the bunker beat a hasty retreat. The left landing gear plowed a furrow in the soft ground and brought the aircraft to a smooth stop. This was considered a "good landing," since I could walk away from the aircraft.

---

[383] Morest or Mobile Arresting Gear - Gear was comprised of two aircraft, carrier, arresting engines on either side of a runway at midfield. Two arresting cables connected the two engines. Engaging either arresting cable with a tailhook stopped the aircraft.

Second Two-wheel Landing

The *USS Midway* (CVA-41) was off Japan for our second qualification attempt. A few landings were made, but not enough to complete a 10-landing qualification.

The Philippines

The runway at Atsugi, Japan was closed for re-surfacing early in 1960 and VMF-251 was moved to Cubi Point in the Philippines. Runway 7/23 was on the south side of Subic Bay, a deep water port used by the US Navy. On a hill above the runway was a long masonry Bachelor Officers Quarters (BOQ) surrounded by tropical jungle. It was an exotic change from cosmopolitan Japan.

Historic Manila Bay, where Admiral George Dewey destroyed the Spanish fleet in 1898, was the next inlet south on the western coast of Luzon. Corregidor Island, where American forces made a heroic last stand against Japanese forces in WW II, guarded its entrance. Relics of global warring abounded in that part of the world.

In March 1960, VMF-251 participated in Operation Blue Star (19-24 March) on Taiwan. This was the largest amphibious operation since WW II,[384] involving ships from the 7th Fleet, the 3rd Marine Division, the 1st Marine Brigade, and the 1st Marine Aircraft Wing.[385] It simulated an invasion of southern Taiwan. We were bivouacked at Ping Tung.

One night we heard that one of the Chinese guards was caught sleeping on watch. His officer was able to get his weapon, and he was immediately put in the back of a truck, taken out, and shot. The Chinese Nationalists were at war, and very serious about their security.

Atsugi runway was re-opened in June, so we returned to the delights of Japan. FMLP practice immediately began, and by August we were ready for "Carquals" on the *USS Ranger* (CVA-61) off Okinawa. The *Ranger* was one of the Forrestal Class super carriers, much larger than the *USS Midway* (CVA-41) or the *USS Oriskany* (CVA-34). The most noticeable differences were the steam catapults. Hydraulic catapult acceleration rates were higher at the beginning of the stroke. Steam cats gave a constant rate, which was much more comfortable.

F-8 on Approach

---

[384] Maritime quest, "Operation Blue Star," http://www.maritimequest.com/misc-pages/sland-terms/slang-o.htm-OperationBlueStar. (accessed July 29, 2011).
[385] *USMC - A Complete History*, Ibid., 527.

After 10 landings we were qualified, and flew our aircraft back to Japan. Four aircraft flew in formation, and were launched from four catapults sequentially. My aircraft was the same one that plowed the field at Atsugi the previous November, and was the fourth to be launched. Atsugi was more than two hours away, so full fuel tanks were needed. This required a higher end speed on the catapult and a higher G acceleration. Being number four, my aircraft was on a waist cat on the angled deck.

The Carrier Air Group aircraft were on the beach during quals, and now were at marshalling points around the ship, waiting for us to leave. Just before launch, the radio announced a mid-air collision between an A-4 and a propeller driven AD. The parachute from the A-4 could be seen descending over my right shoulder. The impact had apparently fired the ejection seat, for the pilot was dead before water entry.

Peter Mersky, in the introduction to his very thorough book, *Vought F-8 Crusader,* had this to say:

> *To its early pilots, the F-8 was a proud, skittish thoroughbred which, if handled properly and respectfully, endowed its rider with a euphoric feeling of godlike invincibility, offering breathtaking speed and grace in the arenas of aerial combat. But, to this same early cadre, the F-8 could be a coffin if poorly flown, especially around its main venue, the aircraft carrier. Many young naval aviators paid for their haphazard operation of the Crusader with their lives.*[386]

Four F-8's in Formation

---

[386] Peter Mersky,*Vought F-8 Crusader,* Ibid., 7.

Blessed

My time in VMF-251 was exceptional for several reasons. The Marine Corps had an excellent program of phase training, with ample time before unit rotation. This provided personnel stability and training that prepared the squadron to function as an efficient team.

Another asset was access to excellent technical schools at El Toro and Dallas. This was enhanced by very competent Chance Vought representatives assigned to the squadron by the manufacturer.

VMF-251 was the most deploying squadron at El Toro, taking advantage of the assets at various facilities.

All this, plus the finest airplane in the world for the job. It took three aircraft carrier decks, but persistence prevailed, and the last hurdle was overcome.

The skipper's final word in his tour book comment was "You're full fledged MARINES, the hard core of the professional Marine Corps."[387]

"We are proud to claim the title of United States Marine!

---

[387] Lt. Col. Al Clark, *VMF-251 Cruise Book – Oct. 1959- Jan. 1961,* from the Commanding Officer's Comments.

EAST ASIA
From Japan to Kijabe – 1961

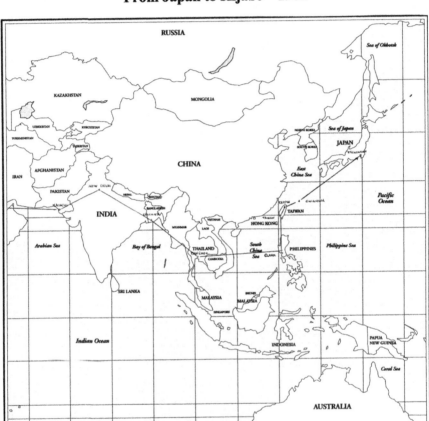

AFRICA
From Japan to Kijabe - 1961

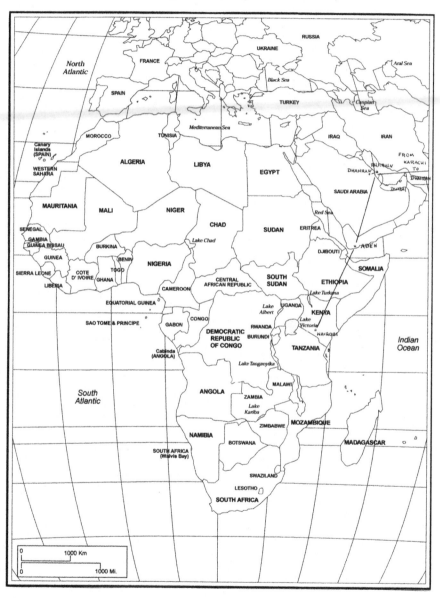

Travels of a Leatherneck

The Marine's long-standing nickname, "Leathernecks," goes back to the leather stock, or neckpiece, which was part of the Marine uniform from 1775-1875. Its purpose was to promote proper posture. Descended from the leather stock is the standing collar on Marine dress blues, whites, and evening dress.[388] It does indeed encourage a military bearing.

Marine Corps Emblem

---

[388] Colonel Robert D. Heinl, Jr., *The Marine Officer's Guide*, (Annapolis, Maryland, United States Naval Institute, 1964), 149.

The history of the Marine emblem is also rooted in the distant past. The globe was borrowed from the British Marines in 1868 by General Zeilin, 7th commandant of the Marine Corps. The globe had been conferred on the Royal Marines in 1827 by King George IV. Because it was impossible to recite all the achievements of Marines on the Corps colors, said the king, "the Great Globe itself" was to be their emblem for Marines had won honor everywhere.[389] The British globe displayed the Eastern Hemisphere whereas the land masses of the Western Hemisphere are superimposed on the US Marine globe. The eagle and foul anchor were added by General Zeilin to leave no doubt the US Marine Corps was both American and maritime.

One of the definitions of an emblem is *a picture with a motto or verses allegorically suggesting some moral truth.*[390] Inasmuch as I believe my entry into the Marine Corps was the result of divine guidance, there are four aspects of the Marine emblem which suggest divine truth. Psalm 2:8 states that the globe of planet earth is to be the possession of the only begotten Son of Him who sits in the heavens. Matthew 5:5 states that the meek shall *inherit* the earth. Spiros Zodhiates, Th. D. says that 'meekness' in this context means *to become angry at sin.* It is the active attitude of the Christian toward sin, combating it instead of a passive, indifferent attitude.[391] History and the Marine Corps Hymn emphasize that Marines are first to fight for right and freedom.

The eagle is referred to in Isaiah 40:31 "...those who hope in the Lord... will soar on eagles wings." (NIV p.1036, Quest Study Bible) Hebrews 6:13-20 emphasizes that we have hope as an anchor, Christ Jesus. And finally, super-imposed above these three is the motto *Semper Fidelis*, reminding us that our God is *always faithful*. One more confirmation of my calling to three dimensional warfare.

Philippines

There were three trips taken while based in the Philippines. One was a weekend in Manila. One memory of Manila persists. Standing on a street corner waiting for traffic, a man behind me tapped me on the shoulder and

---

[389] Ibid., 144.
[390] *Webster's New World College Dictionary*, 4th ed., 464.
[391] Spiros Zodhiates, *The Hebrew-Greek Key Study Bible*, (Grand Rapids, Michigan, Baker Book House, 1984), 1141.

asked in English: "Excuse me sir, are you U.S. Marine?" With a nod in the affirmative, he responded: "I thought so." Perhaps it was my haircut!

The scheduled Rest and Relaxation (R&R) trip to Hong King was an opportunity to buy tailor-made clothes and Rolex watches. Prices there in the 60's were especially reasonable.

Beguio is the summer capital in western Luzon, at an elevation of almost 5,000 feet. Several of the pilots rented a special services station-wagon with driver to take them to this lovely resort. A couple of us were tied up in a court-martial case and couldn't leave with them. However, two pilots checked out the SNB a twin engine Beechcraft, carrying 6-8 passengers, and flew us there that evening.

Higher altitude with lower temperatures was a welcome relief from muggy Cubi Point. A carved wooden figurine of an Asian girl, done by a well-known artist, caught my eye in the market there. It is in my adventurer's room with other keepsakes.

The ride back to Cubi Point was an adventure. Crooked mountain roads with steep drop offs made us appreciate the flight up. A beautiful cathedral on a mountain by the side of the road is still a pleasant memory.

Japan

One of my most vivid memories was a five day trip to Kyoto, the old capital of Japan. It is the only time I ever kept a detailed diary. Traveling alone by train from Tokyo on an all night coach was tiresome to say the least. There was not enough knee room. Seat backs were vertical and flat. Ten hours was a long ride, leaving an aching neck and back.

Eight o'clock in the morning found me at the small hotel the Japan Travel Bureau had booked. Hot green tea and sweet cakes were breakfast. A tatami bed was laid out, my first experience with Japanese sleeping arrangements. Drifting off to sleep, the sound of a roaring lion took me back to my roots. A zoo was next door. That really was a lion roaring me to sleep that morning!

My transportation in Japan was an old 250 cc Honda Dream motorcycle, purchased from a Marine whose tour was over. Gravel truck drivers made open road riding very interesting, but a trip to Lake Ashinoko was worth the effort. At the southern end of this lake, a hotel provided a beautiful view of Mount Fuji, reflected on the lake's surface. My third visit was an overnight Christmas Eve. It was quite festive, with the hotel staff putting on a spirited program.

Mt. Fuji

Because space-available travel was intended, a month's extension was requested for a trip west to Africa, after the holidays. My squadron had rotated back to the States in December, so my new job was officer in charge of the Morest Unit. The group commander had ordered all final landings arrested by the Mobile Arresting Engines. Five enlisted men had been running this operation around the clock. They had performed maintenance the Navy was sure could not be done in the field. But they were Marines, getting the job done. One was a pen and ink artist, who drew a caricature of his commanding officer that still amuses me!

Bangkok Bound

Travel in Japan was relatively easy, with frequent trains and inexpensive taxis. A passport was issued by the American Consul in Yokohama. With passport in hand, embassies in Tokyo were visited. Visas for the Philippines, Pakistan, Kenya, Saudi Arabia, China, and India were acquired.

The last departure from Atsugi was on Sunday evening, 29 January, 1961. My name was not on the space-available list at Tachikawa Air Force

Base, so traveling companions from Atsugi left on the 0100 flight without me.

Space became available on a 0530 flight to Okinawa. The 0530 Air Evac flight was a Convair C-131 Samaratan, a two engine aircraft designed to replace the venerable DC-3 after WW II. It was pressurized and cruised at 280 miles per hour. The limit to piston engine performance was reached with this airplane. We aborted once because of a bad magneto, but finally at 0700 climbed through an overcast sky and were on our way. The flight continued on to Taipei, Taiwan, where we spent the night.

At 0730 the next morning we continued to Tainan, on the southwestern side of Taiwan. By 0900 we were airborne for Clark Air Force Base in the Philippines, arriving at 1300. There were no flights the rest of that day, so BOQ accommodations were provided.

There was space next morning on a C-131 leaving at 0700 for Bangkok, Thailand. Several of the 50 seats were occupied by Filipino military personnel, headed for a Southeast Asian Treaty Organization (SEATO) meeting in Bangkok.

SEATO was formed in 1954 for the purpose of preventing communism from gaining ground in the region. The United States, Great Britain, France, New Zealand, Australia, Pakistan, Thailand, and the Philippines were members. The Philippines and Thailand were the only Southeast Asian nations..

Headquartered in Bangkok, SEATO maintained no military forces of its own, but organized joint military exercises each year. Economic foundations and living standards were strengthened by a variety of meetings, and exhibitions on cultural, religious and historical topics. Non-Asian member states sponsored fellowships for Southeast Asian scholars.

Vietnam, Cambodia, and Laos were excluded from a military alliance by the Geneva Agreements of 1954, after the fall of French Indochina. However, the United States used SEATO as justification for refusing to go forward with the 1956 elections intended to unify Vietnam maintaining the divide at the 17th parallel. As the conflict in Vietnam unfolded, the inclusion of Vietnam as a territory under SEATO protection gave the United States the legal framework for continued involvement there.[392] Thus evolved a global conflict, eventually engulfing United States Marines in a very unpopular 10-year war.

---

[392] "Southeast Asia Treaty Organization (SEATO), 1954,"
http://www.globalsecurity.org/military/world/int/seato.htm, (accessed August 5, 2011).

The Thai government and the United States jointly engaged in a project to evaluate the educational and human resources of the Southeast Asia kingdom.[393] This was under the patronage of the Education Division of the United States Operations Mission (USOM.)[394] Amazingly, my mother's older brother, Dr. Dale W. Houk, was appointed to that post.

After a 1,365 mile flight, I was able to spend three days with Uncle Dale and Aunt Ruth in Bangkok. They moved in the upper echelons of royal society in the Kingdom of Siam. This was a nice respite after four days and 3,500 miles of "three dimensional hitch-hiking."

The US Embassy flight left Bangkok at 0753 on 4 February, 1961. It was another beautiful Lockheed Constellation. After a 90 minute stop at Calcutta, we continued on toward New Delhi. Our flight paralleled the Himalaya Mountains, where glistening snow capped peaks were clearly visible off the right wing. It was an impressive view of the highest mountain range on the planet! We over-nighted in a large hotel in New Delhi where the doorman was a large uniformed Sikh, with a neatly wound colorful turban. My younger sister Ruth painted a picture of one of these characters on black velvet. It, too, is in my museum of keepsakes.

India, no longer part of the British Empire, still reflected the years of British influence. Without British presence, India's history has been characterized by internal conflict.

Our journey continued west to Dhahran, Saudi Arabia with a stop at Karachi, Pakistan. As we descended to land in Arabia, the steward asked for my magazine. I told him I wanted to finish the article I was reading. He replied: "Lieutenant, I have to lock up all literature before we land. It's the law." I thought at first they were wary of pornography, but learned later it was a program of controlled ignorance. The barrier between 10% of the population who owned 90% as slaves had to be maintained. We landed in a sandy desert on the western side of the Persian Gulf at 1500 in the afternoon. The temperature in February was warm, but not uncomfortable. Over-night accommodations at the BOQ were convenient and pleasant.

Bahrain Island was clearly visible from Dhahran, about 30 miles east. There was an RAF base there, with flights heading south. A Gulf Air aircraft left at 0800 the next morning. Twenty minutes later we landed on Bahrain Island. This was the only commercial flight used in my journey

[393] Hugh M. Smythe & Nibondh Sasedhorn, "Educational Planning in Thailand," *Comparative Education Review*, Volume 8, No 1 June 1964.
[394] http://pdh.usaid.gov/pdf-docs/PDACR494.pdf. (accessed August 5, 2011).

home. An RAF flight departed at 1700 that evening, and landed at Aden at 2130 for 90 minutes. Airborne again at 2300, Nairobi was reached at 0300 the next morning. Like Ferdinand Magellan's crew, I had circumnavigated the globe in about three year's time. This Marine was back in the land of Zinj, where life had begun 26 years earlier; home with family, enjoying life at healthful Kijabe. From 30 January to 7 February, 1961 I had flown 10,000 miles and enjoyed three days with relatives in Bangkok, spending very little money. Obviously the Lord was my travel agent!

Kijabe

Chapel Speaker - 1961

School was in session upon my arrival in February, and opportunities presented themselves for recounting adventures, in God's plan for my life. There was an invitation to speak in chapel, sing a solo in church, and teach a science class. As my wife keeps reminding me, FAITH is a Fantastic

Adventure in Trusting Him, and it was fun relating my latest quest. One of my keepsakes is a sweet little note Doc Propst's youngest daughter wrote, thanking me for encouraging her. It was good to be home!

An interesting conversation with one of my schoolmates left an indelible impression. He had been conscripted into the military during the Mau Mau emergency, and had spent a long time in the bush. Time away from the noise of civilization and the tension of pursuit sharpened senses and quickened reflexes. He told of being the last man in a single file patrol, passing through thick brush. Upon hearing a sound behind him, he turned, fired, and killed a waterbuck that landed on top of him, dead! A waterbuck is 50 inches high at the shoulder and can weigh up to 500 pounds. He must have needed help getting out from under that beast!

There are three prominent peaks dominating the view from Kijabe. Suswa is a double volcanic crater rising from the floor of the Rift Valley farthest away. Much closer, and to the right of Suswa, is Mount Longonot, with a crater that is almost perfectly round. A little further to the right is Kijabe Hill, an extension of the escarpment behind Kijabe Station. Early morning color photos were obtained, with these peaks brightly lit by the morning sun. Trees in the foreground were shaded by the escarpment to the east forming a black lacy frame. Prints from these slides decorated my domiciles for decades, graphic reminders of home.

Nairobi

Recollections of Nairobi were rekindled with shopping trips. The quality of wood carvings had definitely improved. Collecting animal wood carvings has been one of my avocations for decades, and it was a pleasure to see antelope with much better proportions. Shops close for the lunch hour, so shoppers frequented hotel dining rooms. The New Stanley Hotel was closest to downtown shopping, and had a beautiful high ceiled dining room. The single price menu consisted of soup, fish, curry, salad, roast beef, fruit, cheese with crackers, and coffee. Eating one's way through the whole menu consumed the full lunch period!

The New Stanley had some beautiful dioramas of miniature African animals, modeled by Louis Paul Jonas Studios, Inc. The details and coloring were works of art. When prices were checked, the only affordable piece for me was a Dik-Dik – one of the smallest antelopes. It is still a treasure!

African animals, carved by Swiss artists in ivory, were intricately detailed, the finest I had seen. Dad later got a cape buffalo and a rhino for me, which enhance my museum.

Farther from the center of town was my favorite. The Norfolk Hotel had been the local watering hole for old time colonials. It was older and more sedate than newer hotels. No one pushed you. You could eat your way casually through another full menu. The Aladdin lamps suspended from the ceiling were nostalgic reminders of days before electricity. It was a relic of the old colonial empire, a fond memory of my formative years.

The most important memories of this visit were the conversations with my Father. Dad was especially busy with school business during the day. But after supper, he made time for me. These discussions went on into the wee hours of the morning. I will never forget his response to my resolution about matrimony. Taking St. Paul's recommendations to remain single, coupled with the danger of my profession, I had resolved that if I were not married by age 25, I should remain single. Dad was quiet for a while, looked down at his outstretched feet, twisted his foot back and forth, and finally said: "Glennie, ever since you were seven years old, I have been praying for your mate." That ended the discussion, but gave me a hope I had never allowed myself before. Of course he was right, as evidenced by 48 years of married life with my best friend "Tweet!"

All too soon my two week vacation came to an end. It was time to continue on to my next duty assignment in Texas. After shopping around for flights, a flight to Aden became available on 21 February, two weeks after my arrival.

The aircraft was a Blackburn Beverly, the largest and most powerful military transport plane ever built in Britain. Until the beginning of the 1960's, the 47 Beverly C-1S was the mainstay of transport command.[395] We were airborne at 0810. My seat was in the troop section above the cargo well. The shadow on the ground clearly revealed extended wheels. Waiting for the landing gear retraction was futile. They were down and welded! They weren't supposed to come up! Seven hours and 20 minutes later we touched down at Aden. There was a window under the cockpit allowing me to watch the touch down close and personal. The runway was just about three feet below. We were back on the Arabian Peninsula.

---

[395] *Rand McNally Encyclopedia of Military Aircraft,* Enzo Angelucci (New York, NY, Military Press, 1983), s.v. "European and American postwar transports: 1947-50."

Next morning the Beverly headed towards Bahrain, stopping at bases in the Trucial States.

British East India Company ships were being attacked and pillaged by a seafaring clan of Arabs known as the Qawasin. An agreement signed in 1798 with the Al-Busaids, arch enemies of the Qawasin, made the British enemies of these seafaring pirates. Based in Ras-Al-Khaima, just west of the Straits of Hormuz in the Persian Gulf, these marauders were defeated by the Royal Navy by 1820. The British imposed a General Treaty of Peace on nine Arab sheikdoms in the southern coast of the gulf, and installed a garrison in the region. A Treaty of Peace in Perpetuity was established in 1853, when the British assumed all responsibility for arbitrating disputes between sheiks in the area. This final truce gave this part of the world its name for the next 120 years: Trucial States.

In the 1890's the British moved to formalize the agreements made with sheiks and rulers throughout the region. The Brits would provide protection in return for promises by these rulers that they would have no dealings with any foreign rulers without the express permission of Britain. This protection served the rulers in one crucial aspect at the end of WW I. Ibn Saud, king of Arabia, was uniting the interior of Arabia, and sweeping all before him. British promises of protection made Ibm Saud hesitate and ultimately bypass this region from his series of conquests. In return, the Trucial States were an extremely quiet and peaceful part of the British Empire, exactly as the Brits wanted it to be.[396]

The Bani Yas was a tribal confederation from the interior, which raised the ire of the British. These Bedouins quickly took over the slave trade routes, as the Royal Navy successfully removed the ocean traders. Keeping a watchful eye on this tribe, the British forced the trade further and further inland, but were unable to stamp it out completely.

One of our stops in the Trucial States was a place called Dubai. In the summer it was a hot, dry, barren land covered with salty sea sand. The only greenery was grown in soil trucked from mountains 20 miles away. Humidity was in the 90's. It looked like one of the worst places on earth. Had someone told me this would be home in 15 years, I would have said: "No way!!"

Some British soldiers boarded the plane as passengers. They wore khaki uniforms with red checked kaffiyeh's. Black cords of camel hair

---

[396]British Empire - The Map Room: Middle East: Trucial Oman, "Trucial Oman," http://www.britishempire.souk/maproom/trucialoman.htm. (accessed August 10, 2011).

called <u>igals</u> crowned their Arab headdress. When they described their sleeping routine in the summer, covering themselves with wet sheets, I would have added a double "No way!"

The Beverly aircraft's final stop, after a long day, was the RAF base on Bahrain Island. This big bird had brought me more than 2,000 miles from home. Two weeks with family and a timely return - another evidence of divine blessing. Gulf Air provided air transportation back to Dhahran in plenty of time to catch the embassy flight leaving on 23 February, 1961.

On my previous visit to Dhahran, a beautiful picture of a cheetah was on a Lufthansa Airlines calendar. One of these calendars was graciously given to me, and five beautiful framed pictures of African animals grace the walls of my museum.

Thursday evening at 2036, 439 pounds of mail was signed over to me as a Courier Officer. Lajes was the destination for 139 pounds, the other 300 pounds for Charleston, South Carolina. This responsibility insured my continuation on that airplane to its destination in the United States. No one at Wheelus in Tripoli, or Lajes would have as high a priority. From Thursday evening, 23 February to Sunday afternoon, C-121 Constellation #40161 was my temporary home. A quartet of Wright 3,400 horse power engines, running day and night, pulled our beautiful airplane through the sky at more than 320 miles per hour. We soared back to the land I defended, back to the land of round doorknobs, back to the most blessed country on the planet!

In November 1960, I purchased a 1961 356B Porsche in Tokyo. It was to be shipped to the States with my personal belongings. After arriving in South Carolina, my next project was traveling to New Orleans, where the car was to be delivered. So, in the "cockpit" of my beautiful heron gray Porsche, I proceeded to my duty station in Kingsville, Texas, well within the time frame of my leave. The whole trip reinforced my confidence in the Planner of my life, and my sensitivity to His leading.

AFRICA
From Nairobi to Charleston, South Carolina – 1961

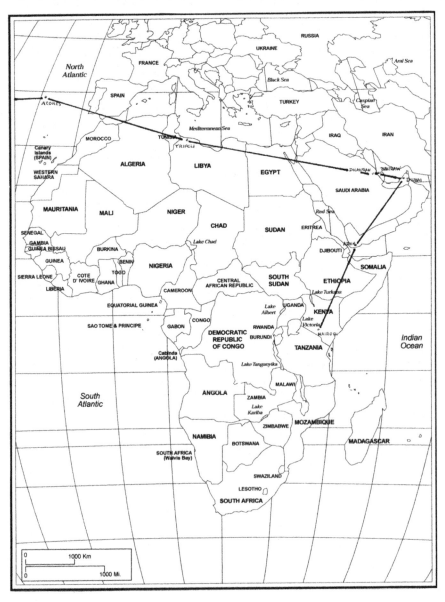

Kingsville

Richard King was born into a poor Irish family in New York City in 1824. At age 11, he ran away from an indentured jewelry apprenticeship, stowing away on a ship. By age 16, he became a steamboat pilot.[397] In 1845, at age 21, he arrived on the Rio Grande River, going into a shipping enterprise with Mifflin Kennedy. Together they made fortunes moving supplies for General Zackary Taylor in the Mexican War (1846-1848), and supplying the growing economy. King began investing in land, beginning with properties in Brownsville, Texas.

In 1852, King rode from the Rio Grande to the Lone Star Fair in Corpus Christi. The Nueces Strip, a coastal area between the Rio Grande and the Nueces Rivers, had very little drinking water. After 124 miles of travel, his party stopped at the first live water they had seen. This was the Santa Gertrudis Creek, a site shaded by large mesquite trees, an oasis offering protection from the sun as well as cool sweet water.

King purchased the property, and with the help of "Legs" Lewis and his Texas Mounted Volunteers, set up a cow camp. It was the opening gambit in his bid to tame the Nueces strip, otherwise known as the Wild Horse Desert. It was a signal of his willingness to battle with marauding Apaches from the north, raiding bandits from south of the Rio Grande, and with the tough intractable land itself. It was the beginning of a dream he was to pursue the rest of his life. This became the cradle of the cattle industry in the United States. Ranching in a land that gave no quarter inspired him to greatness in a way that river-boating never could. It became his quest, his obsession.

Dividing his time between the ranch and the steam-boast business in Brownsville, King formed a deep and long-lasting friendship with a young officer at Fort Brown, Lt. Col. Robert E. Lee, who suggested the location of the first ranch house on the high ground overlooking Santa Gertrudis Creek, a location easy to defend.

Henrietta Chamberlain, a minister's daughter, became King's wife in December 1854. Mrs. King brought gentleness and civilization to the Wild Horse Desert. She gave it a polish and a luster that made the ranch a

---

[397] Richard King (Texas) – Wikipedia, The Free Encyclopedia, "Richard King (Texas)," http://en.wikipedia.org/wiki/RichardKing (Texas). (accessed August 13, 2011).

welcome refuge for weary travelers.[398] She became the mother of King's five children, and outlived her husband by 40 years.

As of 1986, the King Ranch, sprawling across 825,000 acres of South Texas, was part of a modern, diversified agriculture corporation. The stockholders were virtually all descendants of one man, Richard King. He was a tough, stubborn, yet creative man, who had a vision, and was intrepid enough to make it come true. The story of the King Ranch is the story of this man, his dream, his tenacity, plus the daring and determined men and women after him, who through six generations kept the vision alive.[399]

VT-21

Naval Auxilary Air Station (NAAS) Kingsville, an outlying field of the Navy's Corpus Christi training complex, was located virtually in the middle of the King Ranch. Three advanced training squadrons were based there; VT-21 and V-22 two sister squadrons, each flying Grumman F-9s with identical syllabi. VT-23 flew Grumman F-11 fighters, and trained graduates of the other squadrons in advanced fighter tactics.

My original orders to VT-23, were changed to VT-21. This was most fortunate for me, for the syllabus was much broader and more diversified. It included transition to the F-9, Basic Instruments, Navigation, Formation, Night Flying, Bombing, Gunnery, and Car Quals.

Located just east of Kingsville, the NAAS was on flat land, 30 miles from the Gulf of Mexico. The hot sun on land caused a fairly strong breeze flowing from the gulf. Weather was usually good all year round, ideal for flight training.

The Bachelor Officers' Quarters (BOQ) was a two story beige brick building about a mile from the hanger. I had two rooms with a private shower. Just down the hall was a lounge and dining room, where instructors and students ate. Across the parking lot was the Officers' Club with an outdoor swimming pool. The married instructors lived in houses in Kingsville.

There were over 40 F-9's in my squadron. About half were two-seated F9F-8T's. The rest were single seat F-9F8B's. Grumman aircraft were strongly built, and stood up to student pounding better than others. This

---

[398] Jay Nixon, *Stewards of a Vision (A History of King Ranch)*, (Hong Kong, Everbest Printing Co., Ltd., 1986), 10.
[399] Ibid., 7.

was an excellent opportunity to build up single engine flight time, averaging more than 550 hours a year for three years-one of the best opportunities that could have come my way.

In spite of the instructor training program, there were two challenges. The first was analyzing exactly what had been acquired subconsciously in my flying experience. After determining the sequential mental processes required, verbal descriptions had to be stated early enough to have the student respond in time for aircraft control. This required trial and error practice, before the right combination was developed.

The second challenge was evaluating performance. With no previous experience with standards, what was acceptable or unacceptable? One of the squadron's solutions was assigning a student with reasonably good grades from basic to a first time instructor. Actually, my first student was one of my best. He had been a smoke jumper before the Navy, jumping by parachute to fight forest fires. He had no trouble, but should have gotten better grades. With no frame of reference on his part, he probably didn't know the difference.

There were other advantages to being an advanced instructor, over and above the higher performance aircraft. One was the elimination process of incompetent students in basic. Another was student motivation. All advanced students really did want their gold wings. A third benefit was learning maneuvers and procedures used in the fleet.

Flight instruction was an ideal relationship between an instructor and his student. It required much more than the acquisition of knowledge. Motor skill performance, in a three-dimensional environment, was the goal. The full spectrum of human attributes was necessary. These include wisdom, which is knowledge guided by understanding. Understanding is knowing things in their right order. A student must be open to coaching, and teachable. It requires physical strength and strength of character. Knowledge from the right source is foundational. Respect for the laws of nature is critical, and finally, good judgment, or making timely decisions, is vitally necessary.

An important factor in the instruction process was evaluating the student. One student would be so sensitive that any sharp correction caused a temporary cessation in learning. Another would become so focused that a sharp command was necessary to penetrate his concentration. It was interesting how much I learned about myself, as well as flying in this instructor-phase of God's curriculum for me.

Instrument navigation was the core of VT-21's syllabus. Learning to fly without a visible horizon, referring to six different instruments, was not natural. The physiology of three dimensional movements can cause spatial disorientation. Some people are more susceptible than others. Very few are unaffected. The key is *learning to believe the instruments rather than your senses.*

Integrating information from six different instruments requires a systematic *scan*. The secret of smooth instrument flight is trimming control pressures so the airplane will not have to be hand held. It took quite a while, but finally I was able to verbally trim the aircraft so students could learn the art. It definitely improved their *scan*.

The finale of the instrument program was a cross country flight to any part of the United States. Since this usually occurred on weekends, single instructors were drafted. Married guys preferred spending weekends with their families. There wasn't much going on in Kingsville, so I really didn't mind. My favorite airport was El Toro, California. The destination was supposed to be the student's choice, but most were persuadable.

Formation

F-9's – Diamond Formation

Formation flying followed instruments. This was one of the most interesting phases of the whole program. Essentially it was a study in relative motion. Initially, the rendezvous technique was taught. The leader flew in a large circle, allowing the wingman to get inside the arc and close the distance between. This was performed with two aircraft at first, later with four. Once the flight had formed, control was by hand signals.

An exercise called a tail chase was especially exhilarating. The wingman positioned himself behind and below the leader, fairly close but

Capt. G. H. Downing, VT-21 Instructor

with nose to tail clearance. The leader was then free to perform almost any maneuver as long as he didn't go to full power. The wingman needed the extra margin of energy to maintain position.

Landing from a formation was the final exercise. A flight of four was positioned in a right echelon,[400] at least five miles from the runway. At 250 knots airspeed, over the runway, the leader broke to the left with 45 degrees of bank, reduced power, and extended speed brakes. At max gear extension speed, landing gear was lowered. The object was to arrive at the 180 degree position,[401] abeam the runway end, in the landing configuration at the proper approach speed.

Five seconds after the leader broke, the number two man broke, then number three, then four. The whole flight was thus in trail with room to make individual approaches and landings.

After landing, the pilots taxied to the flight line, parked, and shut down the engines. Finally, everyone proceded to the air-conditioned ready room, removed sweaty G-suits, and was graded and debriefed by the instructor. Usually, all were tired but happy!

---

[400] Echelon - A step like formation of aircraft in which each aircraft is on a 45 degree line behind the lead aircraft, slightly stepped down.

[401] Abeam - The touchdown point with 180 degrees of turn to landing runway heading.

Summer – 1962

The summer midshipmen program was designed to acquaint Naval Academy students with various activities of the Navy. NAS Corpus Christi was tasked with a T-34 flight demonstration program. T-34's were ferried from the Pensacola area to Waldron Field, just south of the Naval Air Station. Various instructors were seconded for the summer. I was one of the hapless ones tagged for this chore.

Actually, it worked out advantageously. It involved renting an apartment in Corpus for three months. Ruth Ann was able to come down from Wheaton College, and spend the summer with me. She and I had fun together. It was a summer with many pleasant memories. Attendance at the Presbyterian Church introduced us to a family with an only child. Janet Stevenson became a close friend of the family, visiting us in Ohio, helping us build our house. She attended our children's weddings and was present in Colorado Springs for Jonathan's graduation from the Air Force Academy. She considered herself his surrogate mother. After her parents died, Janet died of cancer and left a substantial bequest to the three families of our children.

"Tweet"

Headquarters Marine Corps entertained applications for the single position of a Marine aviator on the Blue Angels Flight Demonstration Team. Close formation had always interested me, so my application was included with 36 others. My name was selected with four others for interviews. One of the five was a former F-8 squadron mate, who was a Landing Signal Officer (LSO.) Going to Pensacola for "car quals" had given him the right connections, and he was selected without interviewing any one else. Actually, I wasn't sure I could handle the socializing the job entailed. Besides, as it turned out, I got a much better deal that has lasted 48 years.

Lois Teuscher was the oldest of five children from central Illinois. Her parents, Dan and Edna, were Mennonite farmers, owning about 120 acres of the richest, blackest soil you can imagine. These hard working farmers had outgrown the legalistic restrictions of a two dimensional faith, and were seeking to rise into the realm of the Spirit. Their search led them to send Lois to Providence Bible Institute. Her roommate was my sister,

Gayle. The three of us traveled back and forth to school together, and became close friends.

The Teuschers drove to Rhode Island for the graduation of Lois's fiancé, and brought Gayle and me back to Ohio in a four-door Nash sedan. With two parents, two younger brothers, a younger sister, Gayle and me, it was crowded. Thelma, the third daughter, was a 16 year old high school student. While washing dishes with her other sister Mary, the second daughter, Thelma was given the nickname "Tweet." This has become her "name" ever since.

Lois married a Baptist minister of music. In 1963, she sent me a newsletter with a postscript about "Tweet" teaching school in Massachusetts, and included her address.

Most of my cross country flights had been to the west coast or Chicago. A change of destinations was inviting. Besides, a fellow cadet had become an airline pilot in Massachusetts. Why not fly up there and see what changes had taken place since our last trip in the old Teuscher Nash?

A contemporary card was sent on 11 January, 1963 asking: "Where in the world have you been?" She even answered, and a date was set to meet. On Friday, 1 March, a student and I set out for New England, refueling first at Navy, Memphis. The weather at our destination was below limits, so we landed in Virginia and spent the night. The next morning, a tire needed air, air bottles had to be serviced, and the weather still required an instrument flight clearance. A telephone call arranged for "Tweet" to meet me in Providence. We finally arrived that afternoon, in time for our date.

"Tweet" met me outside Quonset operations in her blue and white 1954 Chevy. Our first stop was for food. When her overcoat came off, the light blue sweater and gray skirt revealed positive changes in the past eight years! A visit to Barrington College, dinner in downtown Providence, and a visit with her sister and brother-in-law on Brown Hill completed our time together that Saturday.

Sunday morning, the four of us met for breakfast and drove back to the airport. The sailors recognized "quality goods," and invited "Tweet" to the tower for our take-off. The following week-end, a flight surgeon wanted to visit his family in Philadelphia. My brother Ed was in medical school there, so I invited "Tweet" to meet me in Philly. I wouldn't have been surprised had she been "too busy," but *wonder of wonders*, she jumped on an airplane in Boston and flew down. Ed's med school friends put her up for the night, and we had our second date. By this time, the die was cast! We met at Lois's home in Birmingham, Alabama for Easter. I flew to New

England a couple of times, and visited her in Illinois that summer. Later she flew to Texas to make sure, and began planning our wedding for 31 August, 1963.

Barrington College Chapel

One of the other instructors flew me to Quonset Point, Rhode Island in an F-9, with wedding garments under the gun bay doors up front. The wedding was in the Barrington College Chapel. We honeymooned at the base of the cog railroad up Mount Washington, New Hampshire. We then drove to Texas, visiting friends and relatives enroute. Had the two year Blue Angel's job materialized, it's doubtful "Tweet" and I would have met. After 48 years, she is still fun to "play house" with. So I got the better deal. After 20 years, Dad's prayers produced a winner!

All the pilots in the ready room gathered around at lunch time, seeing what my new bride had packed. There was a certain amount of jealousy when they saw me combine all the ingredients for a salad she had put in separate containers. The big surprise was when she copied a $90 dress for the Marine Corps Ball for less than $10! She then made two eye-popping gowns for a Marine neighbor's wife across the street.

Marine Corps Ball - 1963

That Christmas we drove to Laredo and caught the train to Mexico City. "Tweet" was carrying our first child, and the all night train ride was tiring. Still it was a nice time together in the big city. Silver was one of the bargains there in 1963, so we acquired some nice pieces. While touring the city, we saw Chapultepec Castle, the site of the Marine battle in the War with Mexico in 1847.

The Halls of Montezuma

Texas began a war for independence from Mexico in the winter of 1835-36. General Santa Ana was sent with 4,000 troops to quell the rebellion. Some 200 men determined to defend the city of San Antonio, and retreated to the Alamo. The Mexican Army besieged the Spanish mission for 13 days. Santa Ana showed the red flag of no quarter to the Alamo defenders, and the Mexican bugler played a call of no quarter immediately prior to the attack.[402] All the Texans who fought that day at the Alamo died.[403]

On 18 April, 1836, General Sam Houston caught General Santa Ana's troops by surprise in a quick and decisive battle at San Jacinto, Texas. The next day, the Mexican general was captured and made to sign a treaty giving Texas independence.[404] Under this treaty Texas claimed the Nueces Strip with the Rio Grande as its southern border. The Mexican government later repudiated this border and laid claim to all land south of the Nueces River.[405]

Having won their independence from Mexico, Texas President Sam Houston sought annexation with the United States. Mexico's president, Santa Ana, warned that such an action on the part of the United States would be "equivalent to a declaration of war against the Mexican Republic." Congress passed a joint resolution to invite Texas into the union on 1 March, 1845. The Rio Grande Nueces River border dispute became the flash point, and war was declared on 13 May, 1845.[406]

On 6 August, 1847, Lt. Col. Watson's Marine battalion joined General Winfield Scott's column, which advanced from Vera Cruz toward Mexico

---

[402] B. Forrest Clayton, *Suppressed History III*, (Cincinnati, OH, Armistead Publishing, 2007), 40.

[403] Rebecca Nelson, *The Handy History Answer Book*, (New York, NY, Barnes & Noble Books, 1999), 102.

[404] Ibid., 102-104.

[405] Jay Nixon, *Stewarts of a Vision*, Ibid., 9.

[406] Rebecca Nelson, Ibid., 102-104.

City.[407] The key to the capital was Chapultepec Castle, set on a crag commanding the swamp causeways into the city.[408] This was the scene of the last-ditch Mexican resistance.   Confronted by 5,000 defenders, including cadets from Mexico's military academy, Scott attacked after a heavy artillery bombardment. The defenders resisted in fierce hand-to-hand combat before capitulating.[409]

Meanwhile, Captain Terrett, a company commander of Marines, pressed home a separate assault toward the city. On 14 September, 1847, after a night in the outskirts of Mexico City, the Marines marched into town in the van of their division – the first US troops to enter – and occupied the palace of the Montezumas.[410]

Montezuma II was the last Aztec emperor of Mexico. During his reign, Mexico came into contact with and was eventually conquered by the Spanish. After a four month battle, Hernan Cortes claimed Mexico City and all Mexico, calling it *New Spain* in August, 1521.

It is pertinent to recall Dr. Quigley's statement in *Tragedy and Hope*:

To this day the Arab influence is evident... above all in Spain. Spain and Latin America, despite centuries of nominal Christianity, are Arabic areas.[411]

The two-year Mexican War (1846-1848) was another confrontation between the seeds of Isaac and Ishmael. The significant differences are their governments and concept of work. Ishmael's have never been able to build any system of government except a simple tyranny.[412] The Arab concept of work, as a curse, is in stark contrast to the Christian perception of work being part of our dignity,[413] as exemplified by the King Ranch.

From the Halls of Montezuma to the Shore of Tripoli, these first two lines of the Marine Corps hymn look back on two instances the US Marine Corps was involved in this continuing conflict. The Halls of Montezuma

---

[407] Col. Jon T. Hoffman, USMCR, *USMC-A Complete History,* (Quantico, VA, Marine Corps Association, 2002), 74.
[408] Col. Robert D. Heinl, Jr., *The Marine Officer's Guide,* (Annapolis, Maryland, United States Naval Institute, 1964), 117.
[409] *The New Encyclopaedia Britannica,* 15th. ed., s.v. "Chapultepec."
[410] Col. Robert D. Heinl, Jr., *The Marine Officer's Guide,* Ibid., 117.
[411] Carroll Quigley, *Tragedy and Hope,* (New York, NY, Macmillan Company, 1966), 1120.
[412] B. Forest Clayton, *Surpressed History III,* Ibid., 12.
[413] Darrow Miller, "Godly Endeavors," *World Magazine,* December 5, 2009, 22 & 24.

were occupied after battling the Arab influence from Spain. And the shores of Tripoli were the scene of conflict with Arab Barbary Pirates.

Winding Down

Three years instructing in VT-21 were most rewarding. My proficiency as an aviator was enhanced. Instruction and training techniques were developed for varying personalities. But above all, I found my life partner.

My last few months involved evaluating borderline students. There are three reasons some trainees' performance is sub-standard: (1) they don't know what they are doing incorrectly, and need instruction, (2) they are not motivated, and need to be shown the advantage of learning, (3) they lack the innate pre-requisites, and should not continue.

Marginal students almost invariably require extra instruction. This could be caused by instructor/student personality problems, or the lack of continuity with one instructor. It could be the rate of a student's learning ability. Every opportunity was provided to help a man qualify. If there was a question of his aptitude, he was referred to a Student Pilot Disposition Board (SPD Board.) Evidence was examined by a group of senior instructors. Further remedial instruction could be assigned, or termination determined. If it appeared the man would endanger his own life or others, he was discontinued.

My last few months involved me in this process. One very conscientious man that I recommended for suspension was given a second chance. He was awarded the entire instrument program over again. He qualified, but later through poor judgment, injured himself for life. I was glad decisions were made by a board.

My last trip from Kingsville was a cross country to El Toro, California. Everything went as planned until the landing gear was extended at Kingsville. The nose and left main were down and locked but the right main would not budge. We circled the field, performing all possible emergency procedures. Nothing! Finally, with tail hook down, I picked up a wire linked to two anchor chains along the runway edge. The chains arrested the landing with the right wing tip dragging the aircraft to the right. We stopped just off the edge of the runway in front of a runway distance marker. This was my third two-wheeled landing!

Two-wheel Landing # Three

"Tweet" had driven from our apartment in Kingsville to pick me up. She saw all the crash equipment moving toward the runway, but was unaware that my airplane caused the excitement. She took it in stride!

The next month we left Texas, driving a 1954 Chevy, with the Porsche in tow. "Tweet" was six months pregnant, and straightened her body every time the baby stamped her feet. We had some excitement in Atlanta, Georgia, when a truck dumped a bag of cement in the middle of a free-way in front of us. Hard breaking caused a jack-knife maneuver into the right lane, which fortunately was open. It took a while for our pulse rates to return to normal!

Finally, we arrived at Marine Corps Air Station, Cherry Point, North Carolina, our next duty station, and home for the next few years.

Marine Corps Air Station - Cherry Point

Cherry Point, one of the best all weather jet bases in the world, occupies more than 29,000 acres in eastern North Carolina. The runway system is so large it served as an alternate emergency landing site for the space shuttle launches from Cape Canaveral, Florida. Congress initially authorized the station on 9 July, 1941. Clearing began the next month with extensive drainage and malaria-control work. Construction was started on 20 November, 1941, just 17 days before the Japanese attack on Pearl Harbor. It is home of the Second Marine Aircraft Wing, which supports the Second Marine Division at Camp Lejeune, 25 miles to the southwest.[414]

The Naval Air Depot Cherry Point opened in 1943 as the assembly and repair depot for Marine Corps Air Station. It "has grown into the finest facility of its kind"[415] and is the only one of three NAVAIR Depots in the Naval Air Systems Command to be led by a Marine Corps Officer.[416] It employs 4,000 civilians and military personnel, spending 270 million dollars in wages every year as of 2011. It is primarily focused on vertical take-off aircraft.[417]

Just outside the air station main gate is the town of Havelock, located midway between New Bern and Morehead City. New Bern is the county seat of Craven County and Morehead City is one of North Carolina's two deep-water port cities. Both have fascinating tales that date back hundreds of years.

History – New Bern

The Reformation was the result of Catholic dominance of the governments of Western Europe. Tyranny and corruption of the papacy engendered an ecclesiastical rebellion in a considerable part of Germany.

---

[414] Official Website of MCAS Cherry Point, NC, "About Cherry Point,"
http://www.marines.mil/unit/mcascherrypoint/Pages/meascherrypoint/AboutCP.aspx,
(accessed August 24, 2011).
[415] NAVAIR, "NAVAIR, Cherry Point,"
http://cherrypointallies.com/index.php?option=content&new=article&id=3&Itemid=8,
(accessed August, 25,2011).
[416] Ibid.
[417] Ibid.

The German monk and theology professor, Martin Luther, provided the spark. In 1529, several princes joined the struggle of Luther in the form of a manifesto to Emperor Charles V of Germany. They protested what they considered unjust measures by the Emperor and by the Pope. From this time forward the word "Protest-ants" applied to those opposed to the Pope and his party. This resulted in a 30 year war that ended in 1648.[418]

A third group of people developed in Zurich, Switzerland in 1525. These became known as Anabaptists, meaning those who baptize again. They were convinced that Scripture allowed only the baptism of believers. This was in direct conflict with both Catholic and Protestant practices of infant baptism.[419]

Switzerland was virtually independent of the Holy Roman Empire, and in its free air the Reformation thrived. It produced the undoubted leadership of the whole Protestant cause.[420] While the Protestant movement was a political as well as a spiritual reformation, the Anabaptist movement was wholly spiritual. Making the same mistake of Israel, rejecting the voice of God, Protestants presumed to become defenders of the faith, imposing their dogmas by force. In contrast, the Anabaptists were nonresistant, refusing to fight for any purpose against either Catholics or Protestants. This made them "fair game" for those who saw the opportunity of separating a productive people from their wealth.

For whatever reason, the Anabaptists were driven from Switzerland. Holland was the first to grant refuge and Russia later on.[421] In London families lived in tent cities in the parks, until Protestant Queen Anne Stuart helped them get to her colonies in America.[422] Swiss Baron Christoph De Graffenreid contracted with the city of Bern to move some of the Anabaptists to America. He is credited with settling the New Bern, North Carolina site in 1710, naming the city after his home town of Bern, Switzerland.[423]

---

[418] Daniel Kaufman, "Anabaptists: Mennonite History," Mennonite Publishing House, http://www.anabaptists.org/history/mennohist.html, (accessed August 25, 2011).
[419] Ibid.
[420] John W. Kennedy of India, *The Torch of the Testimony*, (Sargent, GA, Christian Books Publishing House,
   1965), 144.
[421] Daniel Kaufman, "Anabaptists: Mennonite History," http://www.anabaptists.org/history/mennohist.html. (accessed August 25, 2011).
[422] John W. Kennedy of India, Ibid.
[423] New Bern North Carolina History Site, http://www.new-bern.ne.us/HistoryNB/, (accessed August 22, 2011).

Down through the ages, God has prepared a remnant through which a testimony to Him has been maintained, and His purposes worked out. The effects of war and persecution scattered some of the faithful believers into areas where they had a fresh opportunity of witnessing to Christ.[424]

History – Queen Anne's Revenge

On 21 November, 1996 the wreckage of *Queen Anne's Revenge*, Blackbeard's flagship, was located in the shallow water of the Atlantic near Morehead City. The 300-ton vessel, originally named *Concord*, was a frigate built in England in 1710. She was captured by the French one year later, modified to hold more cargo and slaves, and renamed *La Concord de Nantes*. Sailing as a slave ship, she was captured by the pirate Captain Benjamin Hornigold in 1717 near the island of Martinique. Hornigold turned her over to one of his men, Edward Teach, later known as Blackbeard, the pirate.

Blackheard made *La Concorde* his flagship, adding cannon and renaming her *Queen Anne's Revenge*. The name may have come from the War of the Spanish Succession, known in America as Queen Anne's War.[425] This was one of four wars fought between France and England for control of much of North America. The struggle was not settled until the French and Indian War (1754-63) which gave Britain the area east of the Mississippi River as well as French possessions in Canada.[426]

Edward Teach is believed to have fought as a privateer for the British, attacking Spanish and French ships. When Queen Anne, the last of the Stuart dynasty, died in 1714, she was succeeded by the German George I of Hanover. This may have been the reason British privateers began attacking everyone, even their own British ships.[427]

---

[424] John W. Kennedy of India, *The Torch of the Testimony*, Ibid. 144.

[425] Queen Anne's Revenge – Wikipedia, The Free Encyclopedia, "Queen Anne's History," http://en.wikipedia.org/wiki/queenAnne'sReveng. (accessed August 25, 2011).

[426] Rebecca Nelson, *The Handy History Answer Book*, (New York, NY, Barnes & Noble Books, 2003), 87.

[427] National Geographic, " 'Blackbeard's Ship' Yields New Clues to Pirate Mystery," http://news.nationalgeographic.com/news/2005/07/0712-050712-pirateship-2html. (accessed August 24, 2011).

Second Marine Aircraft Wing

Before leaving Kingsville, my orders were to a helicopter squadron. Helicopter pilots on the east coast were spending many months on ships in the Mediterranean that did not count as overseas tours. The result: senior helicopter pilots left the Marine Corps to join the airlines. The Marine Corp's blanket solution was a requirement for all pilots to be dual qualified, and all jet jockeys received orders to helicopters. By May 1964 the east coast squadrons had twice as many pilots as they needed. Fortunately, my orders were changed to the wing staff at Cherry Point. Being Top Secret Control and Plans Officer for the wing, G-3 seemed much better than spending the rest of my career in helicopters.

Most pilots considered "paragraph trooping" a prison sentence. However, there were advantages, such as a regular work schedule with most weekends off. This permitted participation in regular church activities, a luxury not available to squadron pilots. The pastor of a little Presbyterian Church in Havelock invited me to team-teach an adult Sunday school class. This later included directing a small choir. Sunday school was rewarding personally, but frustrating when the desired dynamics of class discussion ended as a lecture.

The author of their study book admitted he wasn't a Christian. I recommended studying the Bible instead. No one objected, so we began with the book of Acts. For the first time, the Holy Spirit became obvious to me. With both grandfathers clergymen, and my parents missionaries, my life had been backstage with church activities; I had never seen the "world turned upside down"[428] by the gospel message. Sensitivity to the Holy Spirit seemed to be the key. Very little emphasis had been placed upon this "Third Person of the Trinity" during my life, and this new emphasis intrigued me.

A pilot at an Officer's Christian Union (OCU) meeting related an experience with an East Indian evangelist. Bakht Singh became a Christian during the depression. His wealthy father had sent him to England for his education. Traveling to Canada with a group of students to harvest crops, he attended a church service aboard ship. To be polite, he overcame his Sikh pride and knelt with them. He was transformed by an encounter with Jesus Christ. Given a Bible on a second visit, he counted the phrase "God

---

[428] Acts 17:6.

said" 500 times and determined to hear God's voice.[429] Could the Holy Spirit direct people in the 20th century as He had in the first?

My background biased me against speaking in tongues. This had been a point of disagreement with Pentecostals at RVA. The problem was resolved with the argument that such signs were superfluous, once the new covenant was established. The enticement of this new quest, however, was 'power.' It had been tremendous power that propelled me into the third dimension of flight. Could there be a similarity in the realm of the Spirit?

One of the effects of focus on Scripture in Sunday school was a change in the pastor's sermons. He began to preach textually rather than topically, on a trail basis. Church attendance increased.

My office was the War Room, on the second floor, in the operations section. Top Secret War Plans were filed there. The room had no windows, files were locked, and the door securely closed after working hours. A large heavy metal box, on strong wheels, sat inside the door. It was about three feet high, three feet wide, and four feet long, with a telephone hand piece on one end. It was called a "scrambler" and was used for classified telecommunications. It chopped words into little pieces and transmitted them piecemeal over telephone lines. A similar box on the other end re-arranged the pieces into intelligible words. Its purpose was to keep information from enemy ears. It occurred to me that this was the purpose of the Holy Spirit's gift of tongues. I was still not convinced, so my quest continued.

In order to acquaint me with the Wings war responsibilities, I was sent on a tour of the Caribbean. This included Guantanamo Bay in eastern Cuba and Vieques Island off eastern Puerto Rico.

Guantanamo Bay ("Gitmo" – located in the Oriente Province on the southeast corner of Cuba) was first leased from Cuba as a coaling station for Navy ships in 1903. The lease was re-negotiated in 1934, with the stipulation that both parities must agree to break the lease before the US could abandon the property. Base relations remained stable through two world wars. Things began to deteriorate after Fidal Castro openly declared himself in favor of the Marxist line, and relations were finally severed by President Dwight Eisenhower in January 1961.[430] By the time of my visit, "Gitmo" was in a high state of defensive alert.

---

[429]T. E. Koshy, *Bakht Singh of India,* (Colorado Springs, CO, Authentic, 2007), 29-30, 32.

[430] The Military Base at Guantanamo Bay: A timeline: NPR, "The Military Base at Guantanamo Bay," http://www.npr.org/templates/story.php?storyId=4715995. (accessed October 10,2011).

In 1942, the US Navy began bombing practice and storing military explosives on Vieques Island. The Navy had acquired 72% [431] of the island and continued to use it as a training area for amphibious invasions, using live ammunition. The base was commanded by a Marine Lieutenant Colonel, and was frequently used by infantry units in 1964.

15 June, 1964, "Tweet" marched into the Naval hospital at Cherry Point for the arrival of our first child. The next morning a beautiful little girl with bright red hair was born. Ann Marie continues to be a channel of blessing to her mother and me. We took her home to our apartment in Married Officer's Quarters (MOQ) F-2. Our baby greatly brightened our lives!

Aviation Safety Officer Course

My request to attend the Aviation Safety Officer Course at the University Of Southern California (USC) was submitted on 9 March, 1963. Two years experience, as assistant safety officer in VT-21, stimulated my interest. One of my motives was to qualify myself for a critical slot in a flying squadron. Finally, after a year at a desk job, my orders to USC came through.

With our 1954 Chevy loaded, we began our journey to the west coast. On the other side of the world, Dad, Mother, and brother Martin left Nairobi enroute to Hawaii to visit brother Ed, an Army doctor at Tripler Hospital. After a visit with Ed and his family on Oahu, the folks flew to Los Angeles where we met and took them to Mission Road in Pasadena. This was home for Dad, Mom, Martin, "Tweet", and Ann while I was in school at USC. An apartment near the campus was home for me and several other students during the week. This was a pleasant and comfortable opportunity for my family to meet, and become acquainted with my new wife and our daughter.

School finished in June, and "Tweet" and I, with Ann and Martin, prepared to drive back to North Carolina. We bought a small travel trailer, and drove up the west coast to Oregon, visiting RVA acquaintances. We were looking for property near Grants Pass as a possible place of retirement for Dad and Mom. A beautiful 10-acre piece, with a 360 degree view, was located and later purchased. It was then time to get back home to Cherry Point.

---

[431] Vieques and the Navy,
http://www.isle-vieques.com/puerto-rico/navy.html, (accessed October 10, 2011).

Marine Composite Squadron Two (VMCJ-2)

My new assignment was Aviation Safety Officer for VMCJ-2. Composite squadrons flew two types of jet aircraft, photo-reconnaissance, and electronic counter measure (ECM) planes. My photo aircraft was the familiar F-8 crusader. The ECM plane was a Korean War night fighter with jamming pods. This was the EF-10 Skynight, a two-place, two-engine mid-wing jet. From mid-July through September, I flew the Skynight. In October my plane was the Crusader again. It was still a pleasure to fly. Instead of armament, it had big cameras and extra fuel. The mission was bomb damage assessment and photo mosaics (picture maps).

The Skynights were used for electronic intelligence. Their mission was to determine an enemy's radar order of battle, and evaluate the quality and maintenance of their radars. We also trained F-4 radar operators. One day after the training mission was complete, the pilot wanted to play. He was never able to get on my tail, because my big wing allowed me to turn inside and keep him on my nose. Finally, he came down hill in a supersonic head on pass. When he passed on the right, that big ugly Phantom appeared covered with white fur from the shock wave. Very impressive!

Late in the year, the squadron deployed to the Naval Air Station, Roosevelt Roads in eastern Puerto Rico. The weather there was much better for photo training. Upon arrival, as I climbed down from my aircraft in Puerto Rico, the Executive Officer pointed his finger at me and said, "You will grow a mustache!"

My obvious response was: "Yes, Sir." It was hot and muggy in Puerto Rico, so we taxied to and from the runway with the canopies up and our oxygen masks off! The wind was always blowing, so it was a new experience to have my bushy red mustache fluttering in the breeze.

After a month, we returned home. "Tweet" came to pick me up at the hangar. As I waited in the parking lot in civilian clothes, she drove right by me, not recognizing that "old man with the mustache." After one good kiss, I shaved the *bloomin* thing off! Separations are good, if for no other reason than the joy of the reunion!

Vietnam Buildup

On 5 May, 1961, President John F. Kennedy announced he was considering using U.S. Forces, if necessary, to aid South Vietnam in resisting Communist aggression. Three months later he declared the

United States would do all it could to save South Vietnam from Communism.[432]

The U. S. Military Assistance Command, Vietnam (USMACV) was established on 8 February, 1962. Its mission: providing support to South Vietnam.

With the tacit approval of the U.S. government, South Vietnam's leader, Ngo Dinh Diem, was killed by Vietnamese generals on 2 November, 1963. The resulting chaos meant that the United States would have to take over the fighting, with tragic consequences.[433]

Less than two weeks later, USMACV announced that 1,000 of the 16,575 U.S. military personnel in Vietnam would be withdrawn due to progress made in training the South Vietnamese armed forces. This was announced on 15 November, 1963. One week later, President Kennedy was assassinated, and President Lyndon Johnson affirmed continued military support for South Vietnam.

North Vietnamese patrol boasts attacked U.S. warships in the Tonkin Gulf on 2-5 August, 1964. Two days later, the Tonkin Gulf Resolution was passed by Congress, authorizing President Johnson to use military force in Vietnam.

On 28 July, 1965 President Johnson announced that an additional 50,000 U.S. troops would go to Vietnam. By the end of the year, 181,000 U.S. personnel were deployed in Vietnam, including 39,000 U.S. Marines.

By 1966 it was obvious that my next orders would be to Vietnam. Inasmuch as there were no plans for VMCJ-2 to be transferred as a unit, it was understood that I would receive individual orders shortly. Mother and Dad invited "Tweet" and Ann to Kijabe, while I was overseas.

"Tweet" applied to the Africa Inland Mission and was accepted as a short term missionary. She would teach fourth grade at RVA, and get a chance to see my home in the land of Zinj.

In order to get our moving started, I switched orders with another pilot who already had a port call date. After storing household effects at Cherry Point, and with Porsche in tow, we headed for New York. "Tweet" and Ann left on a Pan American flight to Nairobi from Kennedy Airport, and I continued to Chicago, towing the Porsche. The vehicles were left with Ruth Ann in Oak Park, Illinois. My travel continued on a commercial flight to San Francisco, with departure for Okinawa on 27 May, 1966.

---

[432] *U S M C - A Complete History*, (Hong Kong, Hugh Lauter Levin Associates, Inc., 2002), 534-536.
[433] Thomas E. Woods, Jr., *The Politically Incorrect Guide to American History*, (Washington, DC, Regnery Publishing, Inc., 2004), 229.

Cherry Point – Post Vietnam

Cherry Point was our home again after our year of separation. Our year apart and reunion will be covered in the next chapter.

On 21 July, 1967, my official title was Second Marine Aircraft Wing Aviation Safety Officer. This was supposed to be filled by a Lieutenant Colonel. As a member of the Wing Commanding Staff, I had open door access to a Two Star General. One of my responsibilities was writing endorsements for his signature on all 2nd MAW accident reports. It was a good job for a young Major, but it was not flying in a tactical squadron. Having recently been promoted and looking at the list of positions for field grade (Major through Colonel) aviators, it became obvious that my proficiency as a competent aviator would never be as high as it had been. The choices were: accept the responsibilities of a two dimension military administrator or leave the active duty Marines and fly for the airlines.

One of the immediate hurdles to the second option was a Marine Corps directive requiring one year's notice before being eligible for resignation. Having completed nine months on an infantry regimental staff in Vietnam, I believed God's plan for me to stay would be indicated by a squadron at Cherry Point. If not, an airline job was the next step. After conferring with "Tweet," my letter of intent was submitted indicating our wedding anniversary, 31 August, 1968 as my final active duty day. And so the "rush" of being a fighter pilot began to diminish.

The regular hours of a staff job again allowed participation in church activities. The Havelock Presbyterian Church again invited me to teach the adult Sunday school class and direct the choir. An interesting turn of events occurred shortly after our return. The pastor had felt called to add a sanctuary to the educational complex. The church had been holding worship services in the fellowship hall, and attendance had increased. He had received a call from a larger church in Norfolk, Virginia. If the Havelock church would agree to build the sanctuary, he would stay. His proposal was rejected, and he left.

The church had hoped to fill their pulpit with chaplains from the air station. The war had reduced the number of chaplains, eliminating that option. A seminary student drove quite a distance on the weekends to preach on Sundays. The former pastor had started a Wednesday evening prayer meeting, which I was asked to lead. It wasn't long before the community learned that the group's prayers were being answered. Interestingly, my quest for Holy Spirit power had been partially answered in Vietnam. Things began to happen that were new experiences for me, and I knew that I was not responsible. For example, "Tweet" was pregnant with our second child. When it came time for her delivery, complications arose requiring an ambulance trip to the large hospital at Camp Lejeune. It appeared that she had a placenta-previa, which would require a C-section. While we were praying, the baby moved into position for a normal delivery. Virginia Ruth was born into our family, and has added so much happiness. Like her older sister Ann, she presently has a special Christian ministry.

Sunday school also produced an interesting development. We were studying the construction of the Tabernacle in the book of Exodus. Again the lesson became a lecture without discussion. The class was made up of the leaders of the church, but participation was nonexistent. One morning, two senior Marine Corps officers from the class stood before the church with plans for a sanctuary, a financial plan, and a schedule of events. The proposal was voted on and passed with two dissenting votes. That church built a sanctuary without a pastor. It was a new experience of God's power for me.

The officer who drew the plans outlined a four pointed star shaped window in the front wall. In the center was a man sized cross. He asked if I could build it. Thinking he had detailed plans, I agreed. The only thing he gave me was the outline. Designing the details and building the window was a real project. It took a big gang to raise a tall 20 foot window into that wall. One of my prize pictures is the communion table highlighted by sunlight through that window with the cross.

When it came time to leave, there were three opportunities before me. Some members of the church offered to send me to seminary, a contractor in the church offered me a lucrative construction job, and the Naval Aviation Safety Center offered me a GS-13 position as an aircraft accident investigator. Deep in my heart was the strong desire for three dimensional flight. I agreed to do whatever God's plan for me entailed, but honestly told Him, "I would like to fly," and He said, "Yes!"

Sunlight through Church Window

EAST ASIA
Ferry F-9 from Iwakuni – 1966

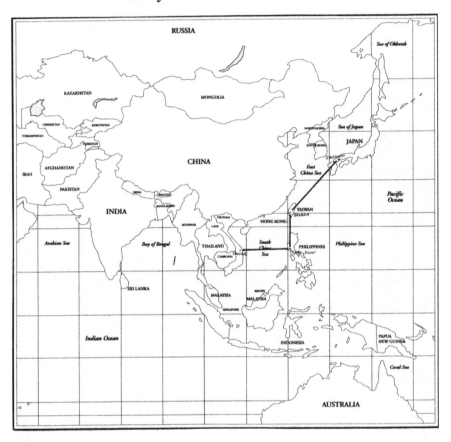

Vietnam

"Let every nation know, whether it wishes us well or ill, that we shall pay any price, bear any burden, meet any hardship, support any friend, oppose any foe, to assure the survival and the success of liberty." ...the most famous words John F. Kennedy was ever to utter.[434]

"In the attempt to protect South Vietnams anti-communist government from overthrow by a Communist insurgency tied to the North, the U.S. government sought to defeat the enemy not in the battlefield but by establishing good liberal[435] government in the South that would win the undisputed allegiance of the South Vietnamese."[436]

President Kennedy's advisers were split as to what kind of changes were first needed in South Vietnam. One group emphasized the importance of a popular government that provided life, liberty, and the pursuit of happiness - the freedoms we were taught to hold dear during WW II. The other group believed that authoritarian regimes should be tolerated as long as they were effective. The latter group prevailed and Vietnam became "the first war in which the United States dispatched its military forces overseas not for the purpose of winning but just to buy time for the war to be won by civilian social programs." [437] Instead of taking the war to the North, and thus attacking the insurgency at its source, American officials sought to export the welfare state to Vietnam.

This was one more example of the persistent conflict between the rule of law and the rule of egalitarianism, between creative excellence, and covetous "fairness," between admiration of achievement versus envy and resentment of it. In my judgment, the American program in Vietnam was a colossal failure. American troops, who had never lost a battle in Vietnam were withdrawn the end of March 1973. In April 1975, the North launched an overwhelming invasion of the South creating a mass exodus of the most effective wealth producers. Some 600,000 South Vietnamese, many of whom had endured French Colonial rule, Japanese occupation, and intense war conditions decided they could not tolerate a Communist

---

[434] Norman Podhoretz, *World War IV*, (New York, NY, Doubleday, 2007), 180.
[435] It should be emphasized that liberal government is the antitheses of liberty. It is the same as the Arab concept of government, 10% of the population hold 90% as slaves.
[436] Thomas E. Woods, *The Politically Incorrect Guide to American History*, (Washington, DC, Regnery Publishing, Inc., 2004), 227.
[437] Ibid., 228-229.

Vietnam. The ensuing bloodbath was typical of tyrannical takeovers down through the ages. The French Revolution, the Russian revolution, Nazism, Communism, and Islamic Imperialism have all had bloody aftermaths.

There were nearly twice as many casualties in Southeast Asia (primarily in Cambodia) the first two years after the fall of Saigon in 1975 than there were during the 10 years the U. S. was involved in Vietnam.[438]

"People of goodwill may disagree about the methods and political wisdom of the Vietnam intervention, but it is no longer possible-if it ever was-to claim, as the hard Left did, that a Communist Southeast Asia would usher in a reign of peace and 'social justice.' On that subject, history has spoken."[439]

VMCJ – 1

My first flight in Vietnam was an EF-10B on 5 June, 1966. By the end of the month, over 27 hours had been logged. Most of these flights were in support of Navy strikes in the Hanoi/Haiphong area of North Vietnam. Our mission was to position ourselves 50 miles out to sea, and monitor enemy frequencies. If an enemy radar controlled anti-aircraft gun came up, the radar officer would jam that frequency. The same thing happened when a surface-to-air missile (SAM) frequency emanated. We were told by attack pilots who saw SAM's, that they looked like telephone poles with a brown cloud of smoke on their tails. After their control frequencies were jammed, their flight paths became erratic. There were no losses to these two weapons while we were on station. Most of the friendly aircraft losses were due to visually controlled anti-aircraft weapons. The Hanoi/Haiphong area was the most heavily defended airspace in the world at that time. It took great courage to brave that firepower, but once attack pilots began their runs, they were focused, ignoring the tracers.

July 27, 1966 was my first Vietnam flight in the RF8. Photo Crusaders were primarily used in South Vietnam for bomb damage assessment. My log book shows only 10 photo flights during my four months in VMCJ–1. John Glenn's *Project Bullet* crossed the United States in a Photo Crusader at the super sonic speed of Mach 1.1 or 725.55 mph, on 16 July, 1957. His aircraft Burean Number was 144608. My log book shows my last RF8 flight

---

[438] Interesting Vietnam War Facts, Statistics & Myths, Capt. Hanson & Capt. Beaton, "Vietnam War: Facts, Stats & Myths,"
  http://www.uswings.com/vietnamfacts.asp. (accessed August 31, 2011).
[439] Thomas E. Woods, *The Politcally Incorrect Guide to American History*, Ibid., 230.

on 5 September, 1966 was in Burean Number 144609, the next RF8 off the Chance Vought factory line.[440]

The second week of August found me at the Marine Corps Air Station at Iwakuni, Japan. F9F8T Aircraft were to be ferried to Vietnam serving as airborne forward air control (FAC) aircraft. An airborne FAC radioed Marines on the ground that needed air support. Airborne attack aircraft were guided onto the target with marking rockets from the F9. The heavy haulers could then use their bombs to neutralize the target. It was like "old home" week flying the venerable F-9 again.

Jungle Survival School was at Cubi Point in the Philippines. This included lectures and a night in the jungle. The survival knives, made from Jeep springs by the Filipino instructors, were effective. One of the lessons was cooking rice in green bamboo. We took bamboo about two inches in diameter, with a closed node on each end. A small piece was cut out of the side, with wedged ends. Rice was put inside with some water and salt. The wedged piece was re-inserted, and the whole section put in the fire. By and by, we had nice fluffy rice!

If it didn't rain, we slept on the ground. That night a "bodacious" thunderstorm moved through. We spent the night on bamboo slats covered by a bamboo roof. Morning was most welcome!

There was a neat hobby shop at Cubi Point. Before returning to Vietnam, I cut parts for a drop-leaf desk from furniture grade tropical plywood. My hooch[441] was the best furnished hooch in the whole air group at Danang. Just about the time it was finished, orders came to send a pilot south to Chu Lai. The 7th Marine Infantry Regiment needed a Major as an Air Liaison Officer. Since I was the junior Major selectee in the squadron, guess who had to go? What a revolting development! I had spent over 10 years learning to use an airplane as a weapons platform. I had volunteered to use my skills in the only war available, and after only four months was ordered to a desk job in an infantry bunker. Don't get me wrong! Two broken wrists reminded me not to remonstrate with the "Planner."

[440] Peter Mersky, *Vought F – 8 Crusader,* (London, England, Osprey Publishing Limited, 1989), 22 - 23.
[441] Hooch - Slang. Chiefly U.S. military, a place to live in; a shack or hut as in Vietnam.

Seventh Marines – Chi Lai

The command post of the 7th Marines was in the foothills west of the Chu Lai Air Base. My office was in a large underground fortification, built into the side of a hill. Our bunker was 12 inch by 12 inch heavy timbers, covered by several feet of dirt. The floor was concrete. The east end housed the Fire Support Coordination Center (FSCC). The Artillery Officer, the Naval Gunfire Officer, and the Air Liaison Officer (ALO) coordinated supporting arms for subordinate units there. The conflict in Vietnam was a guerrilla war with no fixed battle lines. Subordinate battalions were assigned Tactical Areas of Operational Responsibilities (TAOR). Patrols policed these areas.

Each battalion had a company grade (Lt. or Capt.) aviator called a Forward Air Controller (FAC). Marine doctrine required air strikes to be controlled by a qualified pilot. This could be an airborne FAC, or one on the ground. Since battalion activities used multiple patrols, it was impossible to send a FAC with each patrol. Seldom did a battalion FAC control an air-strike; consequently, most were directed from the air.

The battalion was normally under regimental control. In Vietnam the division directed battalion activities, by-passing the regiment. There were only two Marine Aircraft Helicopter Groups to support two Marine Divisions, an Army of the Republic of Vietnam (ARVN) Division, and a Republic of Korea (ROK) Brigade. All of them wanted their troops moved by helicopter. When they got into a bind, they wanted transportation immediately, and became angry when it was previously committed to those who had planned ahead. Airplanes had been much more manageable than "grunts" (infantrymen!)

There were two instances a Tactical Air Control Party (TACP) was needed when the battalion FAC's were all busy. A light reconnaissance airplane ran out of gas and landed on the main highway near the Regimental Command Post (CP). We took my radio jeep and radio operators to the scene, in case air support was needed. A battalion patrol in the area was directed to provide ground defense. Shortly after our arrival, the point man in a worn flak jacket stepped from the bushes. Soon the plane was surrounded by ragged Marines, who would see about 240 days of combat in a year's time. The average infantryman in the South

Pacific in WW II saw about 40 days of combat in four years.[442] Their treatment upon return to the States was heartbreaking.

Later, a U.S. Army destroyer chased a North Vietnamese gunboat ashore several miles south. Since we were the only TACP available, a CH-46 helicopter picked us up at the Regimental Landing Zone (LZ) and deposited us on the beach at the site. After the "brass" had viewed the scene, we were ordered to remain with the infantrymen over night. My three radio operators dug a huge foxhole in the sand. They really looked after me!

The next morning we marched toward the closest Battalion CP. Our radio equipment included a single-side band long distance radio, a UHF radio to talk to attack aircraft, and an FM radio to talk with infantry patrols. My guys had to "hump" this heavy equipment on their backs. We passed through a village that had been "pacified" by the Korean Marines. There was just one very old man living there. The battalion fed us, and drove us back to Chu Lai in trucks. The people in the office thought I'd lost some weight!

There were two operations when the Regimental Staff was displaced from Chu Lai. Operation RIO Blanco took place at Binh San, Quang Ngai in November, 1966. This involved Civilian Irregular Defense Group Troops, Regional Forces, Vietnam Army Troops (ARVN), Vietnam Rangers, Korean Marines, and U. S. Marines.[443] Planning was closely guarded by the U. S. Colonel advising the ARVN troops. There were obvious holes in security when plans were transmitted to higher echelons. As a result of this secrecy, an enemy battalion was "bagged."

Operation Desoto was a search and destroy action against Viet Cong units in southern Quang Nqai Province. This was a 7th Marine operation in the Duc Pho area. Our command post was on top of a hill called Nui Dang. By the time it ended on 7 April, 383 communist troops were killed at a cost of 69 dead and 556 wounded.[444]

The prelude to this move was personally traumatic. In preparation for the operation, a necessary confidential frequency list assigned to me was

[442] Interesting Vietnam War Facts, Statistics & Myths, Capt. Hanson & Capt. Beaton, Ibid., (accessed August 31, 2011).
[443] Military History, Viet Nam, "The CIDG Program Begins To Mature," http://www.ranger95.com/militaryhistory/sfvietnam/chap4middleyears.html. (accessed September 9, 2011).
[444] Col. Jon T. Hoffman, U S M C- A Complete History, (Quantico, VA, Marine Corps Association, 2002), 558.

My Radio Jeep

missing. Misplacing classified information is an egregious error in the military and could end a career. In desperation, I went to my hooch to pray. I shared a code Xed pyramidal tent with another officer. Code X meant it was unacceptable and should have been replaced. I built a canopy over my bed and covered it with a foxhole cover to keep it dry. Alone, I knelt on a plywood floor with holes to let the rain through. Cocky, fighter pilot, Glenn Downing, finally came to the end of his tether. This was the first time I had an emotional experience with the "Boss." It was a turning point and a key in my quest for the Holy Spirit. As I rose to my feet, the sergeant from the Fire Support Coordination Center knocked and asked: "Is this what you were looking for, Major?" It was! Walking with the Lord since, has been much more intimate!

Flight time requirements for flight pay were flown in the F-9. My log book records 14 flights, most of which were visual reconnaissance missions. On at least one, we attacked a target on the ground for some ground troops.

On 11 November, 1966, one of my last students at Kingsville was shot down over North Vietnam. He was on his last scheduled mission before rotation back to the States, and ejected from a crusader. He was captured

Code X "Hooch" – Surrender

by the North Vietnamese, spent the next seven years as a prisoner of war, near Hanoi, and was released in the general prisoner release in 1973. This is only one of the sad tales from Vietnam.

Eleven weeks after I left Vietnam, my cousin, Robert Sawhill, flying an Air Force F-4 out of Ubon Royal Thai Air Force Base in Thailand, was shot down. He became a prisoner of war near Hanoi and was also released in 1973. My wife, two grandsons, and I attended his funeral at Arlington Cemetery in 2009. He considered it a "very maturing experience." He was never bitter about his years in prison.

Seventh Marines – Danang

In April 1967, at the conclusion of Operation Desoto, the 7th Marine Headquarters was moved to Hill 55, southwest of the Danang airport. This was to be my final hooch before leaving Vietnam. Being located close to Danang allowed me to again fly VMCJ-1's EF10B aircraft. From April through June, seven flights were logged. It was especially beneficial when they allowed me to fly to Saigon to get travel documents for my return to the States.

My request for circuitous return to the United States, upon completion of my overseas tour, was signed 21 January, 1967. There were 60 days

AFRICA
From Vietnam to Kijabe – 1967

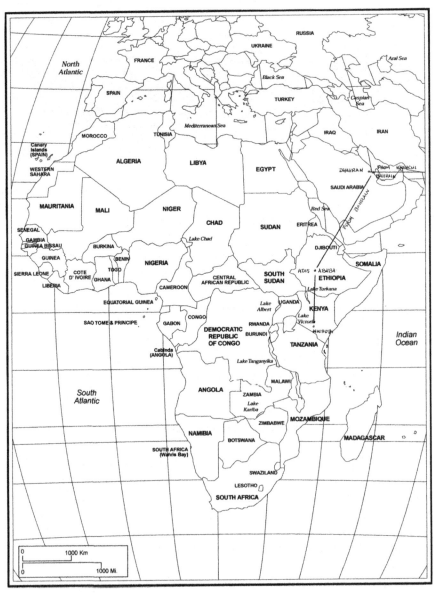

EAST ASIA
Danang to Kijabe – 1967

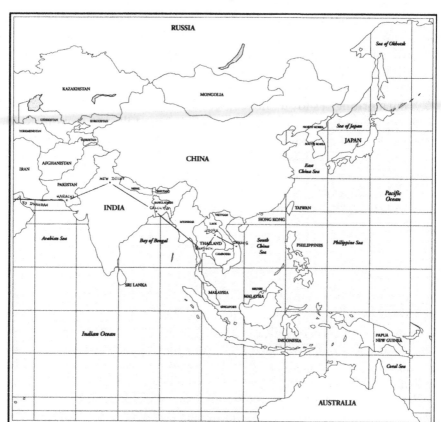

accrued leave on the books. Reimbursement for my personal travel from Nairobi, Kenya to New York via Pan American Airways was requested. Space-available travel to Kenya was also requested.

The 7th Marines were not involved in any major operations from Hill 55 until after I left on 6 June, 1967. Life was fairly routine until then. One episode convinced me of the wrongheaded thinking of the State Department. We were frequently losing Marines to land-mines on patrols. The Vietnamese knew where these were, and avoided them. A simple solution was to have the Vietnamese drive their "cattle" ahead of the patrol.

The State Department objected on the grounds that postwar reconstruction would be negatively affected. So, one more rule of engagement was inflicted upon the military by American officials, seeking to impose a welfare state on the Vietnamese.

The problem was that Congress, which is solely responsible for declaring war, never did so in Korea or Vietnam. When the State Department fails to negotiate peace, and war is declared, the Defense Department displaces them. This never happened because ironically police actions are not considered wars.

One morning, a shot-up helicopter made an emergency landing at the Regimental Landing Zone (LZ) after picking up a Killed in Action (KIA) Marine. When I approached the open door of the helicopter, the remains of the marine lay face down on the floor. The back of the flak jacket was still wet with his sweat. I cannot express the rage that coursed through my body at this obscene waste. I was convinced that *Liberal* thinkers in the country, this kid believed he was protecting, have no regard for shedding American blood.

Reunion

Upon approval of my circuitous return, I departed Danang on a flight to Udorn, Thailand. Almost immediately, there was a seat on an Air American 'Twin Beach' with a Volpar modification. This was the same type of airplane that had taken me from Cubi Point to Boguio, with the exception of turbo-prop engines. Upon arrival in Bangkok, a seat on the embassy flight to Dhahran became available. As on my previous "Odyssey," there were stops at Calcutta, New Delhi, and Karachi. There was time at Karachi to visit the restaurant in the terminal. The diet in Vietnam excluded green salads, so one was ordered from the menu. Big mistake!

Gulf Air took me from Dhahran to Bahrain, and an RAF plane to Nairobi via Aidis Ababa, Ethiopia. So, for the second time, I had rounded the world. The best part of returning to Zinj this time, was the reunion with my wife and daughter. Family separations have only one positive aspect: the joy when the tour is over!

"Tweet" and Ann lived in an apartment behind my parent's house. Younger brother, Martin, objected to having his parents called *grandpa* and *grandma*, so Ann was taught to use the Kikuyu equivalent. The expressions on the faces of Africans in Nairobi, when this curly, red-headed, white girl called a white man <u>Guka</u>, were priceless.

No sooner did I arrive in Kijabe than my Karachi salad caught up with me. One of my worst cases of diarrhea put me in bed, and required my good friend, Doc Propst, to get me back on my feet. Home cooking, tropical fruit, and <u>safe</u> green salads enabled me to enjoy family and home.

Mother and Dad recommended a second honeymoon at one of the game lodges. They offered to care for Ann and lend us their Volkswagen Bug for a trip to Kilaguni Lodge in the Tsavo West National Park. So, off we went like two newlyweds on a four hour drive to 'the place of the young rhino,' Kilaguni. Our lodge was cool, tranquil, and hushed for optimum game-viewing. A thatched central dining area, with a viewing terrace, looked directly down on the water hole 100 yards away. Day or night, elephants could be seen. Our second honeymoon was so great that we have repeated it frequently!

When the waiter in the dining room approached our table, I addressed him in Swahili. "Tweet" was flabbergasted. She had never heard such strange sounds from my mouth. Even more surprising, the waiter responded to these noises. The up-shot of the exchange was a warm friendship. When it came time to return to Kijabe, the waiter's cousin needed a ride to the railroad station at Mtito Andei, 15 miles away. We were happy to oblige.

The road to the railroad station was a winding dirt road on flat ground. Coming around an S curve, a young bull elephant having breakfast was encountered. We stopped and waited for him to move off. He didn't move. Finally, I eased up towards the curve. Just as I started to turn, he threw up his trunk, flapped his ears, and started toward the car! He was only about 35 yards and could have squashed us! Fortunately, our "Bug" accelerated smartly. When I looked back, instead of a black boy in back, there were <u>three</u> white people in that car!

Gatab

My wife was aware of my deep desire to hunt a leopard. It was the only trophy, of the big five game animals in East Africa that interested me. She let Doc Propst know, and plans were set in motion for a hunt. Leopards are nocturnal hunters, so are rarely seen. The most beautiful of all cats, they are a hunting challenge.

Gatab was a pioneer mission station, situated on 7,000 foot Mount Kulal. My best friend from Kijabe and an RVA classmate had both set up the station there, in accordance with Peter Scott's vision. The Africans were losing livestock to these beautiful predators, so were interested in reducing this menace. The problem was complicated by inter-tribal warfare, which closed the hunting blocks in northern Kenya.

Doc Propst was probably the only man to untangle this predicament in a timely fashion. A doctor, he was authorized to visit Gatab's dispensary. He was also an assistant game warden, clearing him to hunt in closed hunting blocks. Finally, he was an engineer, who designed a windmill to generate electricity there. The hunting safari was on!

Two vehicles set out from Kijabe. Doc was driving his International pick-up with three people up front, including "Tweet." The first night was spent at an AIM mission station at Thompson Falls. The second night was by a dry river bed. The following morning, Doc wanted some meat for the Gatab missionaries. A young bull Oryx and two Grants Gazelles were taken, and tied to the back of his truck. We left the main road at the bottom of Mount Kulal, and proceeded up a rough track to the mission station. Our tires rolled over stones the size of a man's head, and the short International springs made our insides ache. It took two hours to go about 15 miles!

The two missionary families lived in dirt-floored corrugated metal buildings. "Tweet" and I had a comfortable tent, but the first night Doc and I set up a bivouac by a babbling brook. The neck of a gazelle was chained to the right side of a large tree-crotch about 20 feet above the ground. That evening we watched until dark. Early the next morning we resumed our vigil. The grating sound of a leopard was heard from the hill below us, but we saw nothing. The sun came up, and the sound of cattle moving out to pasture indicated we had probably missed our chance. I was about to quit, when Doc saw an agitated butcher bird. He said, "Watch!" Just then, this leopard appeared in the tree-crotch, like a house cat. My bullet hit him just to the left of center and he came out of the tree like a sack of meal!

Vietnam

Trophy

Cautiously, we approached the tree. I used Doc's 375 H & H Magnum, the smallest gun authorized on dangerous game. Doc's back-up gun was a 458 Winchester Magnum. Wounded leopards can be extremely dangerous. (Three people were put in the hospital by one near Nairobi.) When we saw the leopard, he was obviously dead. "Tweet" was summoned from her tent to take pictures. She said I acted like a little kid on Christmas morning! It was the most gratifying hunt I could have imagined. I had forgotten how much I enjoyed hunting!

Dad and I spent several hours skinning my trophy. My father had the best hands I knew. He skinned the head skin out to the eyes, without a single cut. There I was, on the top of a mountain with a tremendous view of Lake Rudolph and the distant mountains. I was with three of the most significant people in my life: my wife, my father, and my friend, Doc Propst. Psalm 37:4 meant so much that morning: "Delight yourself in the Lord, and He will give you the desires of your heart." (NASB)

Safari's End

The Vietnam interlude was over. It was time to return to Cherry Point for the final act in the Regular Marine Corps. We boarded a Pan Am 707 in Nairobi to cross the heart of Zinj. Our first stop was Entabbe, Uganda where Harold and Jane Amstutz wished us a pleasant journey. The flight continued towards Monrovia, Liberia, stopping at such places as Logos, Nigeria, and Abidjan, Ivory Coast. Monrovia, operated by Pan Am, was the jumping off point for transatlantic flights. JFK in New York, our intended destination, was weathered in, so we landed in Boston on 17 July, 1967. The Glenn Downing family was finally back in the land of round door knobs.

The best thing that happened to me in Vietnam was complete submission to Him on my knees in a Code Xed pyramidal tent! Life has become more meaningful and rewarding ever since!

AFRICA
Return to Boston – 1967

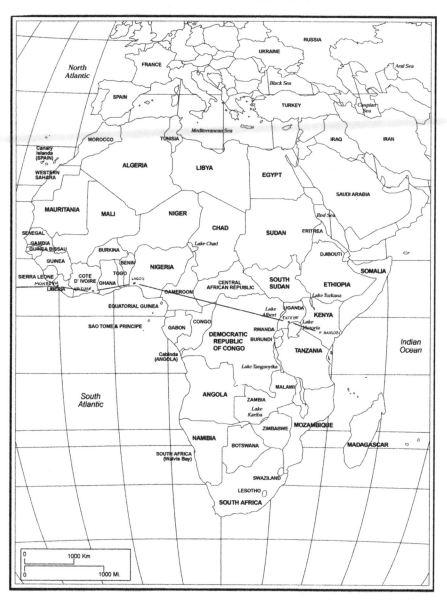

Airlines

The assignment to a staff job at Cherry Point was the fleece[445] that confirmed God's leading me to leave the Marine Corps. My problem was the one year's notice required of Regular Marine Officers before release. The major airlines were hiring pilots, but the maximum acceptable age was 32 years. January 1968 was my 33rd birthday, eliminating these airlines as an option.

Mrs. Barden, of the Pilot Employment Agency, directed me to Mohawk Airlines in Utica, New York. As regional carriers with plans for expansion, they were willing to waive the age to acquire experienced pilots. Within a week of my release on 31 August, 1968, I was in ground school for the Fairchild FH-227. My first flight, as a co-pilot, was 8 October, 1968. By the end of the month I had flown over 60 hours, with more than 70 landings. It was much more interesting than cruising for hours at a time, with an auto-pilot doing the flying. In fact, the FH-227 was a 44 passenger turboprop that did not even have an auto-pilot installed.

Mohawk, with no more than 350 pilots, had seven domiciles. My first assignment was Newark, New Jersey for a month or so, until New York City became our permanent domicile. "Tweet" and the two girls spent September with her family in Illinois. The AIM home in Brooklyn provided temporary accommodations, until one of "Tweet's" relatives arranged for us to occupy the vacant manse of his church. This was a beautiful large home in Flushing, near LaGuardia Airport. It was obviously God's provision for my probation year, since my salary was less than half of Marine Corps pay.

Flying for Mohawk was interesting, but very demanding. In my probationary year, my log book shows almost 600 hours of flight time and 725 landings. New England winters required a lot of instrument flying. A totally new procedure was flying the glide slope on a low visibility approach, using an Instrument Landing System (ILS). All my previous low-ceiling landings were Ground Controlled Approaches (GCA) where radar operators directed you to the runway with voice commands. Learning to trim a hand-flown aircraft was a definite asset.

---

[445] Judges 6:36-40: The wet and dry fleeces were Gideon's means of confirming his perception of God's directive will.

Living in New York City in 1968 was expensive. Feeding a family of four required creative solutions. One of the advantages of the airlines was space-available travel. To encourage air travel, the airlines believed that heads in the windows would attract more paying passengers. This was an industry-wide concept. Interline agreements allowed us to travel beyond Mohawk's route system. One of our creative food solutions was visiting "Tweet's" folks' chicken farm in Illinois. We could carry 12 dozen fresh eggs on the airplane when we returned. These eggs were fresher than eggs we bought in New York. At least that's what my eggspert wife told me!

With such a brief courtship, I didn't know if "Tweet" could cook. This didn't matter, since cooking for myself qualified me to teach her. Teach her?! She was a culinary artist, fixing hamburger so many different gourmet ways, you would think we owned a butcher shop! And frugal? She squeezed every nickel "til the buffalo bellowed!"

God was trimming us down, drawing us closer to Him. One of the more painful lessons involved my Porsche. It needed repairs when we left Cherry Point, and was left in a shop at Camp Lejeune. After we were situated in New York, "Tweet" repeatedly advised me to contact the shop about picking up the car. My work kept me so busy, there didn't seem to be time, and I didn't know when I could get it. When I finally contacted the garage, I was told the car had been declared an 'abandoned vehicle' and sold at a police auction! A visit to the shop showed a letter, addressed to me, with two digits reversed, that had been returned to sender. So, we made do with our 15 year old Chevy for several more years. The lesson for me: listen to Tweet. She was much more sensitive to God's voice than I!

In order to supplement my income, I attempted to join a Marine Reserve A-4 squadron at Floyd Bennet Field in Brooklyn, New York. An unexpected snag reared its ugly head. I needed a certificate of citizenship for a necessary secret clearance to fly the A-4. I was born in East Africa of American parents. The American Consulate in Nairobi recorded my birth on a State Department Birth Certificate (a copy of which was in Washington, D.C.). For decades, this served as appropriate proof of citizenship for passports, entry into the Navy, Marine Corps, and for Top Secret, NATO Crypto Clearances. All of a sudden, a certificate of citizenship, issued by the Justice Department, was necessary. This required acquisition of my grandfather's death certificate, and my father's birth certificate from a foreign government, Kenya. With these, I was able to get a certificate of citizenship for my father and me, after presenting all this foreign evidence to a Justice Department official. Apparently, the

Justice Department didn't trust the State Department. My certificate of citizenship was issued on 3 September, 1969, allowing me to be issued a Secret Clearance in the Reserves of the United States Marine Corps. Bureaucratic nonsense!

I jointed VMA 131 and flew A-4's from Floyd Bennet and from NAS Willow Grove, when the squadron was moved to Philadelphia. It was a neat little airplane. The last flight was March 1971, with a total time of 175 hours.

An opportunity to become caretakers of a transient facility for missionaries, near JFK airport, presented itself in January 1970. The owners were looking for people to look after this ministry, while they served aboard the Operation Mobilization ship *Logos*. The move from Flushing, on an icy winter New Year's Eve, was memorable. The house was in a small residential community off the approach end of Runway 13L. Low, flying jets were uncomfortably noisy when the wind was from the southeast. However, it became a refuge for a host of hungry, weary, traveling missionaries passing through New York's Kennedy Airport.

A man who impacted my Christian growth was Watchman Nee, the Chinese author of the *Normal Christian Life*.[446] His chapter on the meaning and value of Romans 7 was liberating. He had passed through New York City, establishing a church that continued long after his departure. From our first exposure, we were drawn to this community of Believers. Their Sunday services were like nothing we had experienced. An hour of teaching by one of several qualified elders was followed by a spontaneous hour of worship, including communion. A fellowship lunch preceded group discussion of the morning's teaching. There was nothing forced or formal. It was delightfully refreshing.

Things went along nicely for more than two years. After 1,352 hours of flight time for me, Mohawk came to a screeching halt. It appeared that management maneuvered the pilot union into a strike that lasted nine months! After 13 years as a manager in the Marine Corps, it was very humbling to be wearing *strike sandwich boards* at the New York airports. The immediate problem was money. Some pilots resorted to food stamps. When I asked the Lord if this was His solution for our dilemma, checks began showing up in the mail and from people in our Chinese Church. Between Marine reserves pay and God's obvious provision, we survived.

---

[446] Watchman Nee, *The Normal Christian Life*, (Wheaton, IL, Tyndale House Publishers, Inc., 1977).

At the end of the year, the church held a series of meetings focusing on the book of Job. The teaching emphasized Watchman Nee's Biblical perception of the Spiritual Man,[447] formed of two essences, body and spirit, each having three impulses. The body was driven by hunger, survival, and social acceptance. The Spirit, in touch with God's Spirit, was impelled by intuition, conscience, and communion or conversations with God. Interposed between these two entities is the human soul, which also has three functions: mind, emotion, and will. As a result of separation, because of Adam's sin, man is born with a spirit that is not dead, but disconnected. These explanations have been enlightening and helpful for understanding Biblical truths.

One of the elders put his hand into my outer coat pocket after an evening service. I was sure it was another gift and said, "We don't need this."

His reply: "The Lord knows, don't argue!" There was a snow storm that evening, when the phone rang. A couple had been traveling by air continuously for more than a day from Europe. They needed funds from their New Jersey office for travel to Minneapolis. Referred to us, because of hazardous roads, they were picked up at the airport, fed, and bedded down for the night. The next morning they returned to the airport. The church check covered their air fares.

In the summer of 1971 we entertained a lady who had developed a bad cough while attending a school in England. The whole family became ill. Coming into the house from a Marine Corps drill one day, my circumstances finally got the best of me. In anger I asked God, "What more do you want of me? You've taken my career, my job, my families' health, and made us live in this crippled city!" His response to my tantrum was just two words: "Get busy!"

One of our AIM acquaintances worked part time for a chiropractor in Brooklyn, who needed office furniture I had agreed to build. There didn't seem to be much urgency until this confrontation. So, I got busy! The project was finished late Saturday night; I was in Allegheny Airlines ground school the following Monday. Dad's sister, Lucile Sawhill, and her husband, opened their home to me, and a neighbor provided transportation to and from school.

For the next three and a half years, my "office" was in the right seat of a Convair 580. The airframes of these aircraft started out as Connair 340's

---

[447] Watchman Nee, *The Spiritual Man*, (New York, NY, Christian Fellowship Publishers, Inc., 1968).

and 440's. Allison installed 3,750 horsepower turbo prop engines, which were much more powerful than the original reciprocating engines. It cruised at 350 miles per hour and carried 50 passengers. It was heavy to fly, but available power and full reversing propellers made it ideal for icy runways.

With the help of the government, I was able to purchase a small house, across from a new primary school. Red-headed Ann was so enthusiastic about first grade, she gathered younger kids and taught them what she had learned that day. Like my red-headed mother, she was a born teacher.

"Tweet" became pregnant with our third child, and with the help of the Lamaze team effort, delivered a red-headed boy, Jonathan Glenn. His crib was in Ginger's bedroom, and she became his nursemaid. She was quite clever getting him on the table and changing him. We enjoyed life with our little family, and thought it would last for years. This didn't happen!

The 'Oil Crises of 1973' was caused by the oil embargo of the Organization of Petroleum Exporting Countries (OPEC). Many oil-producing states withheld their oil in response to Western support of Israel during the Yom Kippur War.[448] The OPEC oil squeeze coincided with a period of the 1975 steep inflation and severe recession.[449] Job hunting was once again a priority, and Mrs. Barden, at the Pilot Employment Agency, found a pilot position with J. Ray McDermott Dubai, in the United Arab Emirates (UAE).

The next two years were spent flying corporate aircraft in the Middle East. Our experiences were drastically different from either the Marine Corps or the airlines. This will be detailed in the next chapter.

In the summer of 1977, we returned to our home in PA. Allegheny Airlines started a commuter airline, with nine Mohawk 298's. All nine 25-passenger conversions were completed by 1978.[450]

My seniority allowed me a Captain's bid on this equipment, sending me to ground school in Harrisburg, PA. Upon completion, my base assignment was Clarksburg, West Virginia. Since Clarksburg was one of the last to receive aircraft, I waited at home. Before the 262 arrived, a BAC-111 bid opened in Boston, so a second ground school was achieved. Simulator time on the BAC-111 was available for Captain up-grades.

---

[448] Energy Crisis – Wikipedia, The Free Encyclopedia, "Energy Crisis," http://en.wikipedia.org/wiki/Energy crisis. (accessed September 19, 2011).
[449] USAIR – Airmail to Airline, (Washington, D.C., Air Line Pilots Association, 1983), 75.
[450] Jane's Encyclopedia of Aviation, ed. Michael J. H. Taylor (New York, NY., Portland House, 1989), "Frakes Mohawk 298 (USA)."

Allegheny made arrangements for veterans to use their GI Bill to pay for this course, providing me with an FAA-type rating on a mainline aircraft. A type rating was required to fly as Captain in the left seat. Captain's pay was much better than a First Officer's, but flying as Captain was based strictly on seniority, which I lacked.

Commuting to Boston, and sitting as a reserve pilot in a rented room was a pain, but it paid the bills. There were only two reasons to commute: either you couldn't move your family, or you wanted to get away from them. Coraopolis was too nice to leave, and my family was my life. When an opening was available in Pittsburgh, I took it!

After flying the BAC-111 for seven months, a DC-9 bid in Pittsburgh opened. Another ground school. The DC-9 cockpit was the quietest, and best laid out of any previous aircraft, but roll control was not nearly as precise. Douglas persisted in using cables and pulleys for ailerons on their jet aircraft, while others used hydraulics. Had my time on the aircraft been longer, it might have become more comfortable. Five months later, my fourth ground school in 18 months took place at American Airlines training facility in Dallas, Texas.

Late in 1978, Allegheny acquired Boeing 727's from United Airlines, and utilized the American Airlines simulators for training aircrews. My seniority on this equipment was very low, but there were advantages. One big advantage was standing reserve as a First Officer in Ohio, with time to build our house.

Each aircraft type is different, with particular systems procedures and limitations that must be memorized. The first requirement in ground school is to erase all previous aircraft numbers. Next, the various systems must be studied, i.e., the flight controls, hydraulics, fuel controls, electrical, and air conditioning systems. Emergency procedures must be learned, and performance numbers memorized. After weeks of classroom work, a qualified oral examiner determines your mental qualifications.

Next comes simulator training. Simulators are aircraft cockpits on hydraulic jacks, with visual screens that simulate virtual reality. They were perfected to the point of qualifying a pilot for flight in an aircraft, with passengers on his first flight. An instructor pilot was always in the other seat under such circumstances. A successful check ride authorized pilots to fly the line, with paying passengers aboard.

Unlike most other professions, pilots are required to prove their abilities to perform emergency procedures in the simulator at prescribed intervals. This included losing a critical engine on take off, low visibility approaches, and various in-flight emergencies. Recurrent ground school was required for all pilots every year. In addition, pilots must pass a flight physical given by an FAA approved physician every year for First Officers, and every six months for Captains.

Company check-pilots and FAA inspectors rode the cockpit jump seats to insure compliance with operational procedures. If the crew did the right thing every flight, these guys added no stress. My personal philosophy was that people who owned the aircraft had a perfect right to dictate how they wanted them operated.

My first 727 line flight was 26 November, 1978. For the next six years my role as First Officer required flexible diplomacy. The pilot in the left seat was in charge and my responsibility was to make his job as easy as possible. Some accepted assistance, and some preferred response only when requested. It was definitely a learning experience.

On 19 September, 1984 my position changed from the right seat to the left on the Boeing 727. One of the nice things about this development was: I didn't have to ask who the Captain was. It was nice to know what "the guy in the left seat" wanted. This Captain wanted a suitably boring trip with no excitement. Usually, he got what he wanted.

There were two exceptions. On a trip from Pittsburgh to San Francisco, we encountered a line of thunderstorms just west of the Mississippi River. With the help of our radar, and Air Traffic Control Center, we avoided the heavy rain areas by skirting to the south of our desired course. Finally, we came to the western end near Kansas. There was nothing on radar, and center informed us that other aircraft had gone through uneventfully. Just as we passed around the end, we hit some clear air turbulence. A small flight attendant was lifted, bounced against the ceiling, and slammed back into her seat, injuring her back. She wanted to continue to San Francisco, so the cabin crew stretched her out on the aft galley floor. She was taken off the aircraft with a "straight-back"[451] and sent to the hospital. This was the only time a crew member was hurt on my aircraft. The memory is still painful. She later recovered, but provided an anxious experience for me!

On another occasion, we were returning to Pittsburgh from San Francisco on an all-night flight, called "the red eye." Every seat was full. As we climbed to our cruising altitude, two flight attendants appeared on the

---

[451] Straight-back - A wheeled conveyance used for moving disabled passengers down narrow aisles to and from their seats.

flight deck with information that a pregnant passenger, who spoke no English, had gone to the hospital for help. Because she had no insurance, she was sent to her doctor in Pittsburgh. She was then having contractions! When asked what they wanted, they said: "We want to get to Pittsburgh as soon as possible!" Three throttles were pushed up until we were flying as fast as possible. Higher speeds consumed more fuel, but we had plenty with the help of a tail wind.

As we crossed the Iowa border, the flight attendants re-appeared saying the situation required an immediate landing. I requested a vector to the closest paramedic, and was cleared for an approach to Des Moines, Iowa. It took 30 minutes until that woman was in an ambulance.

It was raining, in the middle of the night. We had an airplane full of sleepy passengers, who were not happy with the delay. A fuel truck arrived and we were finally on our way, arriving in Pittsburgh about an hour late. The woman was given something to slow the birth process, and sent to Pittsburgh on a later flight. It was her ninth pregnancy, and a caesarian section was anticipated. The flight attendants were right!

The Boeing 727's were taken from Pittsburgh and moved to Charlotte, North Carolina in June 1991. Rather than commute, a bid on the Boring 737 sent me back to ground school again. This newer aircraft was smaller and slower than the older airplane I had flown for 12 ½ years, and leaving was difficult. The 727 was a pilot's airplane, responsive and fast. The 737's were equipped with integrated glass cockpits that provided comprehensible information more quickly than the "steam gauges" of the 727. New equipment had autopilots that would even land the aircraft by themselves. The Boeing 737 was a good transition into integrated, automated, new technology, which I flew from July 1991 until July 1993.

My last aircraft was the Boeing 757, the most beautiful airplane in 20 years of flying. It had a narrow waist, long legs, and large turbo-fan engines. Its sleek exterior made the cockpit quieter than the 727, and was definitely easier to fly. With gear and flaps up, after take-off, the auto pilot could be coupled to fly the rest of the flight. It could be programmed to climb, level-off, navigate to destination, descend, fly the approach, land, and stop. The only manual requirement of the pilot was extending gear and flaps before landing. The autopilot had to be disengaged before the aircraft could be taxied off the runway centerline. In order to prevent loss of flight proficiency, my practice was to hand fly the aircraft to altitude and fly the approach and landing. My landings were usually smoother than the autopilot's.

Final Airline Flight

The Boeing 757 was unusual, with a dual type rating that included the wide bodied 767. There were little differences between the two cockpits, but the disparity was obvious when the shadow on the taxi way could be seen. The 767 was one big airplane! Spending 13 years in the Marine Corps precluded gaining the seniority to fly the 767 internationally. Most of my flights were domestic flights, with an occasional trip in the big one.

My last trip was to San Francisco on 20 January, 1995. It was scheduled to return to Pittsburgh on Sunday, the 22nd, my 60th birthday. I was suddenly unqualified to fly a commercial passenger aircraft. A younger pilot flew the trip back to Pittsburgh, and my family and I celebrated. It had been an exciting, satisfying career. With more than 19,780 hours of flight time, I had maintained flight proficiency much longer than would have been possible in the Marine Corps.

I had now retired twice; once from the Marine Corps, and now from the airlines. When asked today if I miss flying, my usual reply is, "I miss the views and the exceptional people I worked with."

After retirement, an opportunity to be a simulator instructor became available. Allegheny Airlines had outgrown its regional bailiwick, and changed its name to USAir on 28 October, 1979. With the simulators acquired from constituent regional airline mergers, USAir had extra simulator time. An enterprise, know as Contract Training, was organized to market this asset. "Superannuated" aviators were employed as simulator instructors, and I qualified. Most of us preferred the adventures of actually flying the line. The next best thing was helping others learn to play with the "toys." It was rewarding and fun while it lasted, but like other questionable management decisions, it was terminated. I got to retire for a third and final time!

Dubai

17 February, 1948, an editorial entitled *Atom and Oil* appeared in the <u>New York Post</u>, which, in the light of intervening years, was extremely farsighted. The writer's concern was that the United States had chosen to focus on developing atomic weapons to the exclusion of using atomic energy for the benefit of mankind. The professed reason was preparation for defense of American oil concessions in the Middle East against Russian intrusion.

The writer's argument was that oil is a source of energy that is infinitely inferior to the atomic product. Consider the following anecdote:

There was a conference in France where a number of international engineers were taking part, including French and American. During a break, one of the French engineers came back into the room saying, 'Have you heard the latest dumb stunt Bush has done? He has sent an aircraft carrier to Indonesia to help the tsunami victims. What does he intend to do, bomb them?'

A Boeing engineer stood up and replied quietly. 'Our carriers have three hospitals on board that can treat several hundred people; they are nuclear powered and can supply emergency electrical power to shore facilities; they have three cafeterias with the capacity to feed 3,000 people three meals a day, they can produce several thousand gallons of fresh water from sea water each day, and they carry half a dozen helicopters for use in transporting victims and injured to and from their flight deck. We have eleven such ships; how many does France have?'

You could have heard a pin drop.[452]

Thanks to the efforts of Admiral Hyman Rickover, "the use of nuclear power continued without interruption in the U. S. Navy. Today 83 ships are equipped with 105 reactors, and there have been no accidents. These

---

[452] "You Could Hear a Pin Drop,"
  http://us.mc321.mail.yahoo.com/mc/show Message?/fid=Inbox&sort. (accessed February 8, 2009).

warships are welcomed at 150 foreign ports without encountering the local equivalents of Jane Fonda."[453]

In 1977 President Jimmy Carter signed an executive order that banned the reprocessing of nuclear fuel in the United States. This prevented the production of plutonium used to fuel Breeder Reactors. "At its best, the Breeder Reactor system produces no nuclear waste whatever – literally everything gets used."[454] President Carter's decision created immense piles of long-lived, highly radioactive material that cannot be used for anything, but must be safely stored for more than 25,000 years. France, Britain, and Japan all use Breeder Reactors.[455] For some reason, no one has reversed that counter- productive 1977 decision.

Multinationals

The *Atom and Oil* editorial continued:

In January (1948) of this year, profits from Arabian oil by two foreign corporations owned by two American oil companies were stated to be more than $117,000,000 in disclosures made to the Senate War Investigating Committee. Treasury agents told the committee, however, they saw little chance of obtaining any tax revenues from those profits. Senator Owen Brewster, chairman of the Senate Committee, had presented the facts unearthed before his committee to the Treasury Department on November 21 (1947.)

It appeared that the Texas Company and the Standard Oil Company of California jointly owned the Bahrain Petroleum Company of Canada, which, it was testified, piled up profits of $92,186,107 on an investment of $100,000 and the California Texas Oil Company (Caltex), incorporated in the Bahamas, had a profits of $25,387,673 on an investment of approximately $1,000,000.

---

[453] Tom Bethell, *The Politically Incorrect Guide to SCIENCE,* (Washington, D.C., Regnery Publishing, Inc., 2005), 22. (Admiral Rickover was an Ukranian Jew – brought up in Chicago – led team that adapted nuclear reactor on *Nautilus*.)

[454] Energy Crisis – Wikipedia, The Free Encyclopedia, "Nuclear Waste and Breeder Reactors – Myth and Promise,"

http://argee.net/DefenseWatch/Nuclear%20waste%20and%20Breeder%20Reactors.htm, (accessed September 22, 2011).

[455] Ibid.

No taxes of any kind had ever been paid to the United States or to any foreign government," Senator Brewster told the Treasury Department.

The money and human effort expended on the development of atomic weapons, if devoted to the development of atomic energy for civilian purposes, would relegate oil to a secondary position.

It is obvious, therefore, that the oil industry is leading not only America, and the entire world, but also itself to disaster. In the atomic age no war should be fought for any source of energy whatsoever.[456]

The big oil companies were simply "trading companies" with shifting allegiances, whose overriding aim was to make money. They were basically committees of engineers and accountants preoccupied, like most businessmen with profit margins, safeguarding investments, and avoiding taxation. But many company men, assumed the image of world rulers. Their high sounding assumptions of global responsibility helped deceive both governments and themselves.

In December 1949, the Federal Trade Commission resolved to investigate the foreign agreements of oil companies. In October 1951 their report, entitled *The International Petroleum Cartel,* concluded that seven companies controlled all principal oil-producing areas outside the United States.[457] They collaborated with each other to achieve the highest possible profits, which were enormous. In 1973, EXXON's profit for the whole year was an all time record for any corporation: a total of $2.5 trillion dollars.[458] That kind of money can buy tremendous political influence. As the oldest and biggest of the multinationals, oil companies have become major players in global warring.

Bedouins

The Bedouins, who govern Saudi Arabia, are the heirs of 20 centuries of an economy of banditry. As Ibu Khaldun showed, they scorn work on the land and as craftsmen. Work is not a positive value, not an activity that gratifies the soul. In their system of values and beliefs, it is an activity reserved for inferiors, because to work an industrial job, for example,

---

[456] Immanuel Velikovsky, "The Formation of Israel," Transcribed from the Observer column, *New York Post*, 4-6.

[457] Anthony Sampson, *The Seven Sisters,* (New York, NY., The Viking Press, Inc., 1975), 122-123, 309.

[458] Ibid., 266.

requires conformity to rules and obedience to superiors who are not tribal superiors.[459]

In their conception of the world, every thing comes from Allah. There is no process by which wealth is created. They are predatory nomads, whose nature is to plunder other peoples possessions. They recognize no limit in taking others belongings. When they acquire superiority and royal authority, they have complete power to plunder as they please. There is no political power to protect property, and civilization is ruined.[460]

Since there is no creation of wealth through work, but only transfer of wealth by force, their world is a zero-sum game, in which one grows rich only at the expense of others. There is no productive cooperation or fruitful exchange. This is anti-capitalism.

Had not capitalists located the oil, drilled the wells, and developed the means to market it, these xenophobic desert dwellers would still be starving camel drivers, protected from the rest of the world by an arid, inhospitable wasteland. The intense xenophobia of the Saudis is tied to "an innate sense of spiritual and racial superiority," which produces arrogance and hostility to foreigners. Bedouins look down on others because they are the summit of creation.[461]

Saudi Arabia

The kingdom of Saudi Arabia was unified under King Abd-al-Aziz (Ibn Sa'ud) in 1932,[462] three years before I was born. Between 1902 and 1932, under his leadership, his clan annexed independent territories of Asin, Hijz, and Shammar into "Arabia of the Sands." Today, monopolized by the Al-Saud Clan, this Arabia is not a state, but a family business, the only one in the world with a seat in the United Nations.[463]

For 250 years the Al-Saud Clan has been married to Wahhabism, a strange mixture of paganism, provincial narrow-mindedness, and rhetoric borrowed from Islam. Hardly a generation ago, the Al-Saud family religion was considered, by the Islamic world, as a weird distortion of

---

[459] Laurent Murawiec, *Princes of Darkness*, (Lanham, Maryland, Rowman & Littlefield Publishers, Inc., 2003), 219.

[460] Ibid., 221.

[461] Ibid., 21.

[462] *Flags, Eyewitness Handbooks*, (Chester, UK, DK Publishers, Inc., 1997), 181.

[463] Laurent Murawiec, Ibid., 1.

Islam by exalted visionaries: the backward religion of ignorant and crude Bedonins.[464]

The religious factor distinguished Ibn Saud from other tribal chiefs in Arabia. In the wars between Muslims, he was able to mobilize for his benefit the energies that sprang from Wahhabism to restore not only the emirate but the Saudi Empire.

According to the historian J. B. Kelly, the "means by which he intended to attain (his) goal was the same as that employed by his ancestors to achieve their conquests – the arousal of the latent fanaticism of the Bedouin tribes, its harnessing to their predatory and warlike instincts, and the launching of the resultant engine of destruction upon his neighbors."[465]

Wahhabism embodies the tribe-party of the Al-Sauds. Their ascendancy and their power are inconceivable without the ideology they convey. And this totalitarian religious ideology is intrinsically destructive. Islam is a religion, Wahhabism an ideology, which like the incubus in stories of witchcraft, has entered the body of the bewitched victim.[466]

Ibn Saud died in 1953 at the age of 73, and was succeeded by Saud IV, his eldest surviving son. Saud IV, a weak and irresolute monarch, was finally replaced by his austere half-brother, Faisal, in 1964.[467] King Faisal was a direct descendant of the family of Abd-al-Wahhab, the founder of Wahhabism.[468]

Faisal began by asking the Arabian American Oil Company (ARAMCO) to support him by rescuing the finances of the kingdom. ARAMCO, one of the giants of the global economy and the largest oil company in the world, obliged. Nearly $100 million in guarantees and loans made it possible to avoid defaulting on payments to Arabian creditors which included major New York banks.

From the moment he came to supreme power in 1964, Faisal undertook a series of journeys to Arab countries, visiting nine in nine months. "At each stop the King made the same call to his brother Muslims to join

---

[464] Ibid., 27.
[465] Ibid., 164.
[466] Ibid., 27.
[467] Ibid., 190.
[468] Ibid., 13.

together in a pan-Islamic power bloc that could wield solid influence on the international scene..."[469]

At the pan-Arab conference in Khartoum in 1967, after the disastrous Six Day War, a new and overwhelming Saudi hegemony emerged. The agreed upon policy toward Israel was to be: "Neither peace, nor negotiations, nor recognition." Saudi Arabia was the founder and head of this Rejection Front, and in that role was principally responsible for the 40 years of belligerence that ensued.[470]

From 1967-1973, radicalism of oil producing countries intensified. The OPEC conference in June 1968 adopted the doctrine of "changing circumstances," where the members of the OPEC Cartel reserved the right to change the terms and conditions of sale. All this was justified by the "excessive profits" reaped by the companies. The 'seven sisters' were treated as captive enterprises, unilaterally. OPEC (Organization of Petroleum Exporting Countries) and OAPEC (Organization of Arab Petroleum Exporting Companies) declared that international law did not apply to oil. A great raid was in preparation against the world economy. The raiding spirit of the Bedouins had not subsided. "From being arbiters of the international oil market (the companies) faced relegation to the position of bondservants to the oil states."[471]

In the early weeks of 1973, the oil companies gave up all their rights and placed themselves at the mercy of the members of the twofold cartel OPEC-OAPEC. The lack of reaction or support on the part of Western governments was the decisive factor encouraging the cartel; the risk was minimal and the potential benefits unlimited.

Ibn Saud's ultimate goal was to aggressively Wahhabize the Arab-Muslim world. With the oil crises Faisal secured the means to carry out his father's strategy. Oil was removed from the market, thanks to the archaic, anti-capitalist, Wahhabi monarchy. This had all been prepared and planned, and orchestrated by King Faisal, who was able to consider the rest of the world as the "land of slaves."[472] - - Until his nephew lodged several revolver bullets into his body in 1975.

Immanuel Velikovsky, the author of the 1948 editorial *Atom and Oil,* was right when he remarked 25 years earlier that: "It is obvious, therefore,

---

[469] Ibid., 197.
[470] Ibid., 197-198.
[471] Ibid., 201.
[472] Ibid., 208-209.

that the oil industry is leading not only America, and the entire world, but also itself, to disaster. In the atomic age, no war should be fought for any source of energy."[473]

J. Ray McDermott

OPEC, the biggest financial power in the history of the world,[474] moved the center of oil activity to the Persian Gulf. J. Ray McDermott was an engineering, procurement, construction, and installation (EPCI) company with a base in Dubai, United Arab Emirates. They provided fully integrated EPCI services for upstream field developments, including fixed and floating production facilities, pipelines, and sub-sea systems from concept to commissioning.

In 1975, they were using a nicely furnished 15-year old Fairchild F-27 to transport their engineers around the Gulf and as far a-field as Cairo and New Delhi. They offered me a two-month contract to fly as co-pilot. Leaving my family in Pennsylvania required positive confirmation from the Lord. On 20 March, 1975, I recorded what I believed to be His answer to my dilemma: "I want you to stay close to Me, to obey Me, and trust in Me. Do not be afraid to follow where I lead. I will go before you to make the way plain. Trust Me! My hand is in all that you are experiencing. Do not fear Satan, for he has been defeated, his strength has been shackled. I have adopted you, blessed you, disciplined you, loved you, used you, and I will lead you."

McDermott moved personnel first class on commercial airlines, so my assigned seat was in the first class section of a KLM Boeing 747 from New York to Schiphol airport in Amsterdam. We took off late in the evening, and shortly after take-off were served an evening meal. White table clothes, beautiful china, and metal tableware were used to serve such expensive fare as caviar, smoked salmon, and filet mignon. Isaiah 1:19 & 20 came into focus while waiting for the main course, and became a second confirmation: "Obey with a will and you shall eat the best that earth yields; but if you refuse and rebel, locust-beans shall be your only food, the Lord himself has spoken."[475]

The next morning a second KLM Boeing 747 transported me to Dubai. As an airline pilot, the crew invited me to ride the jump seat for landing.

---

[473] Immanuel Velikovsky, *New York Post,* February 17, 1948.
[474] Anthony Sampson, *The Seven Sisters,* Ibid., 284.
[475] *The New English Bible,* (Cambridge at the University Press).

That aircraft is so long that the cockpit is still high in the air when the main landing gear touches the runway. To help pilots judge their sink rate, an aural signal was heard well before touchdown that descended in pitch. It was a new and interesting experience for one who had flown only relatively small aircraft!

The first trip with McDermott was from Dubai to Tehran on 6 April, 1975. By 28 May, my log book recorded 136 hours with multiple landings in five different countries and eight different airports. Most of our flights were to Saudi Arabia. Dhahran was visited most frequently, being the headquarters of Aramco. McDermott had a barge at Khafji which was also visited, near the Kuwait border. Two trips took us to Riyadh, the capital. Iran was the second most visited country with several visits to Tehran and two to Abadan on the coast. Six trips each were made to Bahrain Island and Doha, the capital of Qatar. The longest flights were the two trips to Cairo.

F-27

After my return to the States in June, the chief pilot in Dubai accepted a position flying the new Gulf stream II for the Sheik of Abu Dhabi. McDermott offered me his position. "Tweet" was reluctant to go to the Middle East to live in "tents with camels and all." But with a nudge from the Lord, she finally agreed.

Dubai

While I was busy getting type-rated in the F-27 and traveling to McDermott's headquarters in New Orleans, "Tweet" was busy packing. She had to sort all our belongings into seven piles: one pile to go with us, one to store, one to sell, one for my folks, one for her folks, one to give away, and one to throw away. She proved to be a good organizer, and got the house ready to rent. Two bachelor businessmen occupied it for the two years we were gone.

Dubai

Life in Dubai was different for all of us, but particularly difficult for "Tweet!" Due to British influence in the Trucial States, Muslim restrictions were not as stringent as Saudi-Arabia. Women were permitted to drive cars, but the Arab ill-feeling toward females was a constant irritant to her. Dubai in July was extremely hot and humid! We arrived about midnight, and "Tweet" was shocked by the temperature when she stepped off the aircraft. She was carrying two-year old Jonathan, who had a six-year old vocabulary. When he saw an Arab in his white dishdasha,[476] he dramatically pointed to the man and announced in a loud voice: "Look Mom, there's Jesus!" She shushed him immediately!

Housing for the family was not immediately available, so we spent several weeks in an old hotel near the airport. Farm girl "Tweet" found the idleness oppressive, so we bought a German sewing machine at the market. She kept herself busy sewing curtains and swimsuits for new acquaintances. After another month or so in an apartment, a villa (house) became available.

My work kept me busy at least six days a week, and though I was home almost every night, "Tweet" was sleeping when I left and returned. The two girls attended the Dubai Petroleum Corporation School, and Jonathan became so popular that I was known in the community as "Jonathan's Daddy!"

The airplane was kept busy until one day the mechanic from Piedmont Airlines drawled: "Ah wont yew ta see this mayess." The F-27 was due for a major inspection that was more than a one man job. There was just enough time to send it to the Avio Fokker plant in Holland.

---

[476] Dishdasha - A long outer garment, worn by Arab men.

McDermott Flight Department

It was a scramble to cover the needed transportation with local charter aircraft. Finally, McDermott in New Orleans authorized wet leasing[477] a Falcon-20 from Unijet in Paris, and sent me to make the arrangements. The aircraft was flown from Le Bourget to Dubai via Istanbul with me aboard. The authorization for our F-27, to penetrate Saudi airspace, was not transferable to any other aircraft, so the hassle of negotiating a new authorization came up every time Unijet replaced their aircraft at Dubai.

McDermott Dubai was finally able to convince McDermott Headquarters in New Orleans of the need for a faster aircraft. So off we went to check out in a new Dassault Falcon 10. Ground school and simulator training were at Teterboro, New Jersey, flight training in New Orleans.

We left New Orleans on 13 November, 1976 for Teterboro, New Jersey. The next day we flew to Reykjavic, Iceland, via Goose Bay, Labrador. We departed Iceland on the morning of the 15th, and landed at Le Bourget in Paris about three hours later. The 16th was a biggie! Leaving Paris, we flew

---

[477] Wet leasing - Includes aircraft, crew, maintenance, and insurance.

1,320 miles to Athens, 774 miles to Cairo, and 1,374 miles to Dubai. A total of 3,468 miles, with 7.4 hours of flying time.

Three days later, we flew to Calcutta and back, a distance of 3,910 miles in 9.3 hours. We had flown 12,292 miles, 27.4 hours in one week. The circumference of the earth at the equator is 24,901.55 miles,[478] So, we had covered almost half the distance in an aircraft under 46 feet long, weighing less than 19,000 pounds, cruising at a true airspeed of more than 490 nautical miles per hour. The Falcon-10 was cute, but cramped in the passenger compartment; you couldn't stand up back there, but it was new, fast, and fun to fly!

Falcon-10

---

[478] "What is the Circumference of the Earth?"
http://geography.about.com/library/faq/blqzcircumference.htm. (accessed October 3, 2011).

Advantages

Despite the filth and flies - the heat and humidity - erratic electricity - pervasive dust storms - the threat of deportation if the God, who had a Son, was mentioned to an Arab – there were advantages to our stay in Dubai.

One of the advantages was buying the property our home has occupied the past 30 years in the "Land of the Free." Another was meeting Christians from various nations who had a common unity, even though clergy was proscribed in the Emirates by Bedouin bigots. Other benefits included developing a tolerance of different people, and seeing life from a different perspective.

We learned that material things should not be held too tightly, anything could be replaced or forgotten. We learned to appreciate things we had taken for granted. For example, we were much better off in Dubai than we would have been in Saudi Arabia. And we learned to appreciate fresh green salads!

Travel benefits opened a whole new world to us. Together, we traveled the canals in Holland, spent a week in the Swiss Alps, spent time in Frankfort, Germany, and saw the Arabian Desert with its sand dunes and camels. Ann traveled to Spain and France with schoolmates. "Tweet" traveled to Iran with fellow teachers from the International School. And I saw India, Pakistan, and Egypt, along with the Gulf States.

Among the most important benefits were the effects upon our family. We grew closer together. We learned to make new friends, and be more flexible. The kids had more confidence, and were stimulated to live adventurous lives. Ann spent two years by herself in the Far East, learning Japanese and Mandarin Chinese. Ginger became a Coast Guard Sailor, sailing both the Atlantic and Pacific Oceans on the Coast Guard bark *Eagle*. Jonathan, who earned his parachute jump wings, a private pilot's license, and owns a Harley Davidson motorcycle, is in Baghdad with the U.S. Air Force.

Although Dubai was different and difficult for the whole family, it was part of God's curriculum for each of us. We were all bigger people, and seeking His plan for our lives, had a harmonious outcome.

Conclusion

John Clark Mead was a New England banker, who from childhood had dreams of making a difference in the world. He was challenged by the enmity of Muslims toward the Western world, and spent 15 years as an anthropologist seeking to understand them. He was advised by an important Muslim leader that: "If you really want to understand the people of this region, you have to gain access to the fundamentalist Islamic leaders. A handful of these men represent millions of followers who would die at a moments notice for them. They are the ones who hold the keys to this culture."[479]

After spending years mastering the language and researching the history of many Islamic societies, Mead made friends with prominent Muslim men, who arranged a meeting with one of these leaders. The result was a friendship which opened doors few in the United States were permitted to enter.[480] Mead's observations present a much clearer picture than the pooled ignorance and confusion of media moguls and government officials. Consider some of his perceptions:

Initially, I was most surprised by the reality that success in these circles is measured not by the accumulation of wealth, but by the number of those associated with the leaders and the degree to which such followers are devoted to Islam... As I spent more time among these Islamic leaders the humble circumstances in which they live never ceased to amaze me. No matter how much I tried to find ulterior motives it became obvious to me that what they said had to be taken at face value. They were in this to serve Allah and for the glory of Islam to be revealed to future generations.[481]

As my research continued and I began to spend more time among Islamic leaders and their followers, my respect for their devotion to their religion grew. There is no question that they understand life to be a struggle and Islam to be that which made it worth living. As time wore on, however, and I began to blend into life among these circles of influence, I became increasingly aware that much of their struggle seemed to be directed against

---

[479] John Clark Mead, *The New World War*, (Fairfax, VA, Xulon Press, 2002), 31. (A behind-the-scenes look at why and how Militant Muslims plan to destroy western civilization.)
[480] Ibid., 56-63.
[481] Ibid., 61.

particular nations of the world. Although most of my personal experiences shared with Muslims within the world of fundamental Islam were very positive indeed, the times in which the darker side of their struggle became evident remain disturbing to this day.[482]

As an American growing up in suburbia... I had no frame of reference with which to compare what I was experiencing. I had never been among a group of people so totally committed to their way of life. The term "intoxicated" is the best I can offer to describe this new world in which I found myself.[483]

Just think for a moment what it would be like to be one of millions who share a common struggle and destiny. To "belong" to a religious community whose roots run deep through the centuries and whose branches seek to encompass the whole of humanity. Imagine feeling solid concrete walls reverberate as one is surrounded by many thousands of Muslims chanting Arabic verse in unison while swept away in intense worship. Regardless of background, a visitor experiencing such a scene is easily overcome with a deep sense of awe. Words cannot convey the visceral power which is present at such a time and place.[484]

The religious influence of a Muslim community is pervasive. Five times a day, beginning just after sunrise, the call to prayer is transmitted from public address speakers from high atop the mosque's minaret. The faithful are reminded of the greatness and oneness of Allah, the one true God, and the role of Muhammad as His prophet. "Come to prayer, come to success." The faithful are often reminded that although their primary allegiance may well be to the community of faith, or "Ummah," within their local area, they must never forget that they are part of the larger Ummah Islam, which encompasses the worldwide community of Muslims.

Rather than looking down upon them from a post-religious pedestal, (Mead continues,) I look across to them as fellow worshipers of Almighty God. Without question, we understand the way to God very differently, and in all honesty realize that our paths are mutually exclusive with regard to

---

[482] John Clark Mead, *The New World* War, Ibid. 62.
[483] Ibid. 49.
[484] Ibid.

394

who will actually make it to heaven. Yet we are very similar in our devotion to God and our adherence to that which we consider to be His Word.[485]

Both Christianity and Islam trace their monotheistic roots back to Abraham. Ishmael, his older son, was a son of the flesh, Isaac, his second son and heir, was the son of God's promise. Both sons were fathers or grandfathers of 12 tribes each, and strife between these two groups has continued for thousands of years. In our day, it has grown to global proportions potentially involving a billion people in a new world war.

Mead breaks down the world of Islam into three meaningful categories with regard to how each group relates to the Quaran. The largest group he calls cultural Muslims, who believe the Quaran was revealed to Muhammad nearly 1,400 years ago. However, the Quaran does not serve as the central determining factor for life decisions. They were born into the Muslim faith and that is all.

The second category: Quaranic Islam, are members who take the teachings of the Quaran very seriously. These people spend a great deal of time studying the Quaran and Hadith, a vast collection of ancient writings concerning the life of Muhammad. The fundamentalist Islamic leaders, who represent millions of followers who would die at a moments notice for them, are in this category.

The third group: Militant Islam is comprised of men of faith, devotion, vision, and action. At present, this group, as the result of OPEC, has access to trillions of dollars to accomplish its goal of world dominance. Throughout history the goat culture (the seed of the serpent, Geneses 3:15) has persistently attempted to restore the utopia of Eden in defiance of God's ejection. In order to reach their goal, everyone on earth must be conquered or destroyed. In my lifetime, this has been true of Nazism, Communism, and now Islam. Mead's chilling conclusion illustrates the enormity of the potential for global conflict Islam represents: He illustrates his analysis with the following diagram.

Inasmuch as Muslims understand that life is a struggle, and every Muslim's primary allegiance is to the "Ummah Islam," any threat to the "community" must be defended in a jihad or holy war. The fundamentalist Islamic leaders, the keys to these decisions, are prone to theological debate rather than hand-to-hand combat.

---

[485] Ibid., 46.

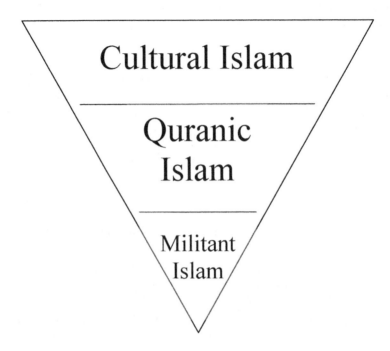

Militant Islam has chosen to adopt what Mead calls "Strategic Provocation and Retaliation" warfare or SPAR for short.[486] The core doctrine of this strategy is based on terrorist attacks against highly symbolic targets located in an enemy's home territory. The purpose is to provoke massive retaliation which would threaten the "Ummah" and mobilize millions of jihadists in global warfare. In this light, the purpose of the attack on the twin towers becomes much more apparent. Fortunately, President George W. Bush was able to convince the "Ummah" that his retaliation was not against Islam but against the terrorists.

The obvious question is: who is their enemy? Before the end of the Cold War or WW III,[487] atheistic communism was the enemy, and though the United States was not Islamic, it was at least monotheistic. As Saudi Arabia's dominance in the Muslim community emerged after 1967, King

---

[486] John Clark Mead, *The New World War,* Ibid., 138-150.
[487] Norman Podhoretz, *World War IV,* (New York, NY, Doubleday, 2007), Mr. Podhoretz defines the Cold War as WW III.

Faisal's Rejection Front identified Israel as the enemy. "Neither peace, nor negotiations, nor recognition" was to be the Islamic policy. Little Israel, hardly the size of New Jersey, seemed inconsequential. However, the resentment and bitterness of Ishmael has continued in his Bedouin bloodline. The United States persistently prevented the Bedouins from pushing Israel into the sea and became identified with Israel as "the enemy."

The Jewish community in the United States is the largest and wealthiest in the world.[488] The ascendancy of the United States could be attributed to God's promise to bless those who bless the seed of Abraham[489] through Isaac and Jacob. However, with this blessing comes the animosity of Isaac's older brother, Ishmael. The United States is therefore now also the enemy of Islam.

It is important to remember that the ascendancy of the British Empire occurred after Cromwell withdrew British barriers to the Jews in 1656, and was quickly reversed when Britain sided with the Bedouins in 1948. The future of the United States could be in jeopardy, should our government make the same mistake.

The consequence of a global Islamic government should be considered by everyone. The Arab work ethic in the past required slaves to do their labor, and the land of Zinj was the source of these workers. In a treaty with Great Britain in 1936, Ibn Saud, King of Arabia, issued a decree ending the importation of new slaves into his country, regulating the condition of existing slaves and providing for manumission (freeing from slavery) under some conditions.[490] King Faisal is credited with abolishing slavery in Saudi Arabia in 1962.[491] However,

...In 1974, oil and its byproducts accounted for 91 percent of Saudi exports. In the year 2000, the figure was 91.4 percent. In a quarter of a century, during which the country was saturated with oil revenues, nothing had changed. No industrialization took place. It is the six million immigrants who do the work—Americans, Europeans, Indians and

---

[488] Martin Sieff, *The Politically Incorrect Guide to the Middle East* (Washington, DC, Regenery Publishing, Inc., 2008), 126.

[489] Genesis 12:3.

[490] Free the Slaves, "Slaves in History," http://www.freetheslaves,net/SSLPage.aspx?pid=303. (accessed October 14, 2011).

[491] MidEast Web, "Brief History of Saudi Arabia," http://www.mideastweb.org/arabiahistory.htm. (accessed October 14, 2011).

Pakistanis, Filipinos, Egyptians and Palestinians, Yemenites, Koreans, all mercenaries deprived of their basic rights, virtual slaves who keep the machines running, who assemble, repair, manage, and construct. From the economic point of view, it is a total loss: the riches produced throughout the entire world, extorted by a monopoly, and poured into this country, have produced absolutely nothing.[492]

The Voice of God

In all of human history, only two men have arrived on planet earth innocent of a capital crime. The first Adam was created by God from the dust of the ground. His first conscious experience was gazing into the eyes of his Creator, breathing life into his nostrils. Adam was given authority to rule the world. His only obligation was to obey the Creator. His domain was a garden that produced seasonal food. One tree was forbidden as food on pain of death.

Adam's partner, Eve, believed a lie of the serpent[493] and ate the fruit of the "Tree of the Knowledge of Good and Evil." Rather than seeking a solution from the Creator, and being fully aware of the consequences, Adam chose to disobey and eat the same fruit. Thus sin, a capital crime, entered the human race.

In order to understand the consequences and aftermath of God's judgment, it is helpful to comprehend what the Bible says of the make-up of created man. Genesis 2:7 says… "The Lord God formed man of dust from the ground and breathed into his nostrils the breath of life: and man became a living being or soul."[494] I Thessalonians 5:23 says: "Now may the God of peace Himself sanctify you entirely; and may your spirit, soul, and body be preserved complete, without blame at the coming of our Lord Jesus Christ."

Since the body was formed from dust and the average adult is composed of 50-66 percent water,[495] it is not wrong to call the human outer

---

[492] Laurent Murawiec, *Princes of Darkness*, (Lanham, Maryland, Rowman & Littlefield Publishers, Inc., 2003), 3-4.

[493] Also referred to as the "dragon, the serpent of old, who is the devil and Satan." Rev. 2:20 (New American Standard Bible Updated.

[494] Genesis 2:7, Ibid.

[495] Boston Globe Online/From the Archives/Health Sense, "What percentage of the human body is water, and how is this determined?"
http://www.boston.com/glove/search/stories/health/how. (accessed October 71, 2011).

shell a *mud body*. The necessities of this shell may be classified into three categories: nourishment, reproduction, and defense.

The soul makes it possible for the spirit and the body to communicate and cooperate.[496] The soul includes the mind, emotion, and will.

The spirit consists of intuition, conscience, and the means of communion with the Creator.[497] This provided Adam with the ability to hear God's voice, before his disobedience. Afterwards, his immortal spirit was disconnected, and he became spiritually deaf. Communion was broken. But God, motivated by love, communicated with His broken creation.

Down through the ages certain men have heard the voice of God and changed the course of history:

Noah listened to God's voice and obeyed Him, saving the human race from complete annihilation. Hebrews 11:7 Abraham obeyed God's voice, and became the means of blessing that continues to this day. Genesis 12:1-3 Joseph's sensitivity to God's voice caused him to be ostracized by his brothers and sold to Ishmaelite slave traders. But God used Joseph to preserve the lives of many people. Genesis 50:20 Moses was obedient to God's voice, and delivered over a million Israelite slaves from Egypt, destroying Pharaoh, his army, and the Egyptian economy in the process. Led by Moses into the Sinai Peninsula, this group of people was invited by God to become priests as special emissaries to the seed of the serpent,[498] the ungodly. Initially, they agreed, but intimidated by thunder, lightning, earthquake, and trumpet blast, they said to Moses: 'Speak to us yourself and we will listen; but do not let God speak to us or we shall die.'[499] The result was the Mosaic Law- 613 rules and regulations, impossible to be kept in their entirety. This was the first of two laws. The history of the nation of Israel can hardly be linked with a blessing that would create envy among all people.[500] They did not listen carefully to Moses.

Two thousand years ago, the seed of the woman arrived,[501] the second righteous man. He had an earthly mother with human blood, to pay the penalty inherited from Adam's crime. He had no human father, or He

---

[496] Watchman Nee, *The Spiritual Man,* (Manassa, VA, Christian Fellowship Publishers, Inc., 1968), 36-37.

[497] Ibid., 33.

[498] Genesis 3:15, "I will put enmity between you (the serpent) and the woman."

[499] Exodus 20:19, The Revised English Bible.

[500] Genesis 12:3. "All peoples on earth will wish to be blessed as you are blessed."

[501] Genesis 3:15.

would have inherited Adam's guilt. Thus God's solution for sin was sending His only begotten Son to redeem His sheep by paying their debt with His own blood. With His resurrection from the dead came the second Law, the Law of Faith.[502]

Matthew 17 describes Peter, James, and John, three of his disciples, witnessing Jesus transfiguration. His face shone like the sun and His clothes were white as light. He was conversing with Moses and Elijah. When Peter intruded into their conversation, a bright cloud overshadowed them and a voice announced: "This is My beloved Son, with whom I am well-pleased: Listen to Him!"[503]

God communed with mankind through Moses and prophets for millennia. Moses was ignored in time, and the prophets were murdered.[504] Jesus came to reconnect the Holy Spirit with man's spirit so that each man could receive God's love.

Jesus Christ's purpose 2,000 years ago was to die as a substitute for the human race. When He comes the second time, He will judge all men and separate those who choose to persist in their rebellion (goats) from those who have chosen Him as their Shepherd.[505] All of Adam's descendants are born as goats. Each has the choice of becoming the Great Shepherd's sheep. The most important proclamation that anyone can make is: "The Lord is my Shepherd!" With this declaration, comes the obligations of obedience to the Creator. It should be emphasized, that this obedience is to His voice, not the keeping of the Law of Moses.

Submission

'Islam,' an Arabic word, comes from a root meaning 'commitment' or 'surrender:' Islam is a religion of submission. Its followers are those who commit themselves in surrender to the will of God (Allah).[506]

Muslims are quick to point out that the Arabic for God, Allah, refers to the same Almighty God (Elohim) who is worshipped by Christians and Jews. Since there is only one Creator, Almighty God, and Master of the Day of Judgment, there is no question that it is the same God we are

---

[502] Romans 3:27, New American Standard Bible Updated Edition.

[503] Matthew 17:5, Ibid.

[504] Matthew 23:31, Ibid.

[505] Matthew 25:31-46, Ibid.

[506] Myrtle Langley, *Religions – A Book of Beliefs*, (Elgin, IL, David C. Cook Publishing Co., 1981), 52.

Conclusion

addressing. This fact notwithstanding, orthodox Muslims and evangelical Christians will agree that our "paths" to that God are mutually exclusive.

Allah is understood within Islam to be the merciful, compassionate creator of all mankind. In fact, Allah loved mankind so much he sent many prophets to show us how to live in order to please Him,[507] by giving man the five pillars of the faith.[508]

The most important teaching in the Quaran is the oneness of God. All manner of sin that an individual commits may be forgiven, except for the sin of ascribing an equal with Allah. This is the unpardonable sin of Islam.[509]

Until Islam accepts God's atonement for sin, Jesus Christ His only Son, it can never be made righteous. Only the Son can re-connect their spirits to the Holy Spirit so they can hear His voice and obey Him, not Mohammed. Islam is not driven by mind, emotion, or will of the soul, but by the *mud body's* drive for defense. There is safety in numbers, and "belonging" to the "Ummah." Engaging in Jihad is the result.

The stage was set for Islamic expansion by a Christian Church that put misplaced faith in Episcopal authority, and in the efficacy of the sacraments to bring salvation. This church insisted on maintaining links with secular power and bringing not only sacred books, but images as well, with its missionary efforts.

... 'Christian' idolatry was little witness to heathen idolaters, and all paved the way for the great wave of Islam which was to sweep over vast territories, blotting out everything in its path. But maybe Islam was but the judgment of God upon a Church which had so degenerated and departed from the truth as it is in Christ Jesus as to have been better destroyed than remain as a reproach to the name of the One it professed to own as Lord.[510]

According to the Scriptures, God uses nations less righteous to discipline His people. He used the Philistines to punish Israel during Saul's reign. Ignoring God's warnings, 10 tribes of Israel were dispersed by Assyria in 720 B.C. Judah was displaced to Babylon in 586 B.C., and the Jews of Jerusalem were scattered by the Romans in A.D. 70.

---

[507] John Clark Mead, *The New World War*, Ibid., 103-104.
[508] Ibid., p 105-108.
[509] Ibid.,105.
[510] John W. Kennedy of India, *The Torch of the Testimony,* (Sargent, GA, Christian Books Publishing House, 1965), 97-98.

401

Though the organized church was inundated by Islam, the torch of God's testimony was carried forward by individuals who heard God's voice.

Much too little importance is usually given to the part played by ordinary men and women in the advance of the Gospel. So often the history of the church is portrayed as simply the organized advance of organized religion. The life of Christ, however, should pre-eminently find its expression in the day-to-day lives of those who have submitted to His Lordship, and this witness should be the most potent power for the extension of the Gospel. This has always been true, and still is where spiritual life has not degenerated to the realm of the purely formal. The fellowship thus established between men and God and between believers together is something much higher and greater than can be expressed in any humanly sustained ecclesiastical system.[511]

The Good Jihad

"Do not fear or be dismayed by this great horde, for the battle is in God's hands not yours."[512]

On 1 April, 1979 the Iranian system of government changed from a constitutional monarchy to a nation governed by Sharia Law. Under the Ayatollah Khomeini, Iran was now the first true Islamic Republic in the history of the world.[513]

"It's ironic that when the Ayatollah Khomeini took power in Iran with his style of Islamic Shiite extremism that the true face of Islam was finally exposed not just to the Christian populace, but to the Muslims themselves. Before 1979, the demand for Bibles in Iran was never that great. Today, Iranians can't get enough of the Bible or biblical teaching... it is as if God used that man, the Ayatollah... to expose Islam for what it is..."[514]

Joel C. Rosenberg says, "I have been able to assemble enough data and anecdotal evidence to paint a picture--albeit an imperfect and incomplete

---

[511] John W. Kennedy of India, *The Torch of the Testimony*, Ibid., 98-99.
[512] II Chronicles 20:15b. The Revised English Bible.
[513] Joel C. Rosenberg, *Inside the Revolution*, (Carol Stream, IL, Tyndale House Publishers, Inc., 2009), 85.
[514] Ibid., 382.

one--that provides a sense of how powerfully the God of the Bible is moving to draw Muslims into His family."[515]

He tells the story of two men driving through the mountains of Iran with a car full of Bibles. The steering wheel jammed and forced them to slam on their brakes. An old man tapped on their window and asked if they had the books. Everyone in his village had had a dream of Jesus. Later this man had another dream in which Jesus told him to wait down the mountain for the books. Jesus is revealing Himself to people in Iran through dreams and visions.[516]

The big untold story is that more Muslims are coming to faith in Jesus Christ today than at any other time in history. In December 2001, a significant Saudi cleric appeared in a live interview on Aljazeera satellite television to confirm that, sure enough, Muslims were turning to Jesus in alarming numbers. "Every day, 16,000 Muslims convert to Christianity," he warned. "Every year, 6 million Muslims convert to Christianity."[517]

One of the believing leaders in Iraq said: "...God is not dependant upon us. This is something He is doing on His own... God is healing Muslims... and... giving Muslims visions of Jesus Christ."[518]

"It is not that the Lord is slow in keeping His promise, as some suppose, but that He is patient with you. It is not His will that any should be lost, but that all should come to repentance."[519]

Learning to Listen

As John Clark Mead broke down the world of Islam into meaningful categories with regard to how Muslims relate to the Quran, the world of Christianity can be similarly analyzed.

---

[515] Ibid.
[516] Ibid., 387-388.
[517] Ibid., 381.
[518] Ibid., 395.
[519] II Peter 3:9. Revised English Bible.

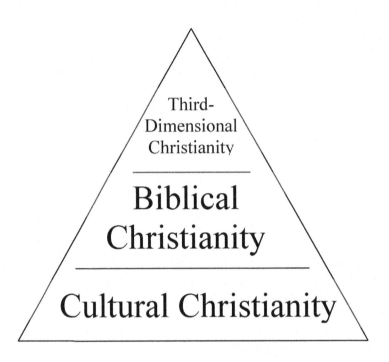

Cultural Christians are born into a society with Christian roots. It is customary to go to church on Sunday morning and join as church members. They are aware of Bible stories and probably have a Bible gathering dust somewhere in their homes. They may believe that the Bible is the Word of God, but it is not the central determining factor for life decisions.

Biblical Christians are those who have chosen to accept Jesus Christ as their Shepherd. They aspire to read the Bible regularly, consider it relevant for today, and actively seek to live their lives accordingly. Oriented more towards written rules than personal divine guidance, they generally solve problems with their minds, emotions, and wills.

Third dimensional Christians have dared to enter the realm of the Spirit. Christ's statement to the Samaritan woman at Jacob's well was: "God is spirit, and those who worship Him must worship in spirit and in truth."[520] These people follow the traditions of men who have heard God's voice, and made a difference in the world.

Learning to hear God's voice is not easy. Because of our "goat" nature we usually have over-developed souls. Learning to accept inputs from our re-energized spirits must be learned. And climbing above our familiar two-dimensional world is scary but rewarding. I've heard people say they don't care how high they fly, "as long as they can keep one foot on the ground." It is essentially a matter of control. Submission to an all-powerful, all-knowing, pervasive, timeless God means giving up control. Getting to know and trust this God takes time. Recognizing His voice is also a learning process. I recall Bill Cosby's story of Noah and the ark. After receiving all of God's instructions about the ark, Noah's question was: "Who is this, really?" On my journey, I believe I have never offended God with my questions or doubts. His ways have been gentle, but positive. If you choose to enter this sphere, allow me to recommend Grandfather Downing's *How May I Know God's Plan for My Life?*, included as Appendix A. And may I add; you are never too old to learn to fly in the realm of the spirit. Moses was 80 years old when he first heard the voice of God.

I am a witness to an exciting, satisfying way of transiting this world in a *mud body.* May I quote Romans 12:1 & 2 from the Phillip's translation: "With eyes wide open to the mercies of God, I beg you, my brothers, as an act of intelligent worship, to give Him your bodies, as a living sacrifice, consecrated to Him and acceptable by Him. Don't let the world around you squeeze you into its own mould, but let God re-mould your minds from within, so that you may prove in practice that the Plan of God for you is good, meets all His demands and moves towards the goal of true maturity."

---

[520] John 4:24. Revised English Bible.

Conclusion

To realize one's Divine Destiny, I believe a person must choose Jesus Christ as a personal Shepherd, attend God's school where the Bible is the textbook and the Holy Spirit the teacher, learn to recognize, listen to, and obey the voice of God.

The urgency of human determination is well presented in the fifth stanza of the poem *The Present Chrisis* by James Russell Lowell:[521]

Once to every man and nation comes the moment to decide,

In the strife of Truth and Falsehood, for the good or evil side;

Some great cause, God's new Messiah, offering each the bloom or blight,

Parts the goats upon the left hand, and the sheep upon the right,

And the choice goes by forever 'twixt that darkness and that light.

---

[521] http://www.readbookonline.net/readOnLine/7194/, James Russell Lowell's poem: "The Present Crisis". (accessed October 30, 2011).

How May I know God's Plan for My Life?

By Rev. Lee H. Downing

D o you know that He has a plan-a plan for your life as definite as that of the architect for a building about to be erected? Before a stone of the foundation is laid the architect has thought through the prepared detailed specifications regarding the shape and size of the building, and of every piece of material entering into its construction. God's plan for your life is no less definite, and His plan is the best that could possibly be made. He understands you better than you understand yourself: knows your limitations and your capabilities better than you know them, and knows also conditions throughout the world, not only those that prevail at the present moment, but all that will arise until the end of time. Is He not, therefore, best qualified to order you life? This He waits to do.

Somewhere in this world He has prepared a niche for you, and when you find that niche you will fit into it as you will into no other. Richer experiences await you there than elsewhere in all the world. "Strength and gladness are in his place" (I Chron. 16:27). "His place" for you, therefore, is the one in which you will be strongest and happiest, the one in which you will experience the highest degree of joy and satisfaction and fruitfulness in service of which you are capable.

Dr. F. B. Meyer once expressed the thought that if such a thing as sorrow were possible in heaven, a sufficient cause for it would be to have God's draft-plan for an individual produced and presented before him that he might compare what God had intended him to do with what he had actually accomplished. The contrast, Dr. Meyer believed, would be so striking as to cause sorrow, if that were possible up there.

Most people finish their course down here without ever having known God's purpose for them. Will You? Does not the very possibility of doing so stir in your heart an intense desire to find an answer to the question: HOW MAY I KNOW GOD'S PLAN FOR MY LIFE?

To some the answer has come through pursuing the course prescribed in the following outline, supported by the Scripture texts inserted:

1. Be assured that He has a plan.
   Eph. 2:10; Acts 15:18; Ps. 37:23; Phil. 2:13; Acts 13:2.
2. Be assured that He will reveal His plan.
   Eph. 5:17; Col. 1:9; Ps. 32:8; Ps. 73:24; Acts 16:6, 7.
3. Afford Him an opportunity by waiting upon Him.
   a) Alone. Matt. 6:6
   b) At an appointed time.
   c) With your whole being yielded to Him. Rom 12:1, 2.
   d) In expectancy - faith. Heb. 11:6.
   e) Recording the impressions.
4. Begin to execute the plan as soon as it is revealed. Acts 26:19, 20.

1. Be Assured That He Has a Plan

This is important, for the Adversary knows that God will be more glorified through our executing His plan for our lives than in the accomplishment of any self-chosen tasks. Therefore he will do his utmost to prevent our knowing the plan, and only a well-grounded assurance of its existence will enable us to persevere until the revelation comes. Such assurance may be had through accepting the truth stated in texts cited above, only one of which will be commented upon.

Ephesians 2:10 declared that "We are–created in Christ Jesus unto good works, which God hath before ordained (R. C., "prepared") that we should walk in them." How long "before," is suggested by the clause in Eph. 1:4, "Chosen–in him before the foundation of the world. " May not the choice and the plan have been simultaneous? If so, then both were made before the foundation of the world. Wondrous thought, that we should be in God's mind, and our lives be planned, before this universe was brought into being! But we are of more value to Him than the material world about us, and it is because we cost Him more.

"That we should walk in them" is the final statement of the verse quoted above–language which suggests that before each of us is a divinely prepared pathway strewn with good works made ready to our hands. Along the one prepared for you will be found all the souls that He expects you to win, all the work that He expects you to accomplish, and all the discipline necessary to fit you for that work. What if you miss that

410

pathway? You will miss God's best for you, and enjoy only His second choice.

"God has His best things for the few that dare to stand the test; God has His second choice for those who will not have His best".

Having become assured that He has a plan for your life, next be assured

2. That He Will Reveal to You That Plan.

"Be ye not unwise, but understanding what the will of the Lord is." We are commanded to know His will, therefore it must be His will to reveal His will, including the part which concerns your life-work.

"That ye might be filled with the knowledge of his will" is one petition in the apostle's prayer for the saints of Colosse. When we are filled with the knowledge of His will, there is no place left for doubt and uncertainty.

Turning to the American Revised Version one finds this interesting series of texts: "Counsel is mine" (Prov. 8:14), "I will counsel thee" (Ps.32:8), "The counsel of Jehovah standeth fast forever" (Ps. 33:11). The marginal rendering in this version of Prov. 8:14 entire affords a powerful incentive to have one's life ordered by the Lord. It is this: "Counsel is mine, and effectual working: I am understanding; I have might. " Get your counsel from God, and He is the Effectual Worker to bring it to pass. He is able to place you where He wants you. The principalities and powers opposed the risen Saviour's return to the Father's right hand, but He brought Him triumphantly through these organized forces of evil arrayed against Him, and placed Him just where He wanted Him. He will do as much for you-that is, He will place you just where He wants you-when your life is wholly at His disposal.

Do not these Scriptures assure you that God has a plan for your life, and that He has pledged Himself to reveal that plan if you will fulfill His conditions? If so, then

3. Afford Him an Opportunity by Waiting Upon Him.

(a) Alone. Jesus said, "Thou, when thou prayest, enter into thy closet, and when thou hast shut thy door, pray to thy Father which is in secret; and thy Father which is in secret shall reward thee openly." In the secret place, shut in with God, we may expect leadings so definite as to assure others later that they were from Him.

When I announced my decision to go to Africa, some friends sought to dissuade me. They knew I was not very strong physically, though passed by the doctor, and to them it seemed a great risk, especially to go under a Faith Mission, which does not guarantee the support of its missionaries. Now, after twenty-three years of service on the field, with every need supplied, not one of them feels that I made a mistake. Little did I realize, as I waited for guidance day after day in the secret place, that the Father would ever reward me so "openly." "He shall bring forth–thy judgment as the noonday" (Ps. 37:6) was verified in my experience.

(b) At an appointed time. Think over your daily schedule and decide when in the twenty-four hours you could be alone with the Lord without interruption, and make up your mind to meet Him every day at that time. The duration of the interview will be determined somewhat by the other duties demanding your attention. A half-hour daily, if more cannot be spared, is better than an hour today, no time tomorrow, and such time the day following as can be conveniently spent in this way. The faithful keeping of this appointment prepares one to receive impressions from the Lord, and brings the consciousness of having definite dealings with Him.

(c) With your whole being yielded to Him. This is absolutely necessary. The one who, on hearing that God has a plan for every life, says, "I would like to look over His plan for me to see if I will accept it," will finish his days down here without ever having seen the plan. God never promised to reveal it on such terms. It is after the body has been presented a living sacrifice that God's will becomes "acceptable" (Rom. 12:1,2).

The experience of a young man in the University of Minnesota illustrates this truth. He was wanted on the varsity football team, and wanted as manager of a branch store by the firm for which he had been working, but God was claiming his life. One evening as the sun was setting, four of us who had spent the day together in his home city went to a nearby place on the shore of Lake Superior and seated ourselves for prayer on a large rock which jutted out a little way into the water. The other three had prayed and he began, but his throat filled; the tears started and the voice stopped; he began to sob and his big body shook with emotion. After a brief silence he said, "Fellows, forgive me, I can't help it." Isaiah 57:15 was quoted to assure him that his present condition was pleasing to God: "For thus saith the high and lofty One that inhabiteth eternity, whose name is Holy; I dwell in the high and holy place, with him also that is of a contrite and humble spirit, to revive the spirit of the humble and to revive the heart of the contrite one." He resumed praying and said, "Lord, Thou didst never have me before where Thou couldst speak to me as Thou canst this evening. Take me and use me in any way that will serve Thy purpose." Nothing was now so "acceptable" to him but this experience followed that of presenting his body a living sacrifice.

(d) In expectancy-faith. "Without faith it is impossible to please Him: for he that cometh to God must believe that He is, and that He is a rewarder of them that diligently seek him." In order therefore to know His plan, one must come to Him in faith, but the faith which He requires He is ready to impart through the means mentioned in Rom. 10:17: "Faith cometh by hearing, and hearing by the word of God." As well might one hope to maintain physical strength without partaking of wholesome food, as to possess faith without pondering the Word of God. The doctor's method of restoring health to an invalid illustrates God's usual method of imparting faith to His children. Specific directions are given by the doctor regarding diet, drugs, exercise, rest, and everything that affects the patient's condition. Through the faithful observance of his directions health is restored. The process may involve months of living strictly in accord with the doctor's orders-abstaining from foods that are prohibited, though pleasing to the palate; retiring at the appointed hour, though further fellowship with friends would be very enjoyable; taking bitter tonics because they are prescribed; and doing other things which the flesh would rather not do—but no self-denial is deemed too great if only health can be restored.

So with faith. It is imparted gradually through ordering the life strictly in accord with the teaching of God's Word. Most people are unwilling to pay the price of faith. They want to receive it in bulk form, as it were, and without cost or delay.

(e) Recording the impressions. Just how God's plan for a particular life will be revealed, no one can say. He does not deal alike with His children, but each may be led on to prayer experiences too rich to be described, and too sacred to be divulged. "If I tried, I could not utter what He says when thus we meet" is the language of every soul accustomed to frequent and sometimes prolonged sessions alone with Him.

My only hope, therefore, is to say something of a general character that may help those who are just beginning to seek counsel of God.

The simple suggestion, made many years ago to a group of Bible students by the General Director of our Mission (the man who by precept and example has helped me more than any other toward a life of absolute dependence upon God), I hope will prove as helpful to you as it has to me.

When desirous of knowing God's will concerning an important matter, especially if it be whether, or not, you should do a particular thing, draw a line through a blank sheet, and on one side of the line write all the reasons against, doing the thing. Pray over these reasons. If necessary revise the list from day to day while alone with Him at the appointed time. Ere long quite a distinct impression will be borne in upon your heart in favor of one side or the other. If the impression which comes today is from the Spirit of God, it will be deeper tomorrow; if not from Him, it will fade out. We should, I believe, regard as from the Lord the impressions that come to us when we are alone with Him and absolutely yielded i.e., perfectly willing to do or not to do the thing about which we are inquiring. An earthly father would not consent to an enemy's answering the question of his son who comes to him for advice; nor will our heavenly Father permit His enemy to enter the secret place and influence the child who is so eager to know His will as to set apart a time and go alone daily to receive the revelation of it. One needs, I know, to speak guardedly on this point. It is easy to become presumptuous and fanatical, but let us remember that we are in God's school, pupils to be taught individually by His Spirit, then seek to discover His method of influencing us personally. I am not emotional; I do not have visions, or hear audible voices, or have such spectacular experiences as I have heard others relate. In my experience the leading comes through gradually deepening inward impressions such as I have already described. Time will reveal to us and others whether or not we have learned to discern His presence, and to understand His impressions.

Here our study ends. Has it been worth while? Are you yet sure that God has a plan for your life, and that you may know it? Has any revelation come as to the way? If so, praise Him, and tell Him you are willing to pay the price of knowing the plan, if only you may have the satisfaction of being consciously in His appointed place, and doing the specific work for which He brought you into the world.

P.S.

In closing permit me to illustrate what I have said with an incident from my own experience. It concerns the securing of funds for our last voyage from Africa to America. To make it intelligible considerable detail must be given. In February 1920, the Field Council of our Mission decided that our family ought to return to America that year. Early in March I wrote the agent of a steamship company at Mombasa to know the prospects for securing passage on one of their steamers to England. He replied that all their boats were booked full for some months, but that as soon as passage was available he would notify us. Days and weeks passed. On July 7th the question occurred to me "Are we sure that God wants us to go to America this year?", since neither room for us on the boats nor funds for the journey has yet been provided. Then I felt condemned for not doing what I had done for years when such an important question was to be decided, namely, set apart a time for waiting upon God to know His will in the matter. Because the Council were unanimously of the opinion that we should go, I had taken it as a matter of course that it was God's will, too. That day time was set apart, and out in the forest where no one could see me I waited upon Him, and wrote down and prayed over the reasons for and against going. That hour the next day found me in the same place, and the next, for several successive days. That it was God's will for us to go became clearer each day. On July12[th] a second letter was received from the agent, saying a boat would be sailing the latter part of August, on which he could book our family-should he do so? Before replying I again sought counsel of the Lord. The former conviction was now so strong, and had been confirmed so often that I wrote "book us," although no funds for the voyage were yet in hand (such boldness needs sure guidance as a little presumption at this point may place one in a most embarrassing situation.) This was a new call to prayer. Going alone day after day, the Spirit so effectually applied promise after promise to my heart that each became God=s message to me as truly as though it had never been His message to any other child of His. Faith was growing and doubts were disappearing. I was becoming "filled with the knowledge of His will."

At this juncture I was sent by our Council to confer with the German Evangelical Lutheran Missionaries who were about to be sent out of East Africa by the British Government, and they wanted our Society to take the oversight of their work until other arrangements could be made. I had precious fellowship with them and was present at their farewell meeting with their native Christians, in which all hearts were deeply stirred, and many eyes filled with tears. The next morning I had my last interview and prayer with their Secretary, and the Lord's presence became blessedly real to us both. Immediately after the interview I went to my room, my heart still aglow with a sense of His nearness, and kneeling down I asked Him to confirm again the conviction that had come regarding funds for the voyage. In a few moments the answer was so definite that I could not ask more. I arose, feeling that the sight of the money with my eyes could scarce be more positive proof that it had already been provided than this inward conviction, confirmed and strengthened day after day, and week after week, until the present moment when the climax was attained.

To reach home I had to travel three hundred miles by rail, then three on foot from the railway to our Mission station. On the train this thought came to me, "if a member of my family meets me at the station, the first news I expect to hear is that the money has come in my absence." On arrival our younger son, twelve years of age, met me. He greeted me cordially and began to speak of what had transpired while I was away, but said nothing about the money. I could not understand it, so frequently had this petition been presented in our family prayers that, had the answer come, I was sure he would mention this first. We walked and talked until almost home. As we neared the house my wife appeared and said, "Kenneth told you the news, did he?" "He has told me considerable news," I replied. "To which item do you refer?" she asked. Then Kenneth spoke up and said, "Oh Mamma, I could hardly keep from telling Papa, but I wanted you to have the pleasure of telling him first," "Yes, it has come," she said. "All that we need for the voyage." I was not surprised, after the prayer experiences already related. Had it not been there, I would have been surprised. We began at once to pack our trunks and prepare for the voyage.

— • —

Rev. Lee H. Downing, my grandfather, was a missionary of the Africa Inland Mission laboring in Kenya from 1901 until his death in 1942.

The Consecrated Life

By F. B. Meyers

When a man is right with God, God will freely use him. There will rise up within him impulses, inspirations, strong strivings, strange resolves. These must be tested by Scripture and prayer; and if evidently of God, they must be obeyed

But there is this perennial source of comfort: God's commands are God's enablings. He will never give us a work to do without showing exactly how and when to do it, and giving us the precise strength and wisdom we need.

Do not dread to enter this life because you fear that God will ask you to do something you cannot do. He will never do that. If He lays aught on your heart, He will do so irresistibly; and as you pray about it, the impression will continue to grow, so that presently, as you look up to know what He wills you to say or do, the way will suddenly open; and you will probably have said the word or done the deed almost unconsciously. Rely on the Holy Ghost to go before you, to make the crooked places straight and the rough places smooth.

Do not bring the legal spirit of "must" into God's free service. "Consider the lilies of the field, how they grow." Let your life be as effortless as theirs, because your faith will constantly hand over all difficulties and responsibilities to your ever-present Lord. There is no effort to the branch in putting forth the swelling clusters of grapes; the effort would be to keep them back.

John 15:4, Scofield note: To abide in Christ is, on the one hand, to have no known sin unjudged and unconfessed, no interest into which He is not brought, no life which He cannot share. On the other hand, the abiding one takes all burdens to Him, and draws all wisdom life and strength from Him. It is not unceasing consciousness of these things, and of Him, but that nothing is allowed in the life which separates from Him.

The Listener's Hymn

By Glenn H. Downing

Father, I am listening, listening
To Your voice within my heart.
I am seeking to hear clearly
All You will impart.

Jesus, I am listening, listening
To your voice that shows you care.
I am finding out the blessing
Of your presence here.

Holy Spirit search inside me,
Purify in every part.
That we all may be united
In the Father's heart.

Holy Trinity of heaven,
Bonded into one by love.
I submit to you completely
Wed me with your love.

Jesus, I am resting, resting
In the joy of what thou art.
I am finding out the greatness
Of Thy loving heart.

To the tune of "Jesus I am Resting, Resting,"
By James Mountain, 1876.
Last verse by Jean S. Pigott